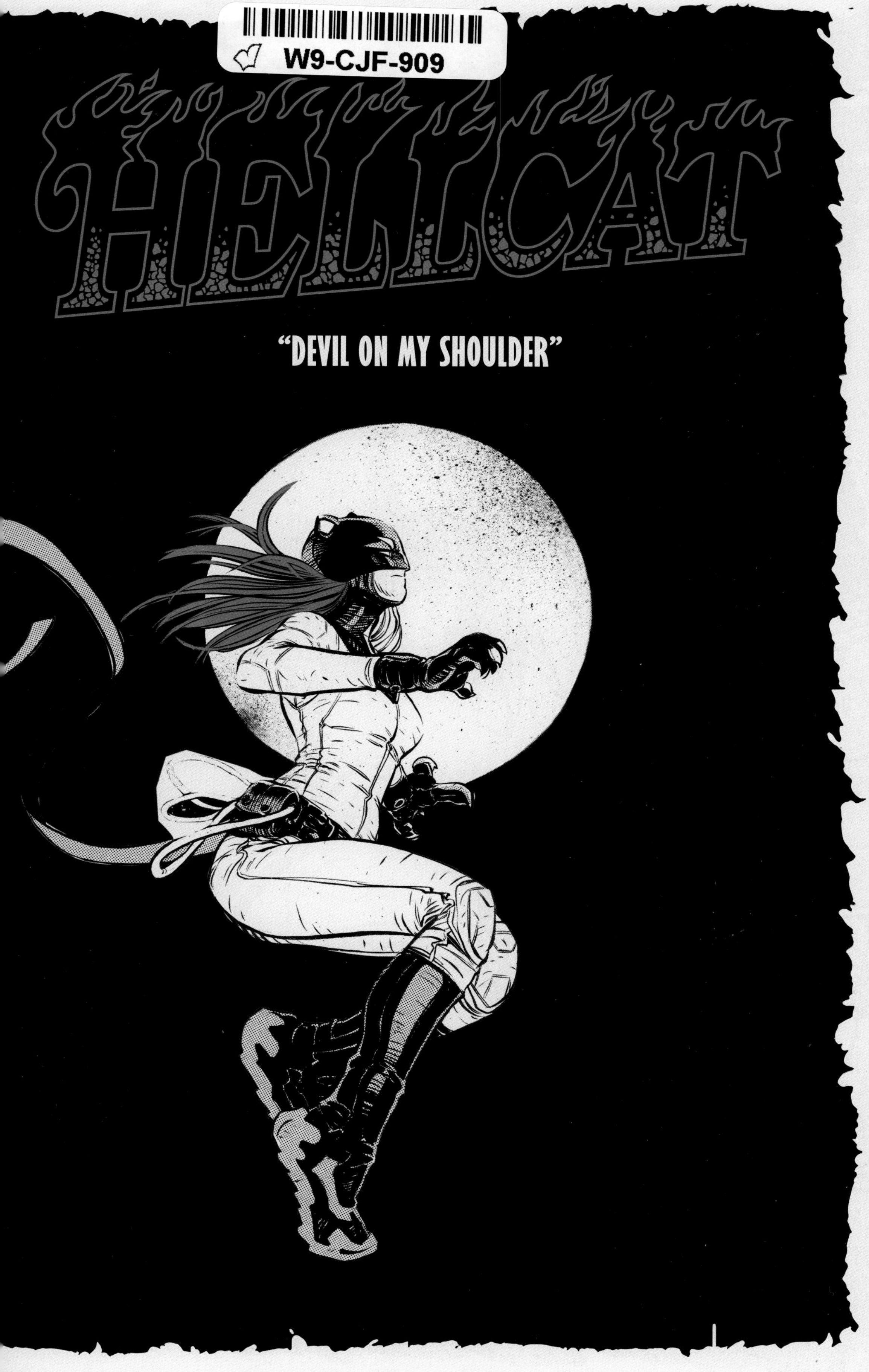
HELLCAT
"DEVIL ON MY SHOULDER"

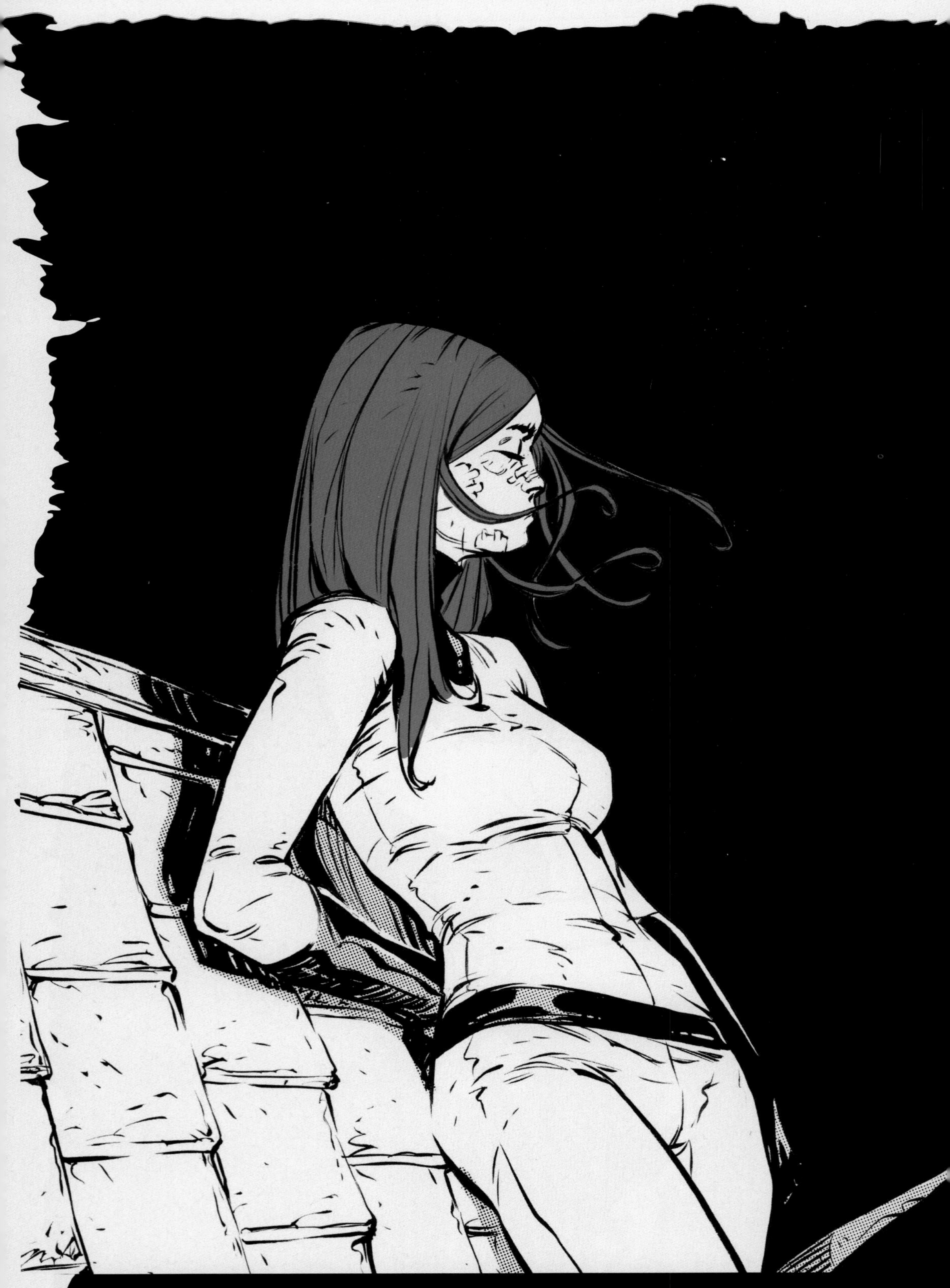

HELLCAT: DEVIL ON MY SHOULDER. Contains material originally published in magazine form as IRON MAN/HELLCAT ANNUAL (2022) #1 and HELLCAT (2023) #1-5. First printing 2023. ISBN 978-1-302-95197-9. Published by MARVEL WORLDWIDE, INC., a su
of MARVEL ENTERTAINMENT, LLC. OFFICE OF PUBLICATION: 1290 Avenue of the Americas, New York, NY 10104. © 2023 MARVEL No similarity between any of the names, characters, persons, and/or institutions in this book with those of any living or dea
or institution is intended, and any such similarity which may exist is purely coincidental. **Printed in the U.S.A.** KEVIN FEIGE, Chief Creative Officer; DAN BUCKLEY, President, Marvel Entertainment; DAVID BOGART, Associate Publisher & SVP of Talent Affai
BREVOORT, VP, Executive Editor; NICK LOWE, Executive Editor, VP of Content, Digital Publishing; DAVID GABRIEL, VP of Print & Digital Publishing; SVEN LARSEN, VP of Licensed Publishing; MARK ANNUNZIATO, VP of Planning & Forecasting; JEFF YOUNGC
of Production & Special Projects; ALEX MORALES, Director of Publishing Operations; DAN EDINGTON, Director of Editorial Operations; RICKEY PURDIN, Director of Talent Relations; JENNIFER GRÜNWALD, Director of Production & Special Projects; SUSAN
Production Manager; STAN LEE, Chairman Emeritus. For information regarding advertising in Marvel Comics or on Marvel.com, please contact Vit DeBellis, Custom Solutions & Integrated Advertising Manager, at vdebellis@marvel.com. For Marvel subs
inquiries, please call 888-511-5480. **Manufactured between 8/11/2023 and 9/12/2023 by SEAWAY PRINTING, GREEN BAY, WI, USA.**

10 9 8 7 6 5 4 3 2 1

Patsy Walker is a former teen celebrity turned super hero with supernatural and psychic powers. During her storied life, she's been an Avenger and private investigator, was married to the Son of Satan, died, went to hell and was resurrected. Having relocated to the West Coast, Patsy is determined to escape the ghosts of her pasts and claw out a new future as…

HELLCAT

"DEVIL ON MY SHOULDER"

writer
CHRISTOPHER CANTWELL

Iron Man/Hellcat Annual #1
Artist:
RUAIRÍ COLEMAN

Color Artist:
TRÍONA FARRELL

Letterer:
VC's JOE CARAMAGNA

Cover Art:
**LOGAN LUBERA &
RACHELLE ROSENBERG**

Hellcat #1-5
Artist:
ALEX LINS

Color Artist:
KJ DÍAZ

Letterer:
VC's ARIANA MAHER

Cover Artists:
**PERE PÉREZ &
MARTE GRACIA**

Editor:
MARTIN BIRO

Executive Editor:
TOM BREVOORT

COLLECTION EDITOR: JENNIFER GRÜNWALD
ASSISTANT EDITOR: DANIEL KIRCHHOFFER
ASSOCIATE MANAGER, TALENT RELATIONS: LISA MONTALBANO
VP PRODUCTION & SPECIAL PROJECTS: JEFF YOUNGQUIST
BOOK DESIGNER: YOUSSIF BAYOR

MANAGER & SENIOR DESIGNER: ADAM DEL RE
LEAD DESIGNER: JAY BOWEN
SVP PRINT, SALES & MARKETING: DAVID GABRIEL
EDITOR IN CHIEF: C.B. CEBULSKI

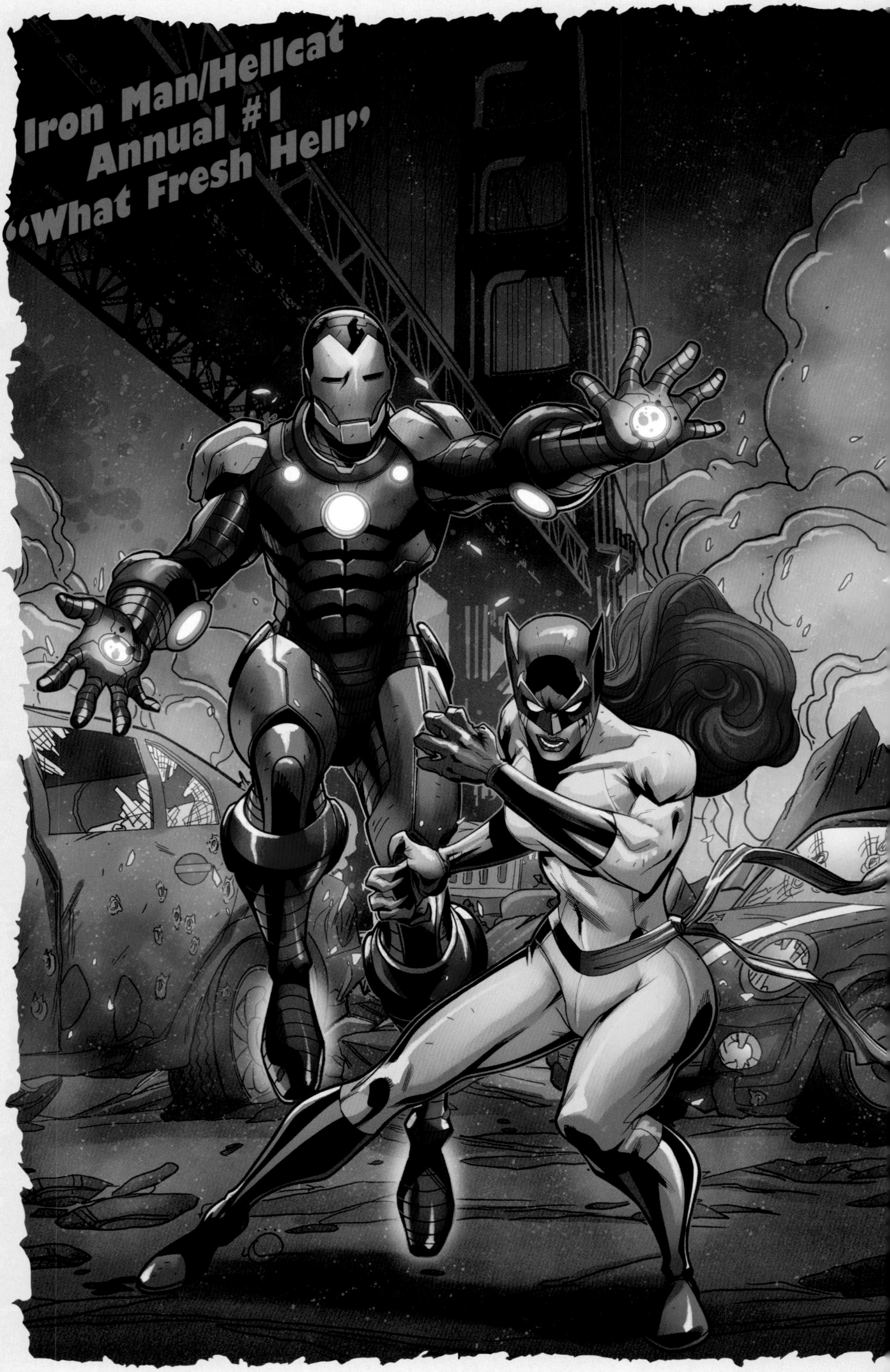
Iron Man/Hellcat
Annual #1
"What Fresh Hell"

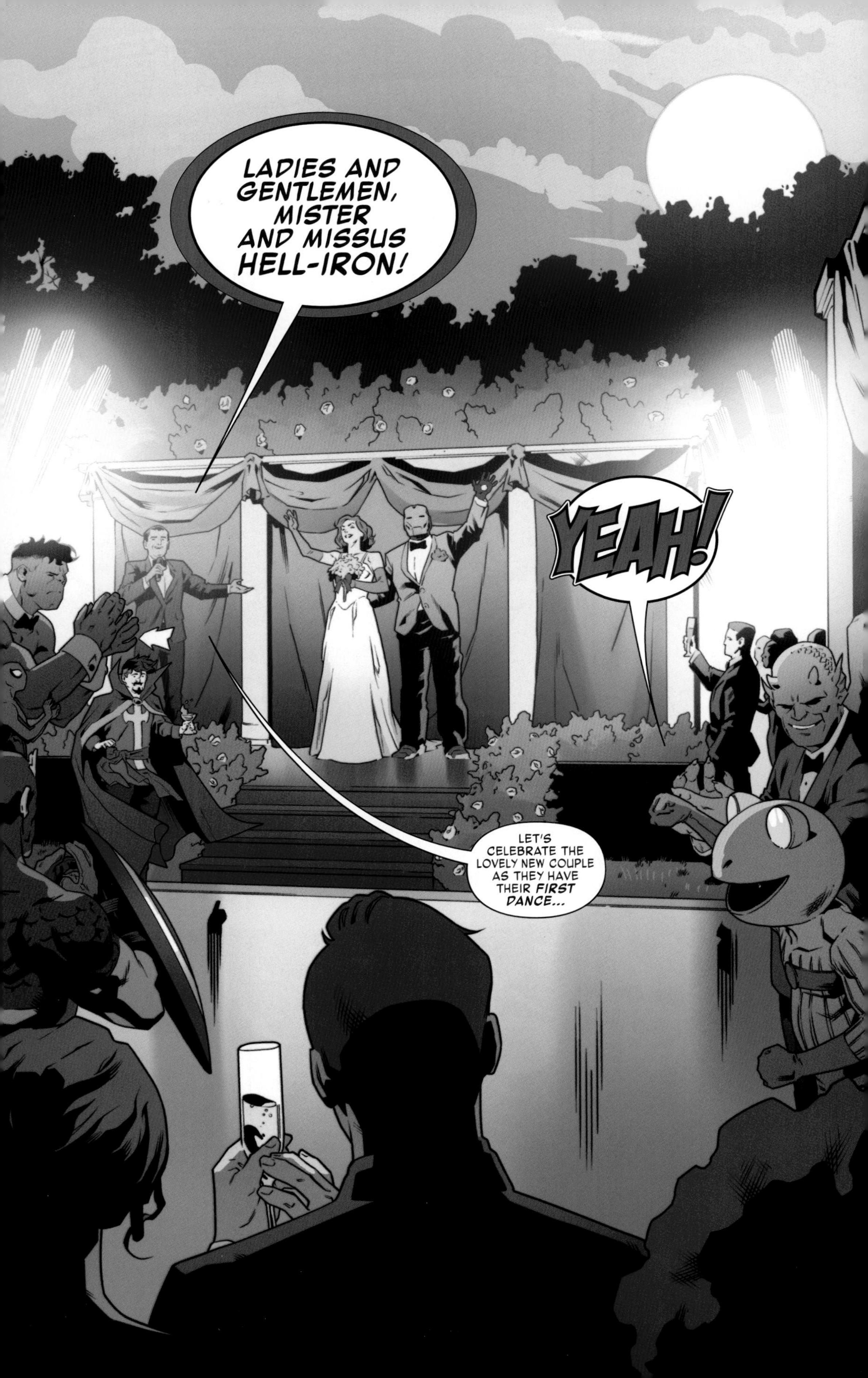
LADIES AND GENTLEMEN, MISTER AND MISSUS HELL-IRON!
YEAH!
LET'S CELEBRATE THE LOVELY NEW COUPLE AS THEY HAVE THEIR *FIRST* DANCE...

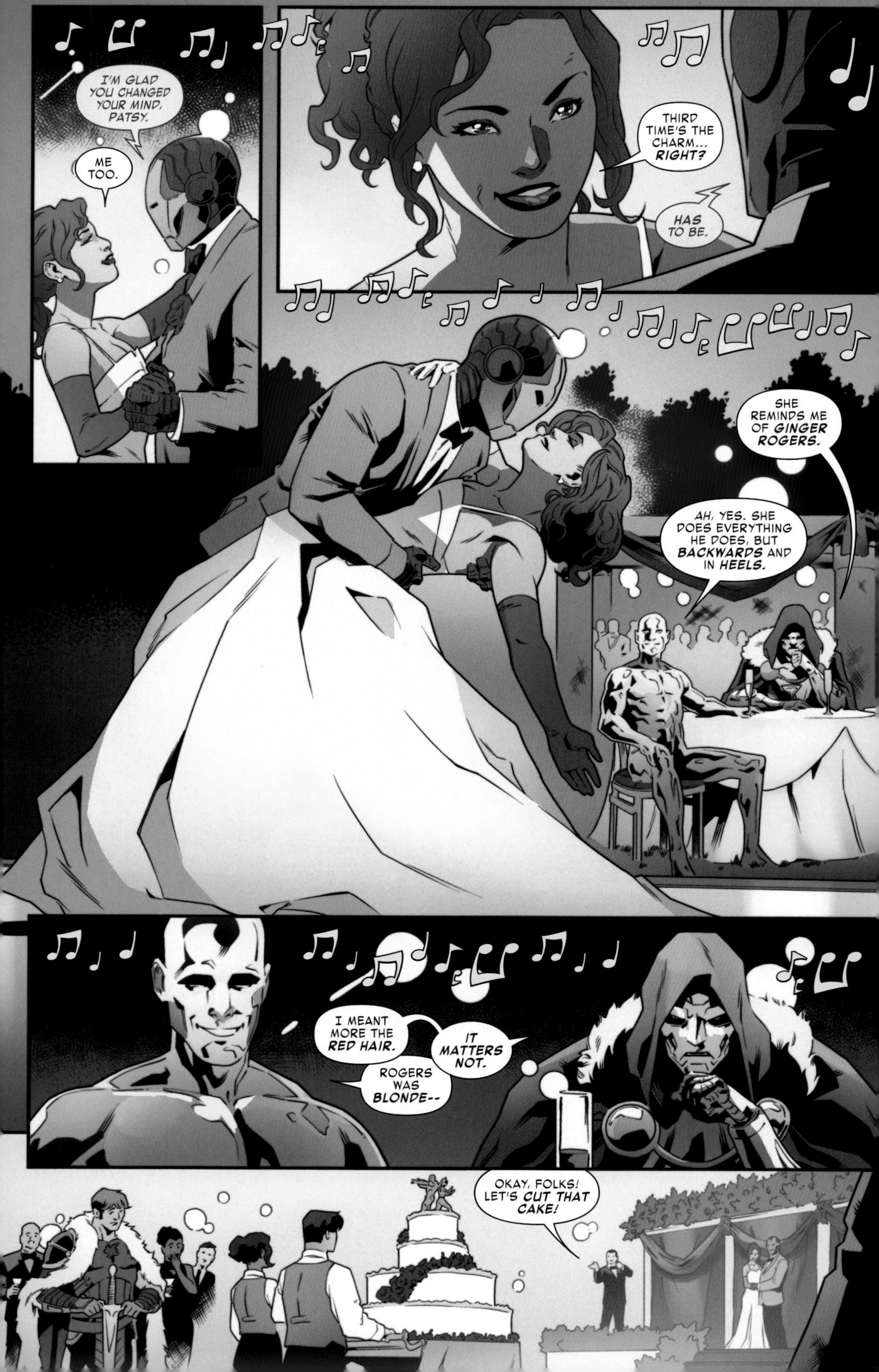

I'M GLAD YOU CHANGED YOUR MIND, PATSY.
ME TOO.
THIRD TIME'S THE CHARM... RIGHT?
HAS TO BE.
SHE REMINDS ME OF GINGER ROGERS.
AH, YES. SHE DOES EVERYTHING HE DOES, BUT BACKWARDS AND IN HEELS.
I MEANT MORE THE RED HAIR.
ROGERS WAS BLONDE--
IT MATTERS NOT.
OKAY, FOLKS! LET'S CUT THAT CAKE!

WE'RE NOT *SHOVING* PIECES IN EACH OTHER'S MOUTHS, RIGHT?

OF COURSE NOT. THIS TUX IS A CUSTOM BRIONI, AND YOU'RE WEARING AN ORIGINAL VERA WANG.

KANGK

UH...

MY...

JUST USE YOUR CLAWS.

...CLAWS?

FWAAASH

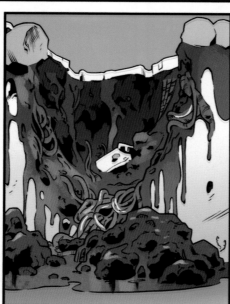

LOOKS DELICIOUS.

I...THINK I'M GONNA BE SICK...

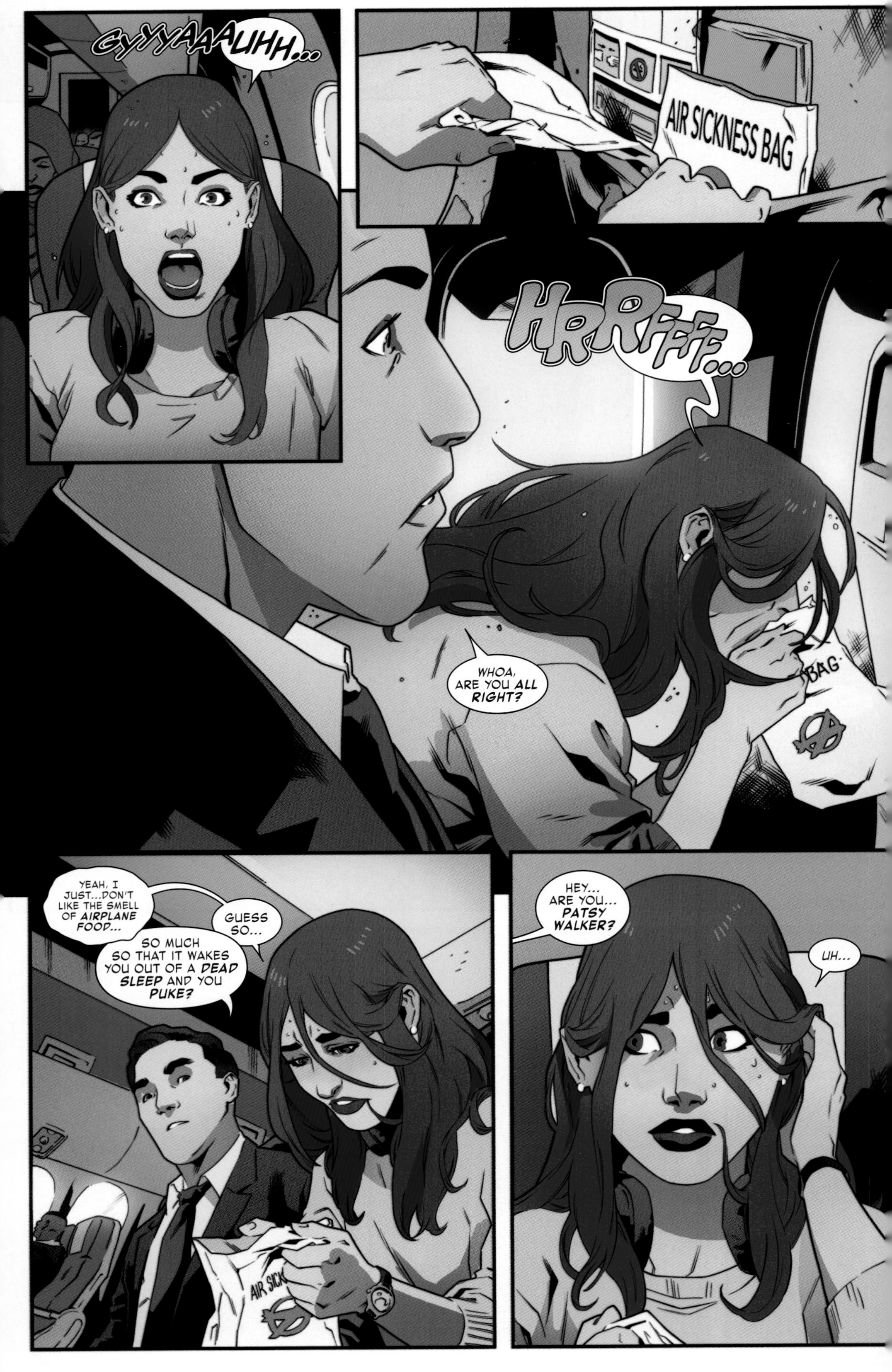
GYYYAAAUHH...
AIR SICKNESS BAG
HRRFFFF...
WHOA, ARE YOU ALL RIGHT?
BAG
YEAH, I JUST...DON'T LIKE THE SMELL OF AIRPLANE FOOD...
GUESS SO...
SO MUCH SO THAT IT WAKES YOU OUT OF A DEAD SLEEP AND YOU PUKE?
AIR SICK
HEY... ARE YOU... PATSY WALKER?
UH...

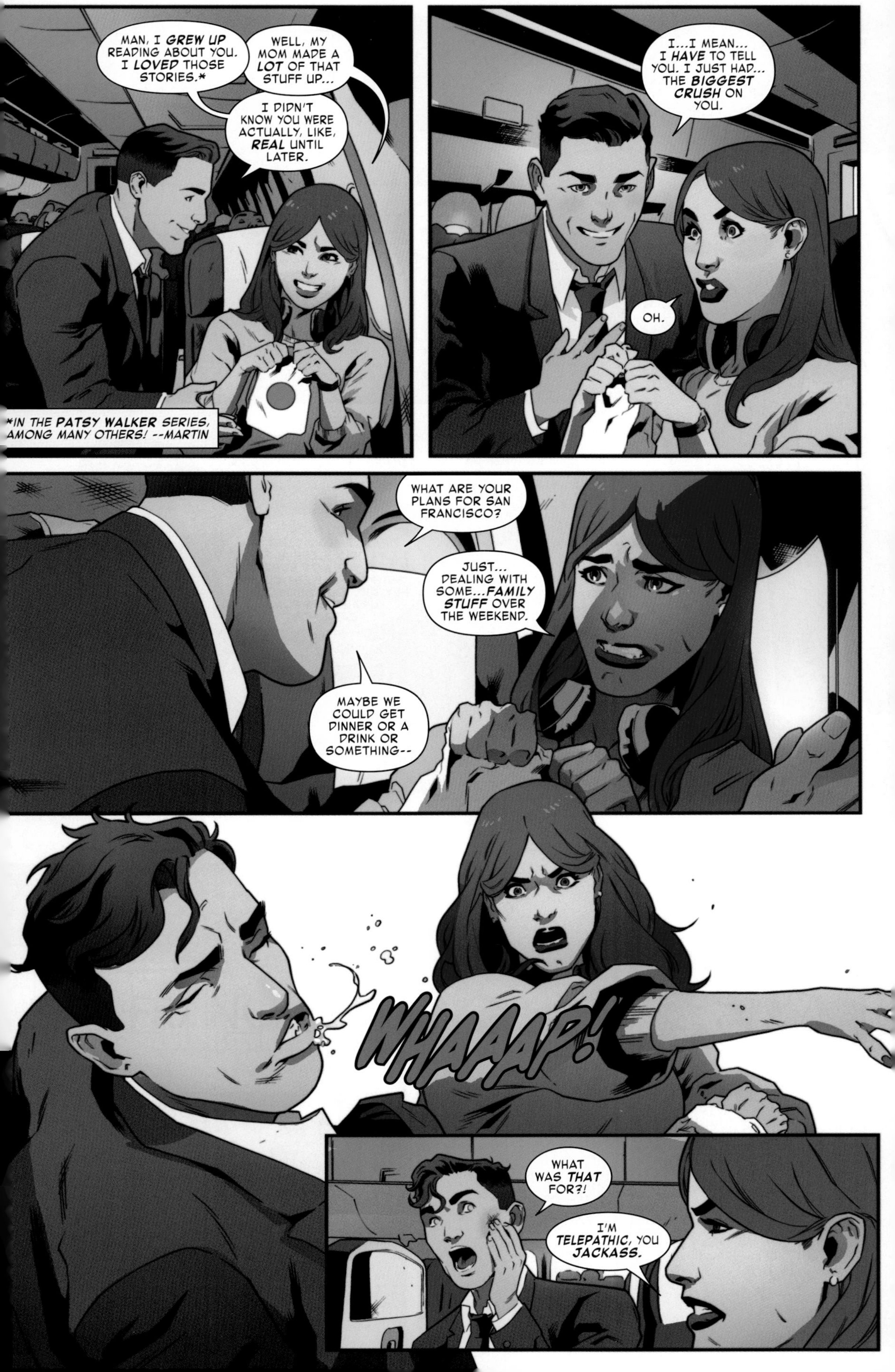
MAN, I GREW UP READING ABOUT YOU. I LOVED THOSE STORIES.*
WELL, MY MOM MADE A LOT OF THAT STUFF UP...
I DIDN'T KNOW YOU WERE ACTUALLY, LIKE, REAL UNTIL LATER.
*IN THE PATSY WALKER SERIES, AMONG MANY OTHERS! --MARTIN
I...I MEAN... I HAVE TO TELL YOU. I JUST HAD... THE BIGGEST CRUSH ON YOU.
OH.
WHAT ARE YOUR PLANS FOR SAN FRANCISCO?
JUST... DEALING WITH SOME...FAMILY STUFF OVER THE WEEKEND.
MAYBE WE COULD GET DINNER OR A DRINK OR SOMETHING--
WHAAAP!
WHAT WAS THAT FOR?!
I'M TELEPATHIC, YOU JACKASS.

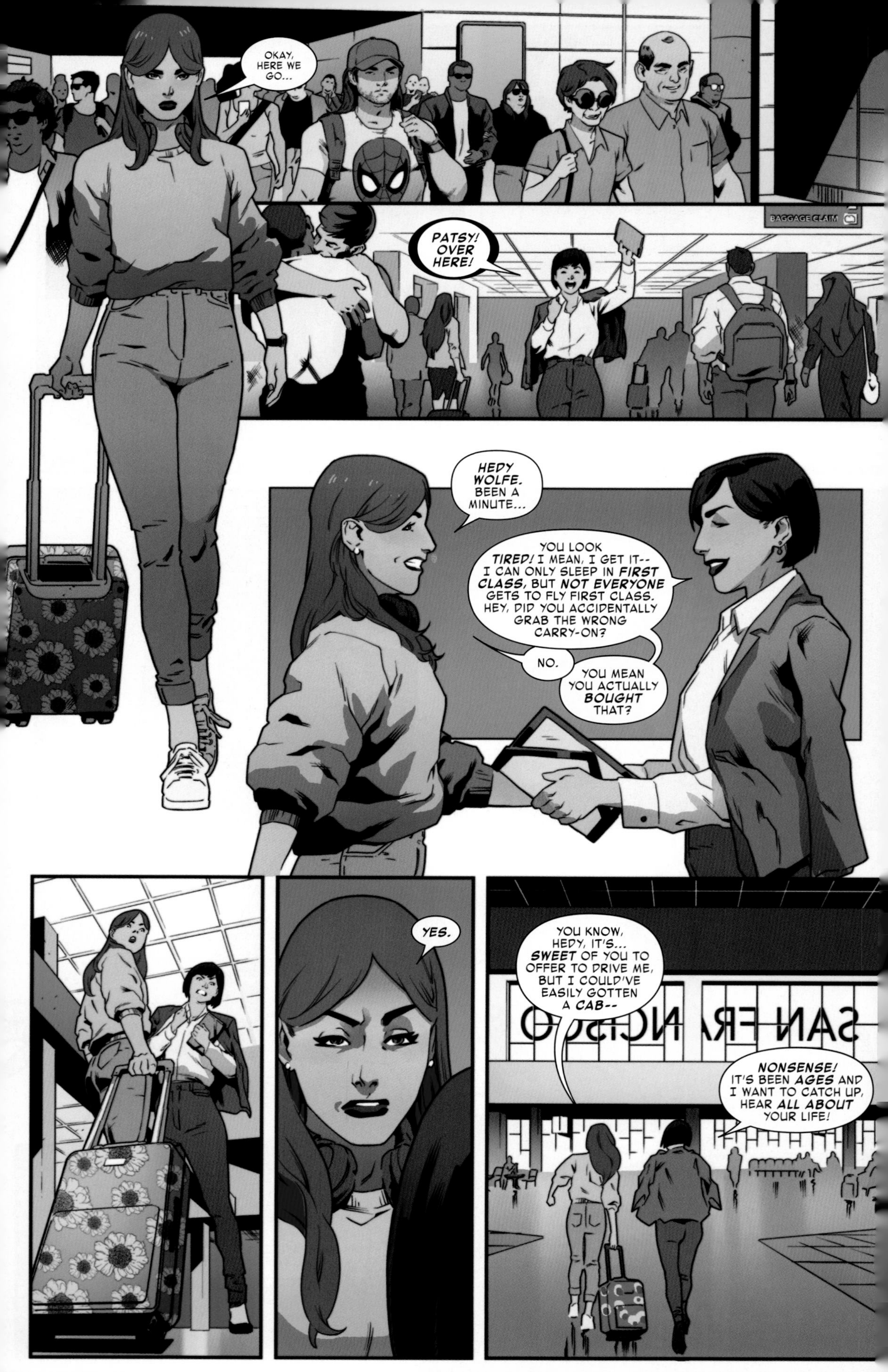
OKAY, HERE WE GO...
BAGGAGE CLAIM
PATSY! OVER HERE!
HEDY WOLFE. BEEN A MINUTE...
YOU LOOK TIRED! I MEAN, I GET IT-- I CAN ONLY SLEEP IN FIRST CLASS, BUT NOT EVERYONE GETS TO FLY FIRST CLASS. HEY, DID YOU ACCIDENTALLY GRAB THE WRONG CARRY-ON?
NO.
YOU MEAN YOU ACTUALLY BOUGHT THAT?
YES.
YOU KNOW, HEDY, IT'S... SWEET OF YOU TO OFFER TO DRIVE ME, BUT I COULD'VE EASILY GOTTEN A CAB--
NONSENSE! IT'S BEEN AGES AND I WANT TO CATCH UP, HEAR ALL ABOUT YOUR LIFE!

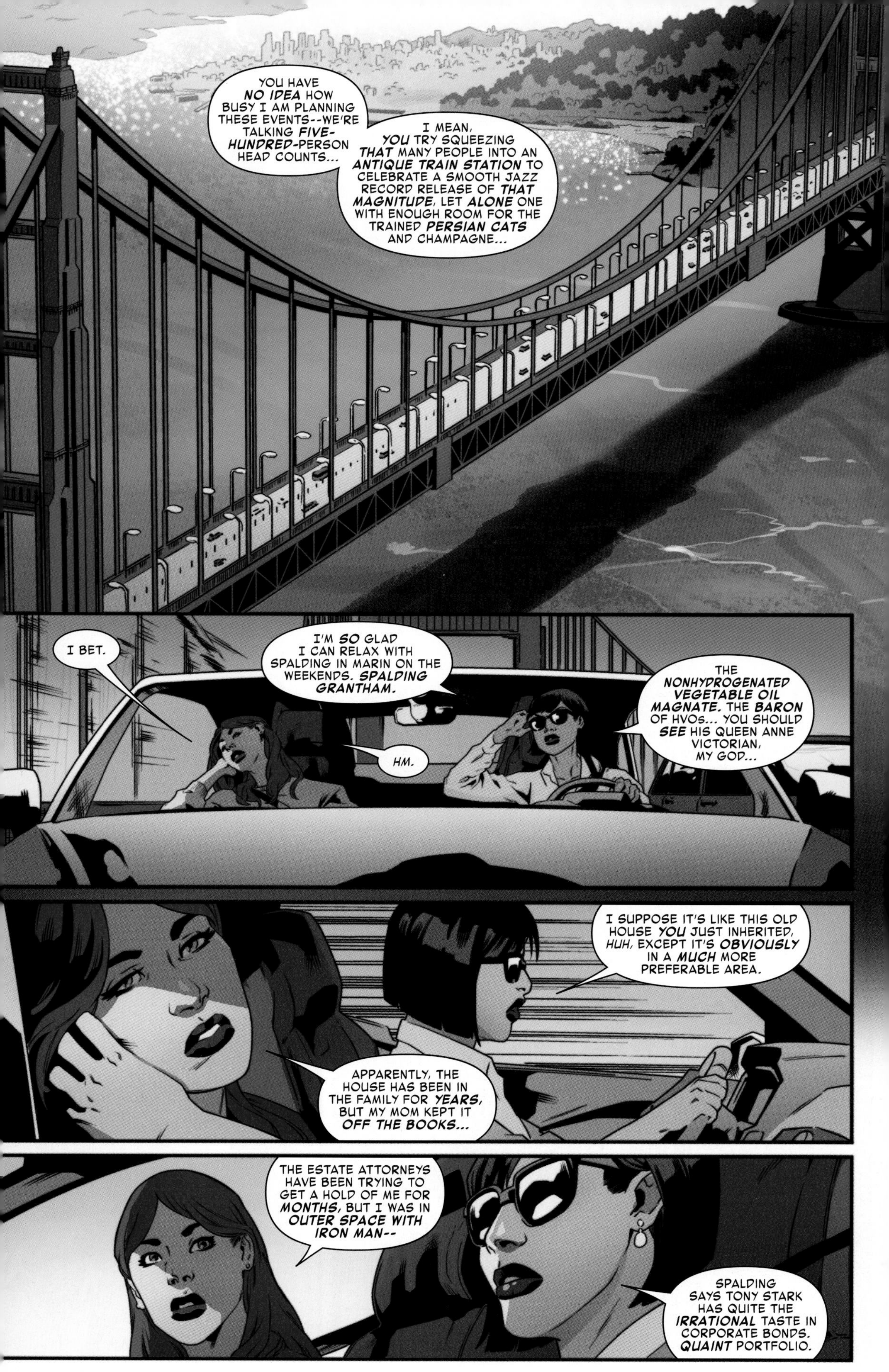
YOU HAVE NO IDEA HOW BUSY I AM PLANNING THESE EVENTS--WE'RE TALKING FIVE-HUNDRED-PERSON HEAD COUNTS...
I MEAN, YOU TRY SQUEEZING THAT MANY PEOPLE INTO AN ANTIQUE TRAIN STATION TO CELEBRATE A SMOOTH JAZZ RECORD RELEASE OF THAT MAGNITUDE, LET ALONE ONE WITH ENOUGH ROOM FOR THE TRAINED PERSIAN CATS AND CHAMPAGNE...
I BET.
I'M SO GLAD I CAN RELAX WITH SPALDING IN MARIN ON THE WEEKENDS. SPALDING GRANTHAM.
HM.
THE NONHYDROGENATED VEGETABLE OIL MAGNATE. THE BARON OF HVOS... YOU SHOULD SEE HIS QUEEN ANNE VICTORIAN, MY GOD...
I SUPPOSE IT'S LIKE THIS OLD HOUSE YOU JUST INHERITED, HUH, EXCEPT IT'S OBVIOUSLY IN A MUCH MORE PREFERABLE AREA.
APPARENTLY, THE HOUSE HAS BEEN IN THE FAMILY FOR YEARS, BUT MY MOM KEPT IT OFF THE BOOKS...
THE ESTATE ATTORNEYS HAVE BEEN TRYING TO GET A HOLD OF ME FOR MONTHS, BUT I WAS IN OUTER SPACE WITH IRON MAN--
SPALDING SAYS TONY STARK HAS QUITE THE IRRATIONAL TASTE IN CORPORATE BONDS. QUAINT PORTFOLIO.

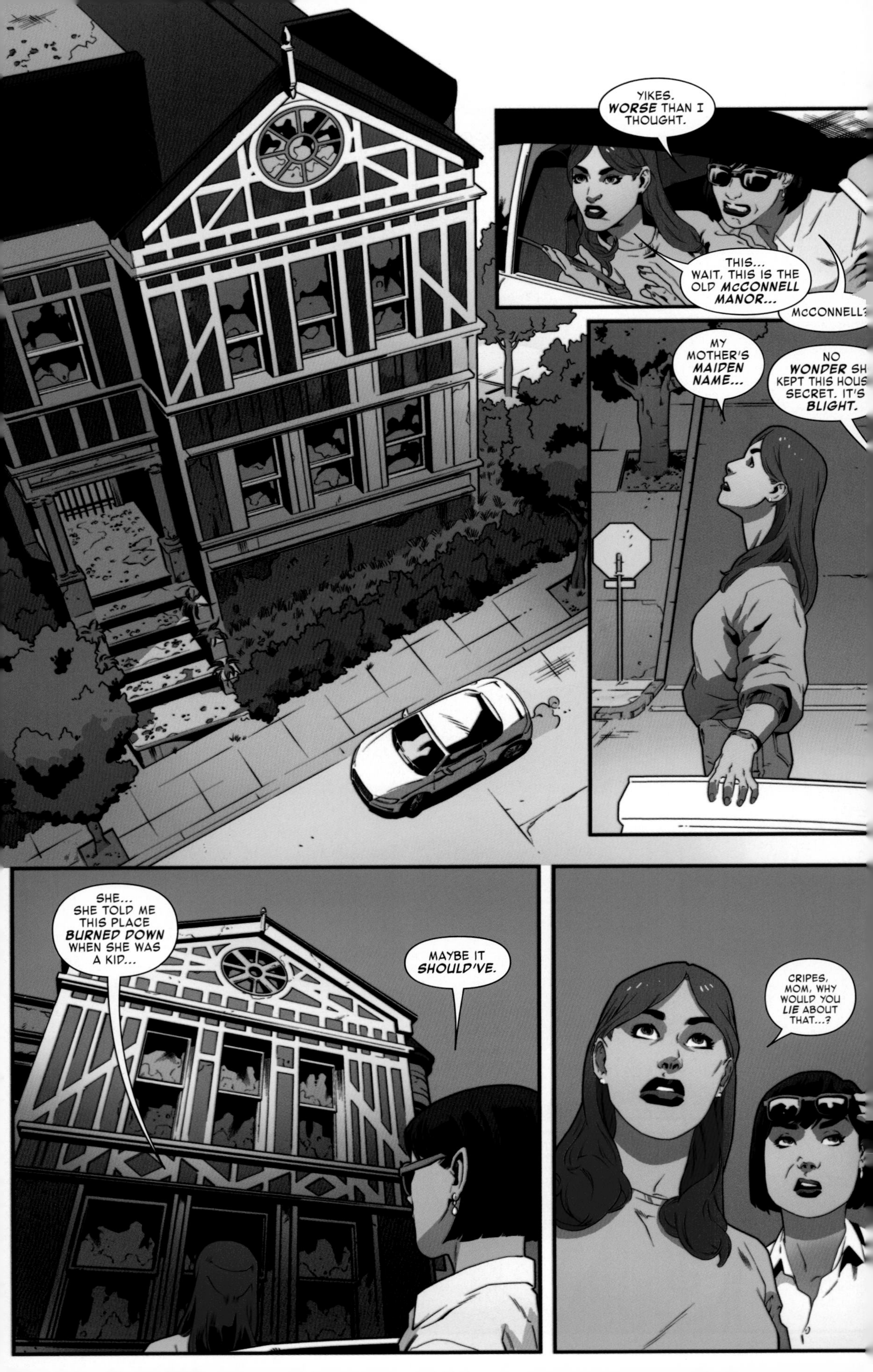
YIKES. WORSE THAN I THOUGHT.
THIS... WAIT, THIS IS THE OLD McCONNELL MANOR...
McCONNELL?
MY MOTHER'S MAIDEN NAME...
NO WONDER SH KEPT THIS HOUS SECRET. IT'S BLIGHT.
SHE... SHE TOLD ME THIS PLACE BURNED DOWN WHEN SHE WAS A KID...
MAYBE IT SHOULD'VE.
CRIPES, MOM, WHY WOULD YOU LIE ABOUT THAT...?

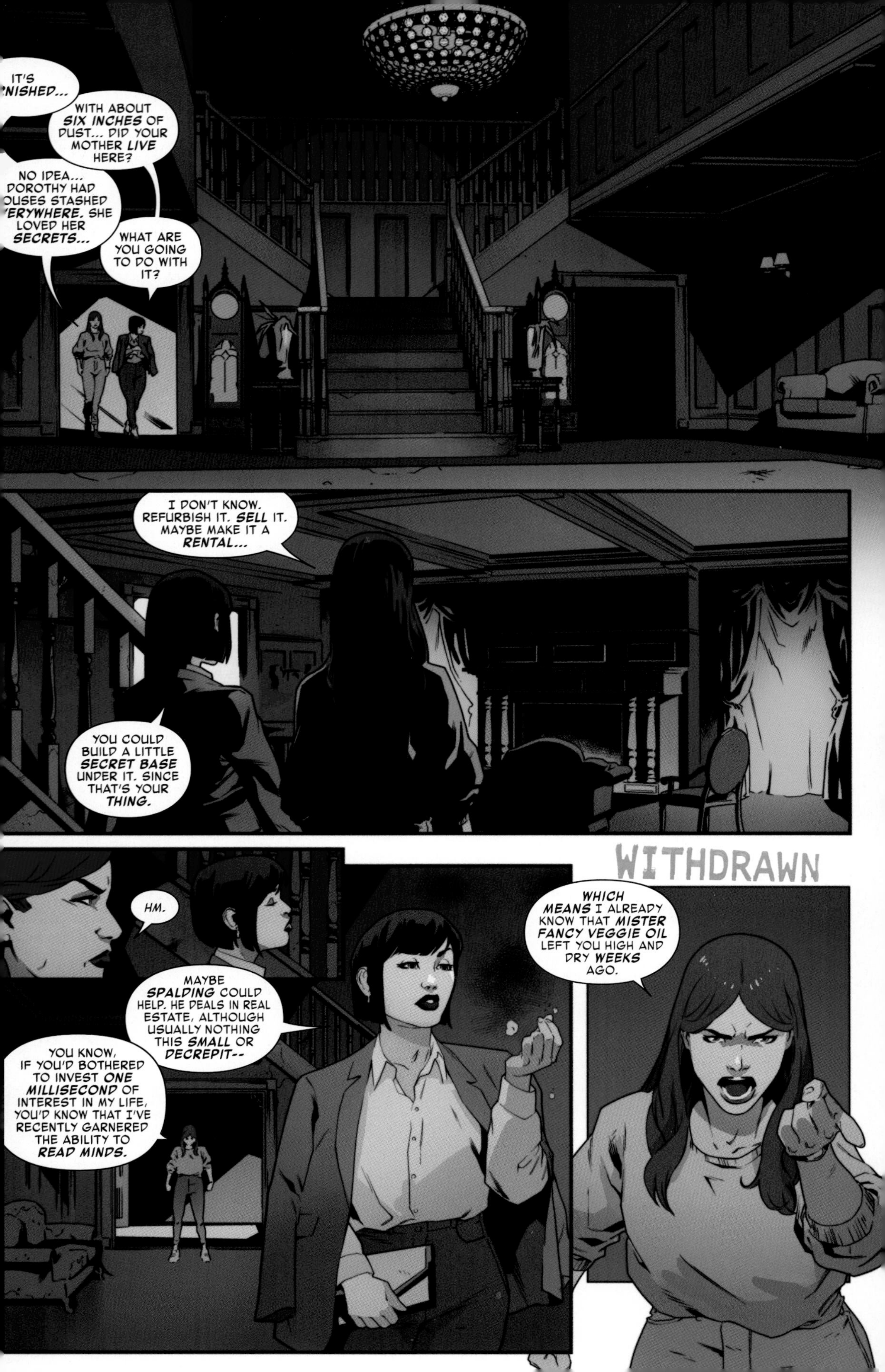
IT'S NISHED...
WITH ABOUT SIX INCHES OF DUST... DID YOUR MOTHER LIVE HERE?
NO IDEA... DOROTHY HAD OUSES STASHED YERYWHERE. SHE LOVED HER SECRETS...
WHAT ARE YOU GOING TO DO WITH IT?
I DON'T KNOW. REFURBISH IT. SELL IT. MAYBE MAKE IT A RENTAL...
YOU COULD BUILD A LITTLE SECRET BASE UNDER IT. SINCE THAT'S YOUR THING.
HM.
MAYBE SPALDING COULD HELP. HE DEALS IN REAL ESTATE, ALTHOUGH USUALLY NOTHING THIS SMALL OR DECREPIT--
YOU KNOW, IF YOU'D BOTHERED TO INVEST ONE MILLISECOND OF INTEREST IN MY LIFE, YOU'D KNOW THAT I'VE RECENTLY GARNERED THE ABILITY TO READ MINDS.
WHICH MEANS I ALREADY KNOW THAT MISTER FANCY VEGGIE OIL LEFT YOU HIGH AND DRY WEEKS AGO.

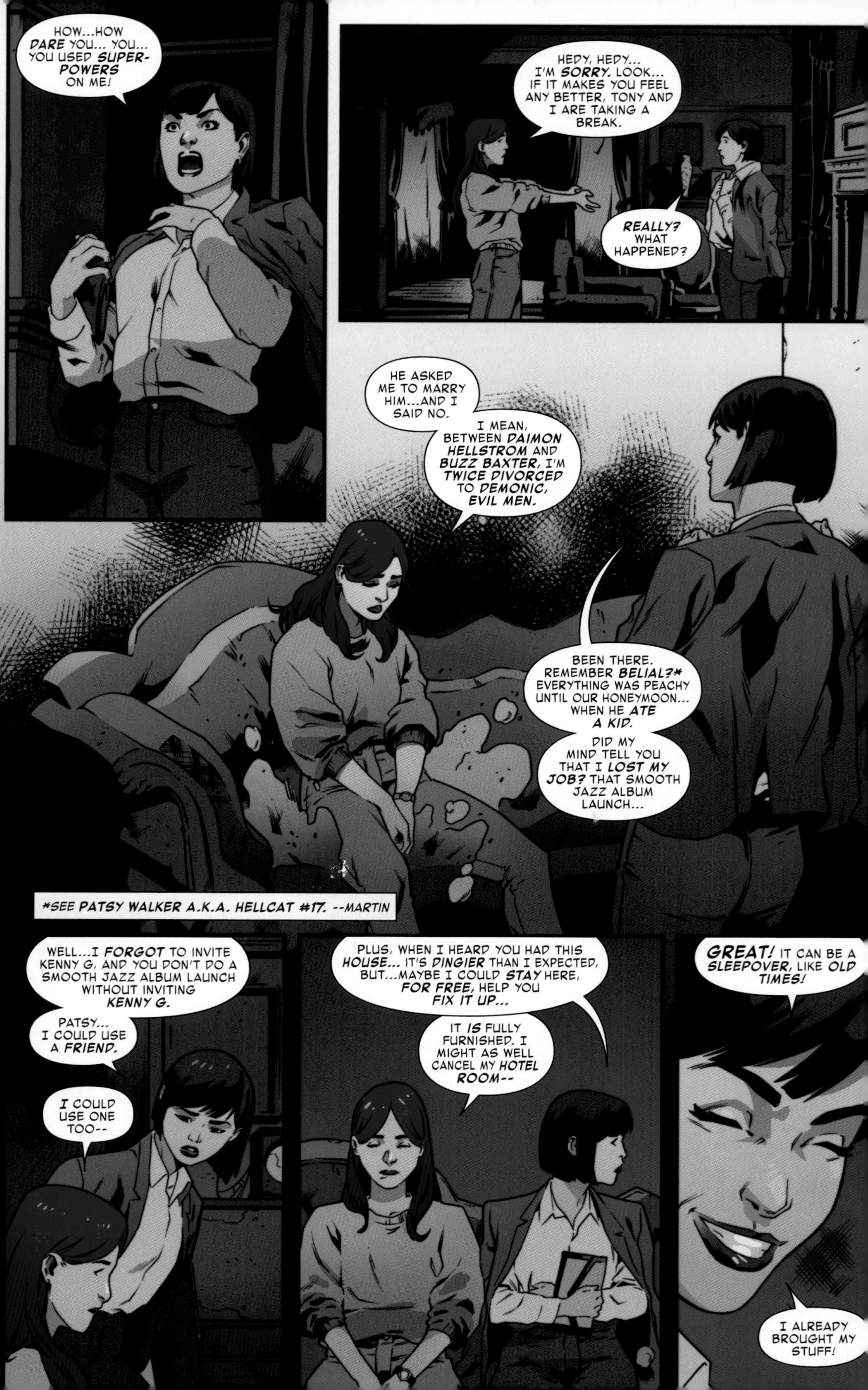

HOW...HOW DARE YOU... YOU... YOU USED SUPER-POWERS ON ME!
HEDY, HEDY... I'M SORRY. LOOK... IF IT MAKES YOU FEEL ANY BETTER, TONY AND I ARE TAKING A BREAK.
REALLY? WHAT HAPPENED?
HE ASKED ME TO MARRY HIM...AND I SAID NO.
I MEAN, BETWEEN DAIMON HELLSTROM AND BUZZ BAXTER, I'M TWICE DIVORCED TO DEMONIC, EVIL MEN.
BEEN THERE. REMEMBER BELIAL?* EVERYTHING WAS PEACHY UNTIL OUR HONEYMOON... WHEN HE ATE A KID.
DID MY MIND TELL YOU THAT I LOST MY JOB? THAT SMOOTH JAZZ ALBUM LAUNCH...
*SEE PATSY WALKER A.K.A. HELLCAT #17. --MARTIN
WELL...I FORGOT TO INVITE KENNY G, AND YOU DON'T DO A SMOOTH JAZZ ALBUM LAUNCH WITHOUT INVITING KENNY G.
PATSY... I COULD USE A FRIEND.
I COULD USE ONE TOO--
PLUS, WHEN I HEARD YOU HAD THIS HOUSE... IT'S DINGIER THAN I EXPECTED, BUT...MAYBE I COULD STAY HERE, FOR FREE, HELP YOU FIX IT UP...
IT IS FULLY FURNISHED. I MIGHT AS WELL CANCEL MY HOTEL ROOM--
GREAT! IT CAN BE A SLEEPOVER, LIKE OLD TIMES!
I ALREADY BROUGHT MY STUFF!

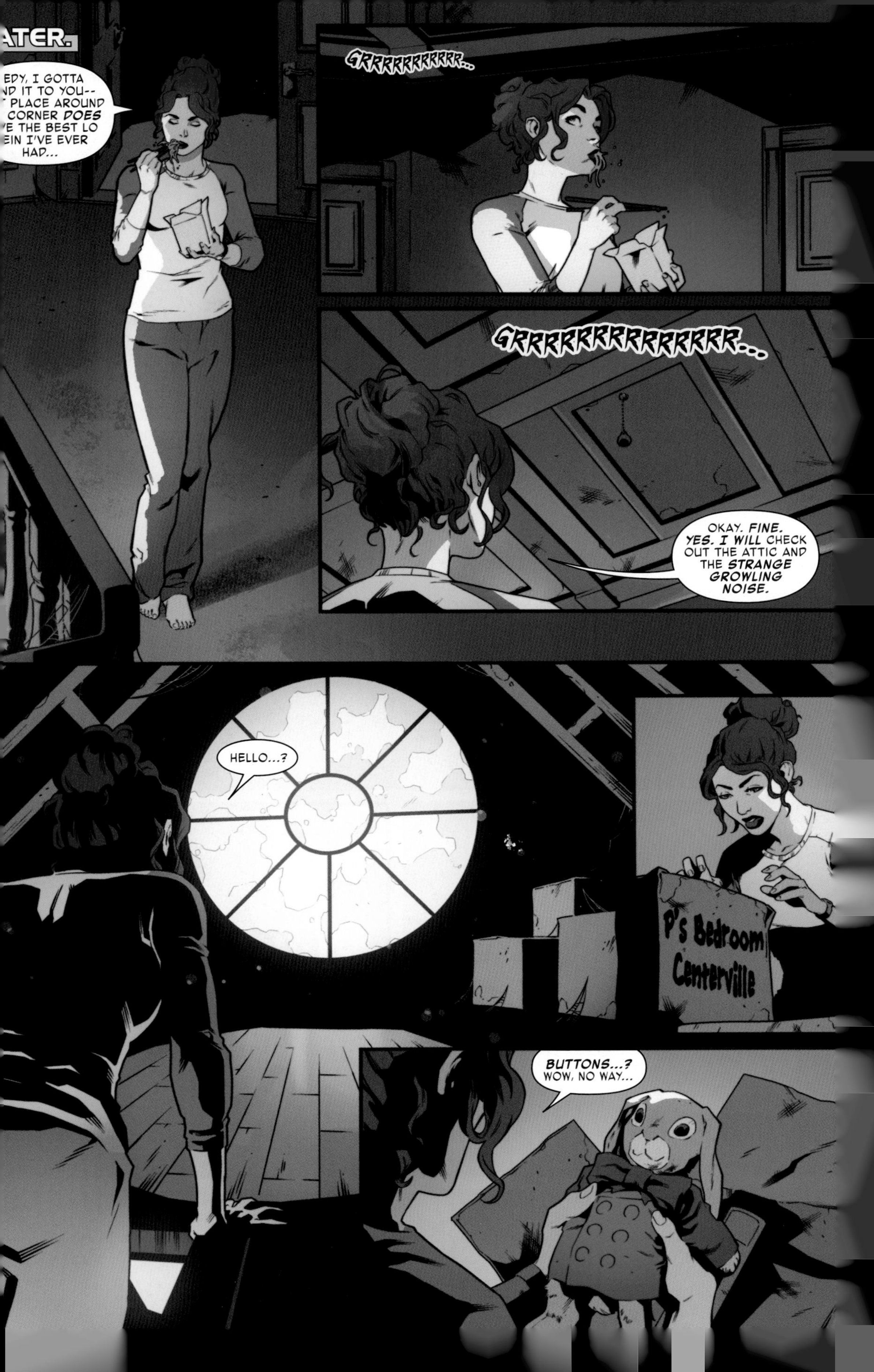
ATER.
EDY, I GOTTA
ND IT TO YOU--
PLACE AROUND
CORNER DOES
E THE BEST LO
EIN I'VE EVER
HAD...
GRRRRRRRRRRR...
GRRRRRRRRRRRRRRR...
OKAY. FINE. YES. I WILL CHECK OUT THE ATTIC AND THE STRANGE GROWLING NOISE.
HELLO...?
P's Bedroom Centerville
BUTTONS...? WOW, NO WAY...

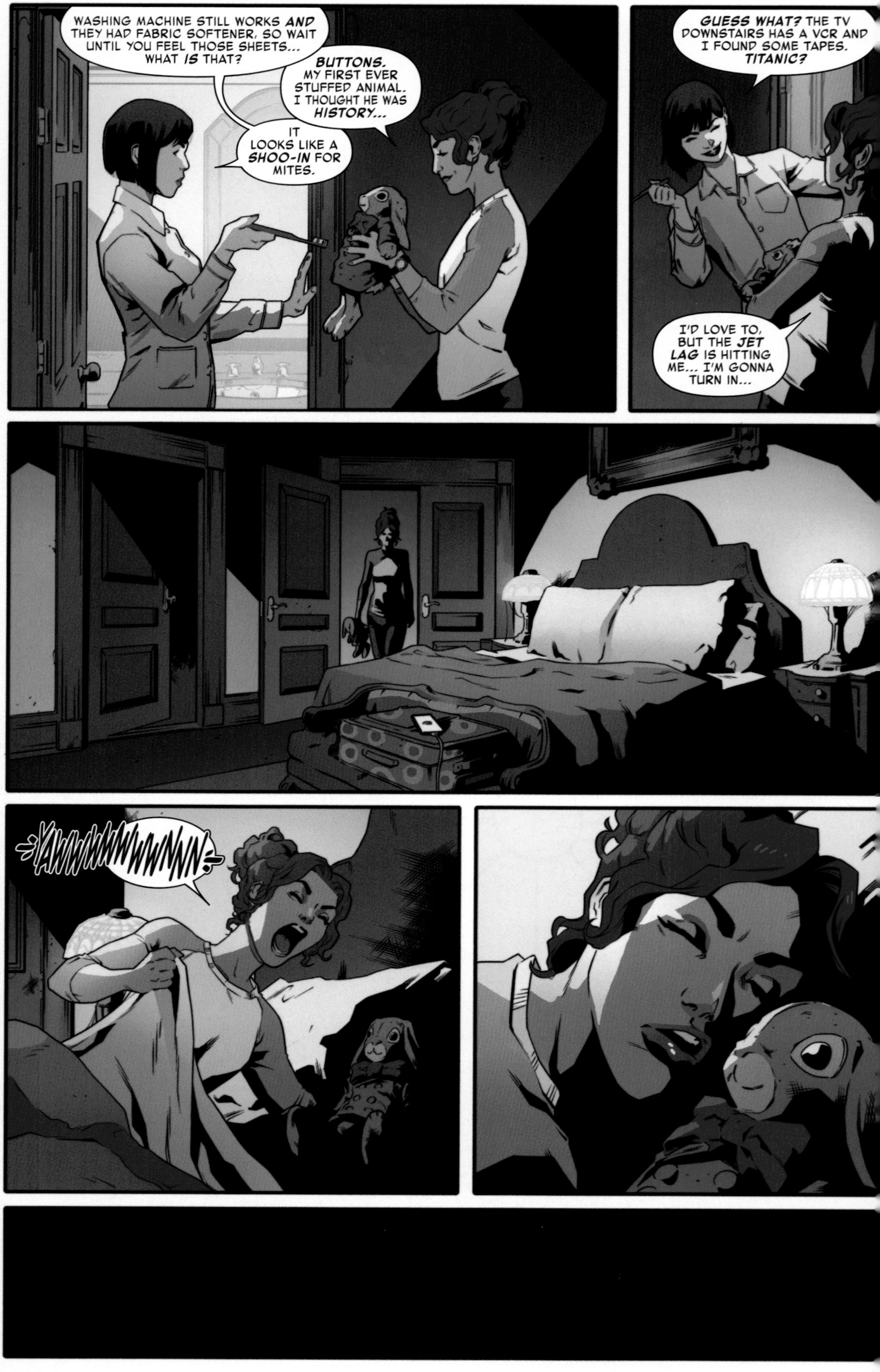
WASHING MACHINE STILL WORKS AND THEY HAD FABRIC SOFTENER, SO WAIT UNTIL YOU FEEL THOSE SHEETS... WHAT IS THAT?
BUTTONS. MY FIRST EVER STUFFED ANIMAL. I THOUGHT HE WAS HISTORY...
IT LOOKS LIKE A SHOO-IN FOR MITES.
GUESS WHAT? THE TV DOWNSTAIRS HAS A VCR AND I FOUND SOME TAPES. TITANIC?
I'D LOVE TO, BUT THE JET LAG IS HITTING ME... I'M GONNA TURN IN...
YAWWWWWWWNNN

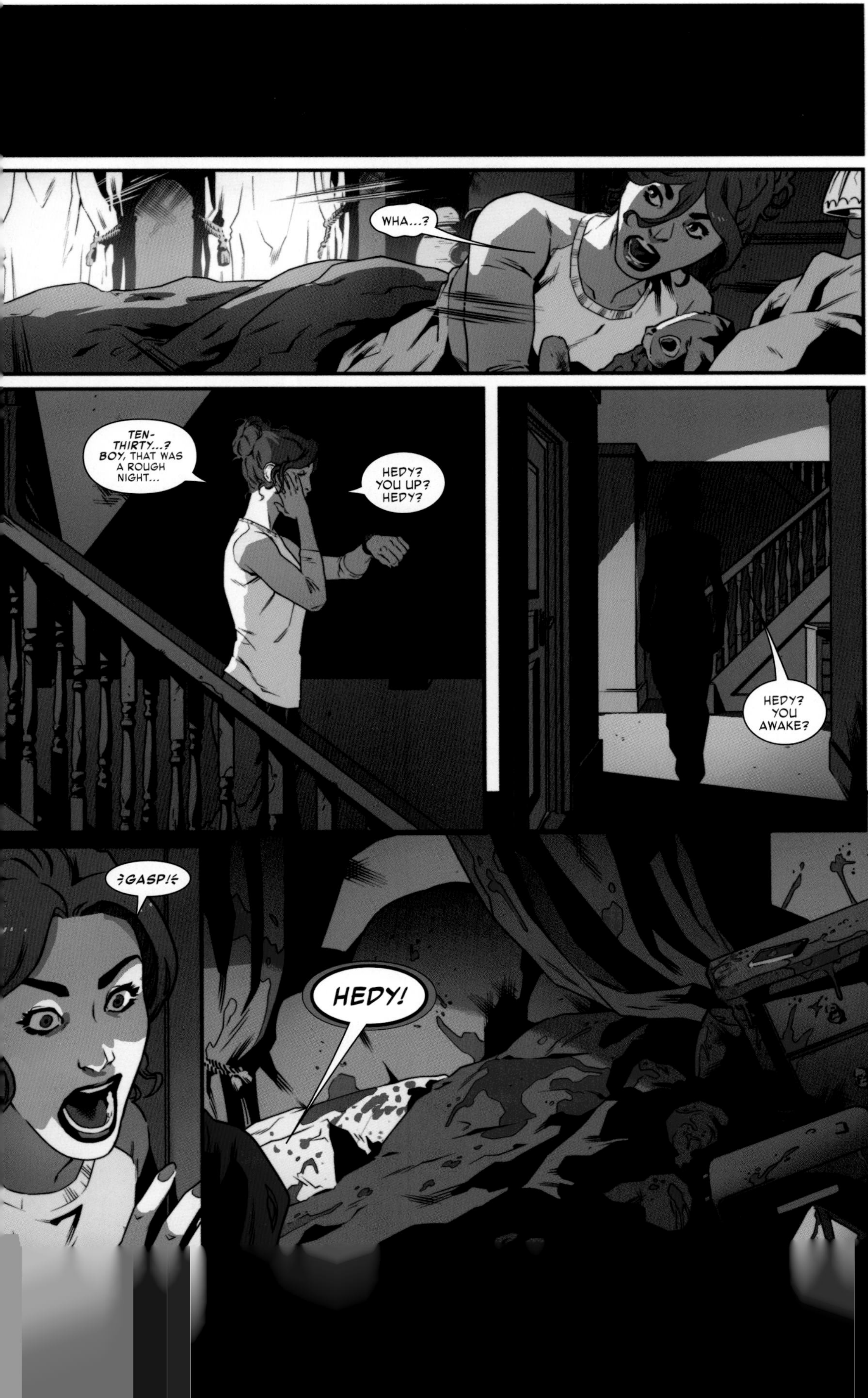
WHA...?
TEN-THIRTY...? BOY, THAT WAS A ROUGH NIGHT...
HEDY? YOU UP? HEDY?
HEDY? YOU AWAKE?
GASP!
HEDY!

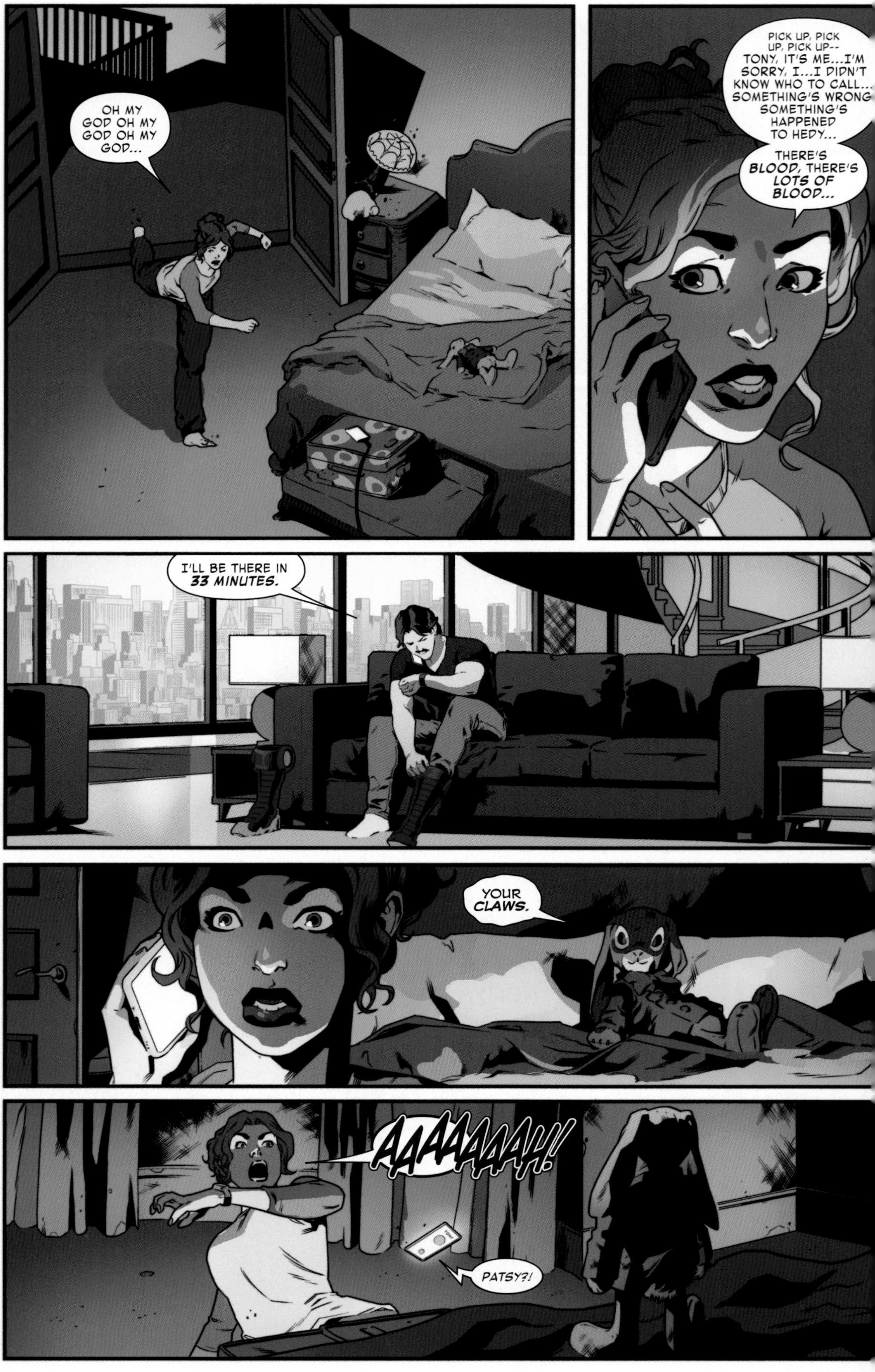
OH MY GOD OH MY GOD OH MY GOD...
PICK UP, PICK UP, PICK UP-- TONY, IT'S ME...I'M SORRY, I...I DIDN'T KNOW WHO TO CALL... SOMETHING'S WRONG SOMETHING'S HAPPENED TO HEDY...
THERE'S BLOOD, THERE'S LOTS OF BLOOD...
I'LL BE THERE IN 33 MINUTES.
YOUR CLAWS.
AAAAAAAAH!!
PATSY?!

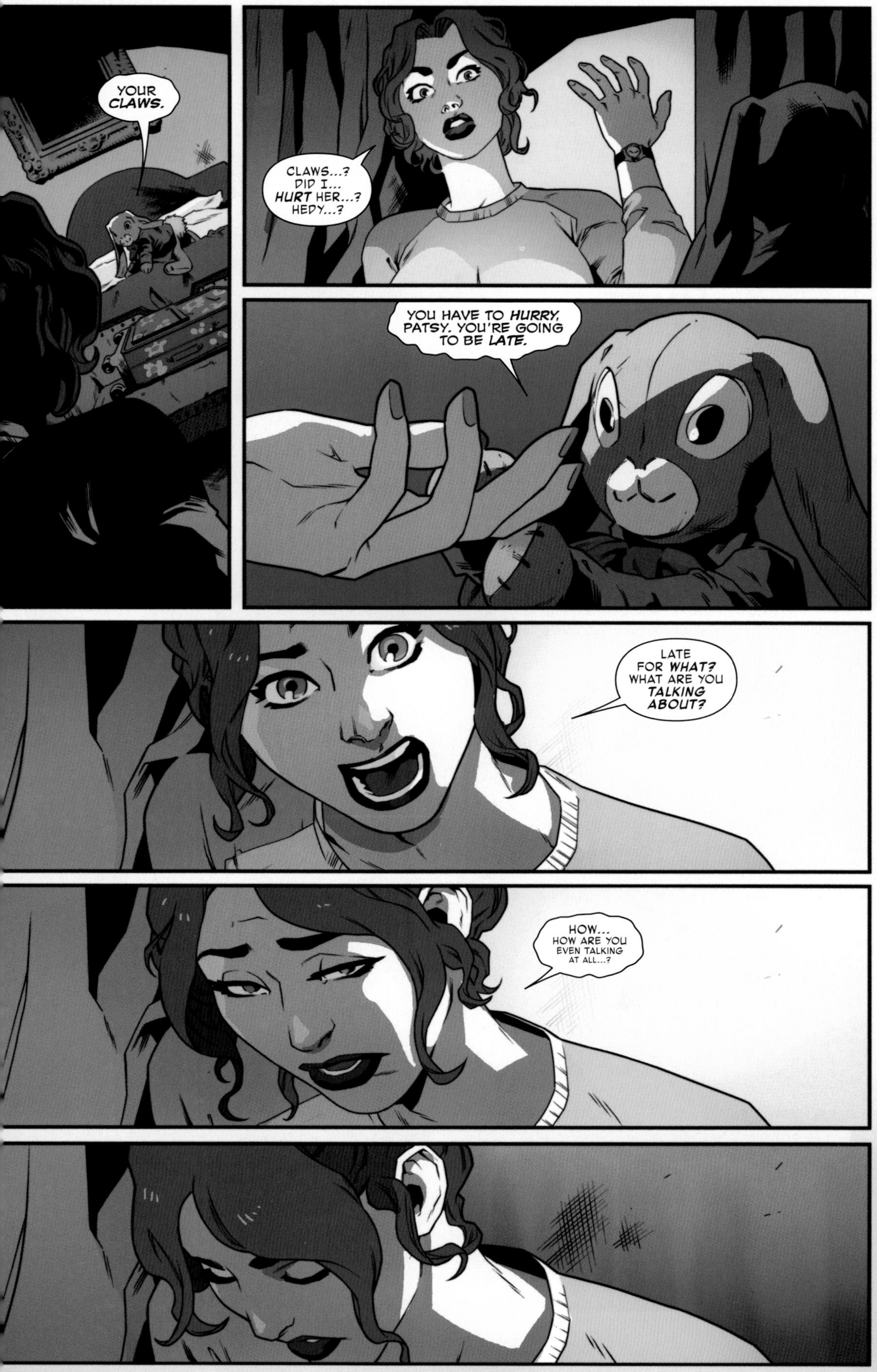
YOUR CLAWS.
CLAWS...? DID I... HURT HER...? HEDY...?
YOU HAVE TO HURRY, PATSY. YOU'RE GOING TO BE LATE.
LATE FOR WHAT? WHAT ARE YOU TALKING ABOUT?
HOW... HOW ARE YOU EVEN TALKING AT ALL...?

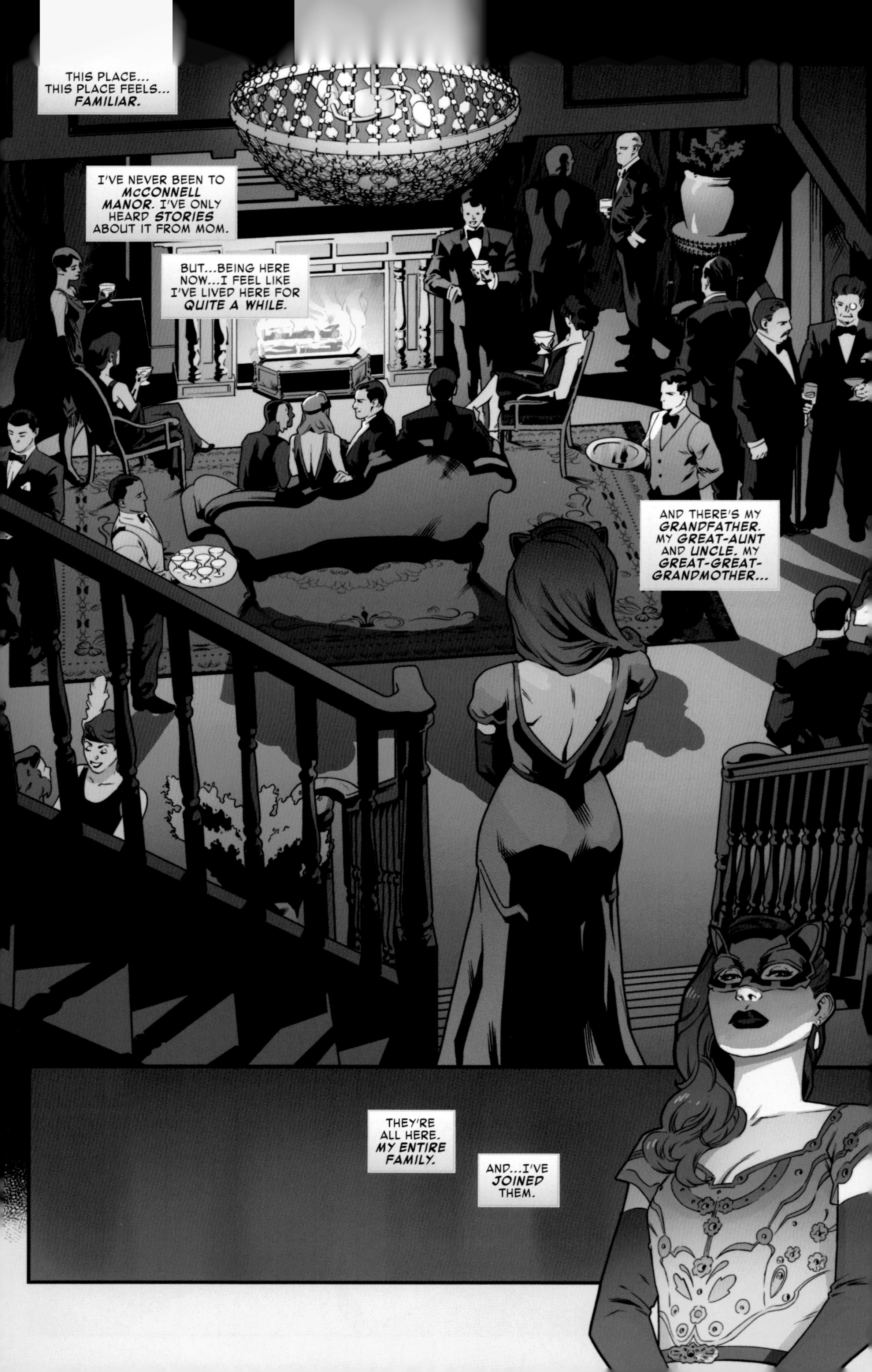
THIS PLACE... THIS PLACE FEELS... FAMILIAR.
I'VE NEVER BEEN TO McCONNELL MANOR. I'VE ONLY HEARD STORIES ABOUT IT FROM MOM.
BUT...BEING HERE NOW...I FEEL LIKE I'VE LIVED HERE FOR QUITE A WHILE.
AND THERE'S MY GRANDFATHER. MY GREAT-AUNT AND UNCLE. MY GREAT-GREAT-GRANDMOTHER...
THEY'RE ALL HERE. MY ENTIRE FAMILY.
AND...I'VE JOINED THEM.

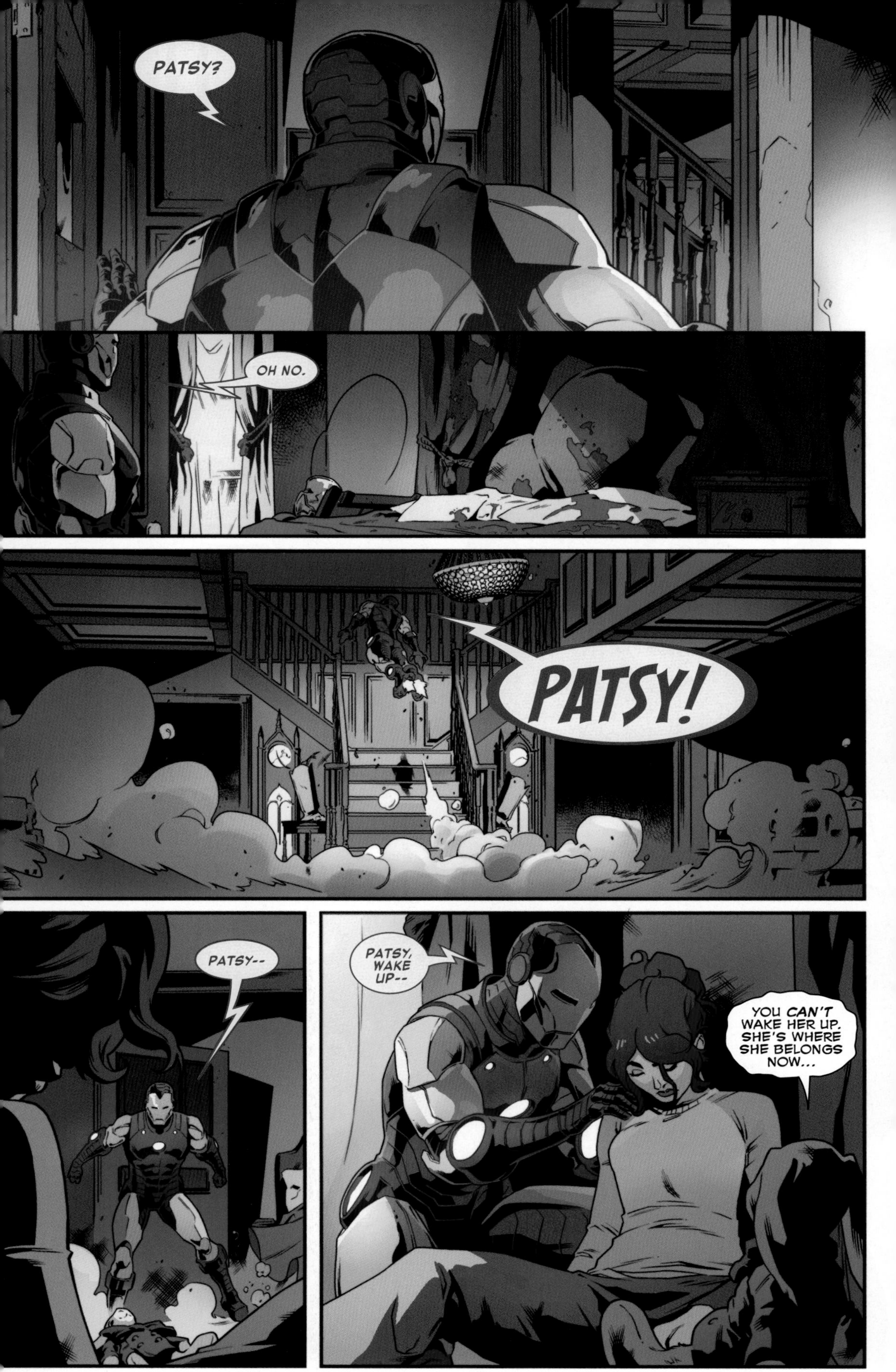
PATSY?
OH NO.
PATSY!
PATSY--
PATSY, WAKE UP--
YOU CAN'T WAKE HER UP. SHE'S WHERE SHE BELONGS NOW...

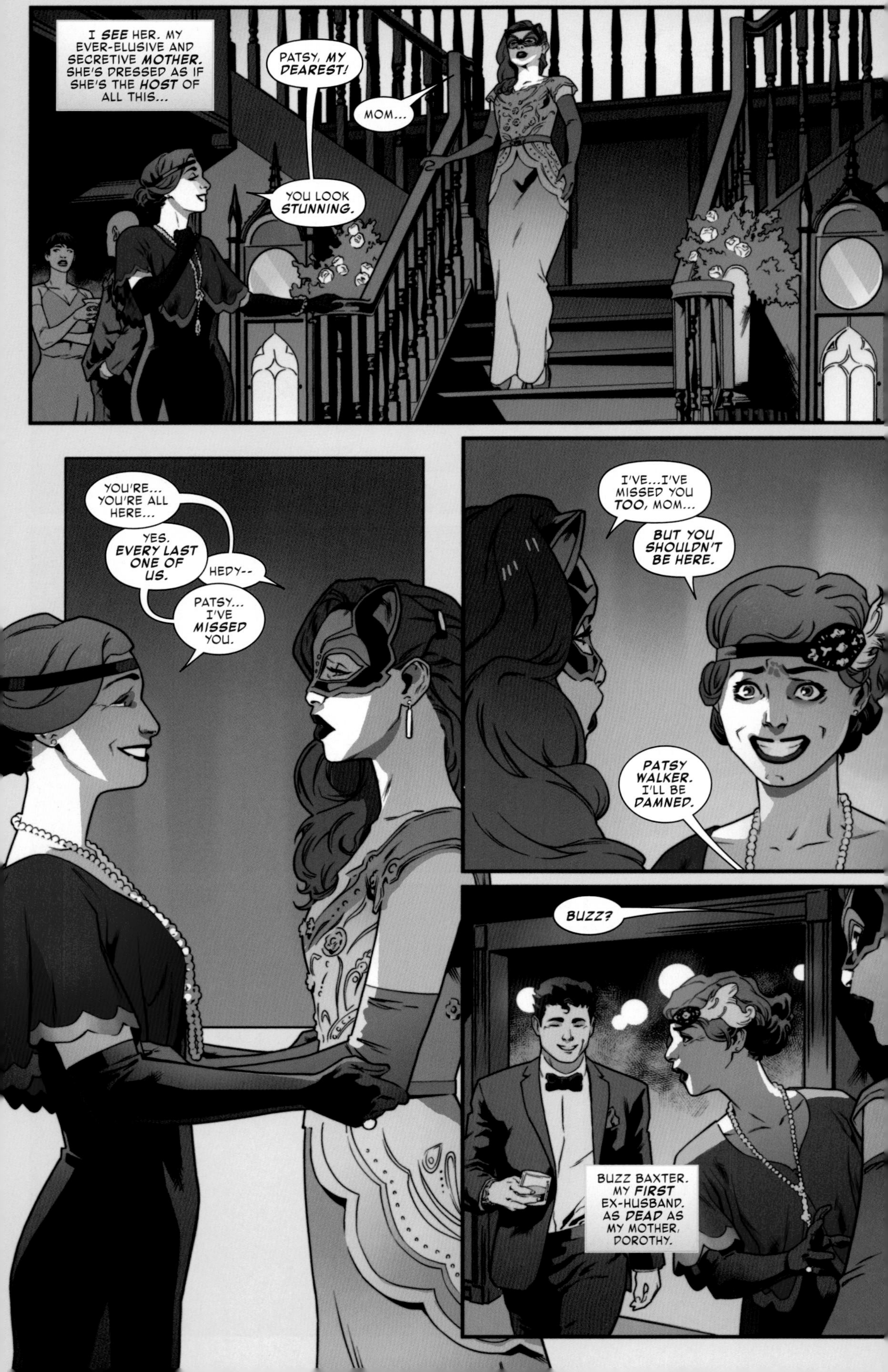
I SEE HER. MY EVER-ELUSIVE AND SECRETIVE MOTHER. SHE'S DRESSED AS IF SHE'S THE HOST OF ALL THIS...
PATSY, MY DEAREST!
MOM...
YOU LOOK STUNNING.
YOU'RE... YOU'RE ALL HERE...
YES. EVERY LAST ONE OF US.
HEDY--
PATSY... I'VE MISSED YOU.
I'VE...I'VE MISSED YOU TOO, MOM...
BUT YOU SHOULDN'T BE HERE.
PATSY WALKER. I'LL BE DAMNED.
BUZZ?
BUZZ BAXTER. MY FIRST EX-HUSBAND. AS DEAD AS MY MOTHER, DOROTHY.

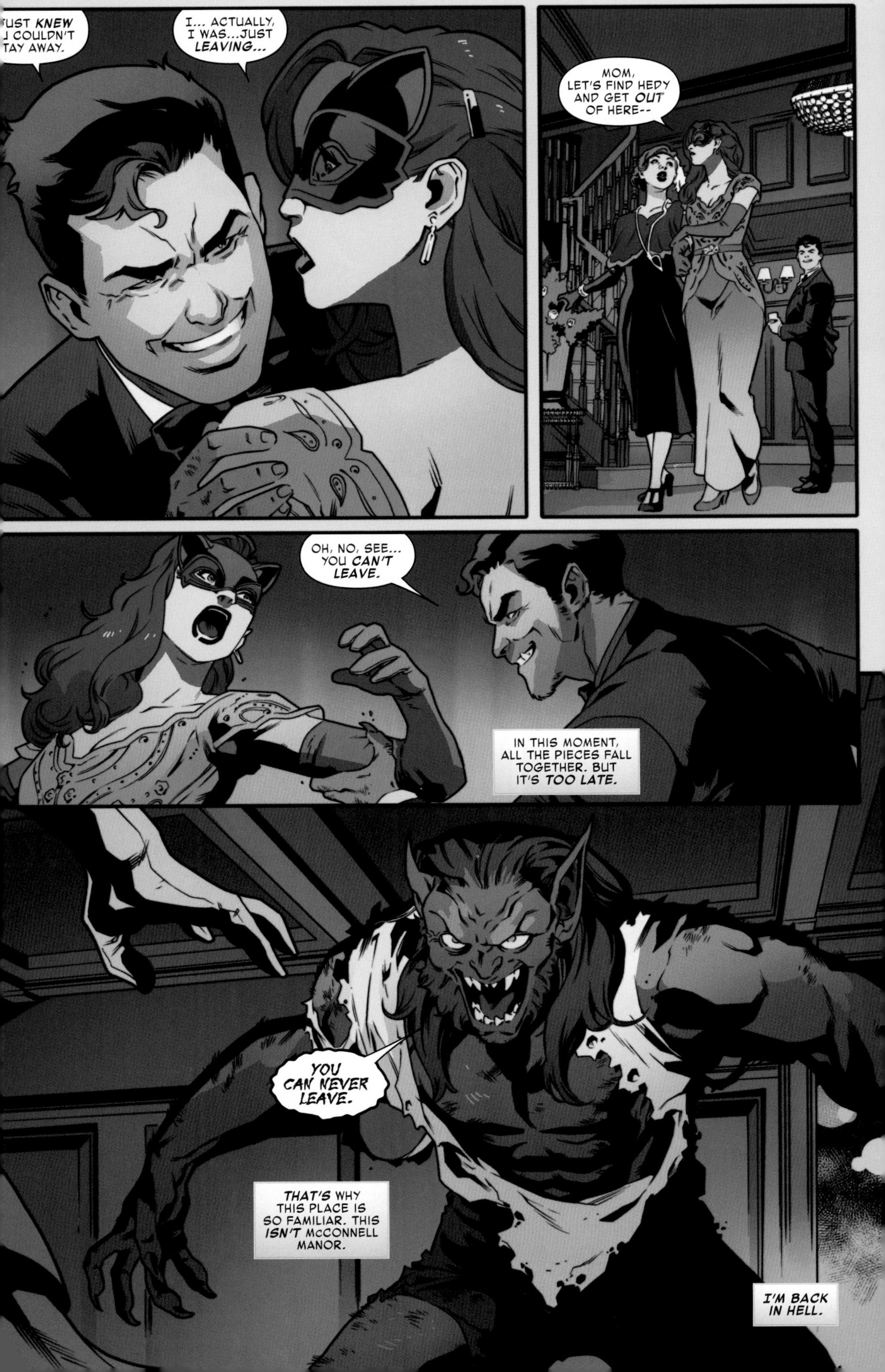

JUST KNEW
U COULDN'T
TAY AWAY.
I... ACTUALLY, I WAS...JUST LEAVING...
MOM, LET'S FIND HEDY AND GET OUT OF HERE--
OH, NO, SEE... YOU CAN'T LEAVE.
IN THIS MOMENT, ALL THE PIECES FALL TOGETHER. BUT IT'S TOO LATE.
YOU CAN NEVER LEAVE.
THAT'S WHY THIS PLACE IS SO FAMILIAR. THIS ISN'T McCONNELL MANOR.
I'M BACK IN HELL.

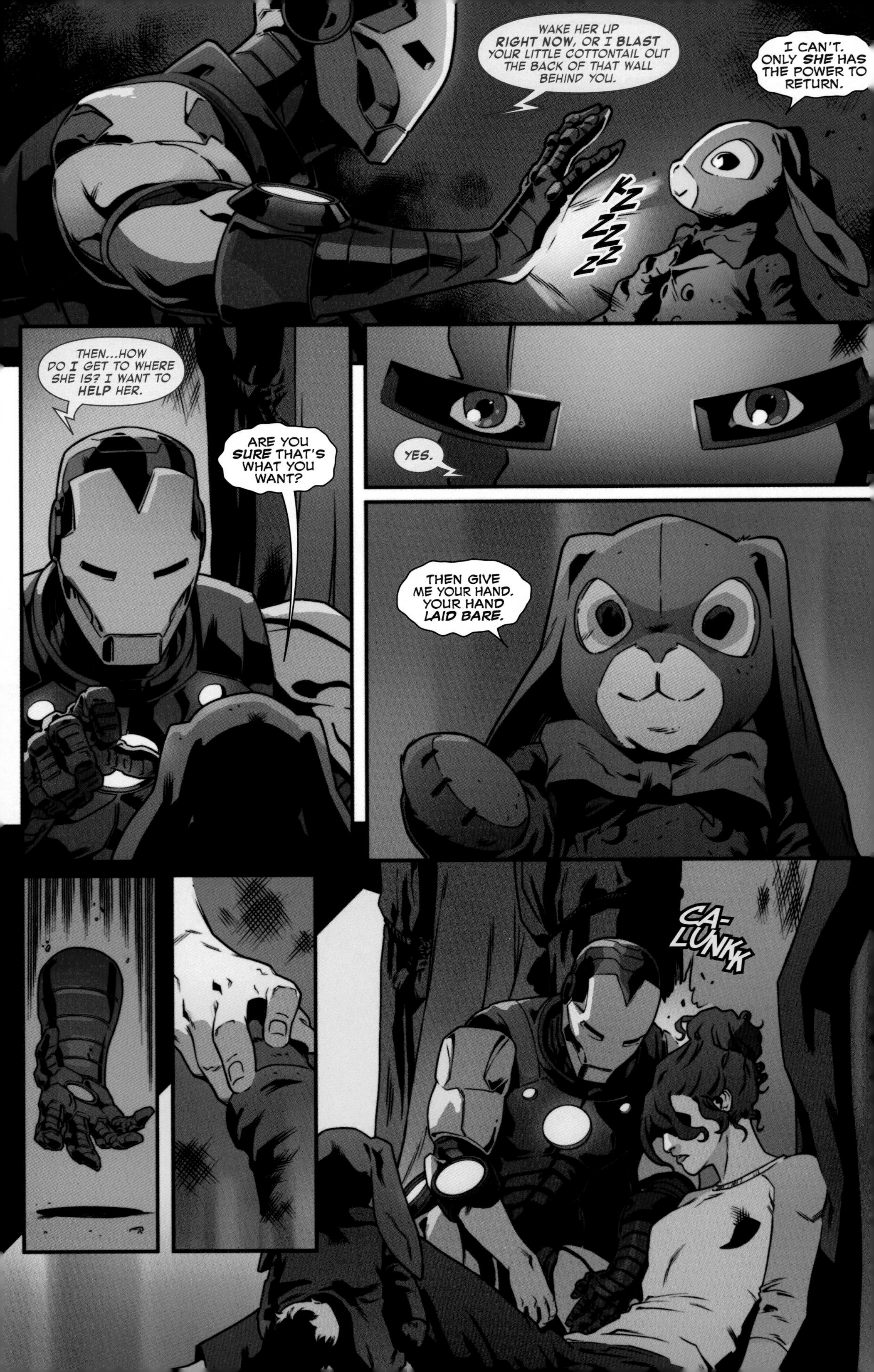
WAKE HER UP RIGHT NOW, OR I BLAST YOUR LITTLE COTTONTAIL OUT THE BACK OF THAT WALL BEHIND YOU.
KZZZZZ
I CAN'T. ONLY SHE HAS THE POWER TO RETURN.
THEN...HOW DO I GET TO WHERE SHE IS? I WANT TO HELP HER.
ARE YOU SURE THAT'S WHAT YOU WANT?
YES.
THEN GIVE ME YOUR HAND. YOUR HAND LAID BARE.
CA-LUNKK

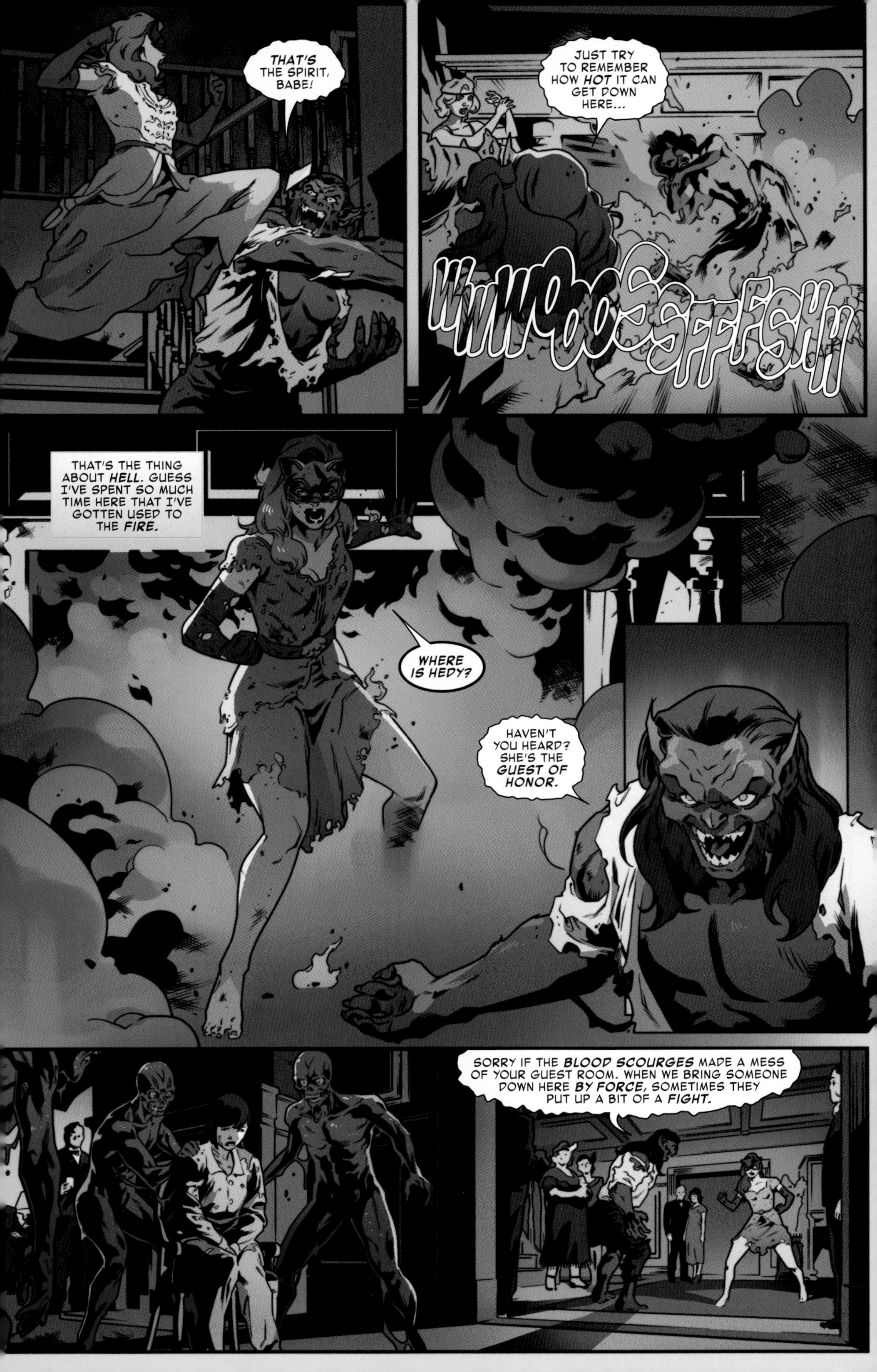
THAT'S THE SPIRIT, BABE!
JUST TRY TO REMEMBER HOW HOT IT CAN GET DOWN HERE...
WWWOOOSSFFFSHH
THAT'S THE THING ABOUT HELL. GUESS I'VE SPENT SO MUCH TIME HERE THAT I'VE GOTTEN USED TO THE FIRE.
WHERE IS HEDY?
HAVEN'T YOU HEARD? SHE'S THE GUEST OF HONOR.
SORRY IF THE BLOOD SCOURGES MADE A MESS OF YOUR GUEST ROOM. WHEN WE BRING SOMEONE DOWN HERE BY FORCE, SOMETIMES THEY PUT UP A BIT OF A FIGHT.

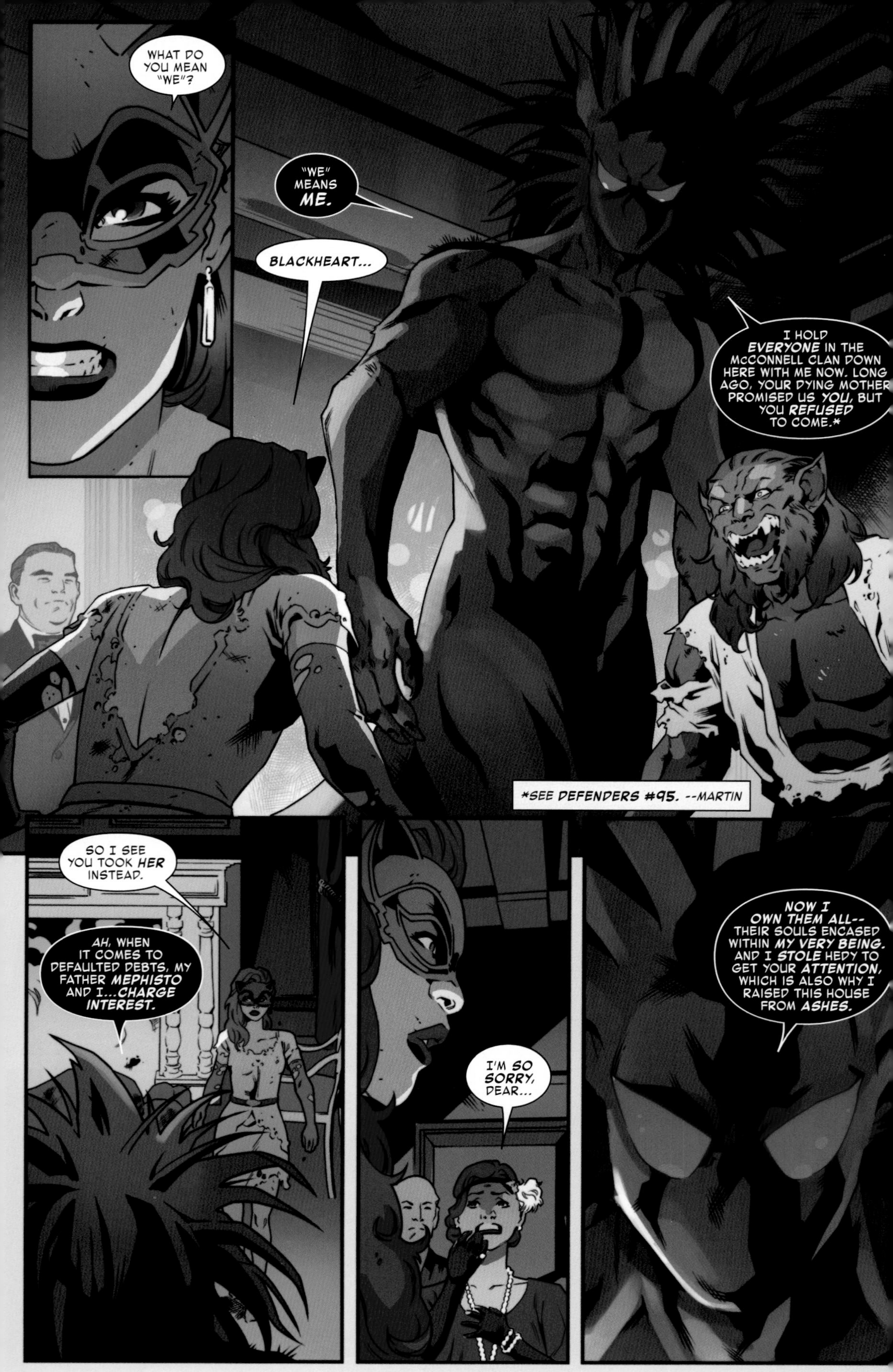
WHAT DO YOU MEAN "WE"?
"WE" MEANS ME.
BLACKHEART...
I HOLD EVERYONE IN THE McCONNELL CLAN DOWN HERE WITH ME NOW. LONG AGO, YOUR DYING MOTHER PROMISED US YOU, BUT YOU REFUSED TO COME.*
*SEE DEFENDERS #95. --MARTIN
SO I SEE YOU TOOK HER INSTEAD.
AH, WHEN IT COMES TO DEFAULTED DEBTS, MY FATHER MEPHISTO AND I...CHARGE INTEREST.
I'M SO SORRY, DEAR...
NOW I OWN THEM ALL-- THEIR SOULS ENCASED WITHIN MY VERY BEING. AND I STOLE HEDY TO GET YOUR ATTENTION, WHICH IS ALSO WHY I RAISED THIS HOUSE FROM ASHES.

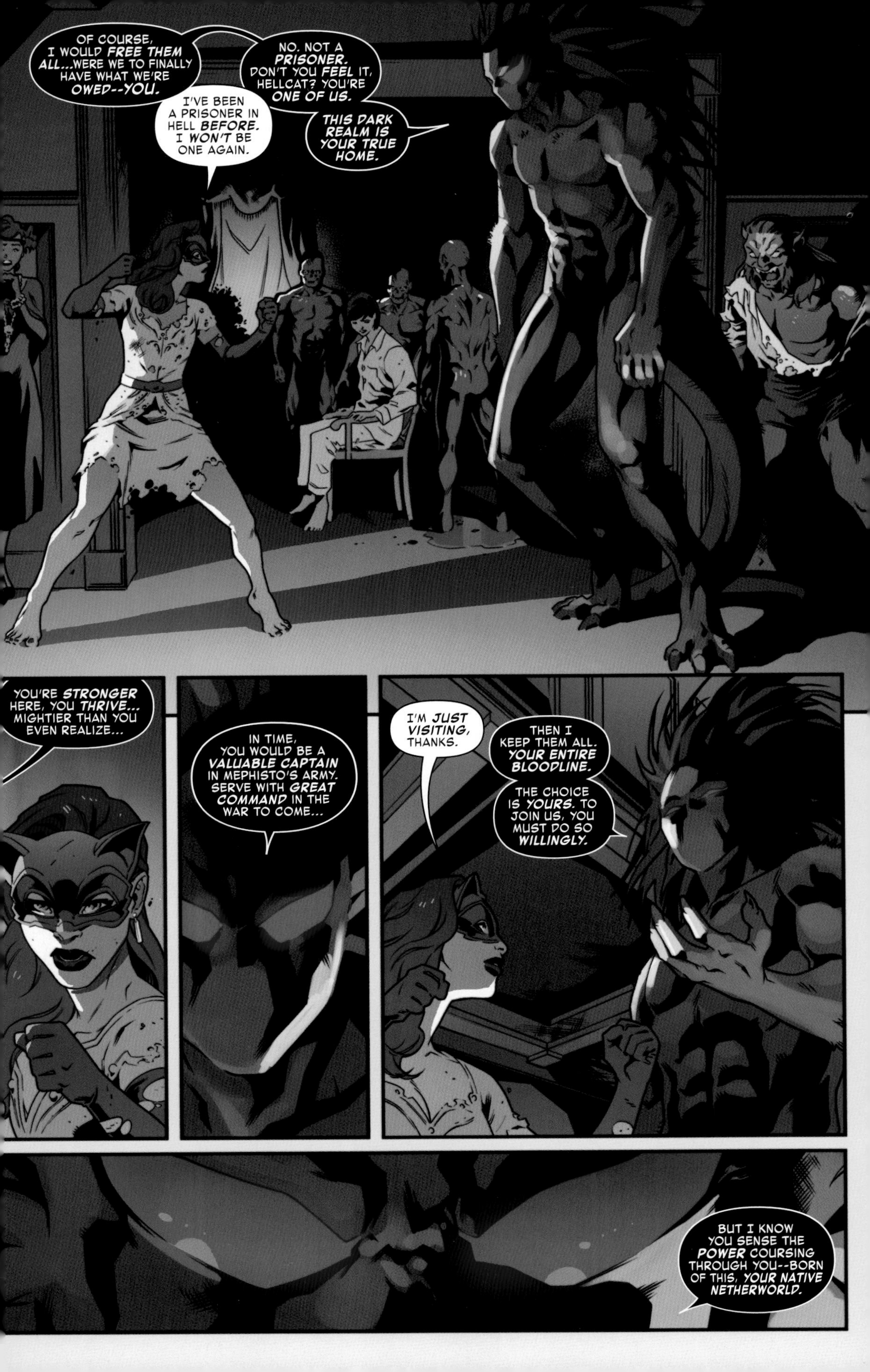

OF COURSE, I WOULD FREE THEM ALL...WERE WE TO FINALLY HAVE WHAT WE'RE OWED--YOU.
I'VE BEEN A PRISONER IN HELL BEFORE. I WON'T BE ONE AGAIN.
NO. NOT A PRISONER. DON'T YOU FEEL IT, HELLCAT? YOU'RE ONE OF US.
THIS DARK REALM IS YOUR TRUE HOME.
YOU'RE STRONGER HERE, YOU THRIVE... MIGHTIER THAN YOU EVEN REALIZE...
IN TIME, YOU WOULD BE A VALUABLE CAPTAIN IN MEPHISTO'S ARMY. SERVE WITH GREAT COMMAND IN THE WAR TO COME...
I'M JUST VISITING, THANKS.
THEN I KEEP THEM ALL. YOUR ENTIRE BLOODLINE.
THE CHOICE IS YOURS. TO JOIN US, YOU MUST DO SO WILLINGLY.
BUT I KNOW YOU SENSE THE POWER COURSING THROUGH YOU--BORN OF THIS, YOUR NATIVE NETHERWORLD.

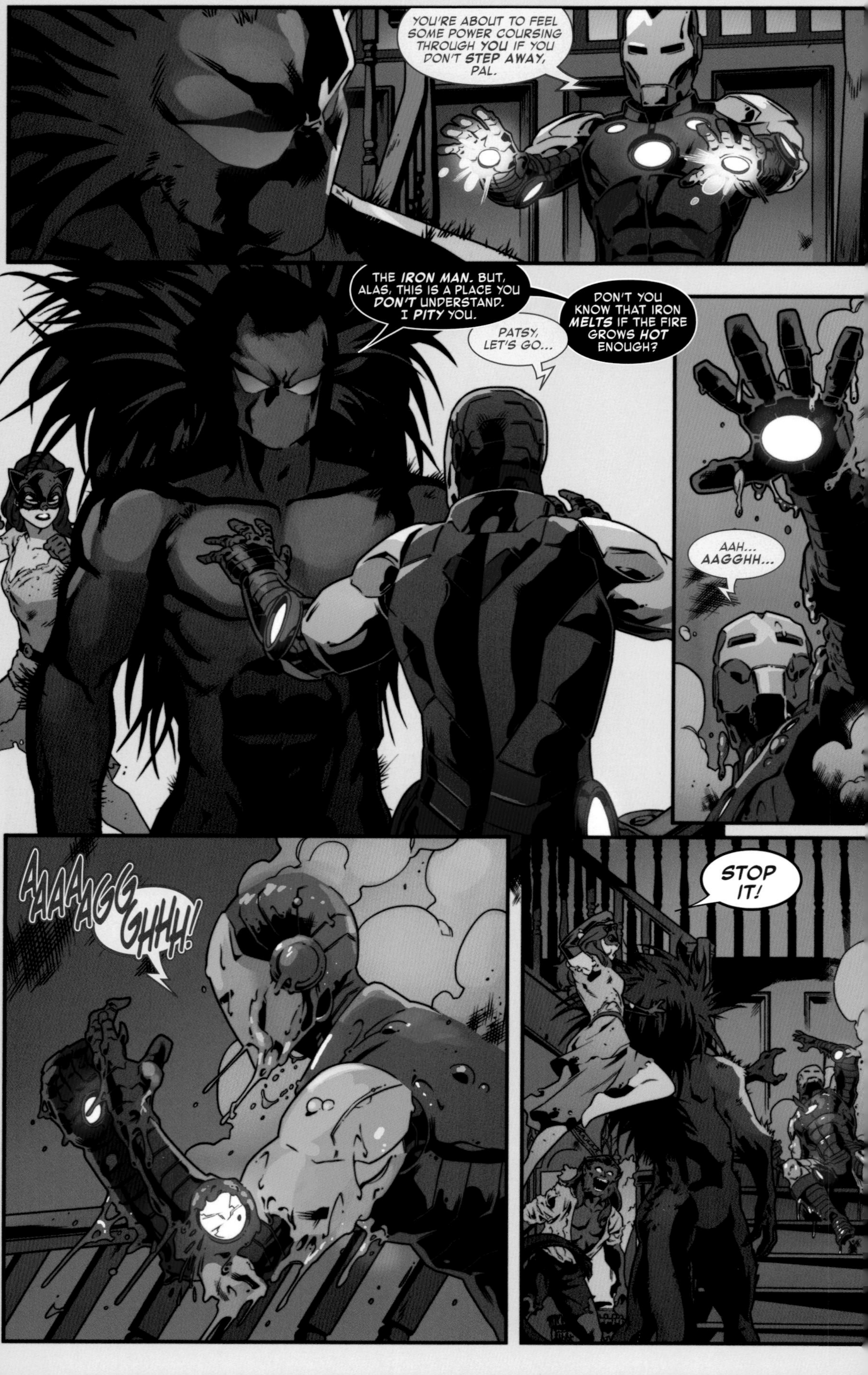
YOU'RE ABOUT TO FEEL SOME POWER COURSING THROUGH YOU IF YOU DON'T STEP AWAY, PAL.
THE IRON MAN. BUT, ALAS, THIS IS A PLACE YOU DON'T UNDERSTAND. I PITY YOU.
PATSY, LET'S GO...
DON'T YOU KNOW THAT IRON MELTS IF THE FIRE GROWS HOT ENOUGH?
AAH... AAGGHH...
AAAAAGGGHHH!
STOP IT!

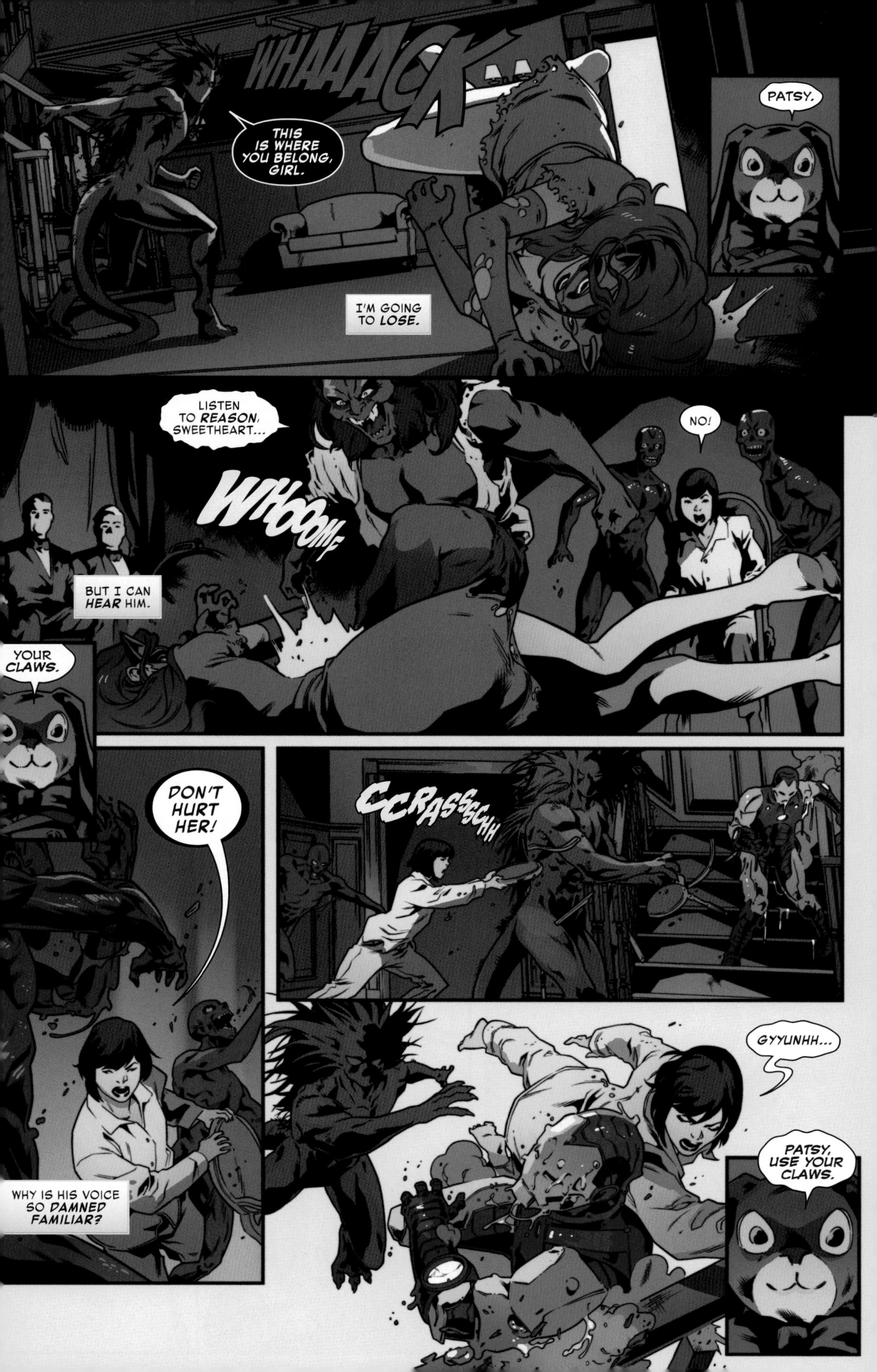
WHAAAACK
THIS IS WHERE YOU BELONG, GIRL.
PATSY.
I'M GOING TO LOSE.
LISTEN TO REASON, SWEETHEART...
WHOOOMF
NO!
BUT I CAN HEAR HIM.
YOUR CLAWS.
DON'T HURT HER!
CCRASSSCHH
GYYUNHH...
WHY IS HIS VOICE SO DAMNED FAMILIAR?
PATSY, USE YOUR CLAWS.

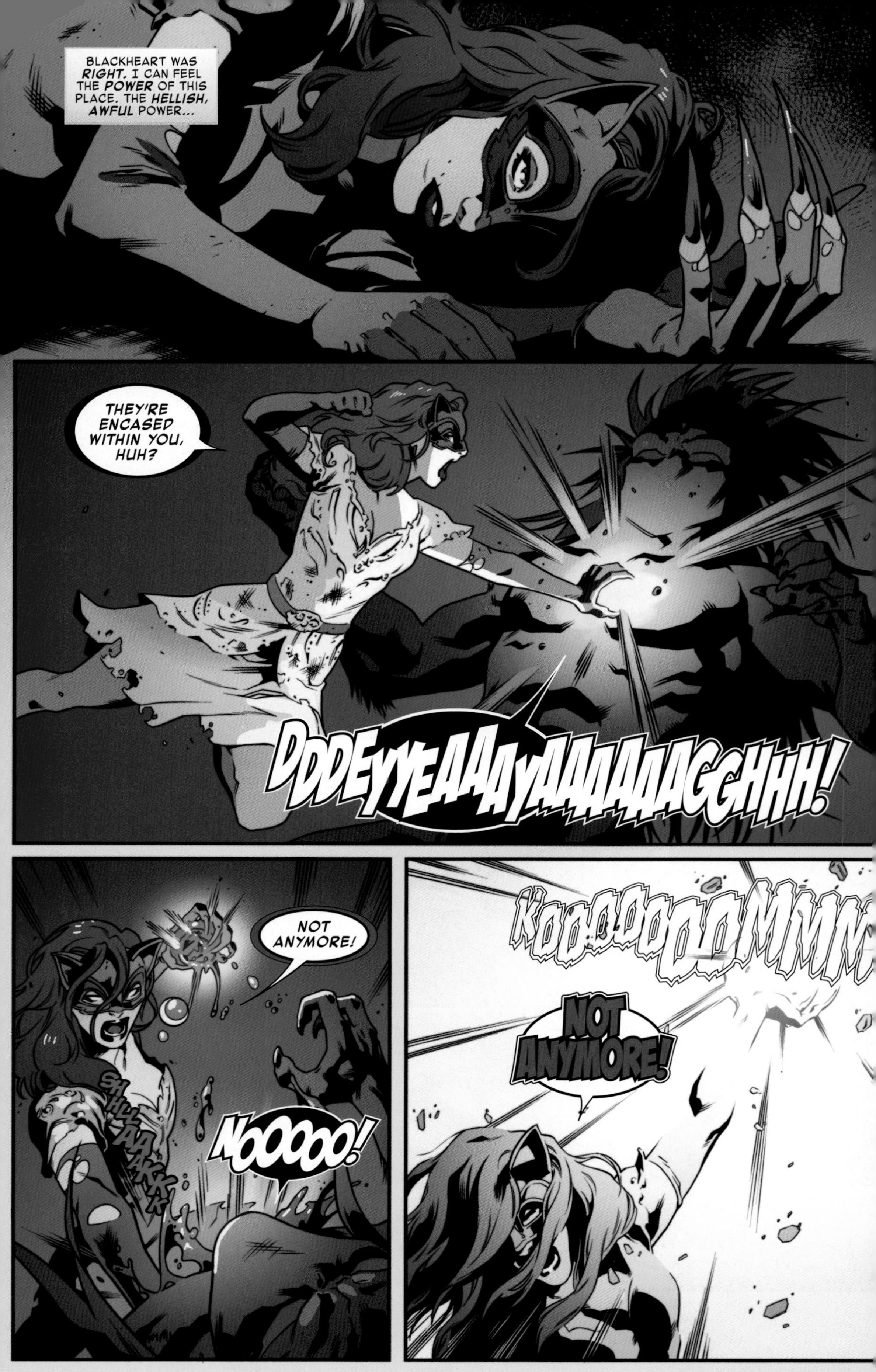

BLACKHEART WAS RIGHT. I CAN FEEL THE POWER OF THIS PLACE. THE HELLISH, AWFUL POWER...
THEY'RE ENCASED WITHIN YOU, HUH?
DDDEYYYEAAAAYAAAAAAAGGHHH!
NOT ANYMORE!
SHHLLAAAKKK
NOOOOO!
KOOOOOOOOMMMN
NOT ANYMORE!

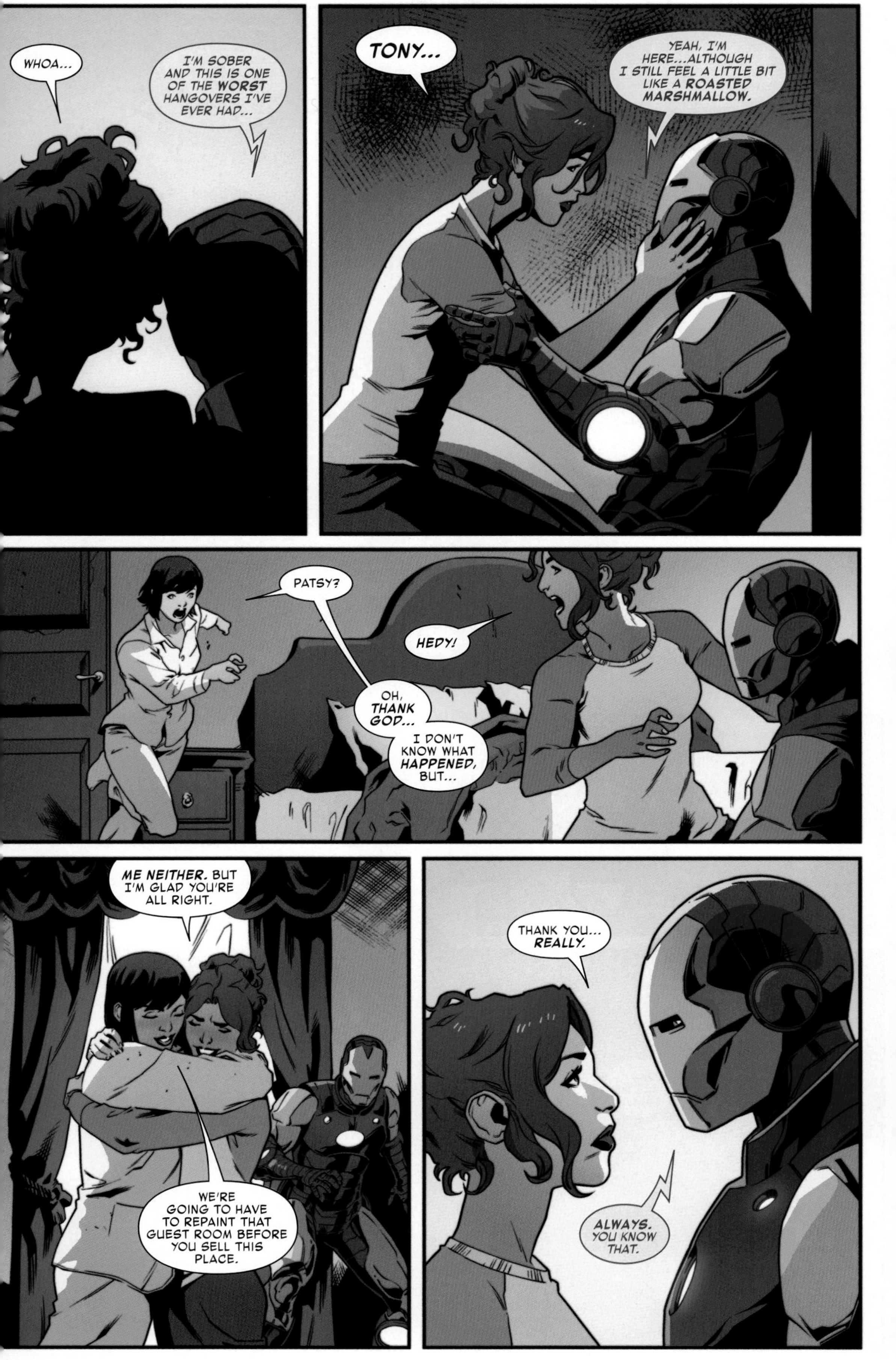
WHOA...
I'M SOBER AND THIS IS ONE OF THE WORST HANGOVERS I'VE EVER HAD...
TONY...
YEAH, I'M HERE...ALTHOUGH I STILL FEEL A LITTLE BIT LIKE A ROASTED MARSHMALLOW.
PATSY?
HEDY!
OH, THANK GOD...
I DON'T KNOW WHAT HAPPENED, BUT...
ME NEITHER. BUT I'M GLAD YOU'RE ALL RIGHT.
WE'RE GOING TO HAVE TO REPAINT THAT GUEST ROOM BEFORE YOU SELL THIS PLACE.
THANK YOU... REALLY.
ALWAYS. YOU KNOW THAT.

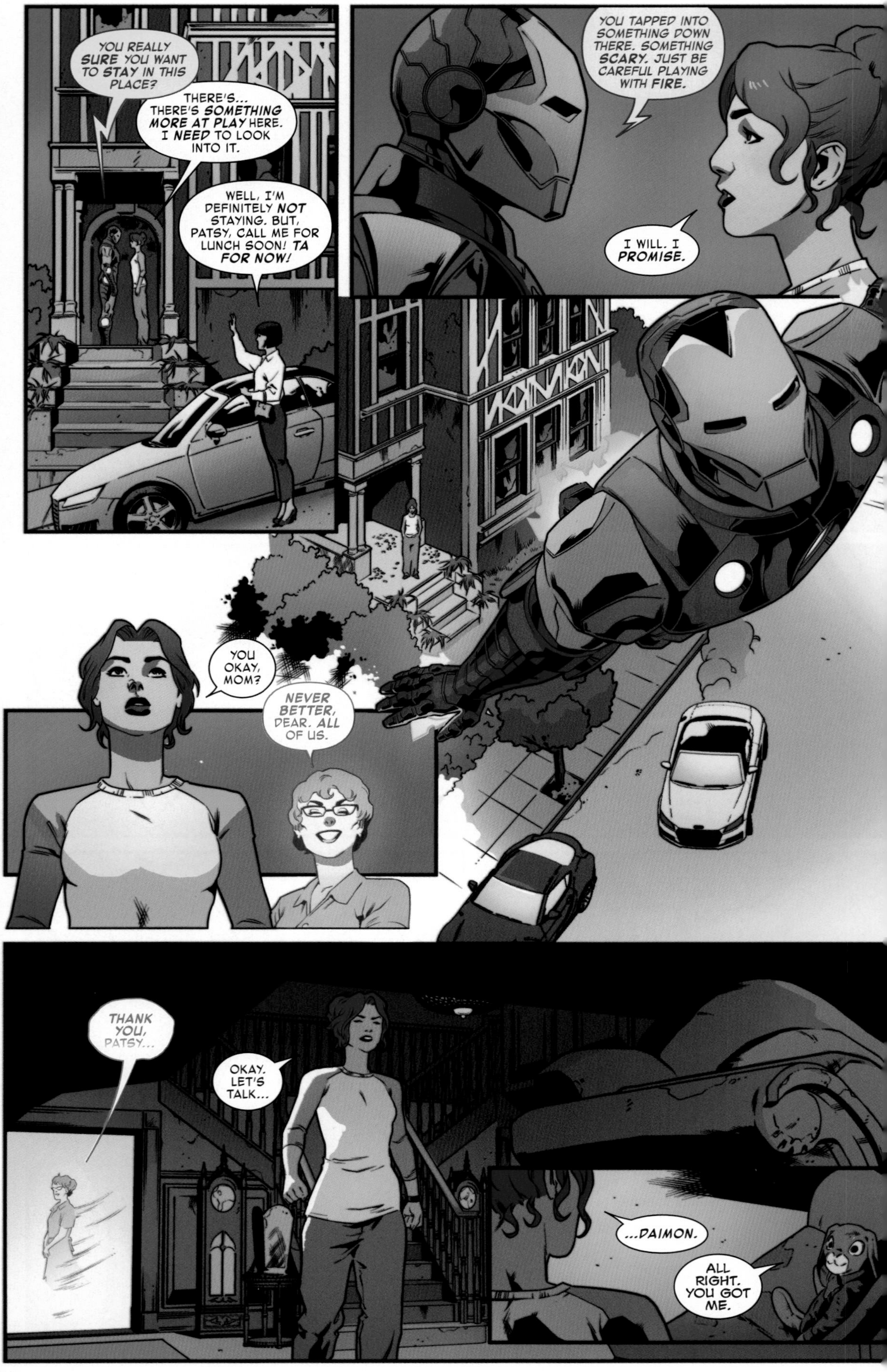
YOU REALLY SURE YOU WANT TO STAY IN THIS PLACE?
THERE'S... THERE'S SOMETHING MORE AT PLAY HERE. I NEED TO LOOK INTO IT.
WELL, I'M DEFINITELY NOT STAYING. BUT, PATSY, CALL ME FOR LUNCH SOON! TA FOR NOW!
YOU TAPPED INTO SOMETHING DOWN THERE. SOMETHING SCARY. JUST BE CAREFUL PLAYING WITH FIRE.
I WILL. I PROMISE.
YOU OKAY, MOM?
NEVER BETTER, DEAR. ALL OF US.
THANK YOU, PATSY...
OKAY. LET'S TALK...
...DAIMON.
ALL RIGHT. YOU GOT ME.

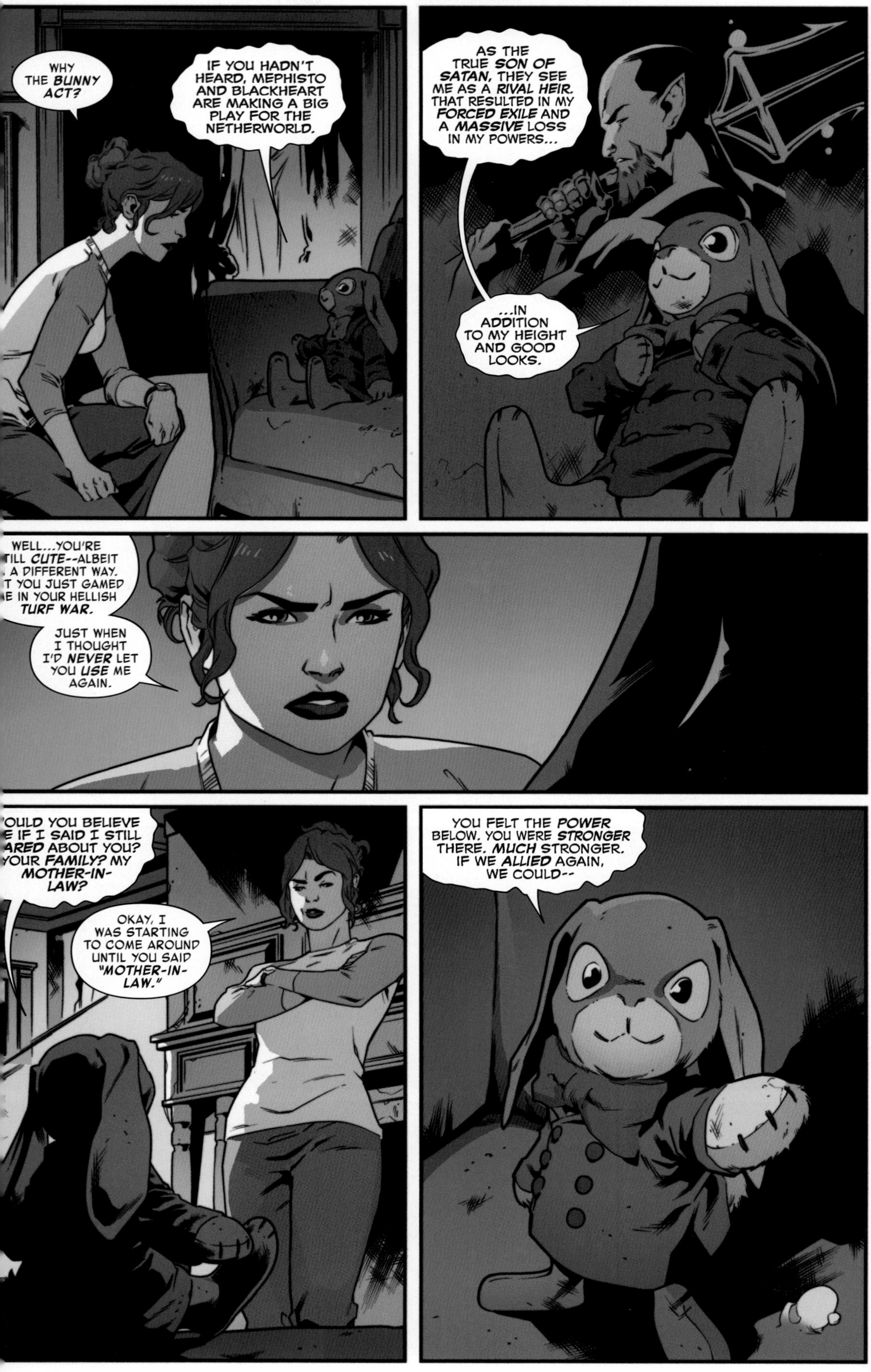

WHY THE BUNNY ACT?
IF YOU HADN'T HEARD, MEPHISTO AND BLACKHEART ARE MAKING A BIG PLAY FOR THE NETHERWORLD.
AS THE TRUE SON OF SATAN, THEY SEE ME AS A RIVAL HEIR. THAT RESULTED IN MY FORCED EXILE AND A MASSIVE LOSS IN MY POWERS...
...IN ADDITION TO MY HEIGHT AND GOOD LOOKS.
WELL...YOU'RE TILL CUTE--ALBEIT A DIFFERENT WAY. T YOU JUST GAMED E IN YOUR HELLISH TURF WAR.
JUST WHEN I THOUGHT I'D NEVER LET YOU USE ME AGAIN.
OULD YOU BELIEVE E IF I SAID I STILL ARED ABOUT YOU? YOUR FAMILY? MY MOTHER-IN-LAW?
OKAY, I WAS STARTING TO COME AROUND UNTIL YOU SAID "MOTHER-IN-LAW."
YOU FELT THE POWER BELOW. YOU WERE STRONGER THERE. MUCH STRONGER. IF WE ALLIED AGAIN, WE COULD--

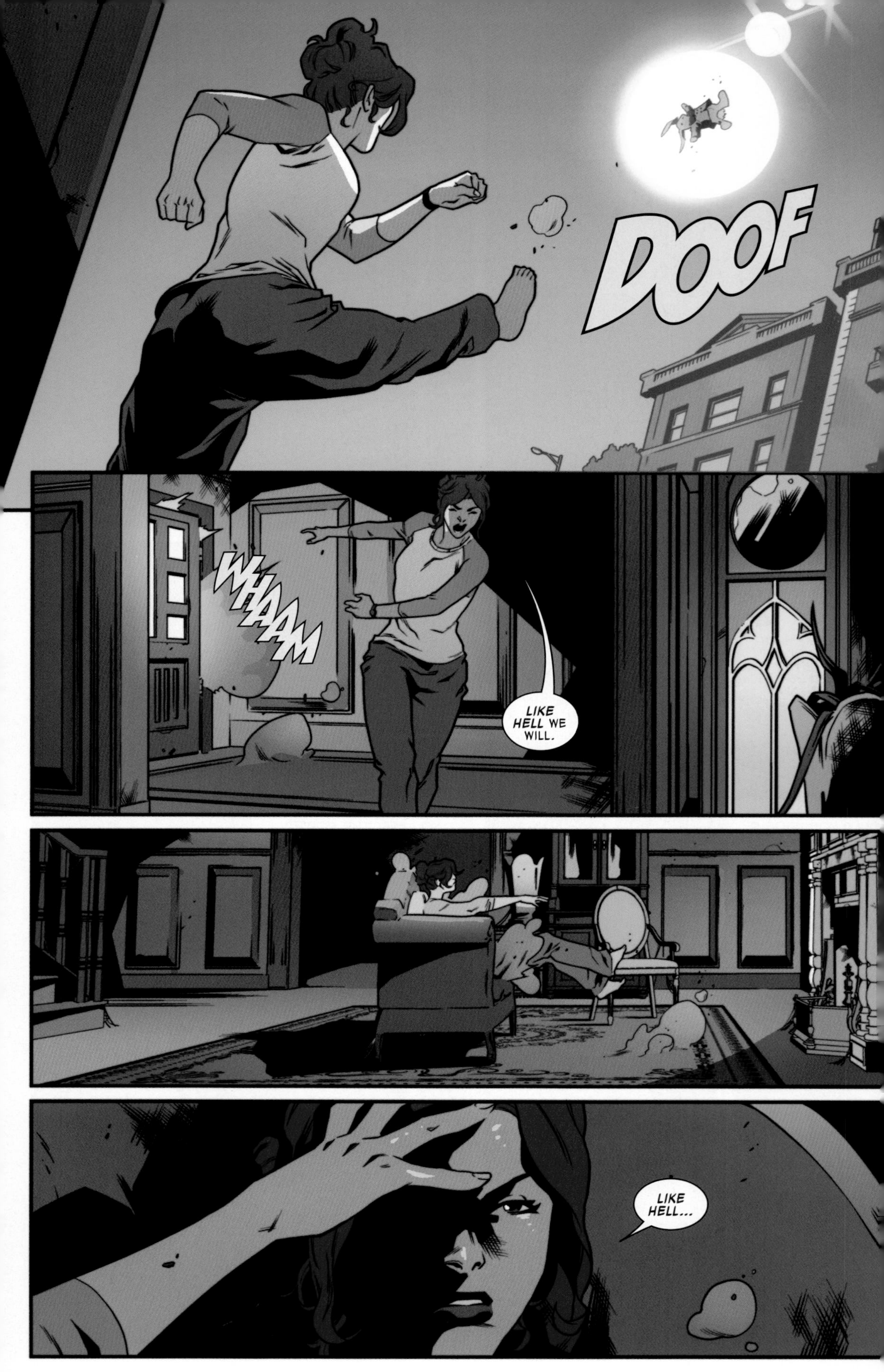
DOOF
WHAAM
LIKE HELL WE WILL.
LIKE HELL...

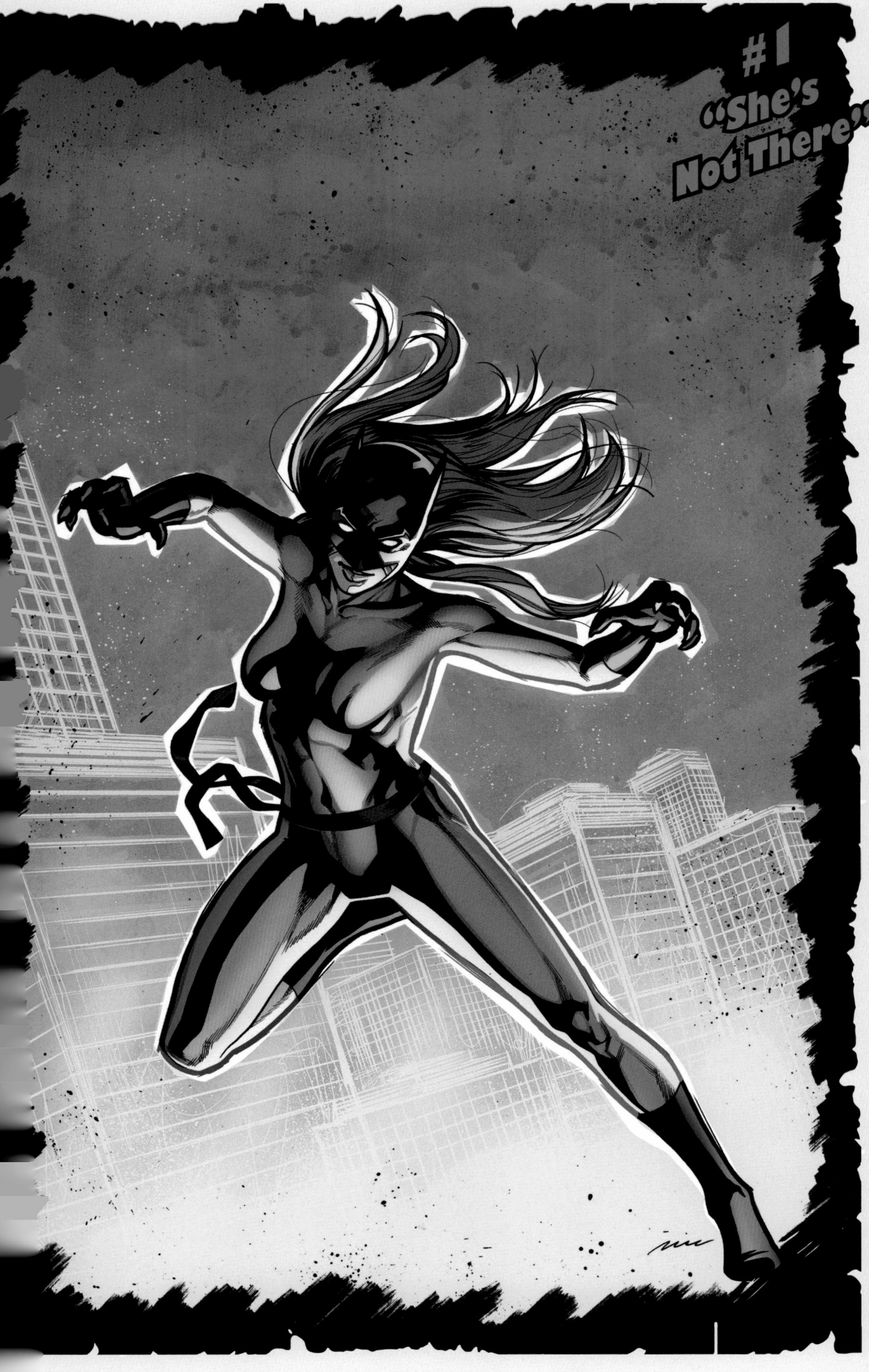
#1
"She's
Not There"

AM I GOOD?

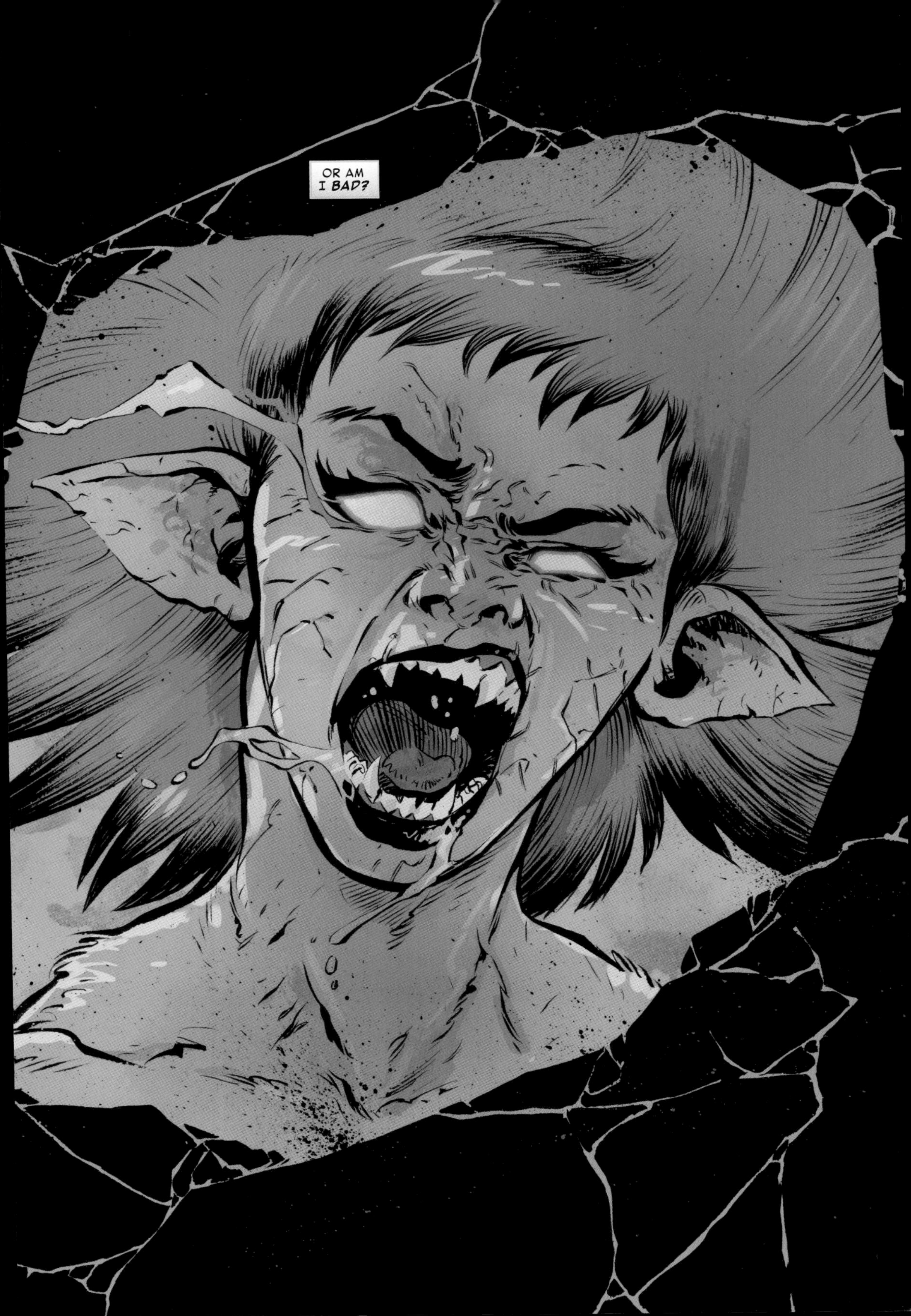
OR AM
I BAD?

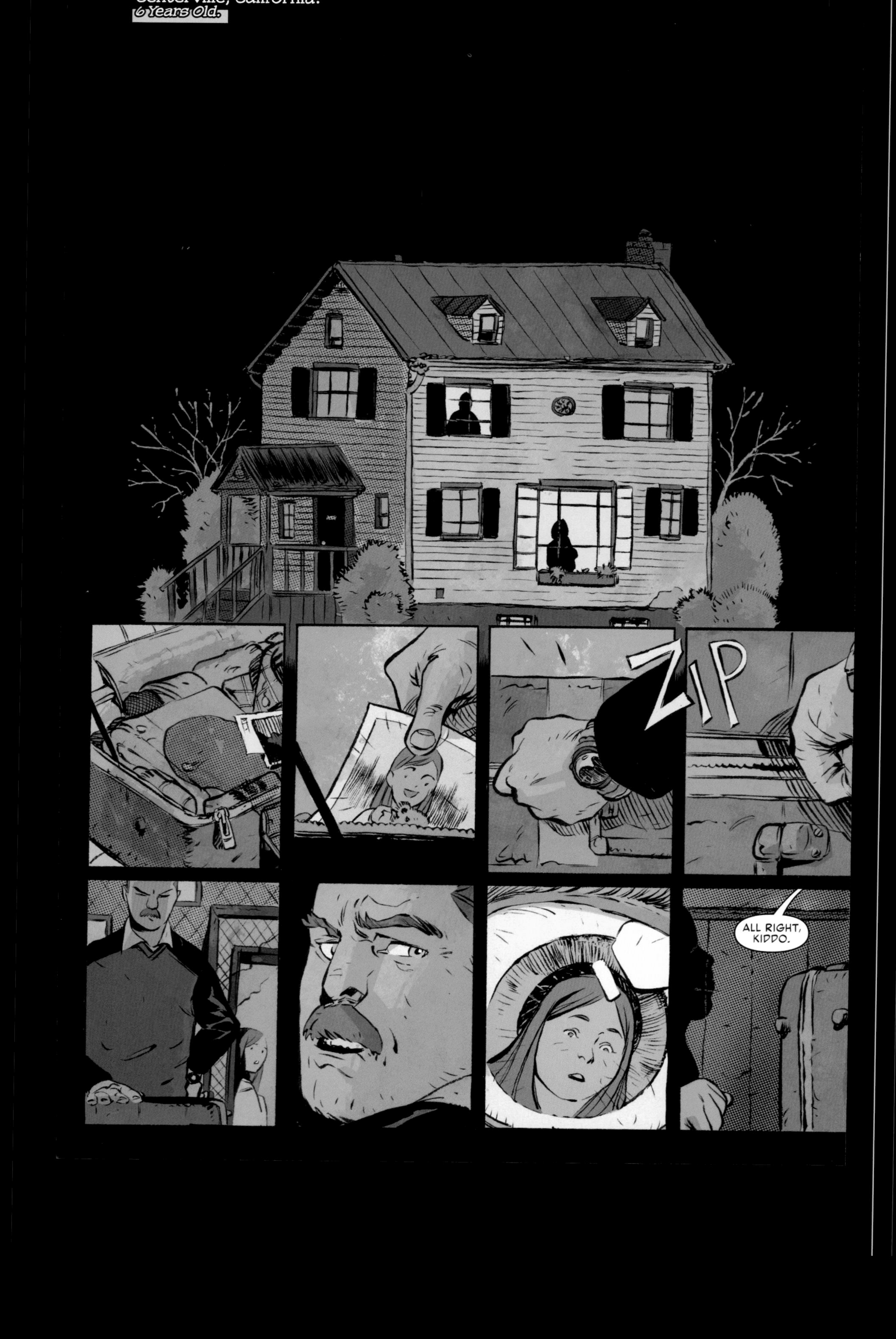
6 Years Old.
ZIP
ALL RIGHT, KIDDO.

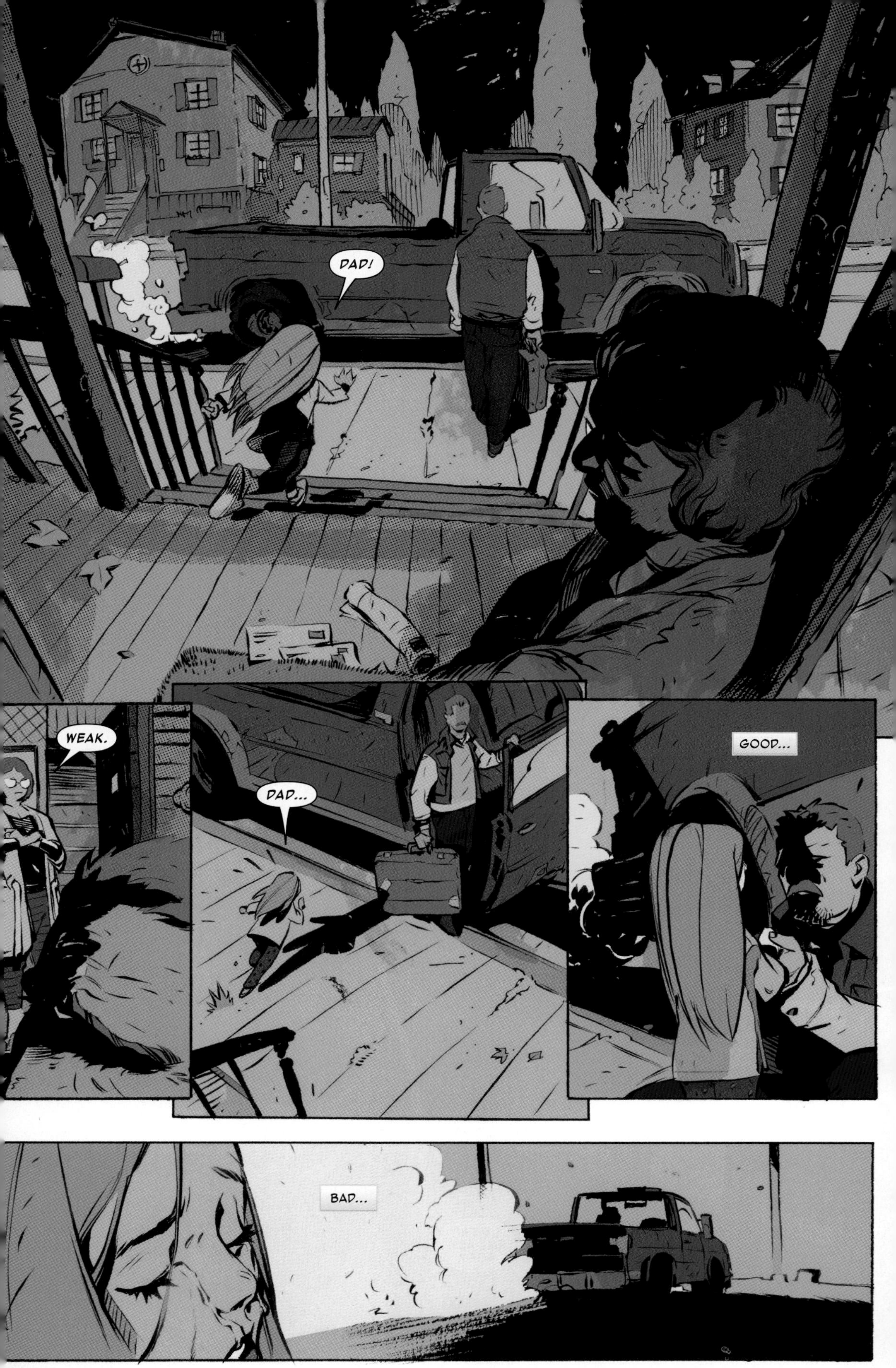
DAD!
WEAK.
DAD...
GOOD...
BAD...

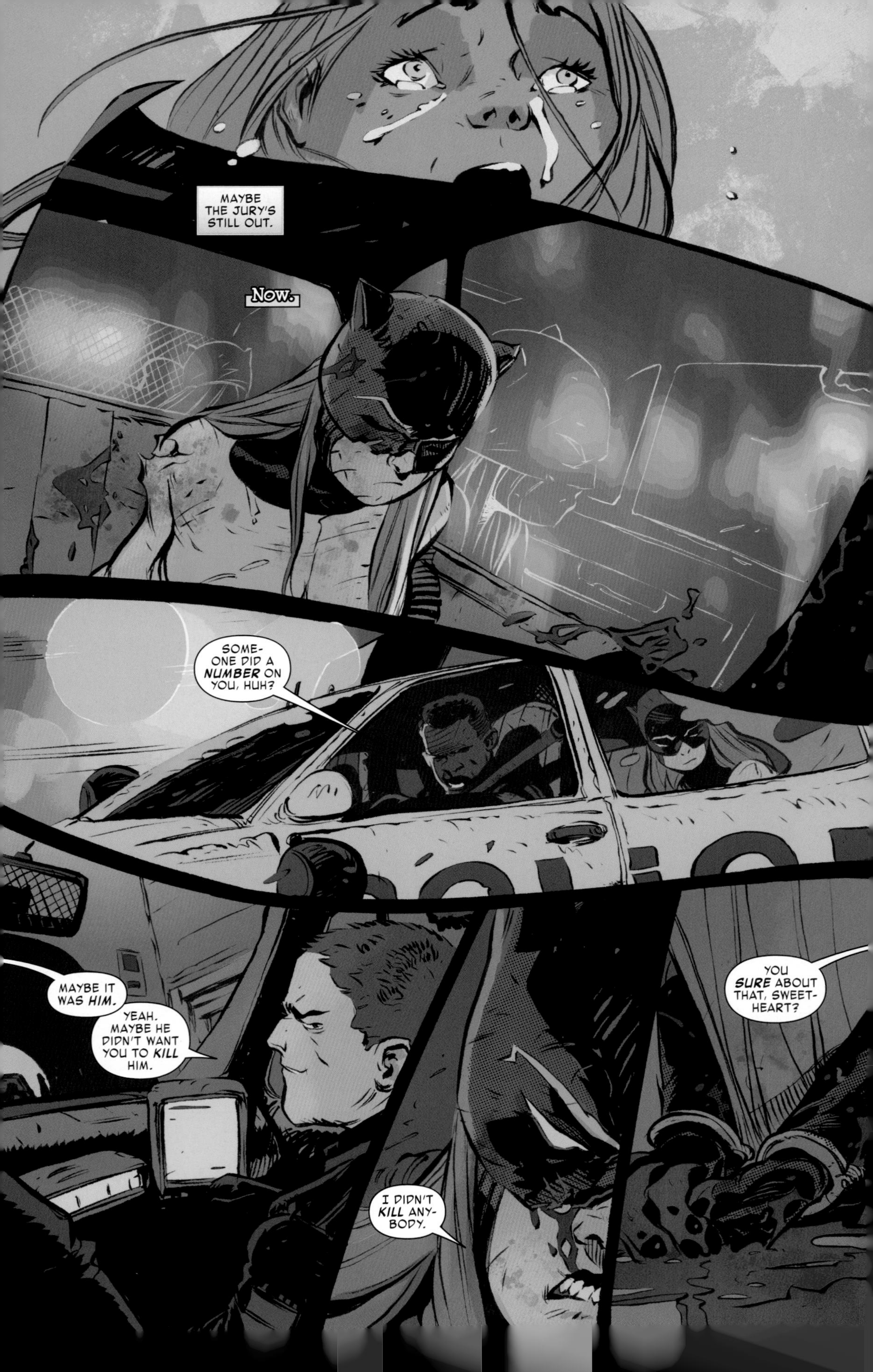

MAYBE THE JURY'S STILL OUT.
Now.
SOME-ONE DID A NUMBER ON YOU, HUH?
MAYBE IT WAS HIM.
YEAH. MAYBE HE DIDN'T WANT YOU TO KILL HIM.
YOU SURE ABOUT THAT, SWEET-HEART?
I DIDN'T KILL ANY-BODY.

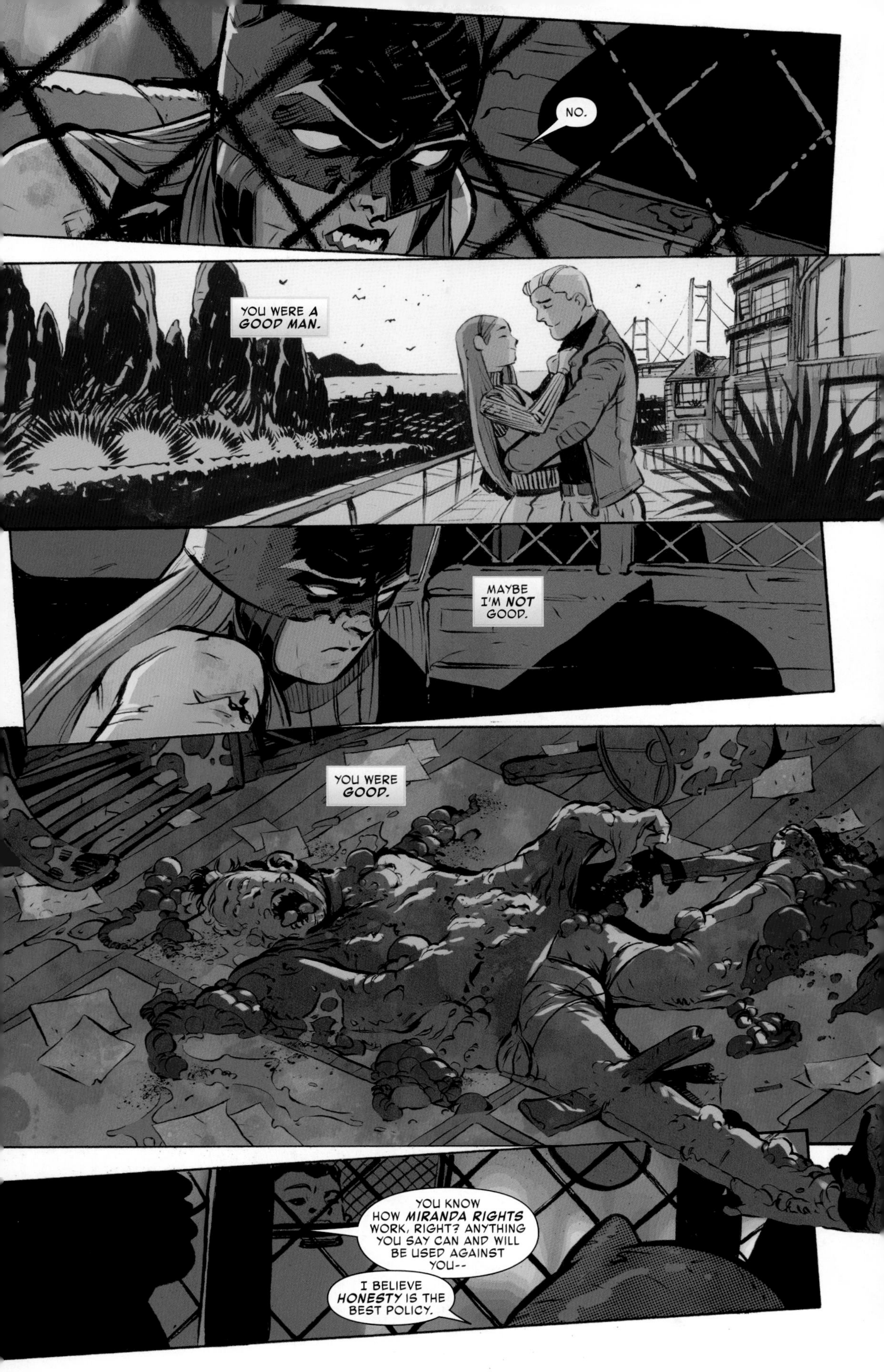
NO.
YOU WERE A GOOD MAN.
MAYBE I'M NOT GOOD.
YOU WERE GOOD.
YOU KNOW HOW MIRANDA RIGHTS WORK, RIGHT? ANYTHING YOU SAY CAN AND WILL BE USED AGAINST YOU--
I BELIEVE HONESTY IS THE BEST POLICY.

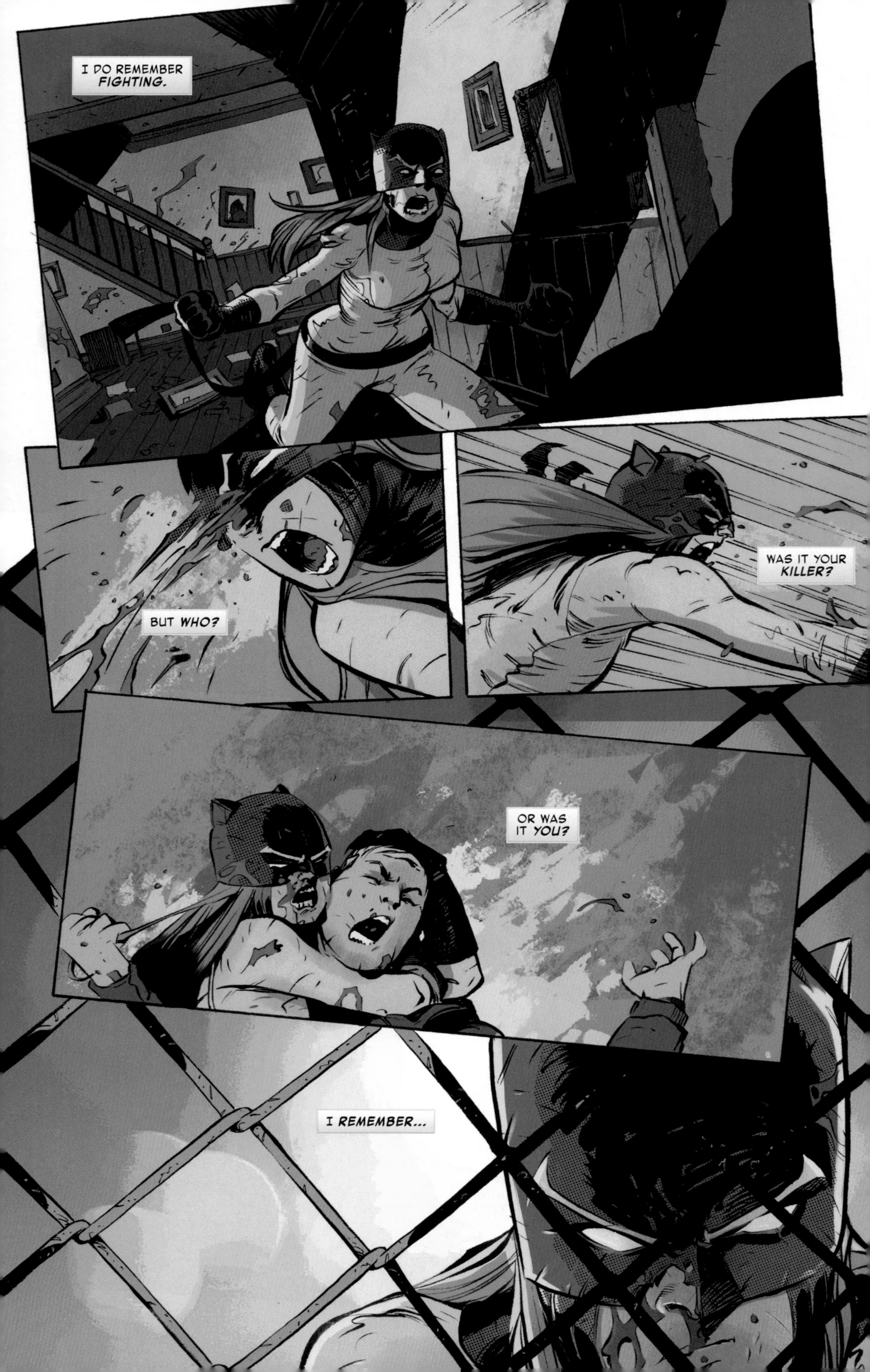
I DO REMEMBER FIGHTING.
BUT WHO?
WAS IT YOUR KILLER?
OR WAS IT YOU?
I REMEMBER...

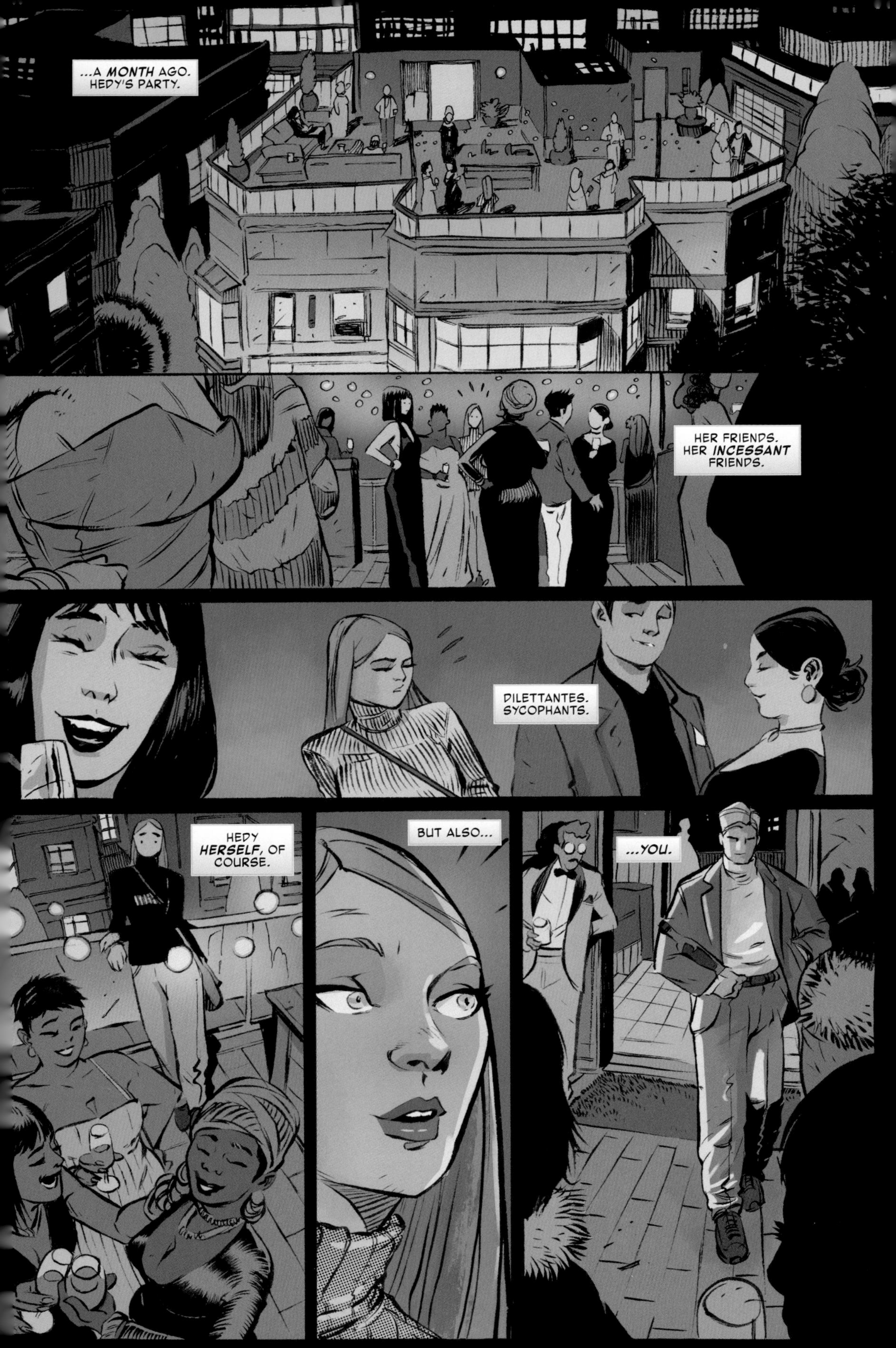
...A MONTH AGO. HEDY'S PARTY.
HER FRIENDS. HER INCESSANT FRIENDS.
DILETTANTES. SYCOPHANTS.
HEDY HERSELF, OF COURSE.
BUT ALSO...
...YOU.

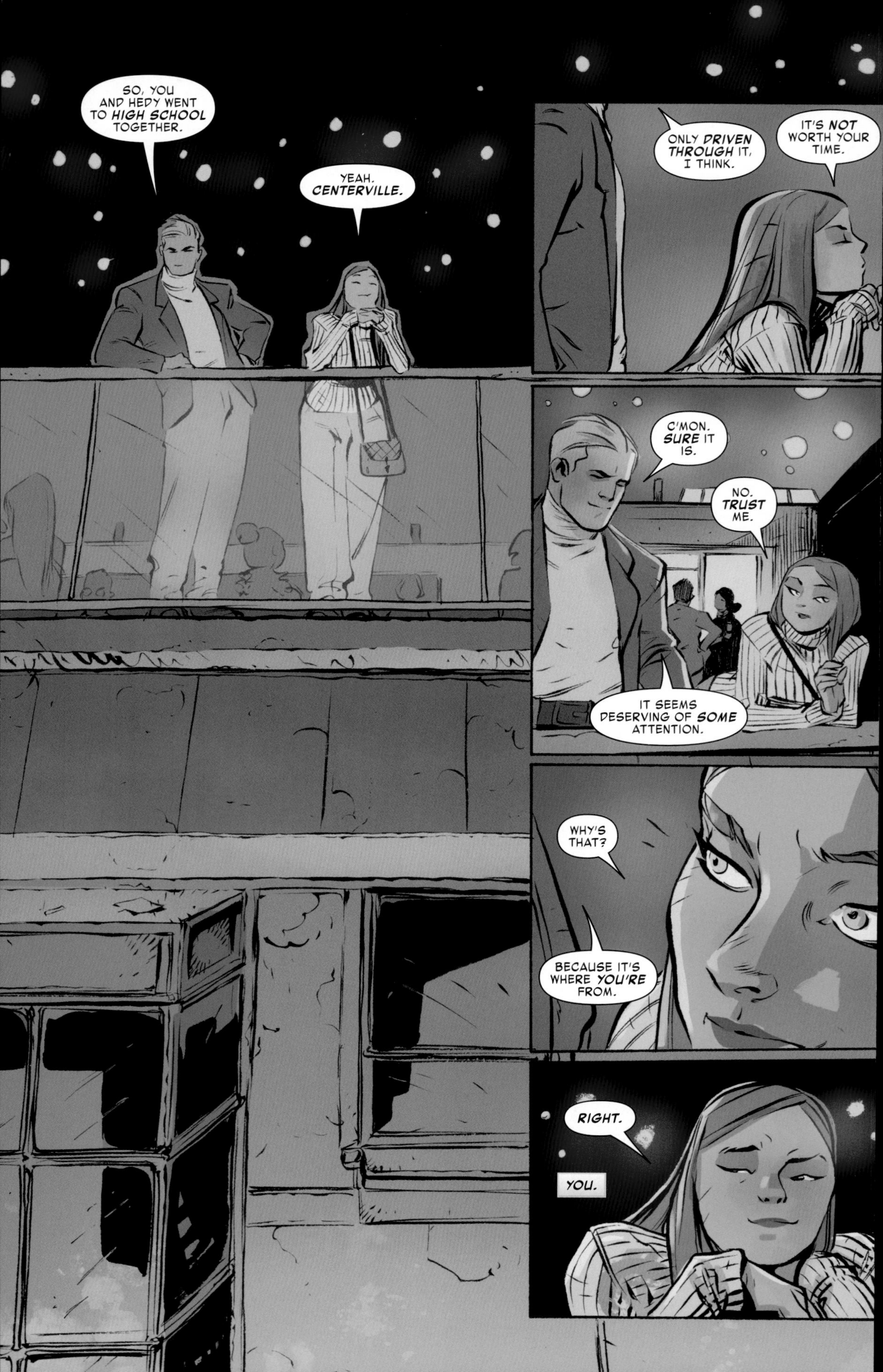
SO, YOU AND HEDY WENT TO HIGH SCHOOL TOGETHER.
YEAH. CENTERVILLE.
ONLY DRIVEN THROUGH IT, I THINK.
IT'S NOT WORTH YOUR TIME.
C'MON. SURE IT IS.
NO. TRUST ME.
IT SEEMS DESERVING OF SOME ATTENTION.
WHY'S THAT?
BECAUSE IT'S WHERE YOU'RE FROM.
RIGHT.
YOU.

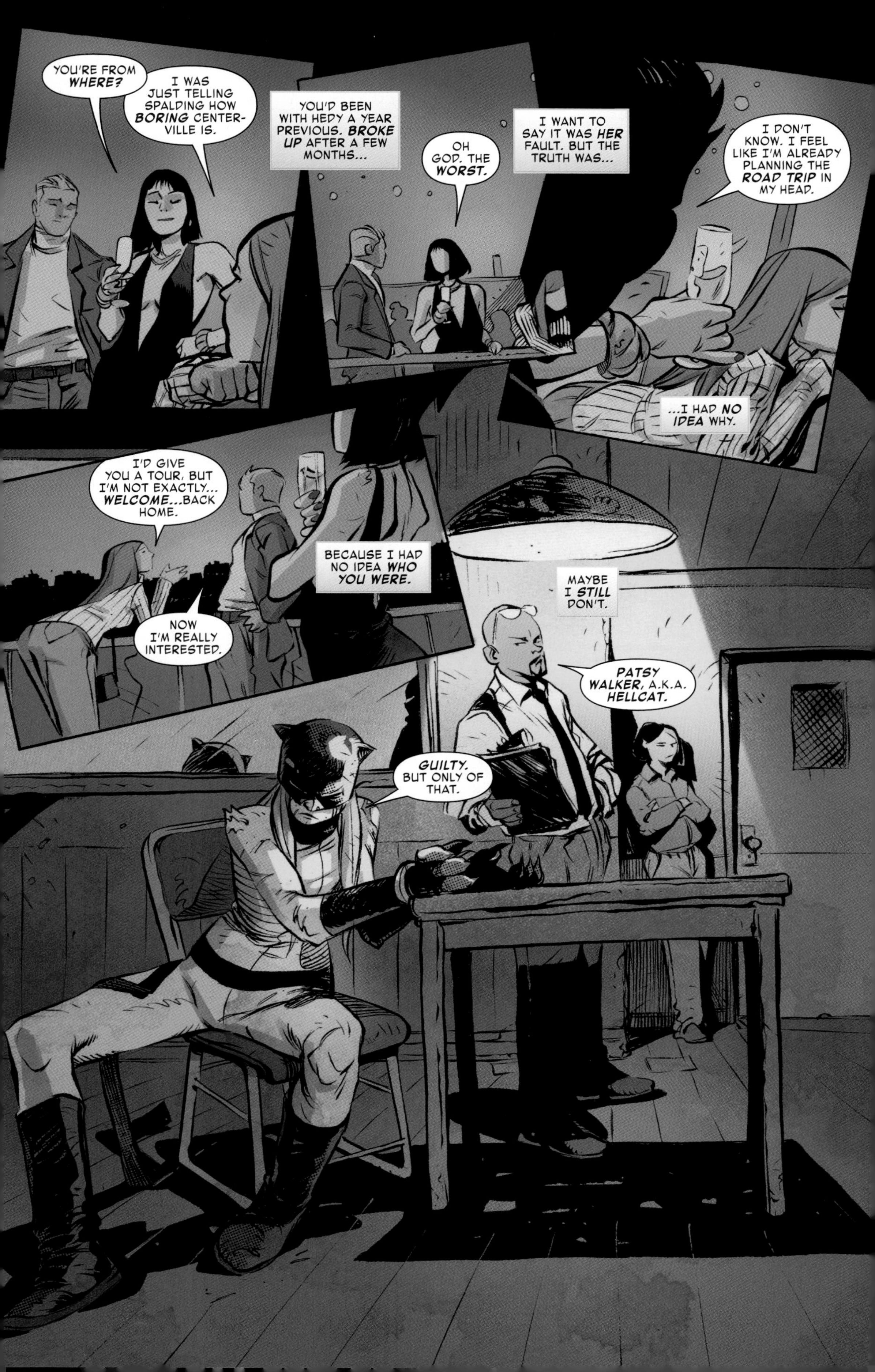
YOU'RE FROM WHERE?
I WAS JUST TELLING SPALDING HOW BORING CENTERVILLE IS.
YOU'D BEEN WITH HEDY A YEAR PREVIOUS. BROKE UP AFTER A FEW MONTHS...
OH GOD. THE WORST.
I WANT TO SAY IT WAS HER FAULT. BUT THE TRUTH WAS...
I DON'T KNOW. I FEEL LIKE I'M ALREADY PLANNING THE ROAD TRIP IN MY HEAD.
...I HAD NO IDEA WHY.
I'D GIVE YOU A TOUR, BUT I'M NOT EXACTLY... WELCOME...BACK HOME.
BECAUSE I HAD NO IDEA WHO YOU WERE.
NOW I'M REALLY INTERESTED.
MAYBE I STILL DON'T.
PATSY WALKER, A.K.A. HELLCAT.
GUILTY. BUT ONLY OF THAT.

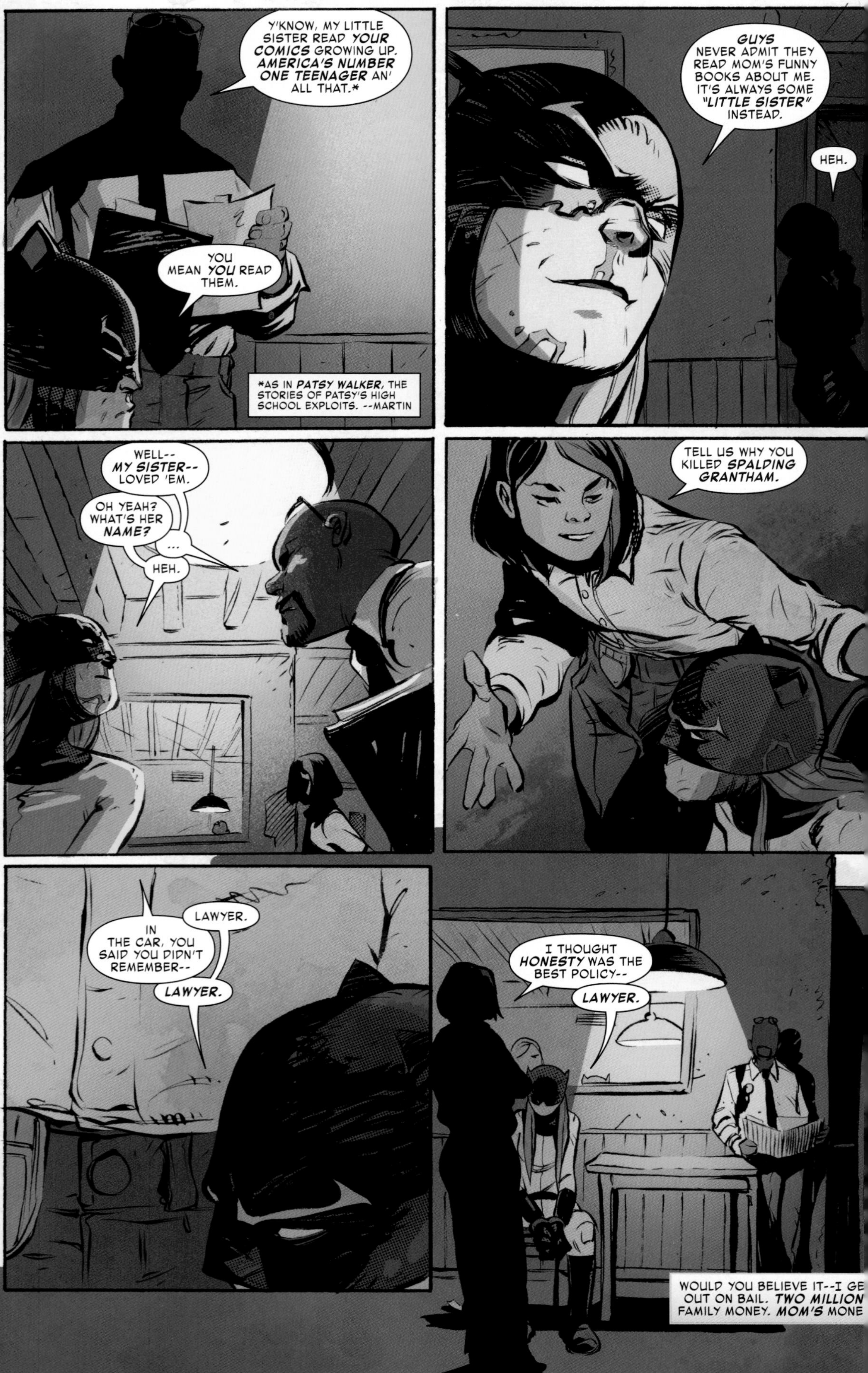
Y'KNOW, MY LITTLE SISTER READ YOUR COMICS GROWING UP. AMERICA'S NUMBER ONE TEENAGER AN' ALL THAT.*
YOU MEAN YOU READ THEM.
*AS IN PATSY WALKER, THE STORIES OF PATSY'S HIGH SCHOOL EXPLOITS. --MARTIN
GUYS NEVER ADMIT THEY READ MOM'S FUNNY BOOKS ABOUT ME. IT'S ALWAYS SOME "LITTLE SISTER" INSTEAD.
HEH.
WELL-- MY SISTER-- LOVED 'EM.
OH YEAH? WHAT'S HER NAME?
...
HEH.
TELL US WHY YOU KILLED SPALDING GRANTHAM.
IN THE CAR, YOU SAID YOU DIDN'T REMEMBER--
LAWYER.
LAWYER.
I THOUGHT HONESTY WAS THE BEST POLICY--
LAWYER.
WOULD YOU BELIEVE IT--I GE
OUT ON BAIL. TWO MILLION
FAMILY MONEY. MOM'S MONE

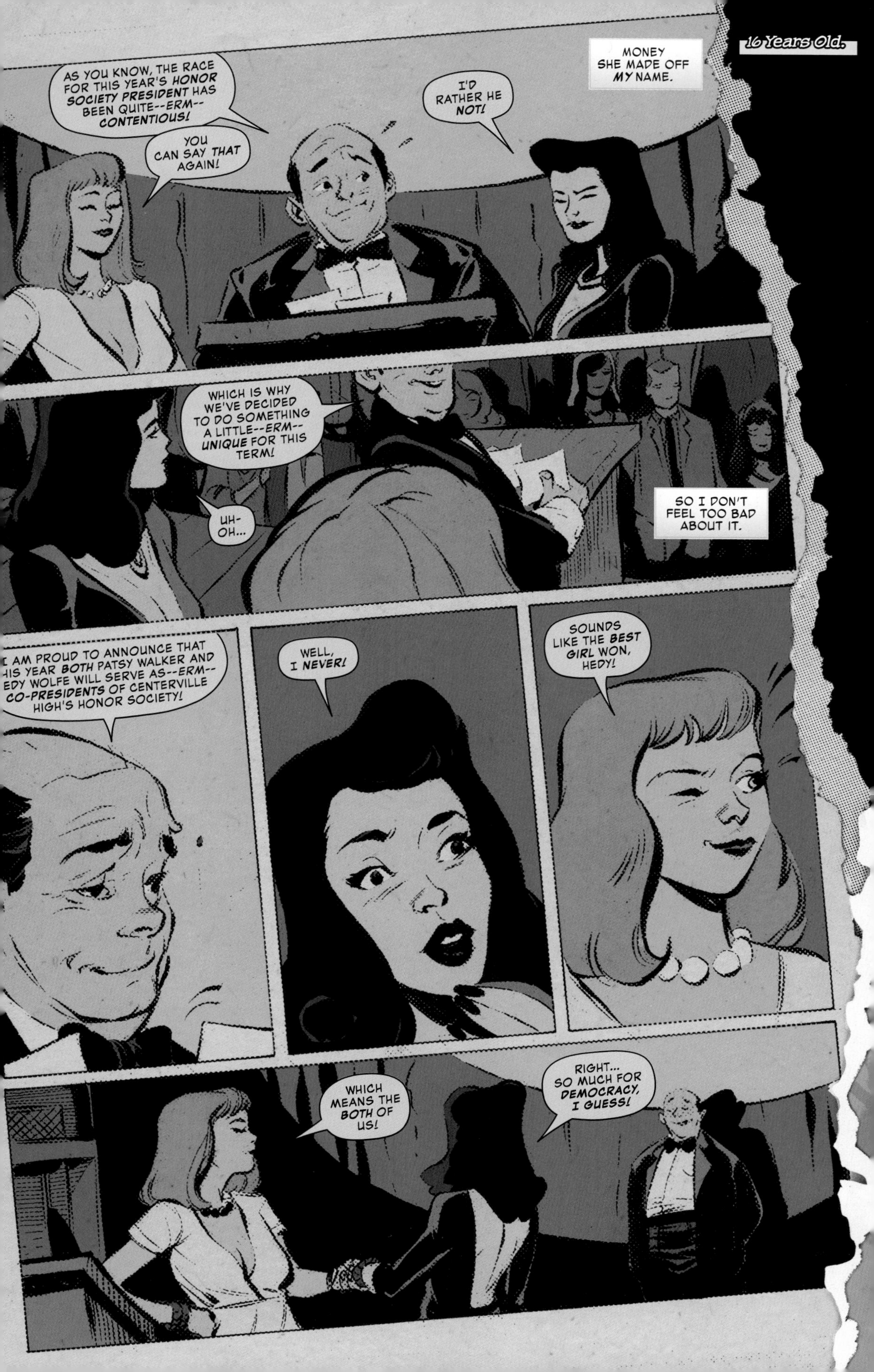
16 Years Old.
MONEY SHE MADE OFF MY NAME.
AS YOU KNOW, THE RACE FOR THIS YEAR'S HONOR SOCIETY PRESIDENT HAS BEEN QUITE--ERM--CONTENTIOUS!
YOU CAN SAY THAT AGAIN!
I'D RATHER HE NOT!
WHICH IS WHY WE'VE DECIDED TO DO SOMETHING A LITTLE--ERM--UNIQUE FOR THIS TERM!
UH-OH...
SO I DON'T FEEL TOO BAD ABOUT IT.
I AM PROUD TO ANNOUNCE THAT THIS YEAR BOTH PATSY WALKER AND HEDY WOLFE WILL SERVE AS--ERM--CO-PRESIDENTS OF CENTERVILLE HIGH'S HONOR SOCIETY!
WELL, I NEVER!
SOUNDS LIKE THE BEST GIRL WON, HEDY!
WHICH MEANS THE BOTH OF US!
RIGHT... SO MUCH FOR DEMOCRACY, I GUESS!

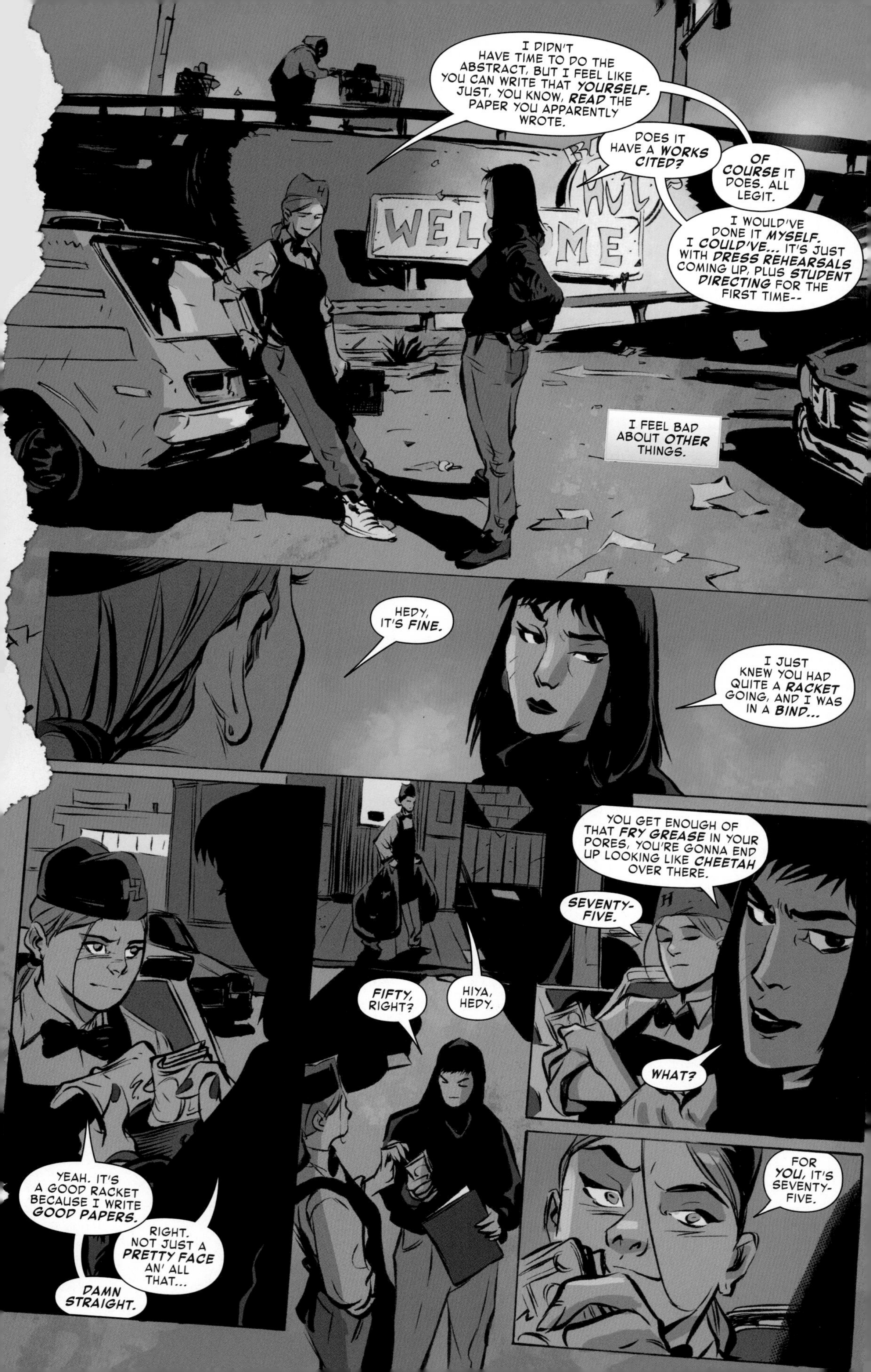
I DIDN'T HAVE TIME TO DO THE ABSTRACT, BUT I FEEL LIKE YOU CAN WRITE THAT YOURSELF. JUST, YOU KNOW, READ THE PAPER YOU APPARENTLY WROTE.
DOES IT HAVE A WORKS CITED?
OF COURSE IT DOES. ALL LEGIT.
I WOULD'VE DONE IT MYSELF. I COULD'VE... IT'S JUST WITH DRESS REHEARSALS COMING UP, PLUS STUDENT DIRECTING FOR THE FIRST TIME--
WELCOME
I FEEL BAD ABOUT OTHER THINGS.
HEDY, IT'S FINE.
I JUST KNEW YOU HAD QUITE A RACKET GOING, AND I WAS IN A BIND...
HIYA, HEDY.
FIFTY, RIGHT?
YEAH. IT'S A GOOD RACKET BECAUSE I WRITE GOOD PAPERS.
RIGHT. NOT JUST A PRETTY FACE AN' ALL THAT...
DAMN STRAIGHT.
YOU GET ENOUGH OF THAT FRY GREASE IN YOUR PORES, YOU'RE GONNA END UP LOOKING LIKE CHEETAH OVER THERE.
SEVENTY-FIVE.
WHAT?
FOR YOU, IT'S SEVENTY-FIVE.

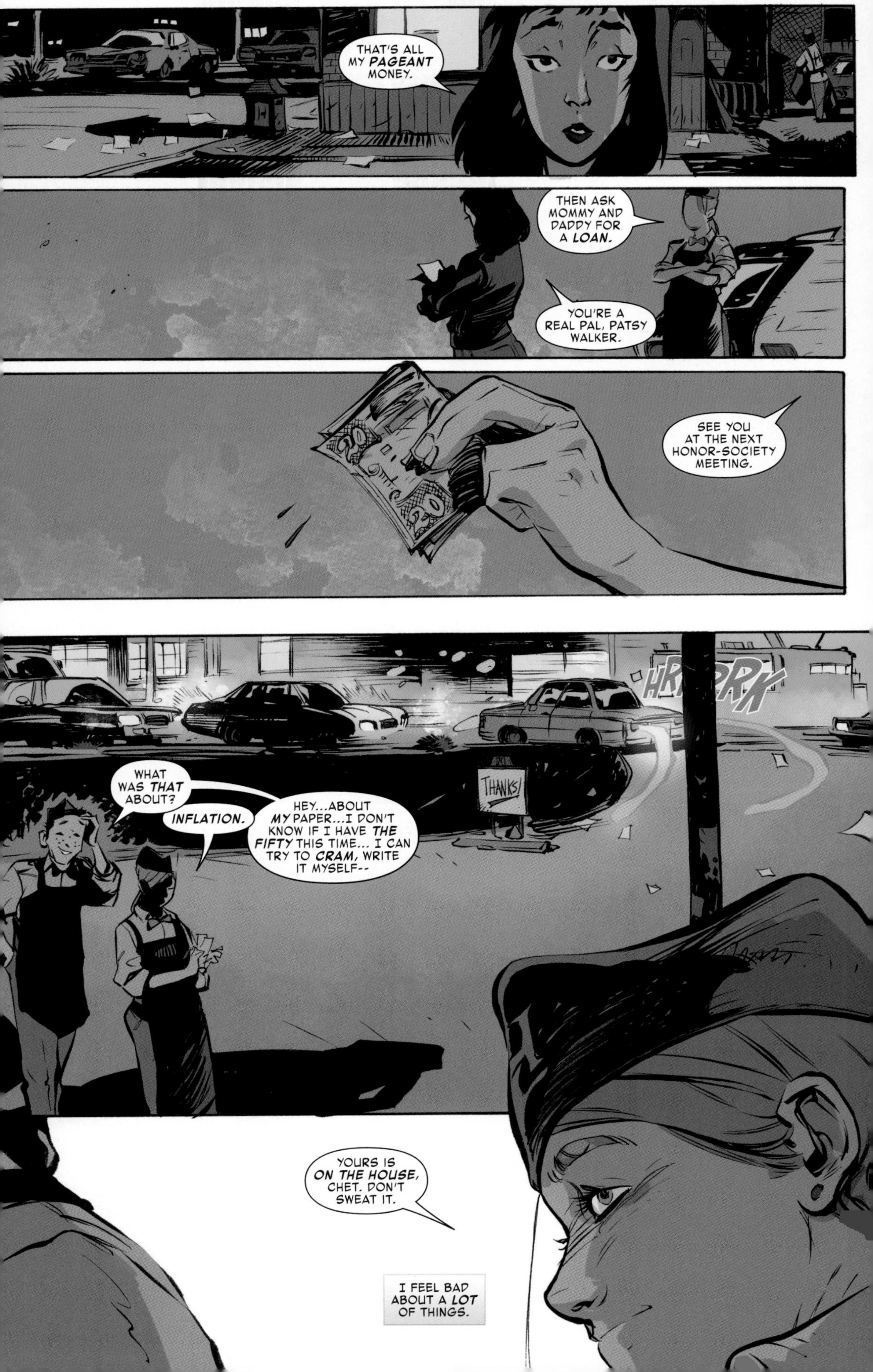
THAT'S ALL MY PAGEANT MONEY.
THEN ASK MOMMY AND DADDY FOR A LOAN.
YOU'RE A REAL PAL, PATSY WALKER.
SEE YOU AT THE NEXT HONOR-SOCIETY MEETING.
HRRRRK
THANKS!
WHAT WAS THAT ABOUT?
INFLATION.
HEY...ABOUT MY PAPER...I DON'T KNOW IF I HAVE THE FIFTY THIS TIME... I CAN TRY TO CRAM, WRITE IT MYSELF--
YOURS IS ON THE HOUSE, CHET. DON'T SWEAT IT.
I FEEL BAD ABOUT A LOT OF THINGS.

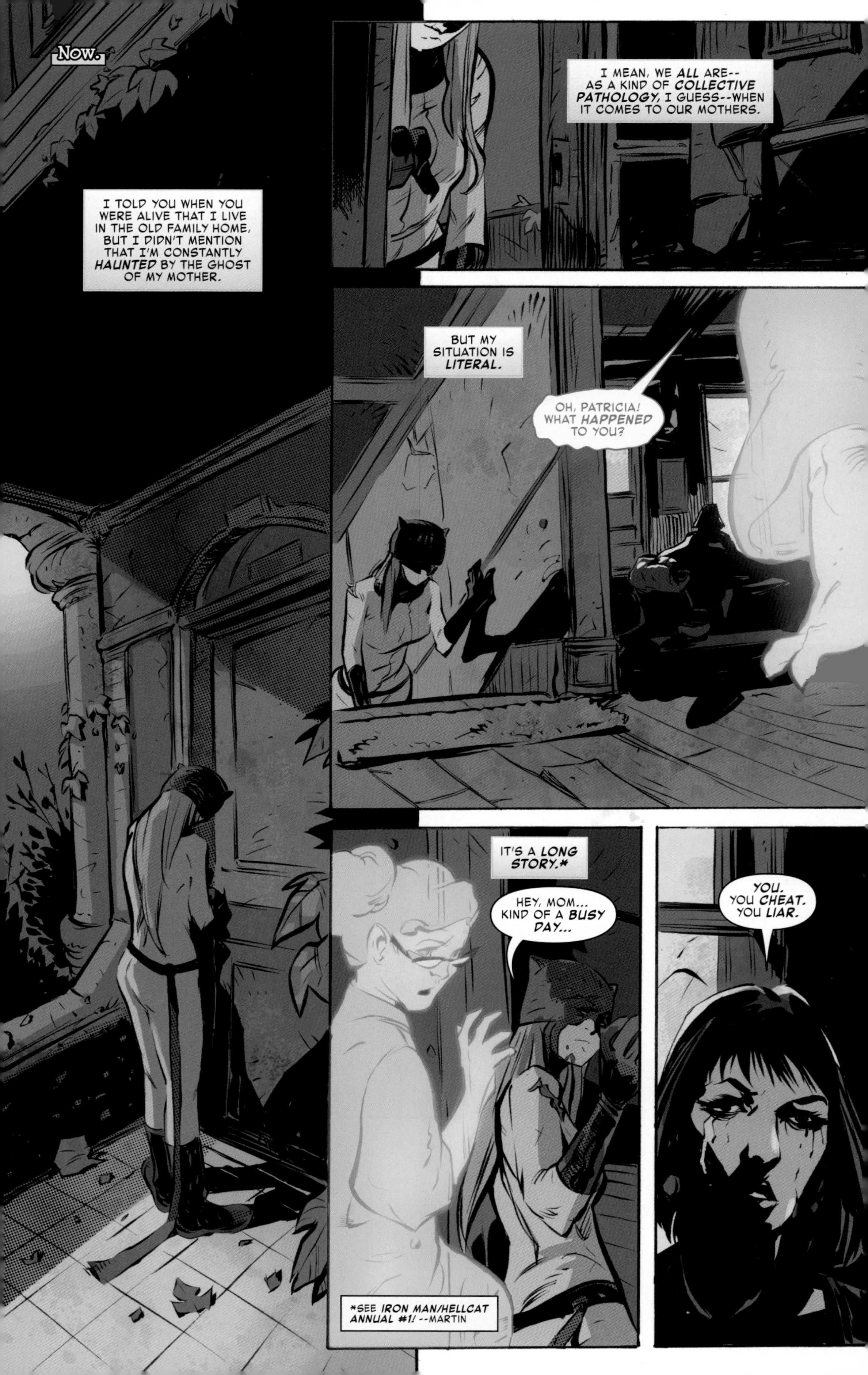
Now.
I TOLD YOU WHEN YOU WERE ALIVE THAT I LIVE IN THE OLD FAMILY HOME, BUT I DIDN'T MENTION THAT I'M CONSTANTLY *HAUNTED* BY THE GHOST OF MY MOTHER.
I MEAN, WE *ALL* ARE-- AS A KIND OF *COLLECTIVE PATHOLOGY,* I GUESS--WHEN IT COMES TO OUR MOTHERS.
BUT MY SITUATION IS *LITERAL.*
OH, PATRICIA! WHAT *HAPPENED* TO YOU?
IT'S A *LONG STORY.**
HEY, MOM... KIND OF A *BUSY* DAY...
*SEE *IRON MAN/HELLCAT ANNUAL #1!* --MARTIN
YOU. YOU *CHEAT.* YOU *LIAR.*

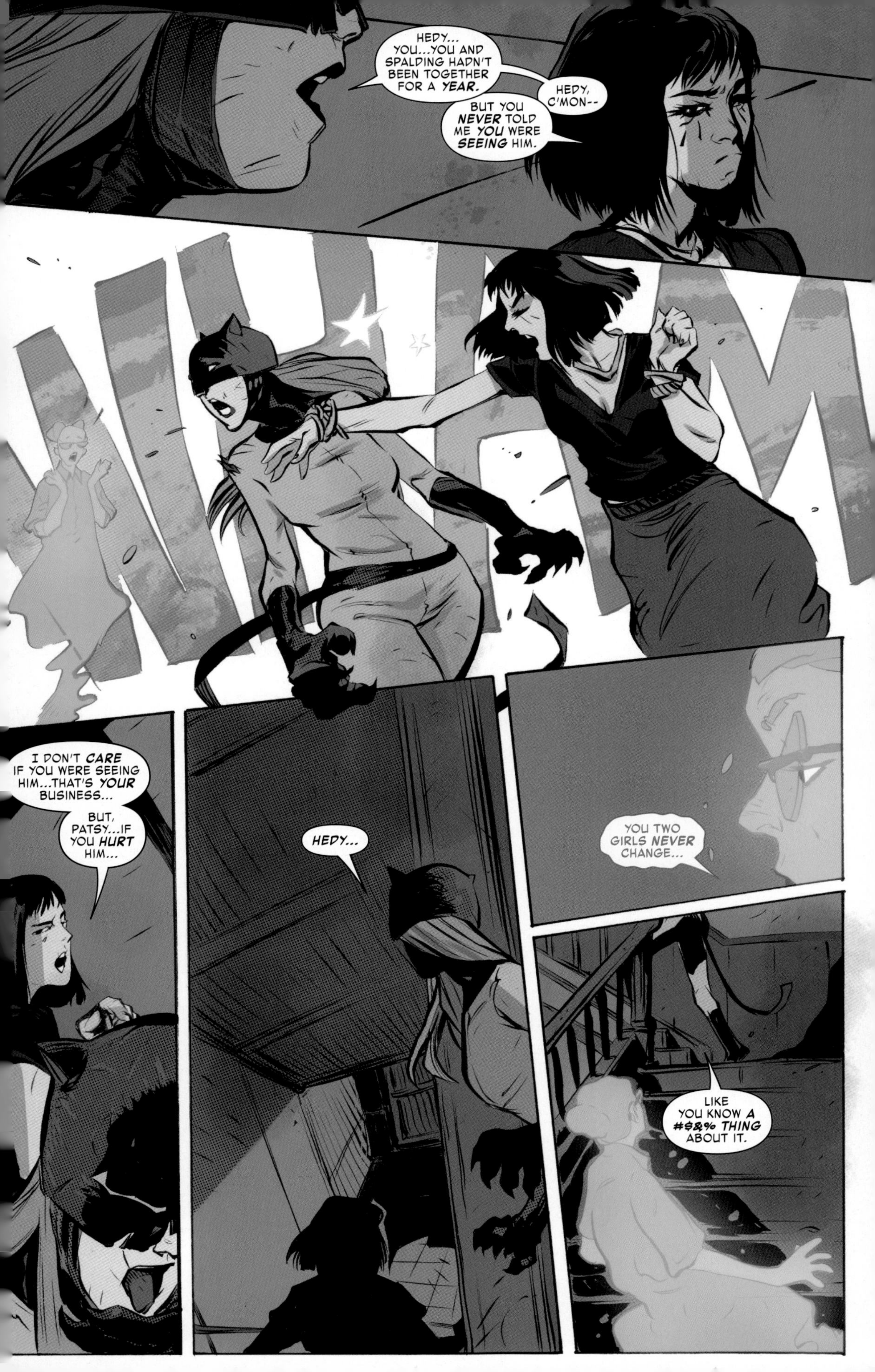
HEDY... YOU...YOU AND SPALDING HADN'T BEEN TOGETHER FOR A YEAR.
HEDY, C'MON--
BUT YOU NEVER TOLD ME YOU WERE SEEING HIM.
I DON'T CARE IF YOU WERE SEEING HIM...THAT'S YOUR BUSINESS...
BUT, PATSY...IF YOU HURT HIM...
HEDY...
YOU TWO GIRLS NEVER CHANGE...
LIKE YOU KNOW A #$&% THING ABOUT IT.

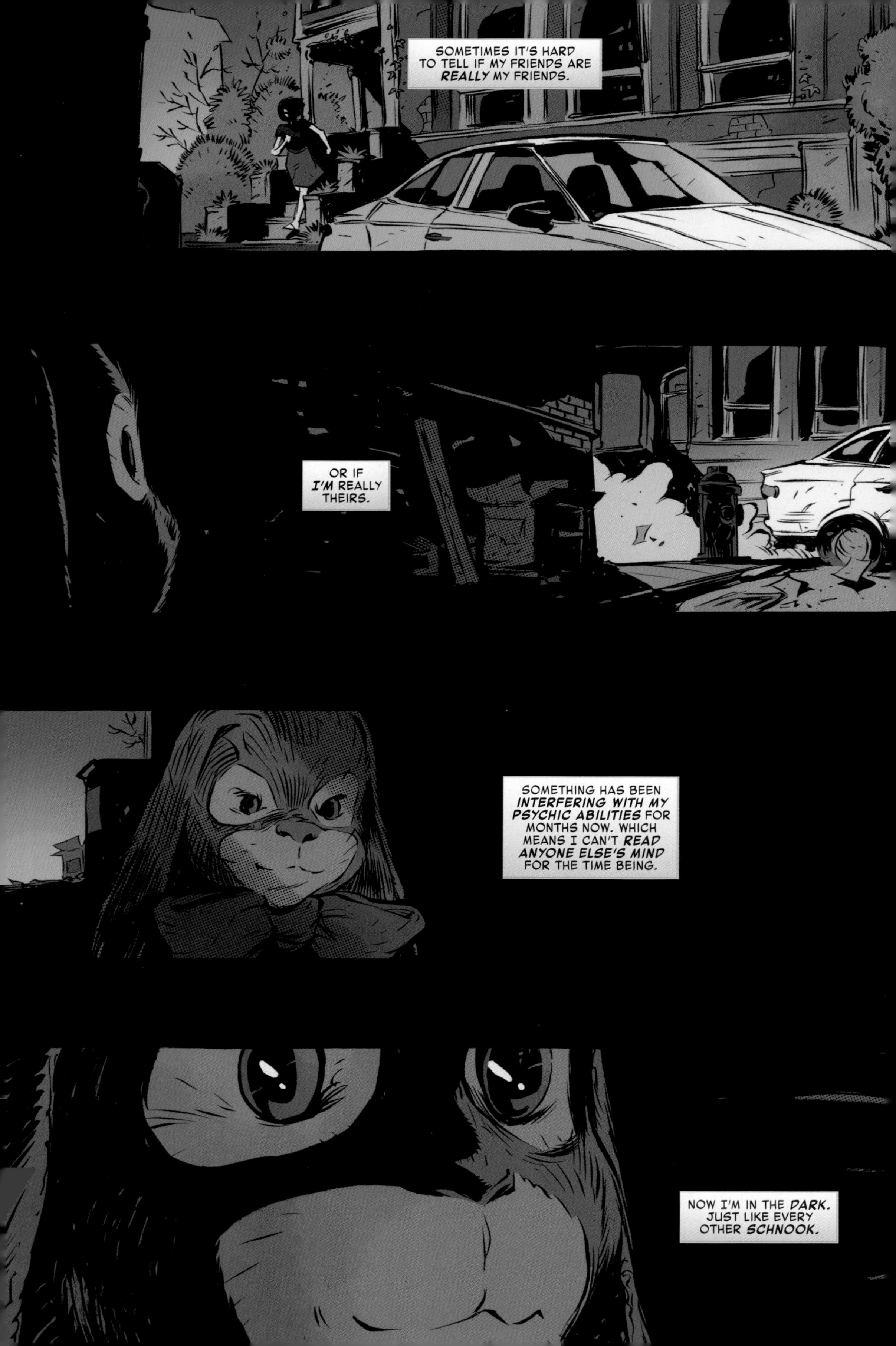
SOMETIMES IT'S HARD TO TELL IF MY FRIENDS ARE REALLY MY FRIENDS.
OR IF I'M REALLY THEIRS.
SOMETHING HAS BEEN INTERFERING WITH MY PSYCHIC ABILITIES FOR MONTHS NOW. WHICH MEANS I CAN'T READ ANYONE ELSE'S MIND FOR THE TIME BEING.
NOW I'M IN THE DARK. JUST LIKE EVERY OTHER SCHNOOK.

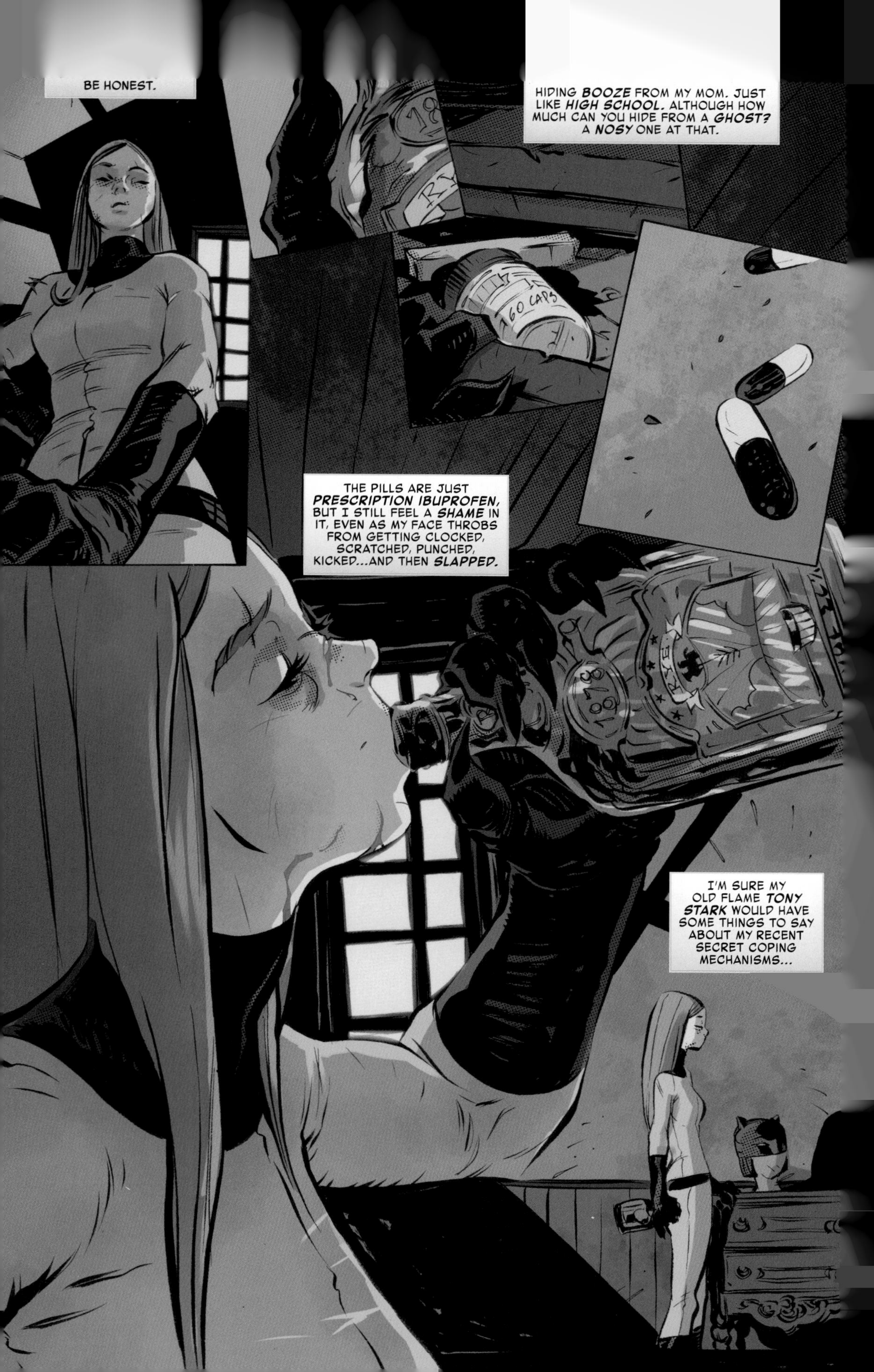
BE HONEST.
HIDING BOOZE FROM MY MOM. JUST LIKE HIGH SCHOOL. ALTHOUGH HOW MUCH CAN YOU HIDE FROM A GHOST? A NOSY ONE AT THAT.
THE PILLS ARE JUST PRESCRIPTION IBUPROFEN, BUT I STILL FEEL A SHAME IN IT, EVEN AS MY FACE THROBS FROM GETTING CLOCKED, SCRATCHED, PUNCHED, KICKED...AND THEN SLAPPED.
I'M SURE MY OLD FLAME TONY STARK WOULD HAVE SOME THINGS TO SAY ABOUT MY RECENT SECRET COPING MECHANISMS...

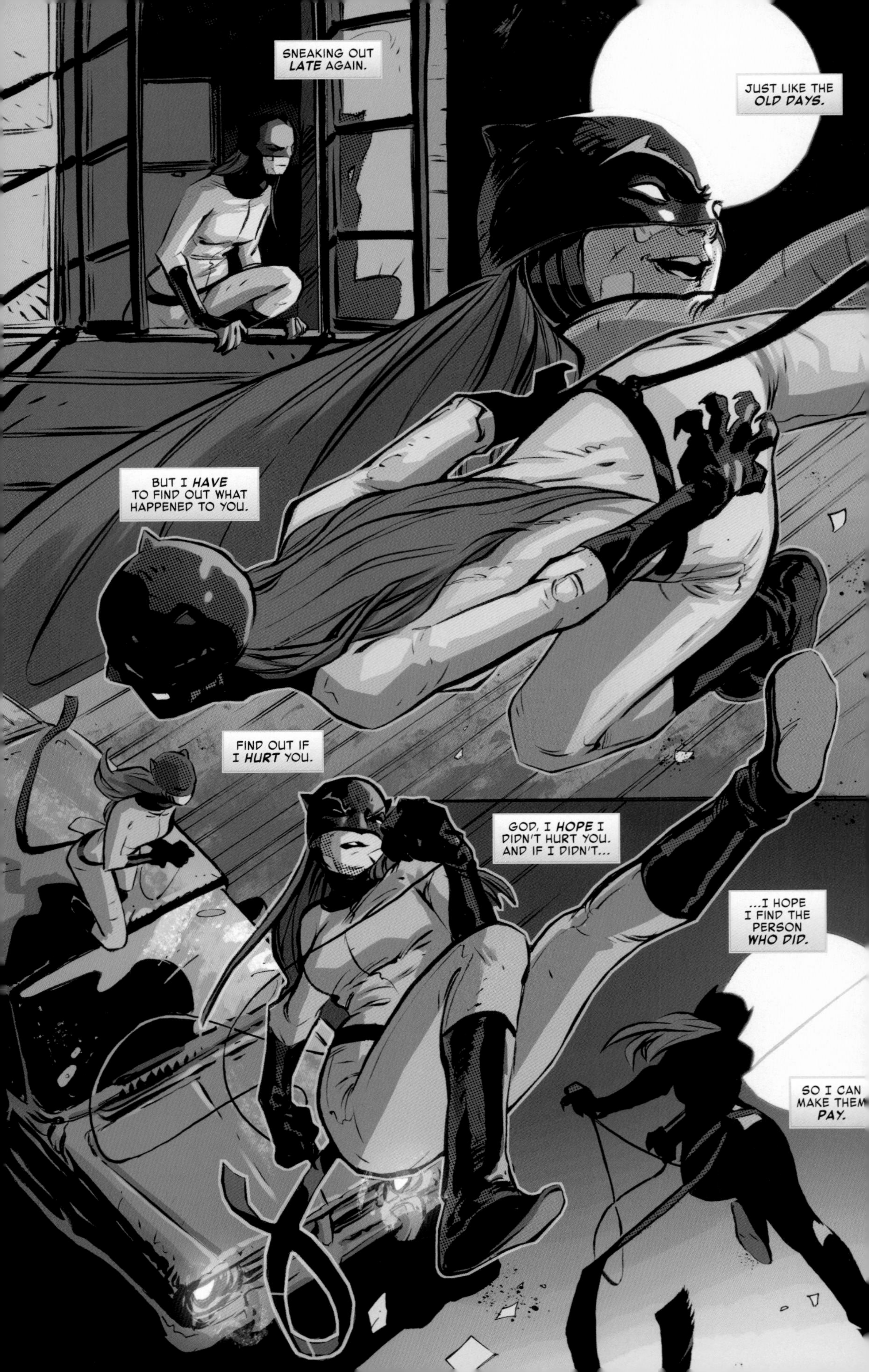
SNEAKING OUT LATE AGAIN.
JUST LIKE THE OLD DAYS.
BUT I HAVE TO FIND OUT WHAT HAPPENED TO YOU.
FIND OUT IF I HURT YOU.
GOD, I HOPE I DIDN'T HURT YOU. AND IF I DIDN'T...
...I HOPE I FIND THE PERSON WHO DID.
SO I CAN MAKE THEM PAY.

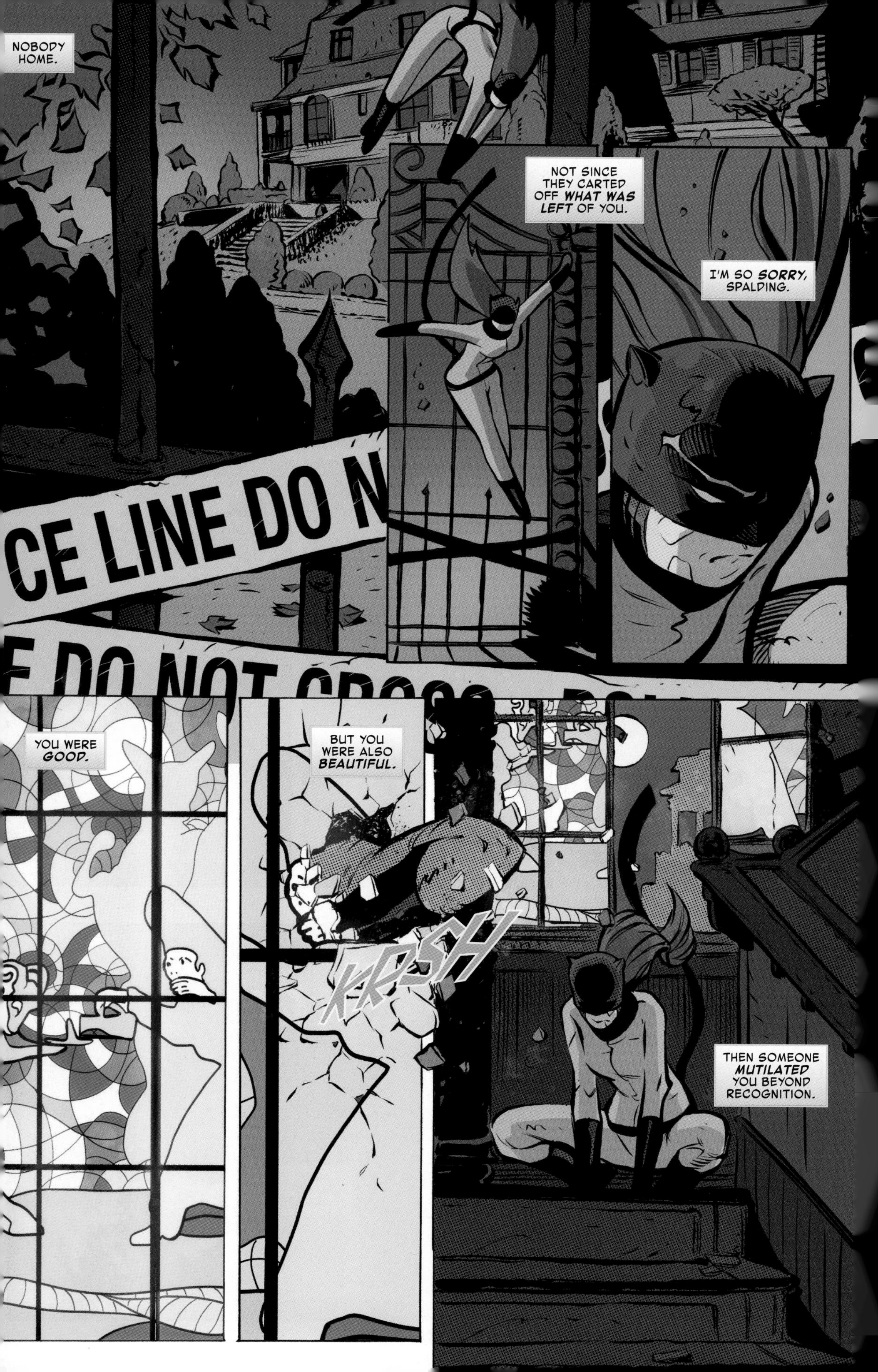
NOBODY HOME.
NOT SINCE THEY CARTED OFF WHAT WAS LEFT OF YOU.
I'M SO SORRY, SPALDING.
CE LINE DO N
E DO NOT CROSS
YOU WERE GOOD.
BUT YOU WERE ALSO BEAUTIFUL.
KRSH
THEN SOMEONE MUTILATED YOU BEYOND RECOGNITION.

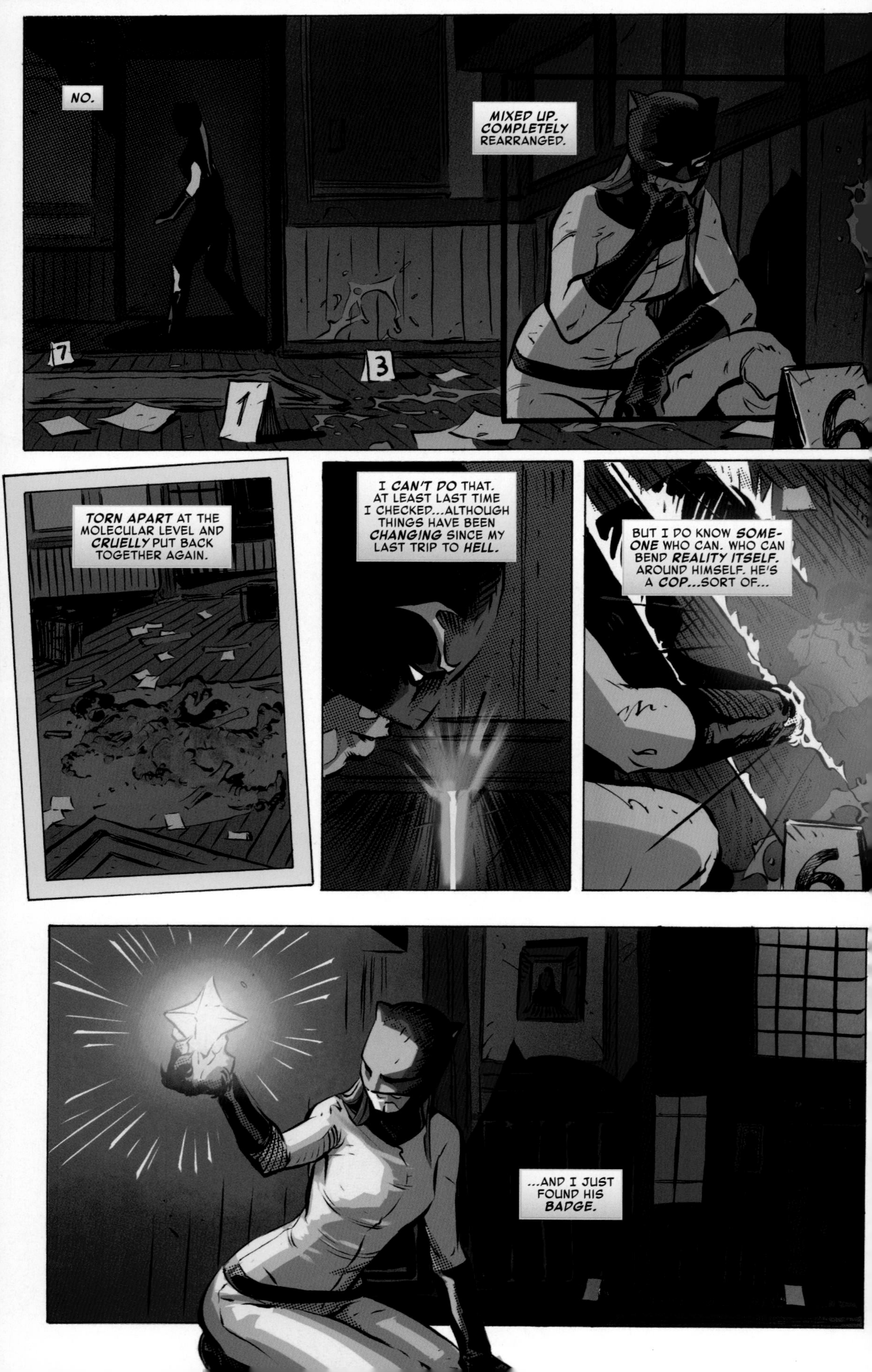
NO.
MIXED UP. COMPLETELY REARRANGED.
TORN APART AT THE MOLECULAR LEVEL AND CRUELLY PUT BACK TOGETHER AGAIN.
I CAN'T DO THAT. AT LEAST LAST TIME I CHECKED...ALTHOUGH THINGS HAVE BEEN CHANGING SINCE MY LAST TRIP TO HELL.
BUT I DO KNOW SOME-ONE WHO CAN. WHO CAN BEND REALITY ITSELF. AROUND HIMSELF. HE'S A COP...SORT OF...
...AND I JUST FOUND HIS BADGE.

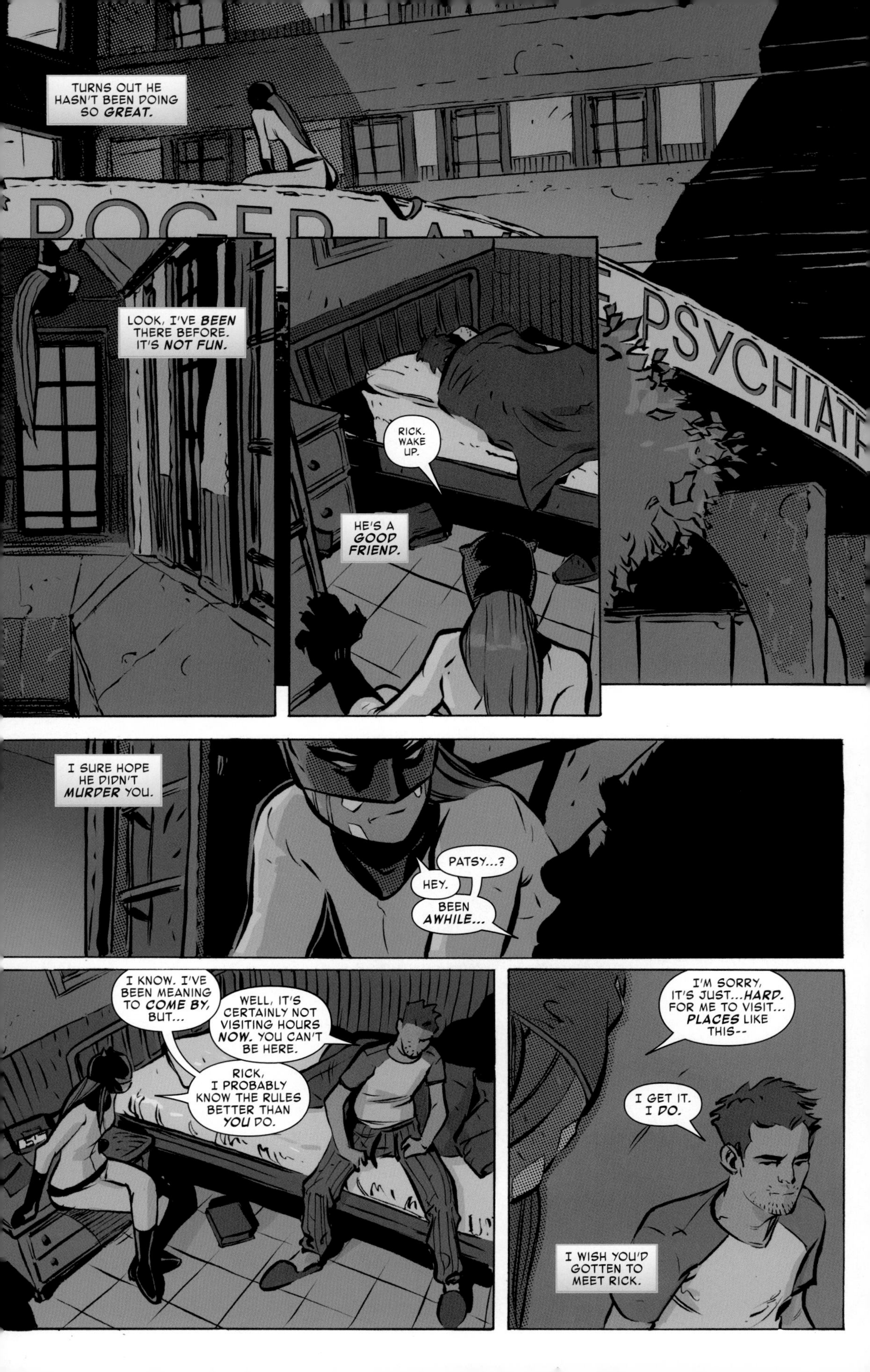

TURNS OUT HE HASN'T BEEN DOING SO GREAT.
ROGER LA...
PSYCHIATR...
LOOK, I'VE BEEN THERE BEFORE. IT'S NOT FUN.
RICK. WAKE UP.
HE'S A GOOD FRIEND.
I SURE HOPE HE DIDN'T MURDER YOU.
PATSY...?
HEY.
BEEN AWHILE...
I KNOW. I'VE BEEN MEANING TO COME BY, BUT...
WELL, IT'S CERTAINLY NOT VISITING HOURS NOW. YOU CAN'T BE HERE.
RICK, I PROBABLY KNOW THE RULES BETTER THAN YOU DO.
I'M SORRY, IT'S JUST...HARD. FOR ME TO VISIT... PLACES LIKE THIS--
I GET IT. I DO.
I WISH YOU'D GOTTEN TO MEET RICK.

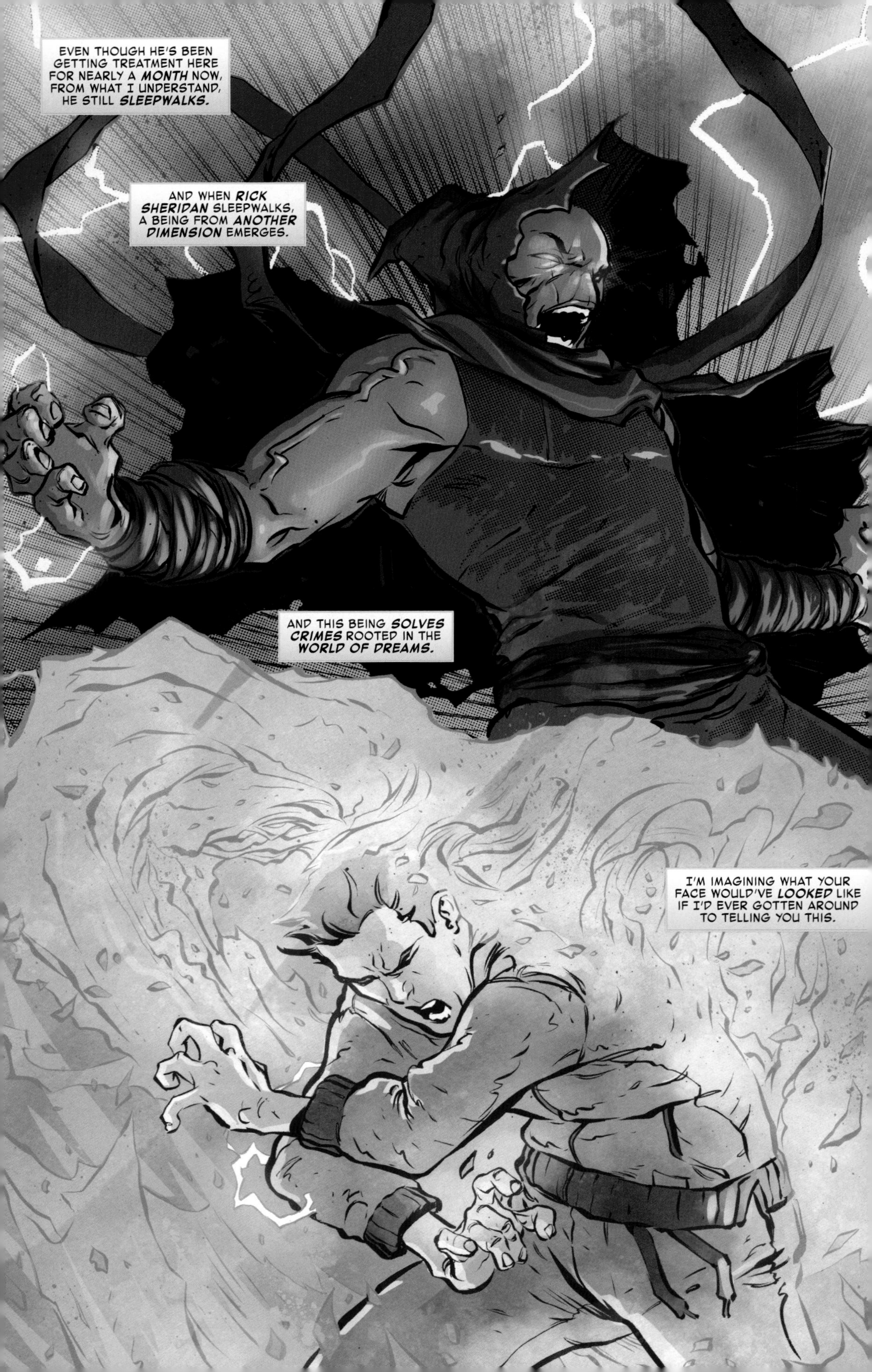
EVEN THOUGH HE'S BEEN GETTING TREATMENT HERE FOR NEARLY A MONTH NOW, FROM WHAT I UNDERSTAND, HE STILL SLEEPWALKS.
AND WHEN RICK SHERIDAN SLEEPWALKS, A BEING FROM ANOTHER DIMENSION EMERGES.
AND THIS BEING SOLVES CRIMES ROOTED IN THE WORLD OF DREAMS.
I'M IMAGINING WHAT YOUR FACE WOULD'VE LOOKED LIKE IF I'D EVER GOTTEN AROUND TO TELLING YOU THIS.

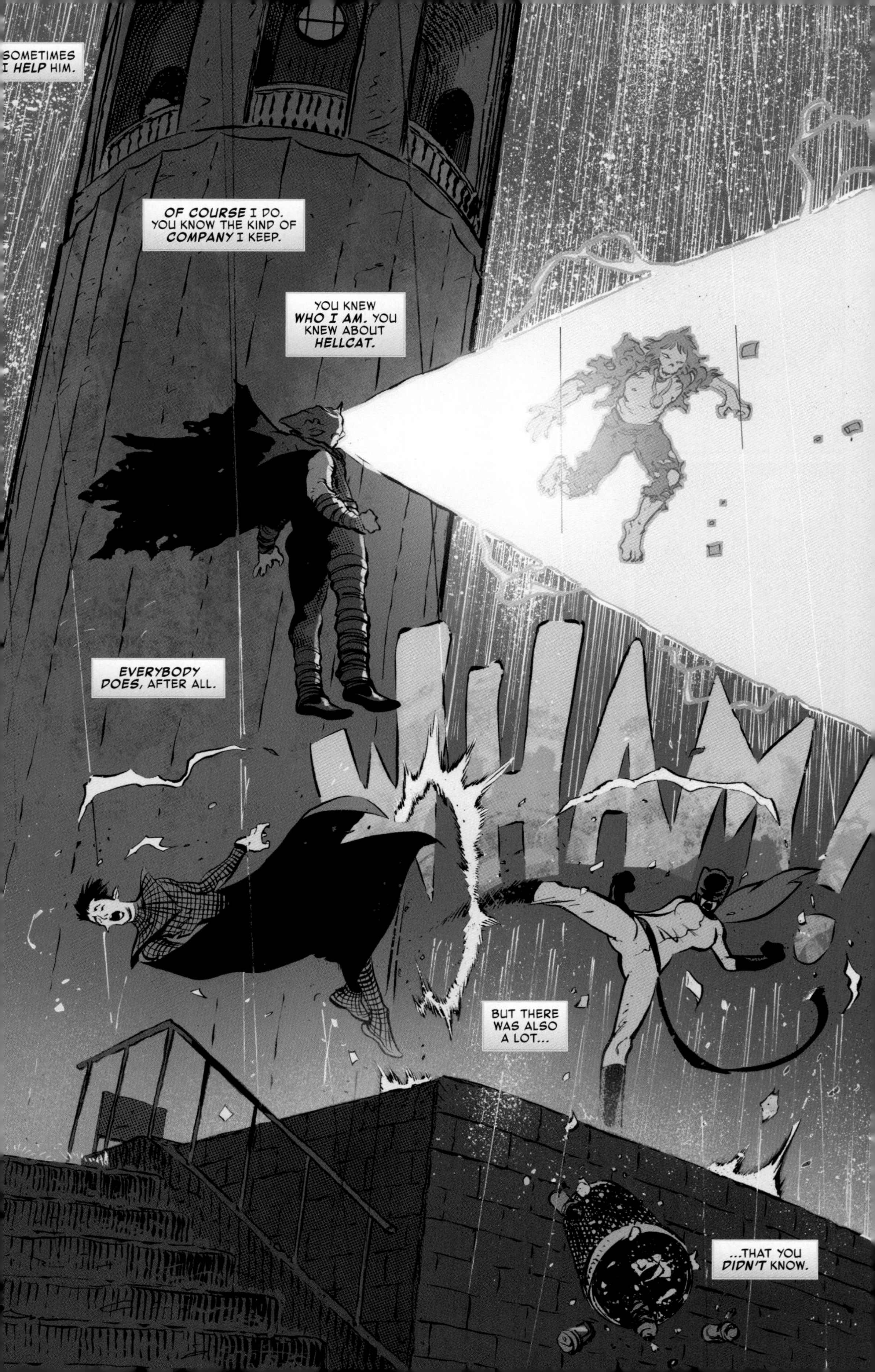
SOMETIMES I HELP HIM.
OF COURSE I DO. YOU KNOW THE KIND OF COMPANY I KEEP.
YOU KNEW WHO I AM. YOU KNEW ABOUT HELLCAT.
EVERYBODY DOES, AFTER ALL.
WHAM!
BUT THERE WAS ALSO A LOT...
...THAT YOU DIDN'T KNOW.

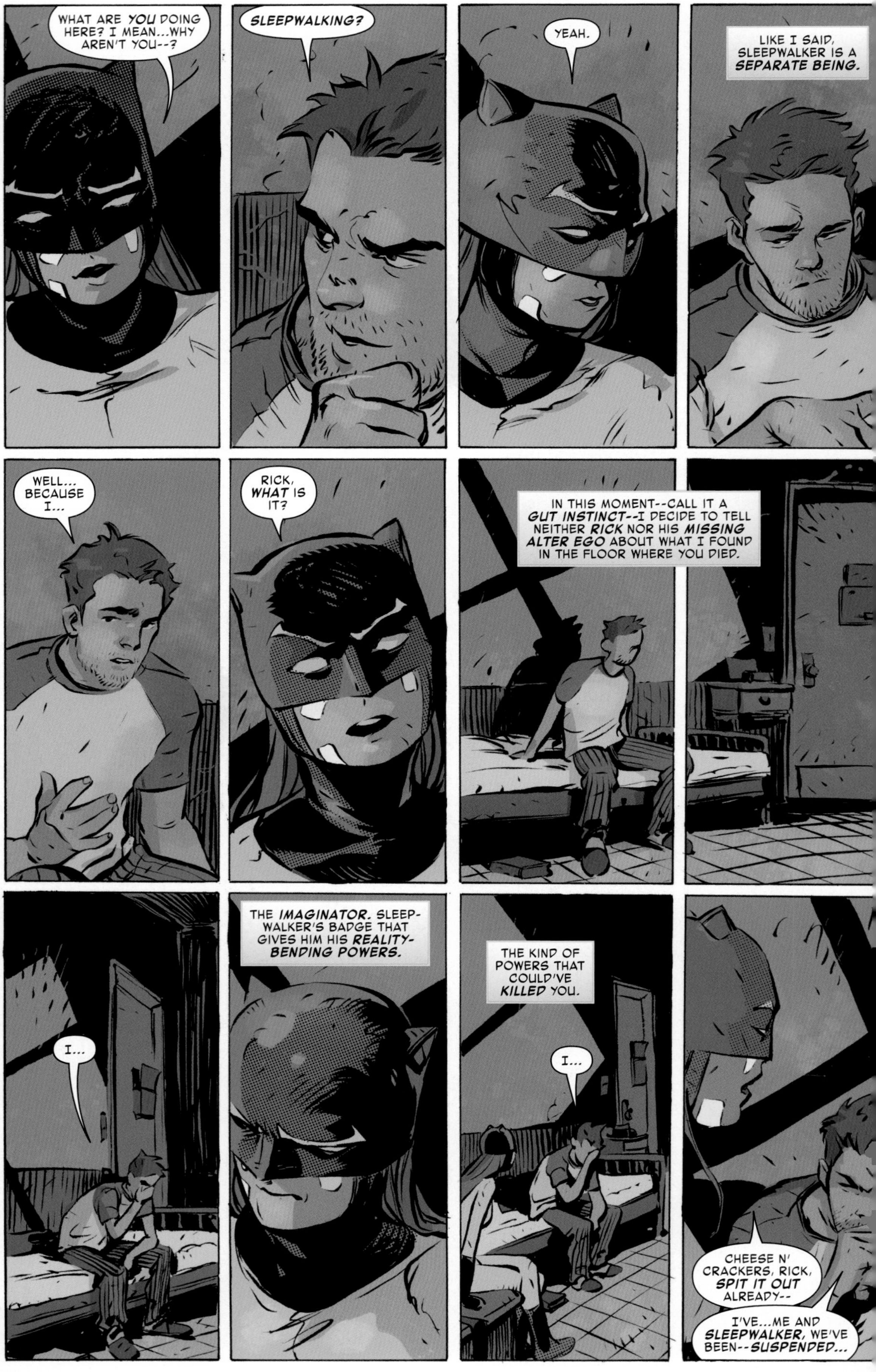
WHAT ARE YOU DOING HERE? I MEAN...WHY AREN'T YOU--?
SLEEPWALKING?
YEAH.
LIKE I SAID, SLEEPWALKER IS A SEPARATE BEING.
WELL... BECAUSE I...
RICK, WHAT IS IT?
IN THIS MOMENT--CALL IT A GUT INSTINCT--I DECIDE TO TELL NEITHER RICK NOR HIS MISSING ALTER EGO ABOUT WHAT I FOUND IN THE FLOOR WHERE YOU DIED.
I...
THE IMAGINATOR. SLEEP-WALKER'S BADGE THAT GIVES HIM HIS REALITY-BENDING POWERS.
THE KIND OF POWERS THAT COULD'VE KILLED YOU.
I...
CHEESE N' CRACKERS, RICK, SPIT IT OUT ALREADY--
I'VE...ME AND SLEEPWALKER, WE'VE BEEN--SUSPENDED...

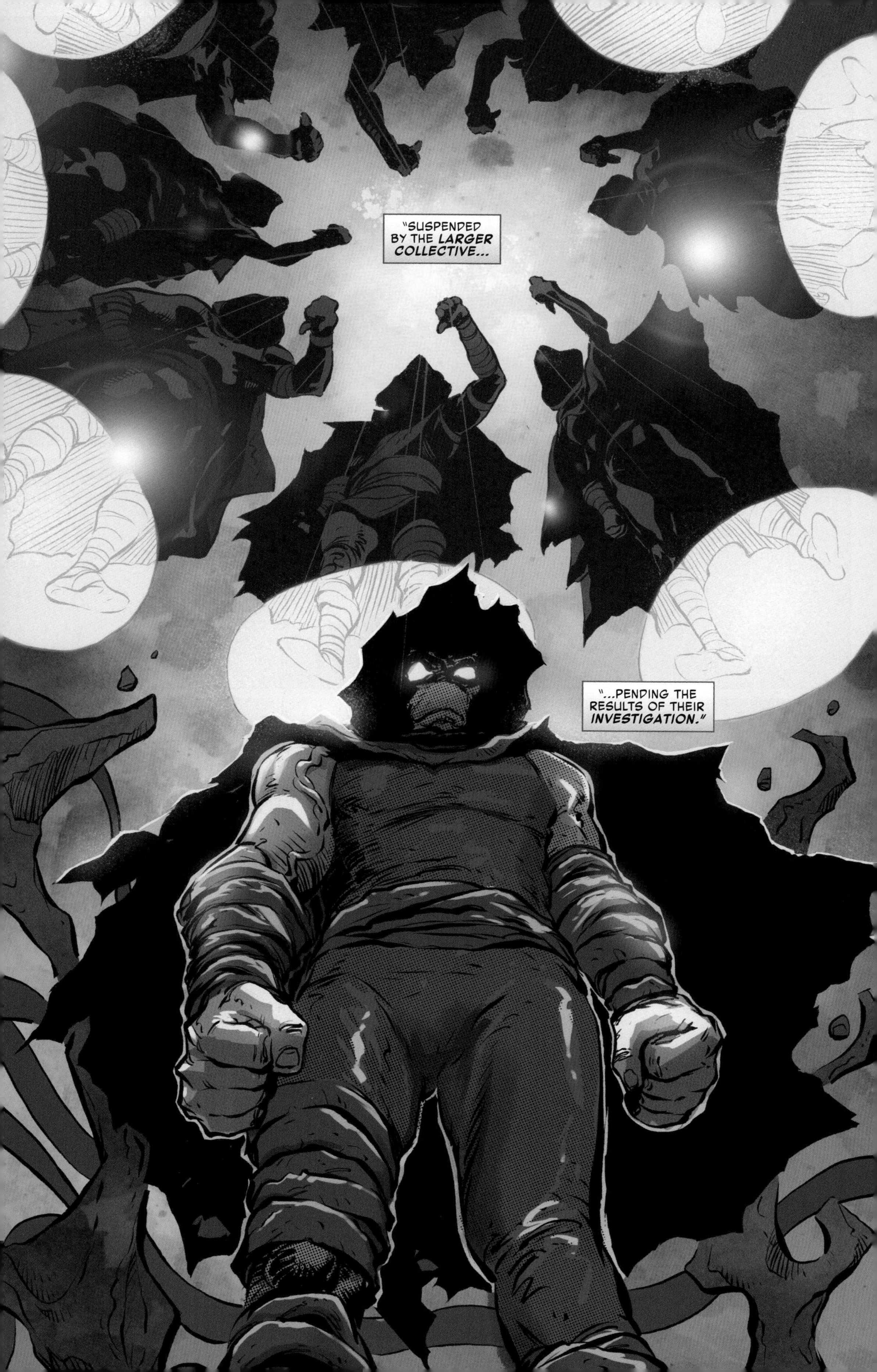
"SUSPENDED BY THE *LARGER COLLECTIVE*...
"...PENDING THE RESULTS OF THEIR *INVESTIGATION*."

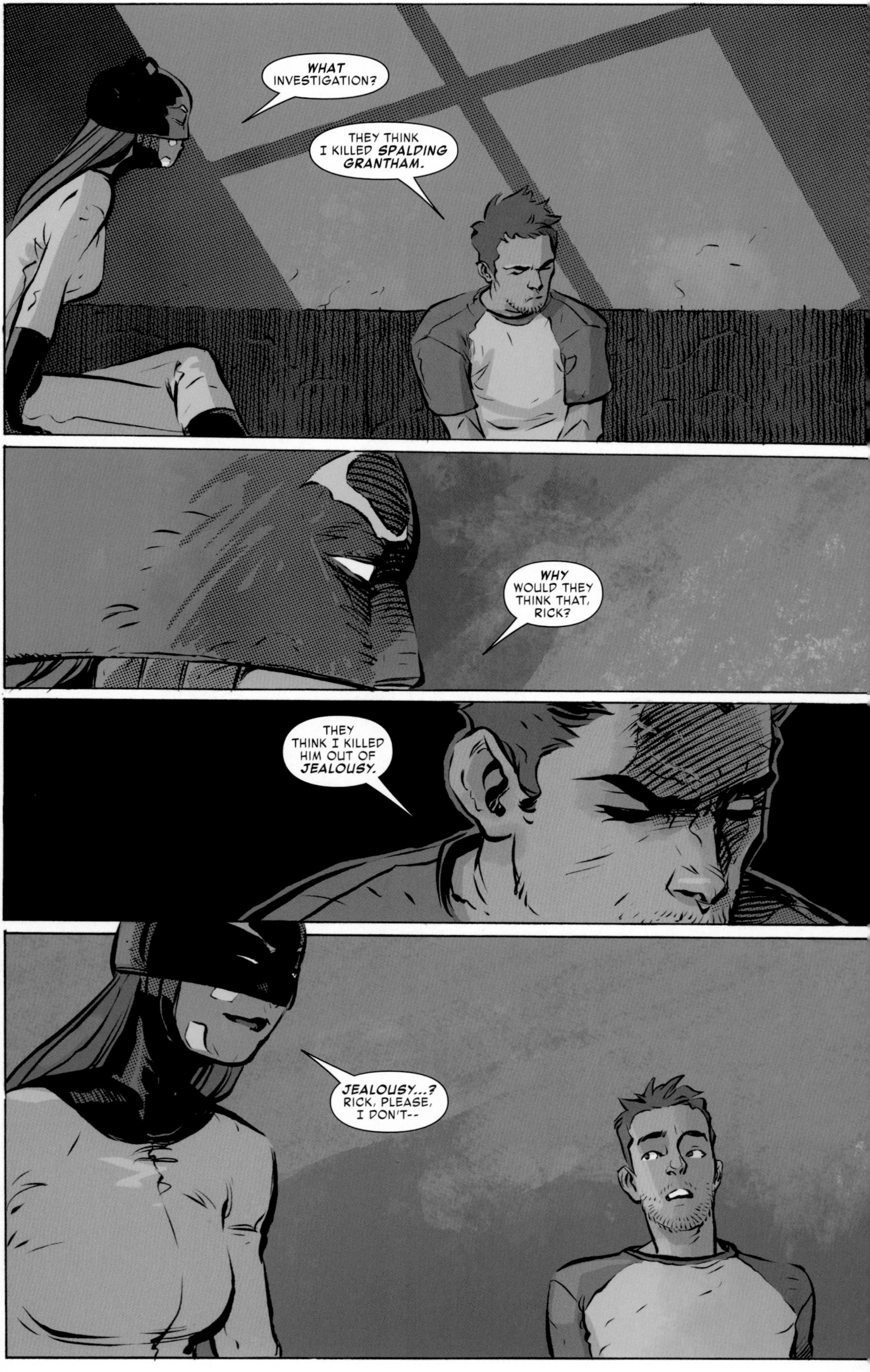
WHAT INVESTIGATION?
THEY THINK I KILLED SPALDING GRANTHAM.
WHY WOULD THEY THINK THAT, RICK?
THEY THINK I KILLED HIM OUT OF JEALOUSY.
JEALOUSY...? RICK, PLEASE, I DON'T--

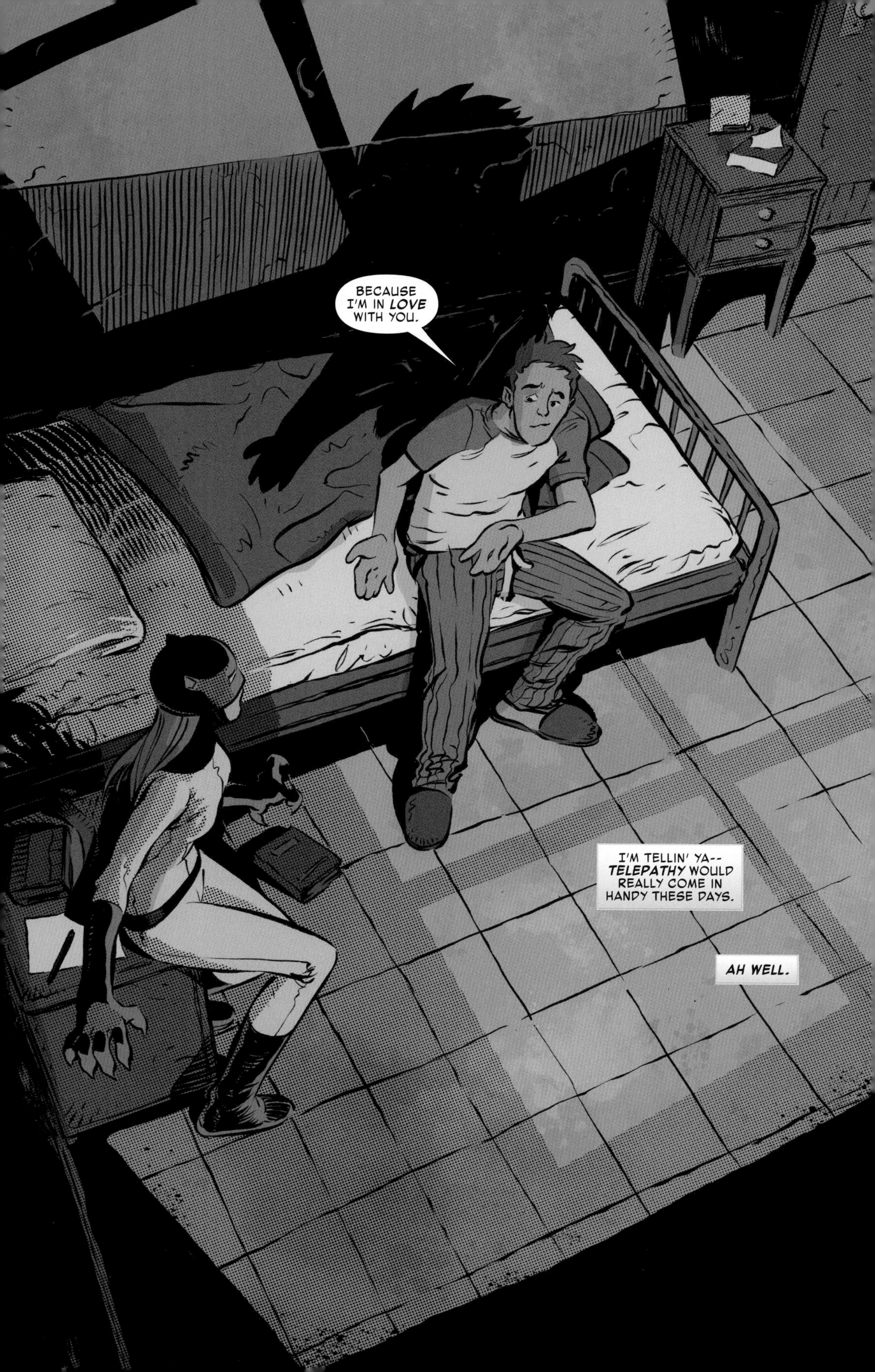
BECAUSE I'M IN LOVE WITH YOU.
I'M TELLIN' YA-- TELEPATHY WOULD REALLY COME IN HANDY THESE DAYS.
AH WELL.

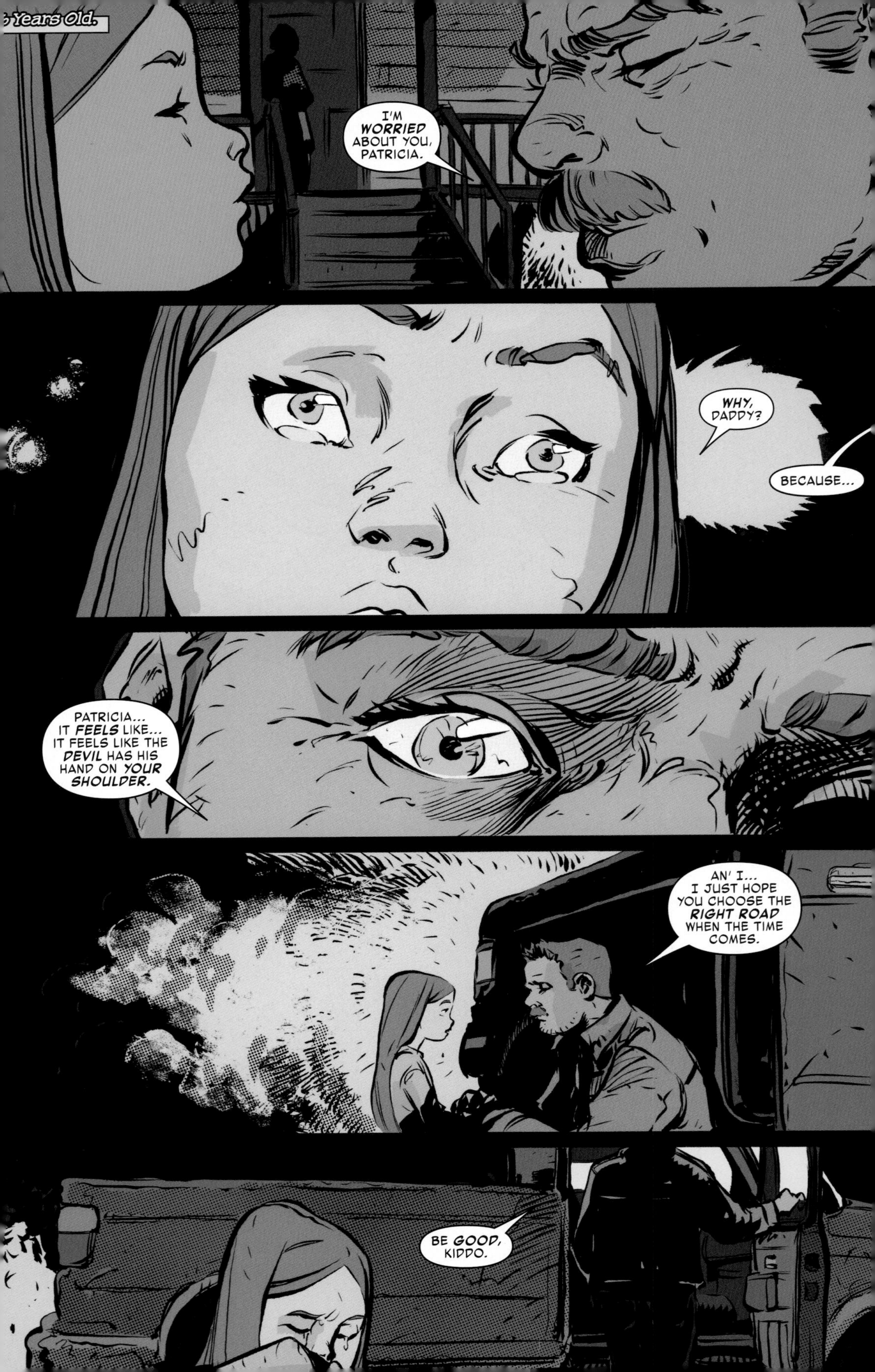

6 Years Old.
I'M WORRIED ABOUT YOU, PATRICIA.
WHY, DADDY?
BECAUSE...
PATRICIA... IT FEELS LIKE... IT FEELS LIKE THE DEVIL HAS HIS HAND ON YOUR SHOULDER.
AN' I... I JUST HOPE YOU CHOOSE THE RIGHT ROAD WHEN THE TIME COMES.
BE GOOD, KIDDO.

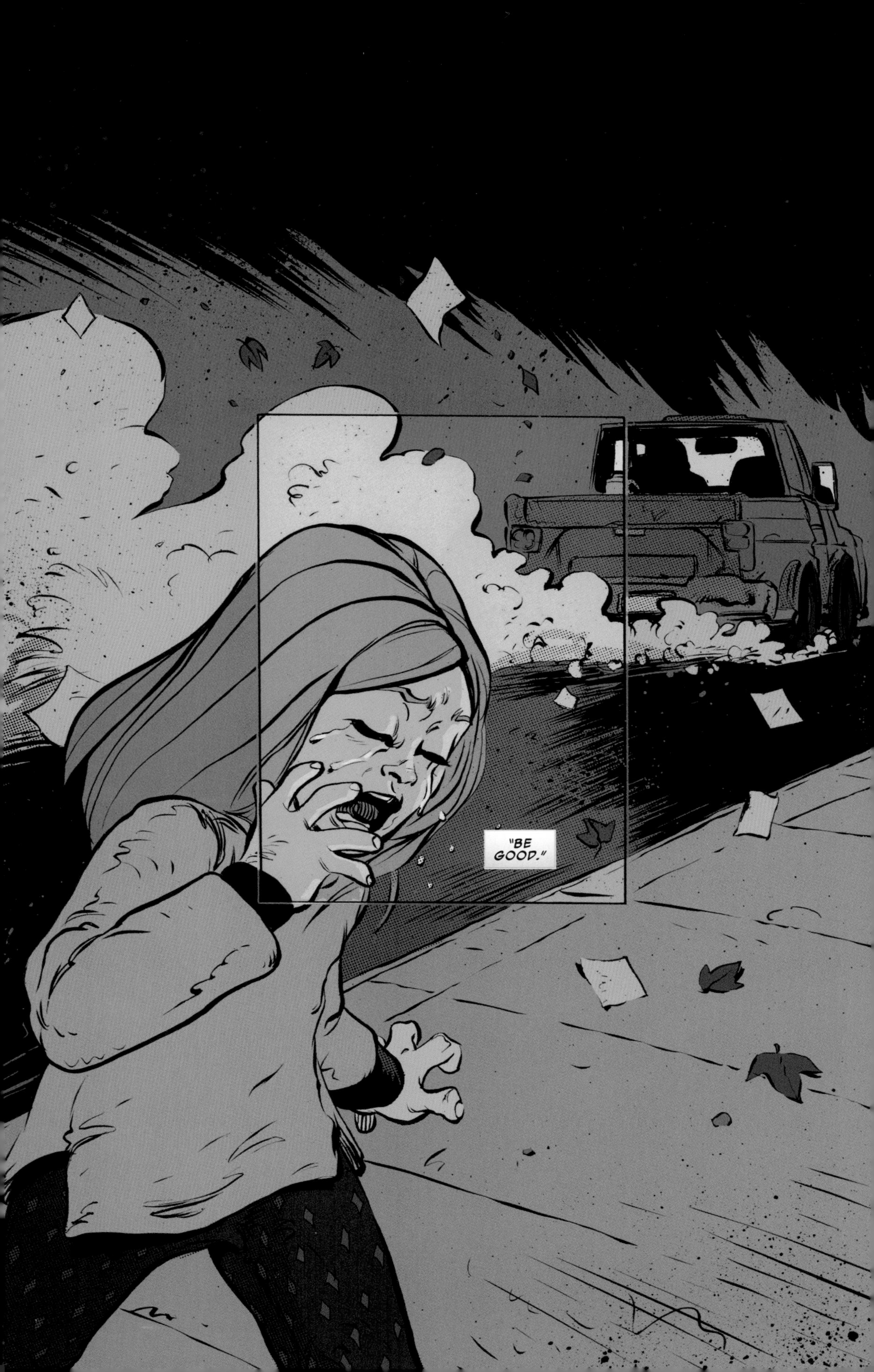
"BE GOOD."

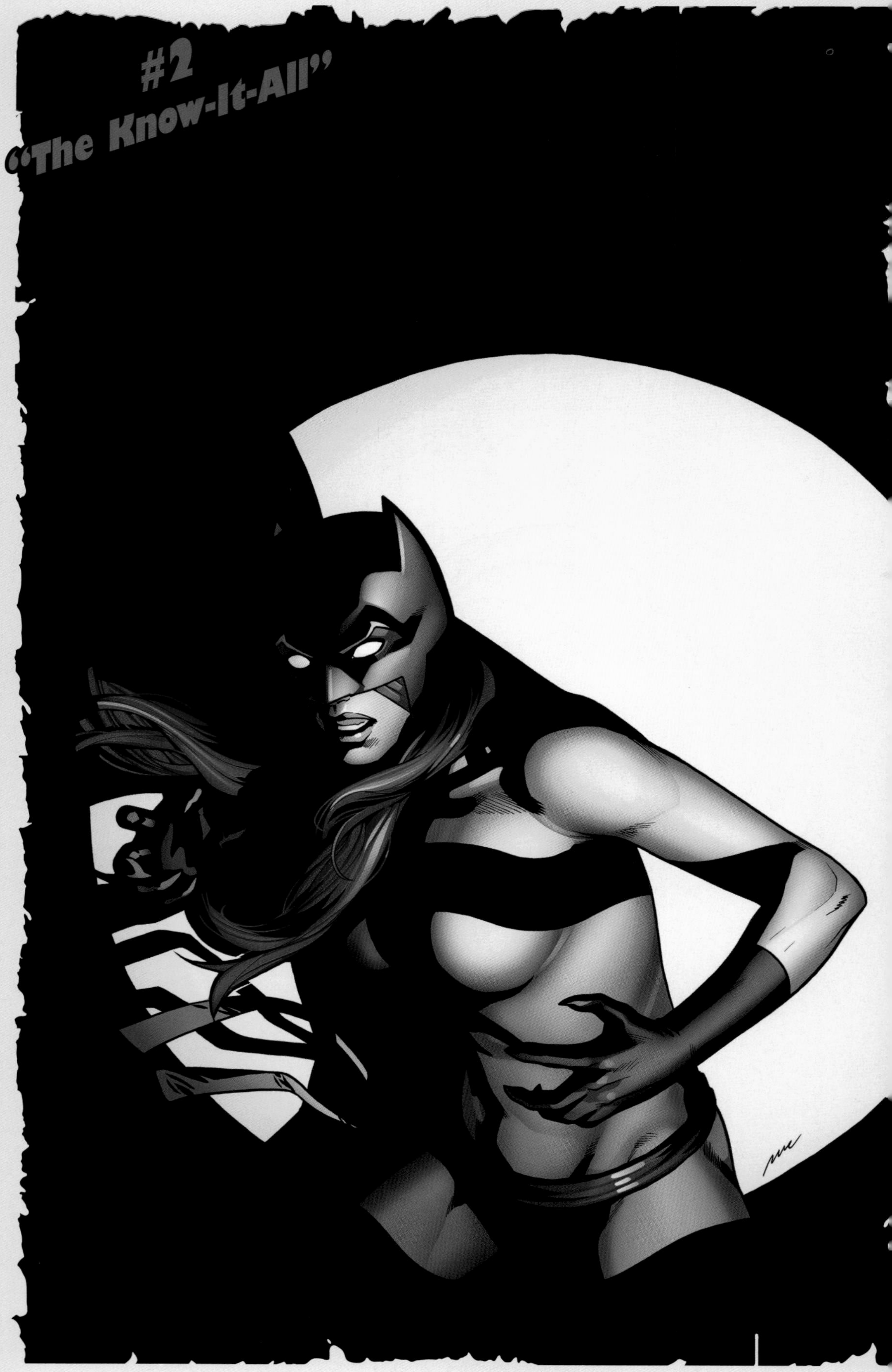
#2
"The Know-It-All"

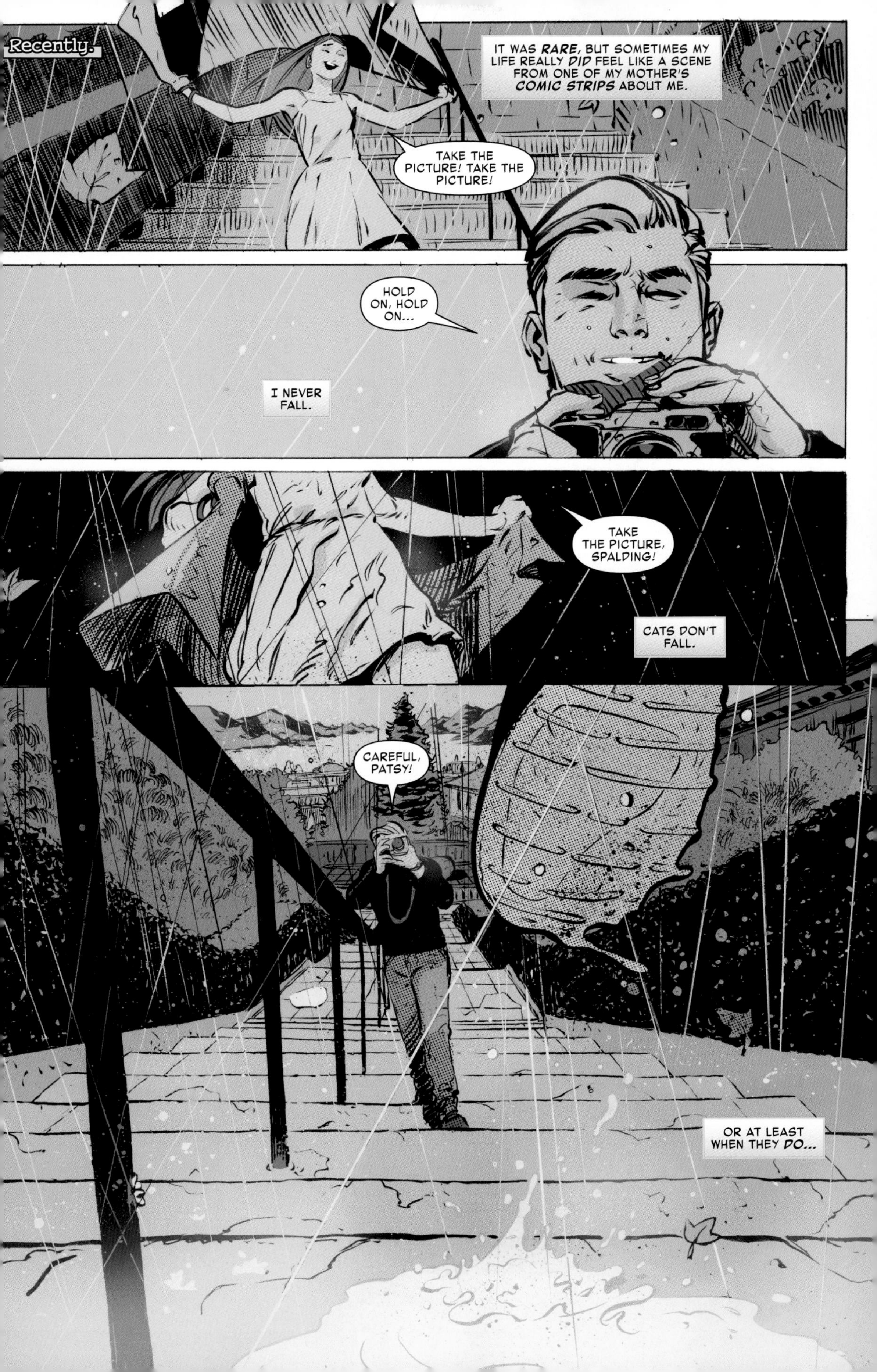
Recently.
IT WAS RARE, BUT SOMETIMES MY LIFE REALLY DID FEEL LIKE A SCENE FROM ONE OF MY MOTHER'S COMIC STRIPS ABOUT ME.
TAKE THE PICTURE! TAKE THE PICTURE!
HOLD ON, HOLD ON...
I NEVER FALL.
TAKE THE PICTURE, SPALDING!
CATS DON'T FALL.
CAREFUL, PATSY!
OR AT LEAST WHEN THEY DO...

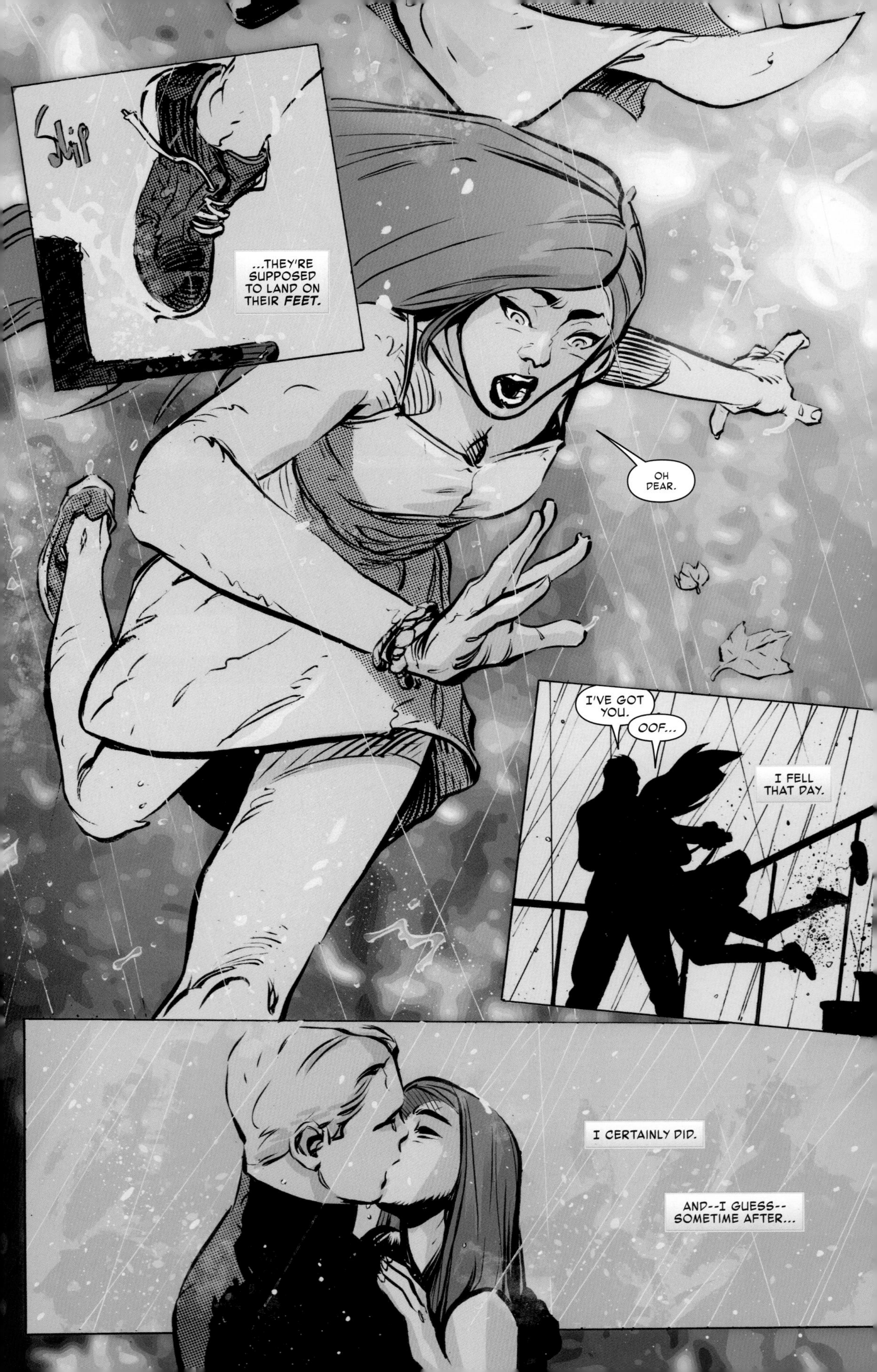
SLIP
...THEY'RE SUPPOSED TO LAND ON THEIR FEET.
OH DEAR.
I'VE GOT YOU.
OOF...
I FELL THAT DAY.
I CERTAINLY DID.
AND--I GUESS-- SOMETIME AFTER...

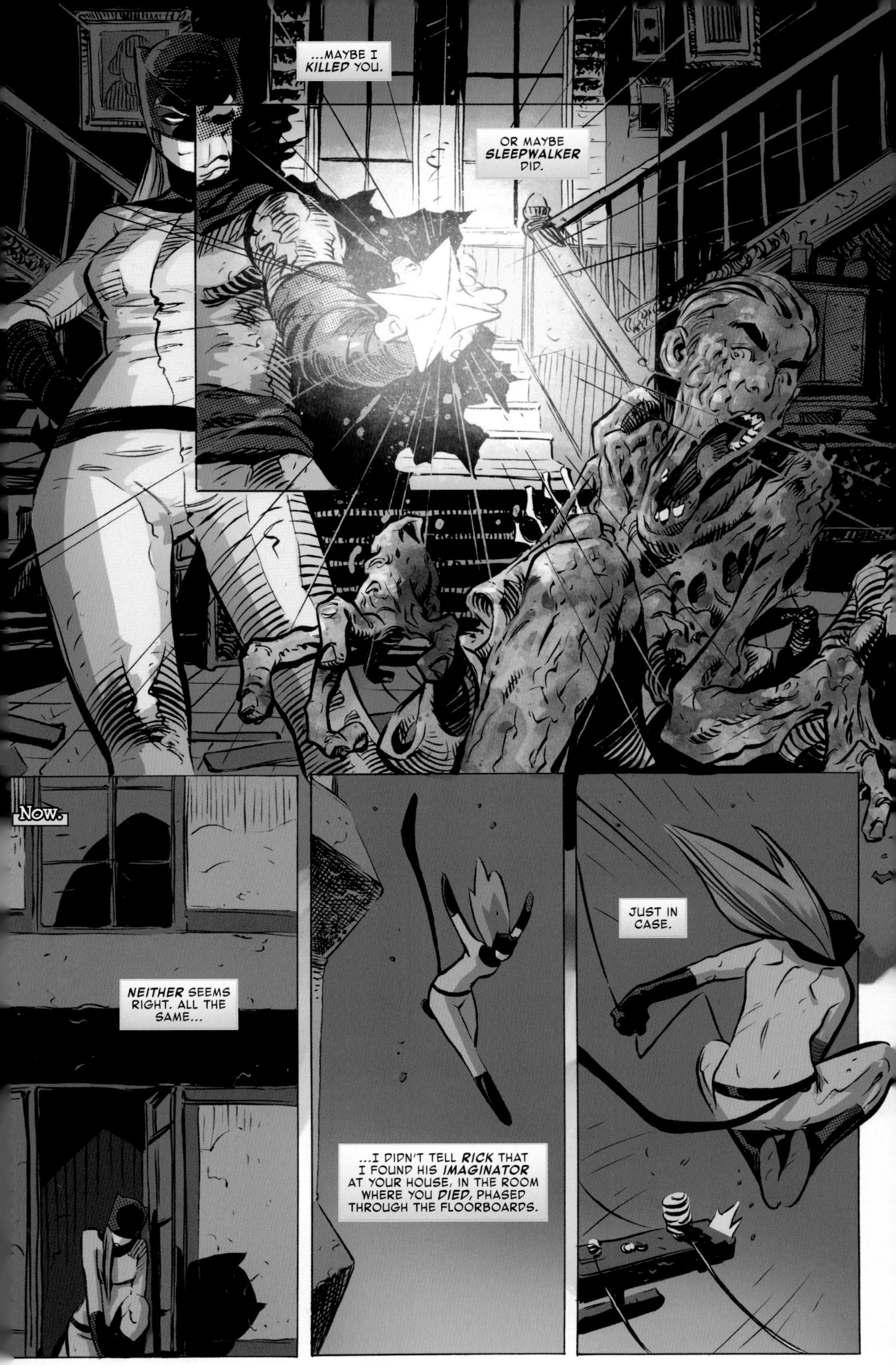
...MAYBE I KILLED YOU.
OR MAYBE SLEEPWALKER DID.
Now.
NEITHER SEEMS RIGHT. ALL THE SAME...
...I DIDN'T TELL RICK THAT I FOUND HIS IMAGINATOR AT YOUR HOUSE, IN THE ROOM WHERE YOU DIED, PHASED THROUGH THE FLOORBOARDS.
JUST IN CASE.

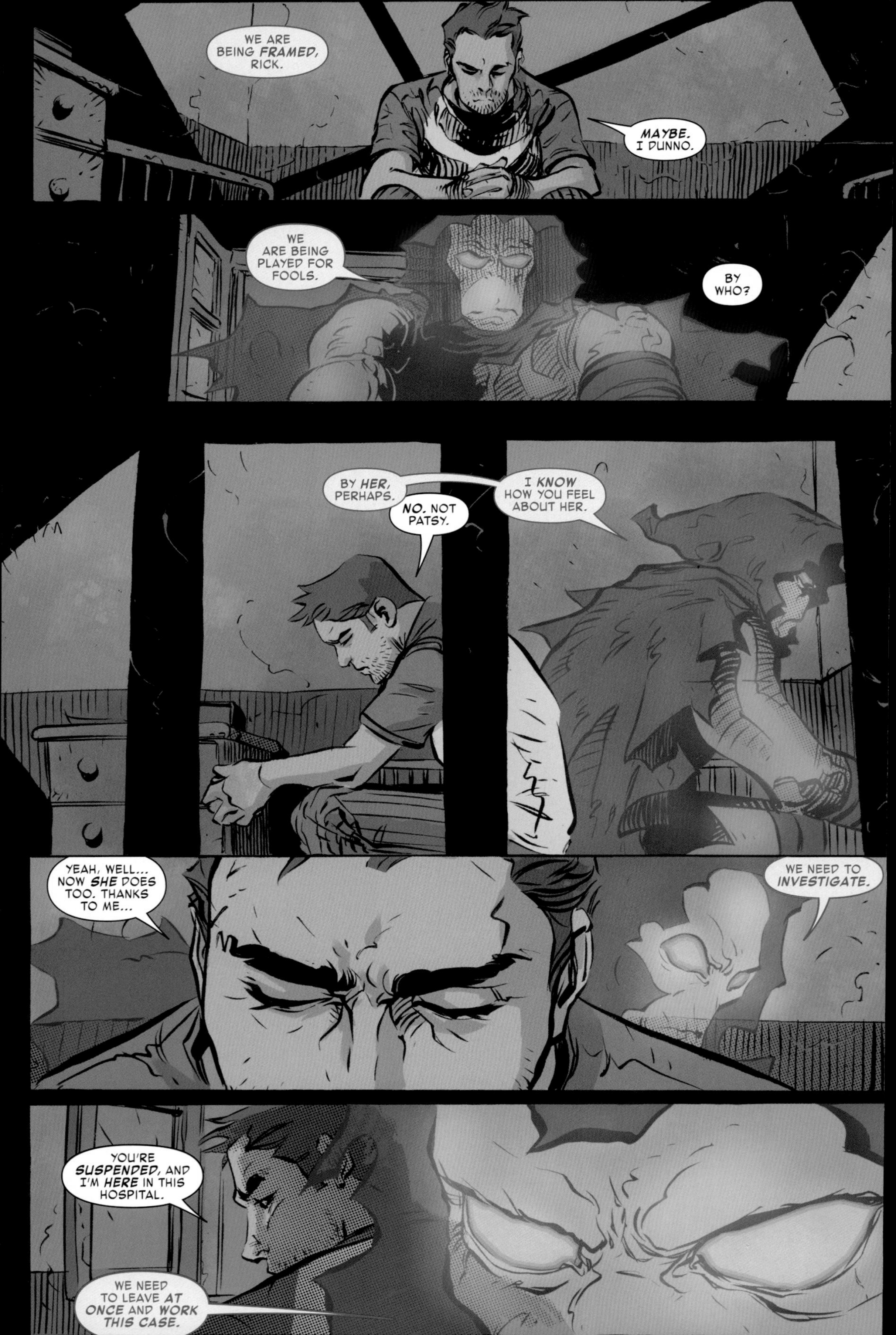
WE ARE BEING FRAMED, RICK.
MAYBE. I DUNNO.
WE ARE BEING PLAYED FOR FOOLS.
BY WHO?
BY HER, PERHAPS.
NO. NOT PATSY.
I KNOW HOW YOU FEEL ABOUT HER.
YEAH, WELL... NOW SHE DOES TOO. THANKS TO ME...
WE NEED TO INVESTIGATE.
YOU'RE SUSPENDED, AND I'M HERE IN THIS HOSPITAL.
WE NEED TO LEAVE AT ONCE AND WORK THIS CASE.

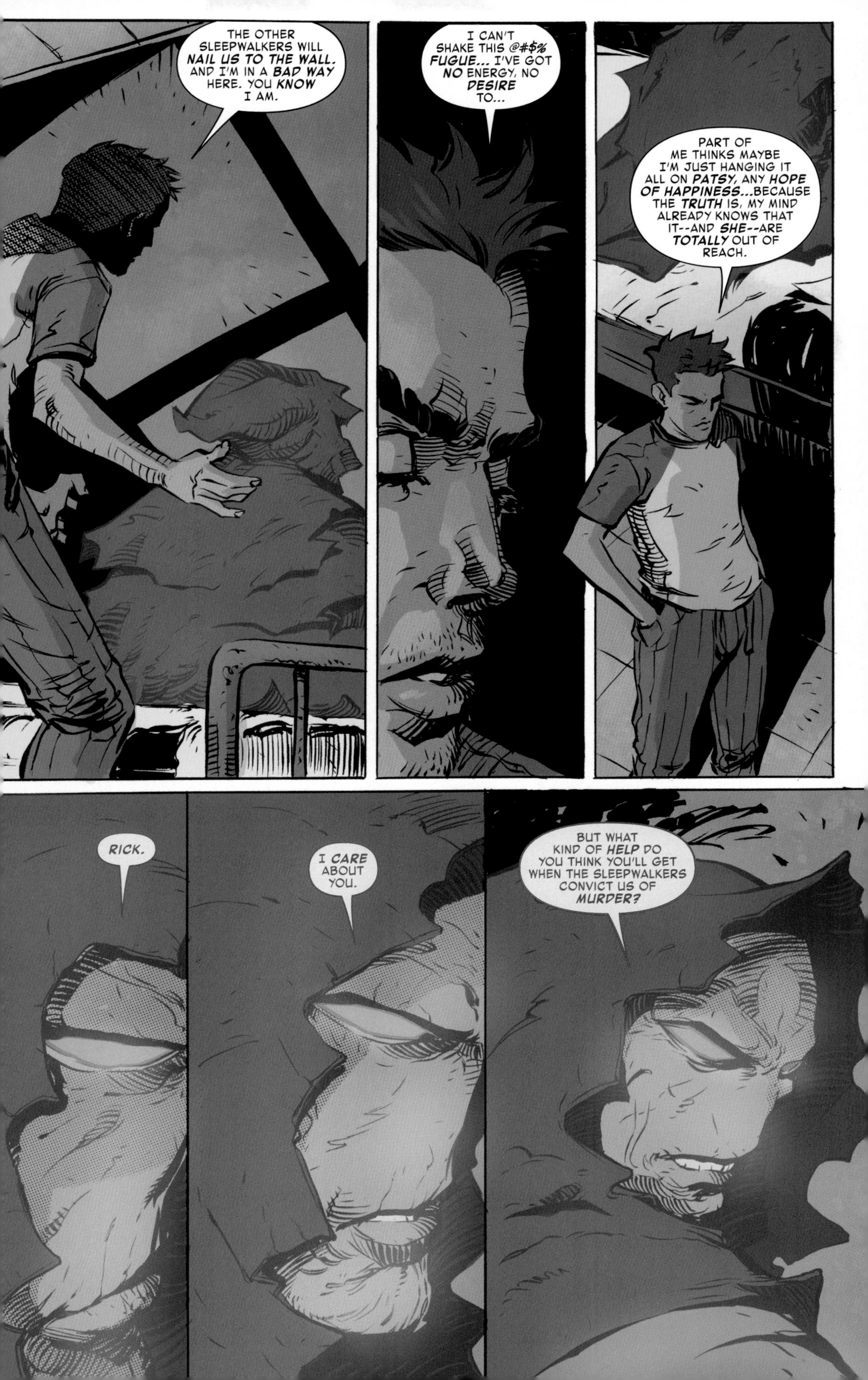
THE OTHER SLEEPWALKERS WILL NAIL US TO THE WALL. AND I'M IN A BAD WAY HERE. YOU KNOW I AM.
I CAN'T SHAKE THIS @#$% FUGUE... I'VE GOT NO ENERGY, NO DESIRE TO...
PART OF ME THINKS MAYBE I'M JUST HANGING IT ALL ON PATSY, ANY HOPE OF HAPPINESS...BECAUSE THE TRUTH IS, MY MIND ALREADY KNOWS THAT IT--AND SHE--ARE TOTALLY OUT OF REACH.
RICK.
I CARE ABOUT YOU.
BUT WHAT KIND OF HELP DO YOU THINK YOU'LL GET WHEN THE SLEEPWALKERS CONVICT US OF MURDER?

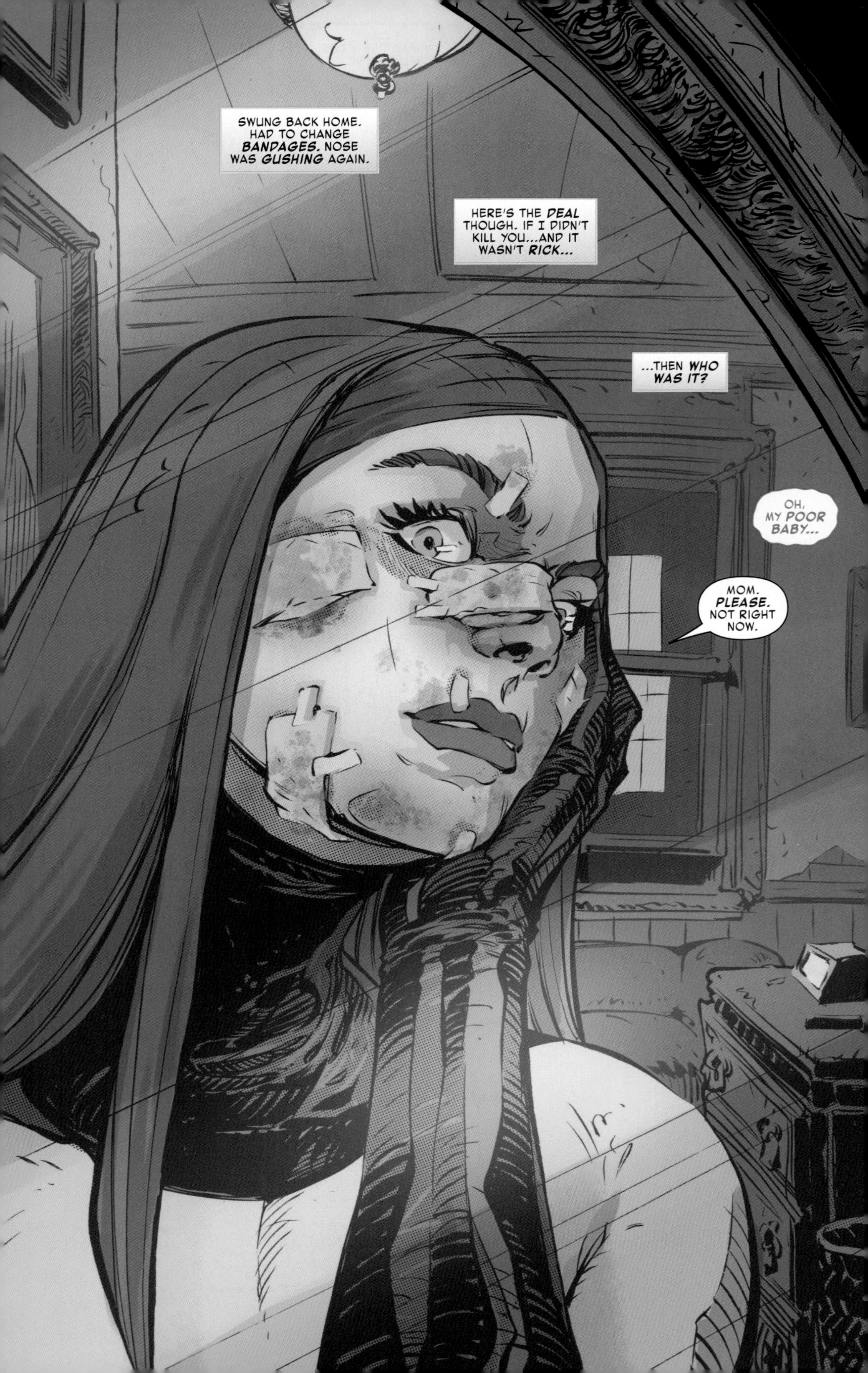
SWUNG BACK HOME. HAD TO CHANGE BANDAGES. NOSE WAS GUSHING AGAIN.
HERE'S THE DEAL THOUGH. IF I DIDN'T KILL YOU...AND IT WASN'T RICK...
...THEN WHO WAS IT?
OH, MY POOR BABY...
MOM. PLEASE. NOT RIGHT NOW.

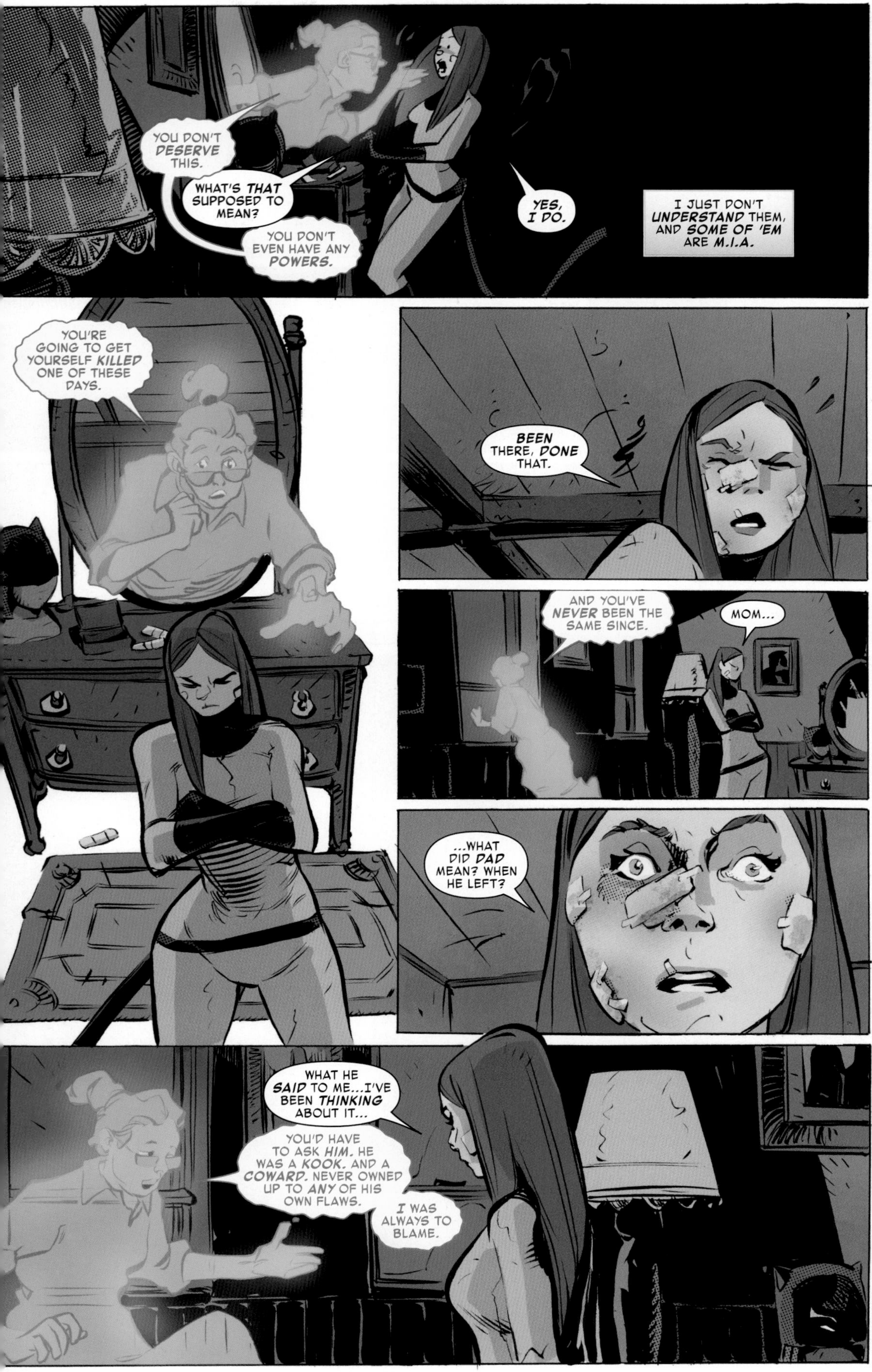
YOU DON'T DESERVE THIS.
WHAT'S THAT SUPPOSED TO MEAN?
YOU DON'T EVEN HAVE ANY POWERS.
YES, I DO.
I JUST DON'T UNDERSTAND THEM, AND SOME OF 'EM ARE M.I.A.
YOU'RE GOING TO GET YOURSELF KILLED ONE OF THESE DAYS.
BEEN THERE, DONE THAT.
AND YOU'VE NEVER BEEN THE SAME SINCE.
MOM...
...WHAT DID DAD MEAN? WHEN HE LEFT?
WHAT HE SAID TO ME...I'VE BEEN THINKING ABOUT IT...
YOU'D HAVE TO ASK HIM. HE WAS A KOOK. AND A COWARD. NEVER OWNED UP TO ANY OF HIS OWN FLAWS.
I WAS ALWAYS TO BLAME.

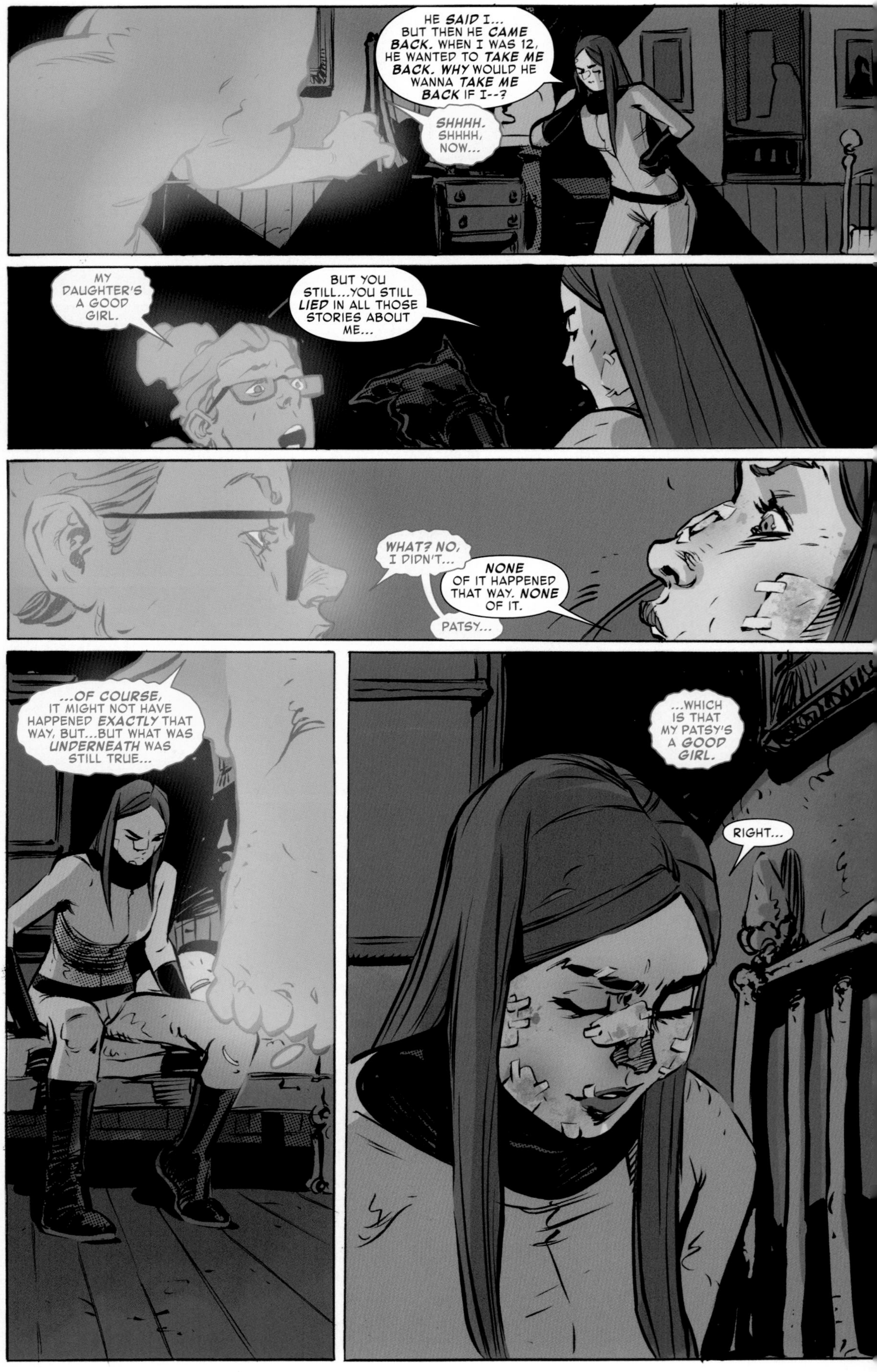
HE *SAID* I... BUT THEN HE *CAME BACK.* WHEN I WAS 12, HE WANTED TO *TAKE ME BACK. WHY* WOULD HE WANNA *TAKE ME BACK* IF I--?
SHHHH. SHHHH, NOW...
MY DAUGHTER'S A GOOD GIRL.
BUT YOU STILL...YOU STILL *LIED* IN ALL THOSE STORIES ABOUT ME...
WHAT? NO, I DIDN'T...
NONE OF IT HAPPENED THAT WAY. *NONE* OF IT.
PATSY...
...OF COURSE, IT MIGHT NOT HAVE HAPPENED *EXACTLY* THAT WAY, BUT...BUT WHAT WAS *UNDERNEATH* WAS STILL TRUE...
...WHICH IS THAT MY PATSY'S A *GOOD GIRL.*
RIGHT...

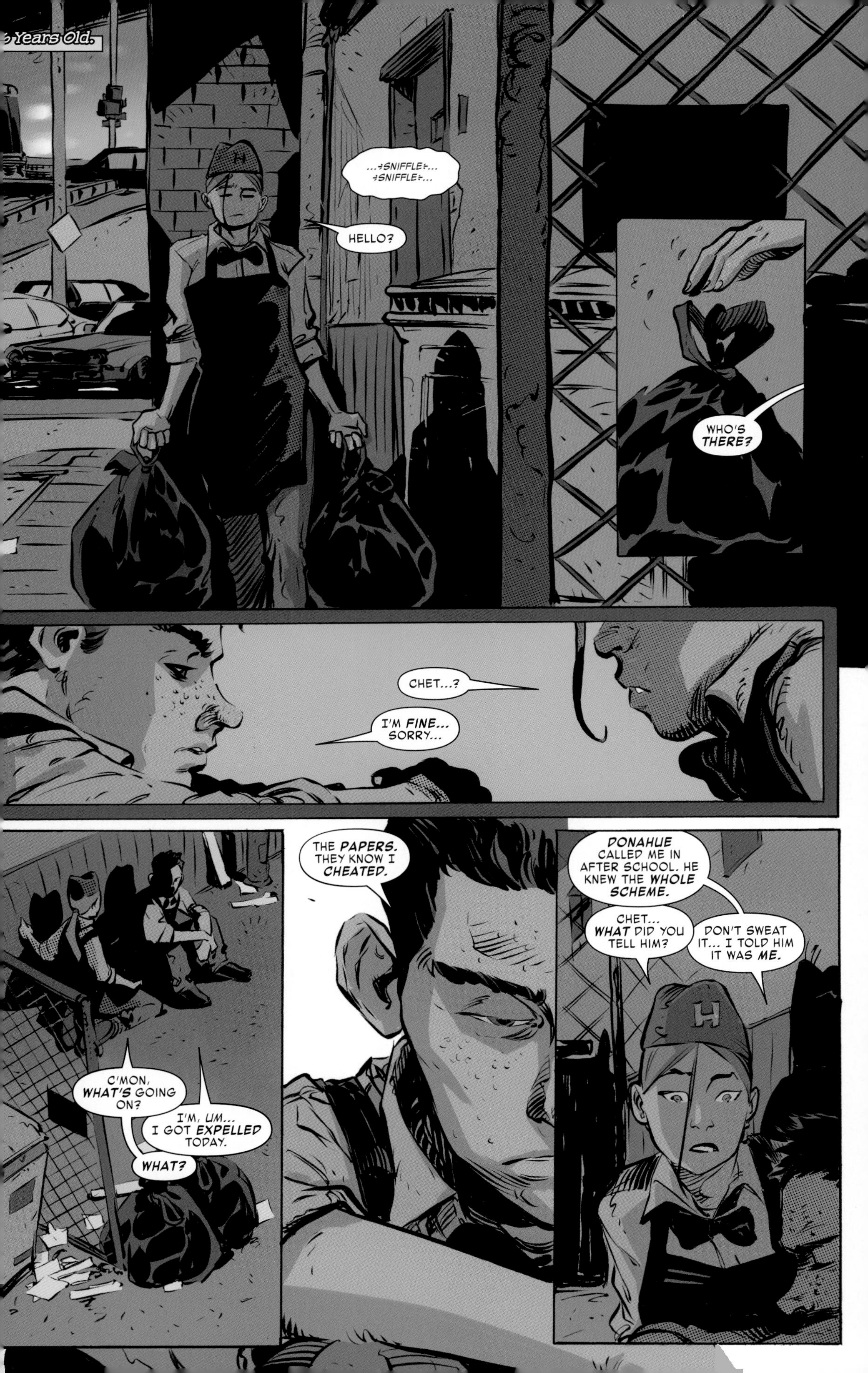
Years Old.
...SNIFFLE...
SNIFFLE...
HELLO?
WHO'S THERE?
CHET...?
I'M FINE... SORRY...
C'MON, WHAT'S GOING ON?
I'M, UM... I GOT EXPELLED TODAY.
WHAT?
THE PAPERS. THEY KNOW I CHEATED.
DONAHUE CALLED ME IN AFTER SCHOOL. HE KNEW THE WHOLE SCHEME.
CHET... WHAT DID YOU TELL HIM?
DON'T SWEAT IT... I TOLD HIM IT WAS ME.

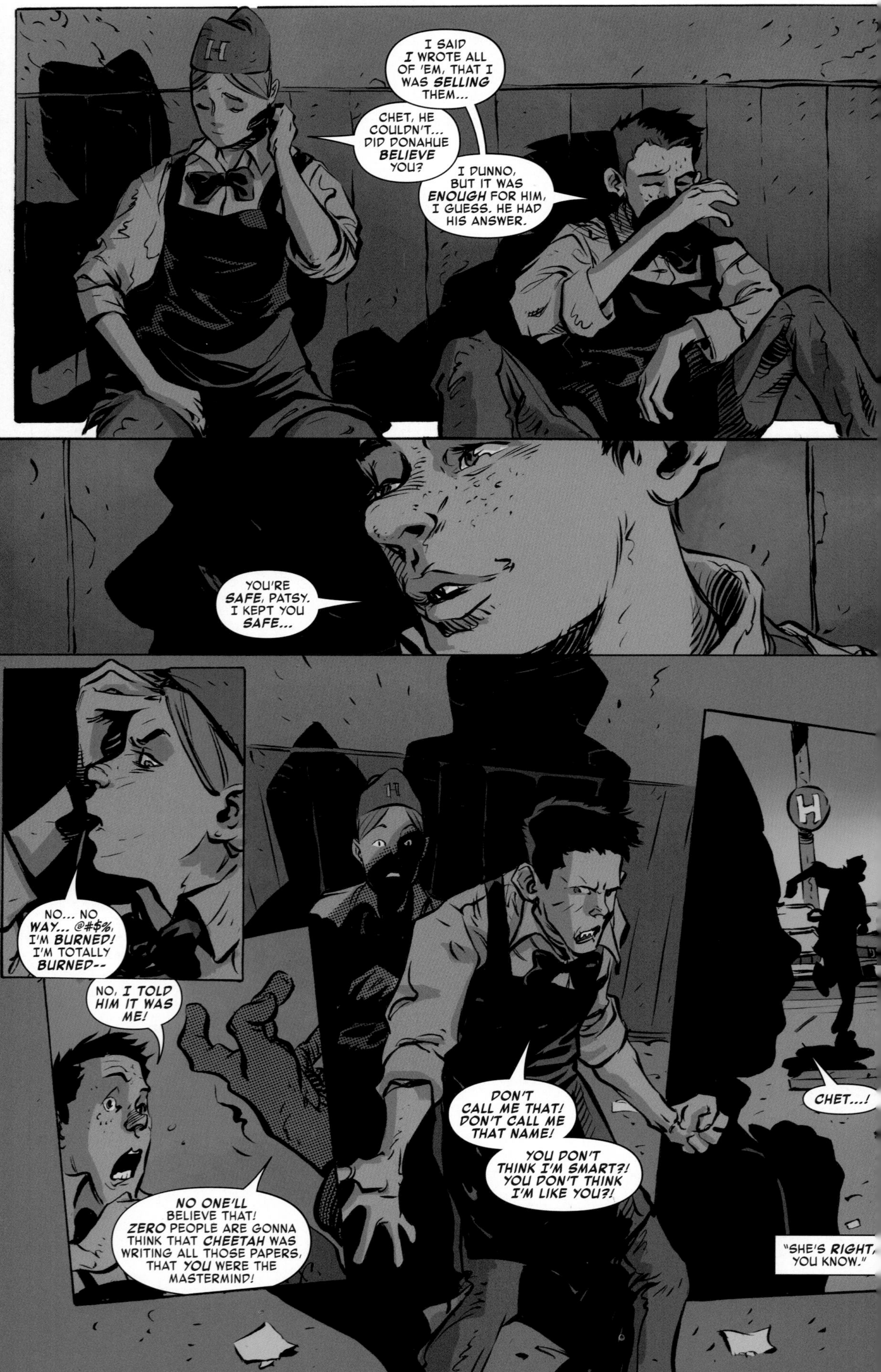
I SAID I WROTE ALL OF 'EM, THAT I WAS SELLING THEM...
CHET, HE COULDN'T... DID DONAHUE BELIEVE YOU?
I DUNNO, BUT IT WAS ENOUGH FOR HIM, I GUESS. HE HAD HIS ANSWER.
YOU'RE SAFE, PATSY. I KEPT YOU SAFE...
NO... NO WAY... @#$%, I'M BURNED! I'M TOTALLY BURNED--
NO, I TOLD HIM IT WAS ME!
NO ONE'LL BELIEVE THAT! ZERO PEOPLE ARE GONNA THINK THAT CHEETAH WAS WRITING ALL THOSE PAPERS, THAT YOU WERE THE MASTERMIND!
DON'T CALL ME THAT! DON'T CALL ME THAT NAME!
YOU DON'T THINK I'M SMART?! YOU DON'T THINK I'M LIKE YOU?!
CHET...!
"SHE'S RIGHT, YOU KNOW."

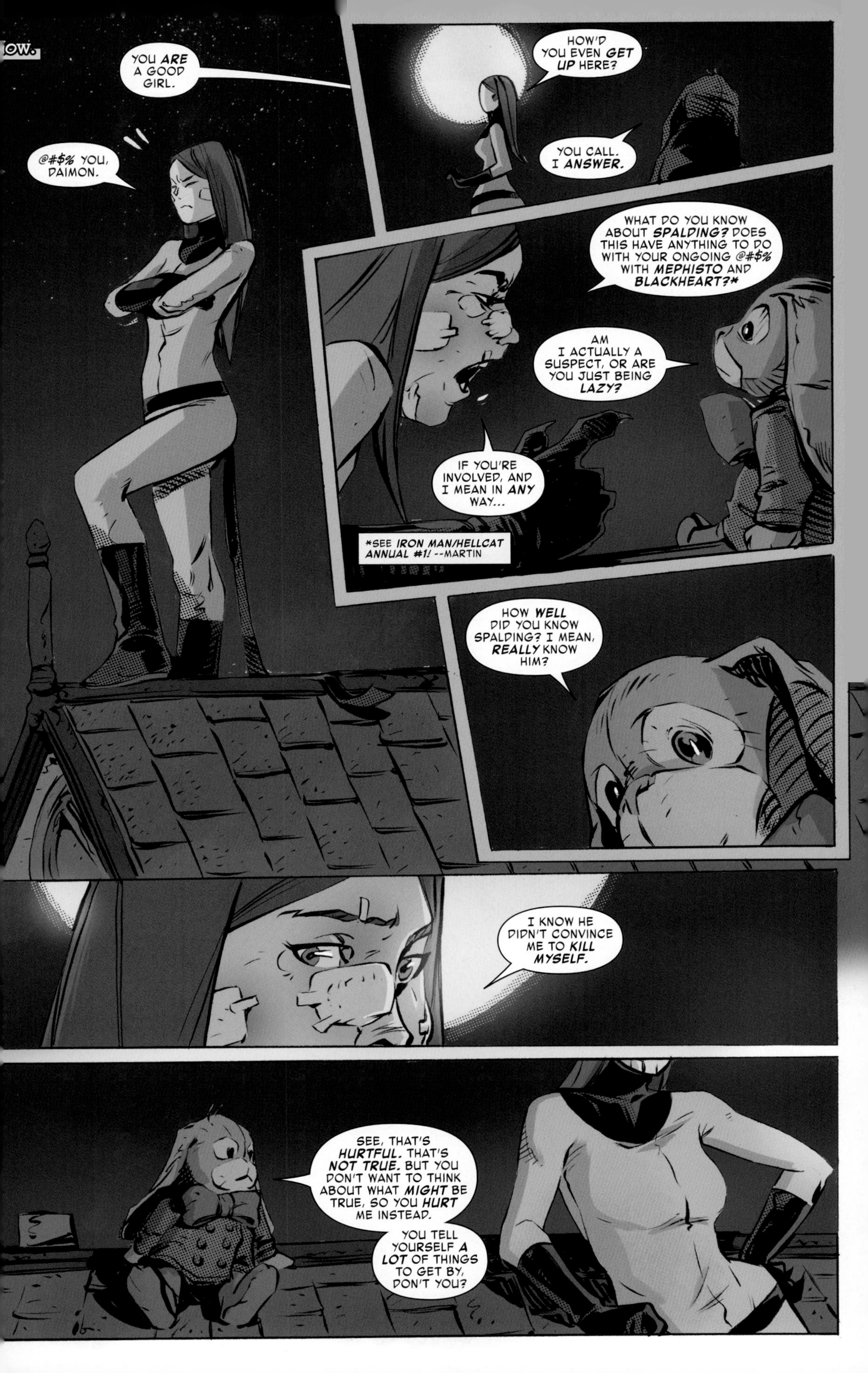

OW.
YOU ARE A GOOD GIRL.
@#$% YOU, DAIMON.
HOW'D YOU EVEN GET UP HERE?
YOU CALL. I ANSWER.
WHAT DO YOU KNOW ABOUT SPALDING? DOES THIS HAVE ANYTHING TO DO WITH YOUR ONGOING @#$% WITH MEPHISTO AND BLACKHEART?*
AM I ACTUALLY A SUSPECT, OR ARE YOU JUST BEING LAZY?
IF YOU'RE INVOLVED, AND I MEAN IN ANY WAY...
*SEE IRON MAN/HELLCAT ANNUAL #1! --MARTIN
HOW WELL DID YOU KNOW SPALDING? I MEAN, REALLY KNOW HIM?
I KNOW HE DIDN'T CONVINCE ME TO KILL MYSELF.
SEE, THAT'S HURTFUL. THAT'S NOT TRUE. BUT YOU DON'T WANT TO THINK ABOUT WHAT MIGHT BE TRUE, SO YOU HURT ME INSTEAD.
YOU TELL YOURSELF A LOT OF THINGS TO GET BY, DON'T YOU?

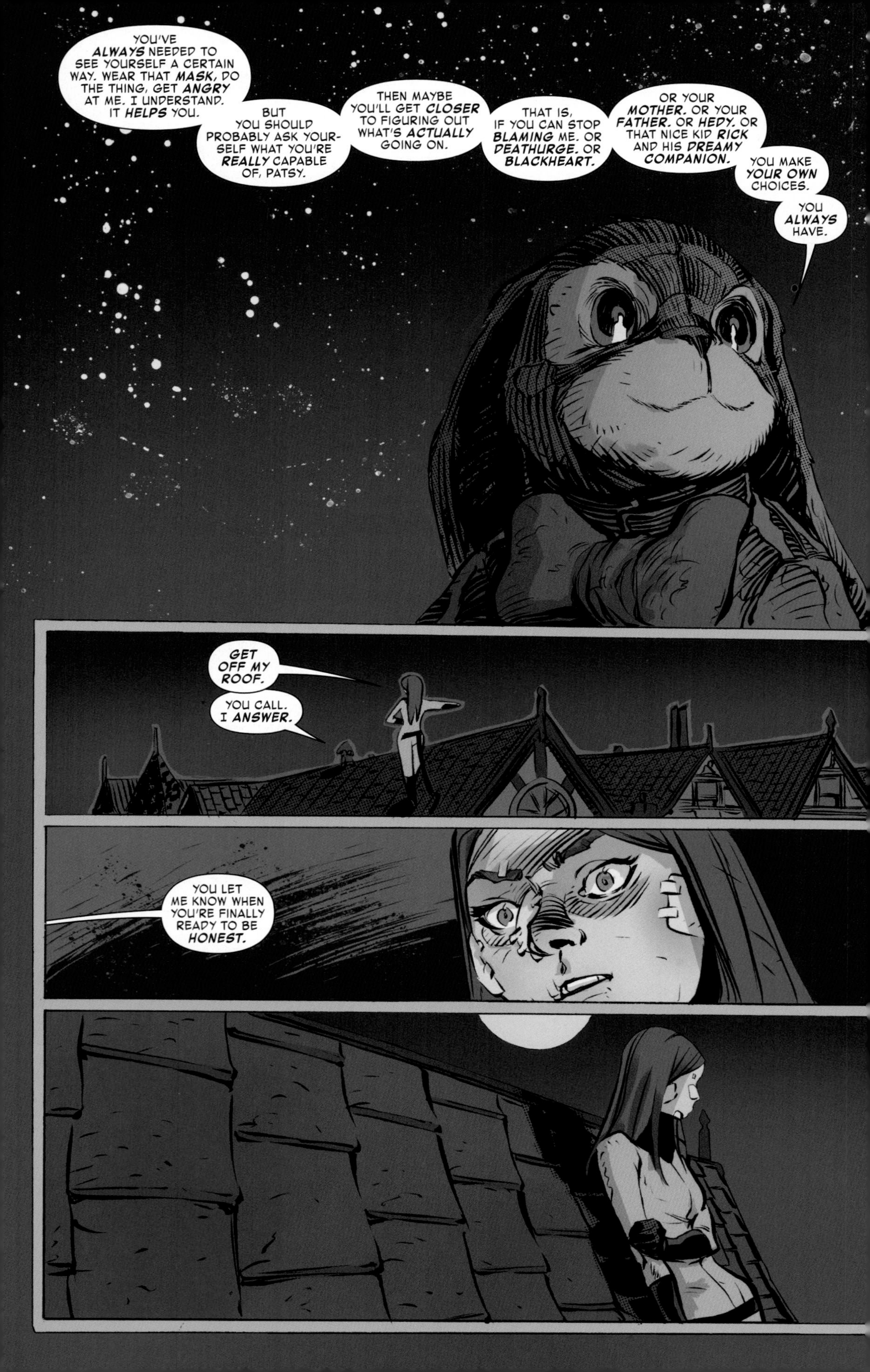
YOU'VE ALWAYS NEEDED TO SEE YOURSELF A CERTAIN WAY. WEAR THAT MASK, DO THE THING, GET ANGRY AT ME. I UNDERSTAND. IT HELPS YOU.
BUT YOU SHOULD PROBABLY ASK YOURSELF WHAT YOU'RE REALLY CAPABLE OF, PATSY.
THEN MAYBE YOU'LL GET CLOSER TO FIGURING OUT WHAT'S ACTUALLY GOING ON.
THAT IS, IF YOU CAN STOP BLAMING ME. OR DEATHURGE. OR BLACKHEART.
OR YOUR MOTHER. OR YOUR FATHER. OR HEDY. OR THAT NICE KID RICK AND HIS DREAMY COMPANION.
YOU MAKE YOUR OWN CHOICES.
YOU ALWAYS HAVE.
GET OFF MY ROOF.
YOU CALL. I ANSWER.
YOU LET ME KNOW WHEN YOU'RE FINALLY READY TO BE HONEST.

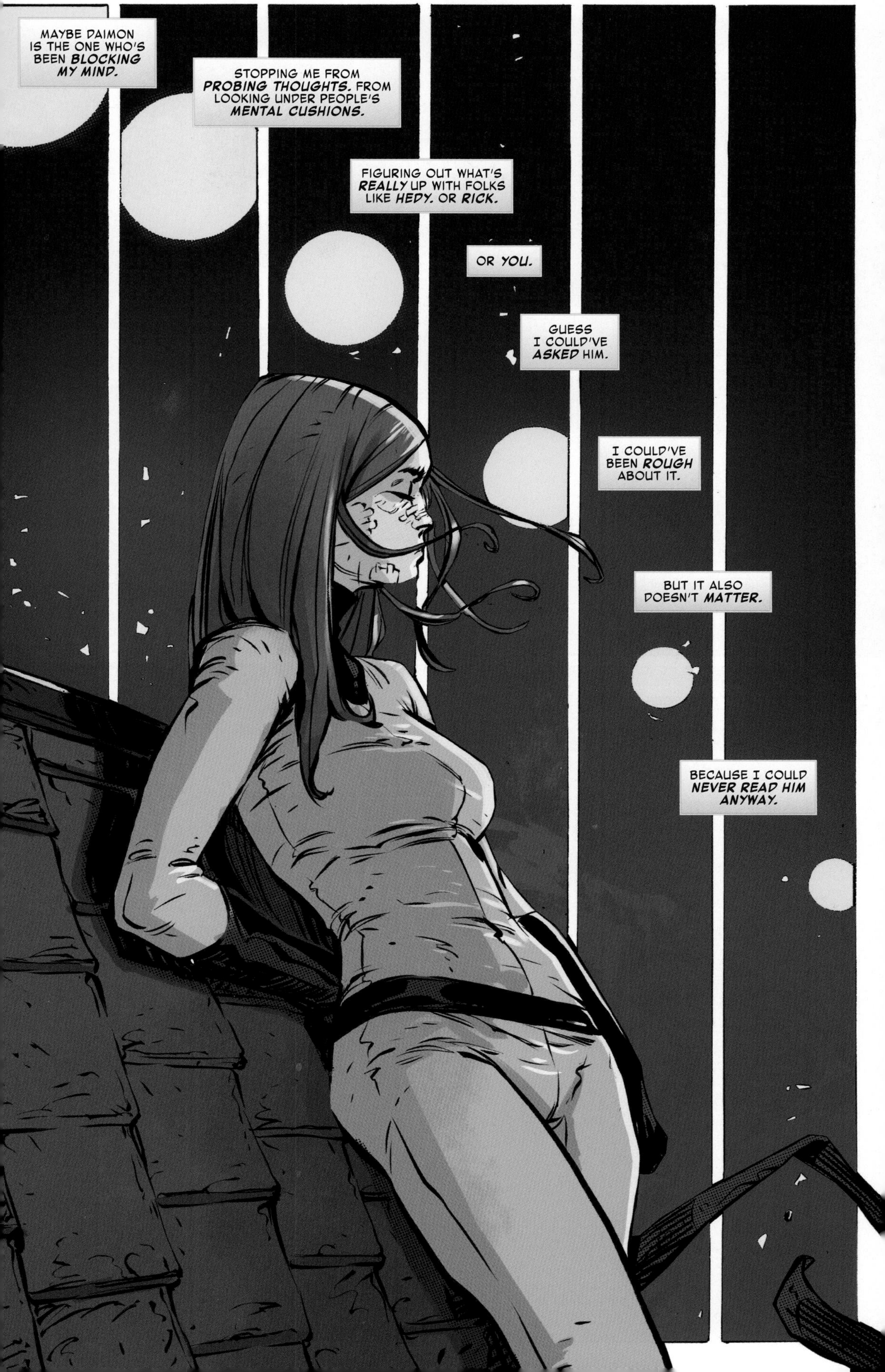
MAYBE DAIMON IS THE ONE WHO'S BEEN BLOCKING MY MIND.
STOPPING ME FROM PROBING THOUGHTS. FROM LOOKING UNDER PEOPLE'S MENTAL CUSHIONS.
FIGURING OUT WHAT'S REALLY UP WITH FOLKS LIKE HEDY. OR RICK.
OR YOU.
GUESS I COULD'VE ASKED HIM.
I COULD'VE BEEN ROUGH ABOUT IT.
BUT IT ALSO DOESN'T MATTER.
BECAUSE I COULD NEVER READ HIM ANYWAY.

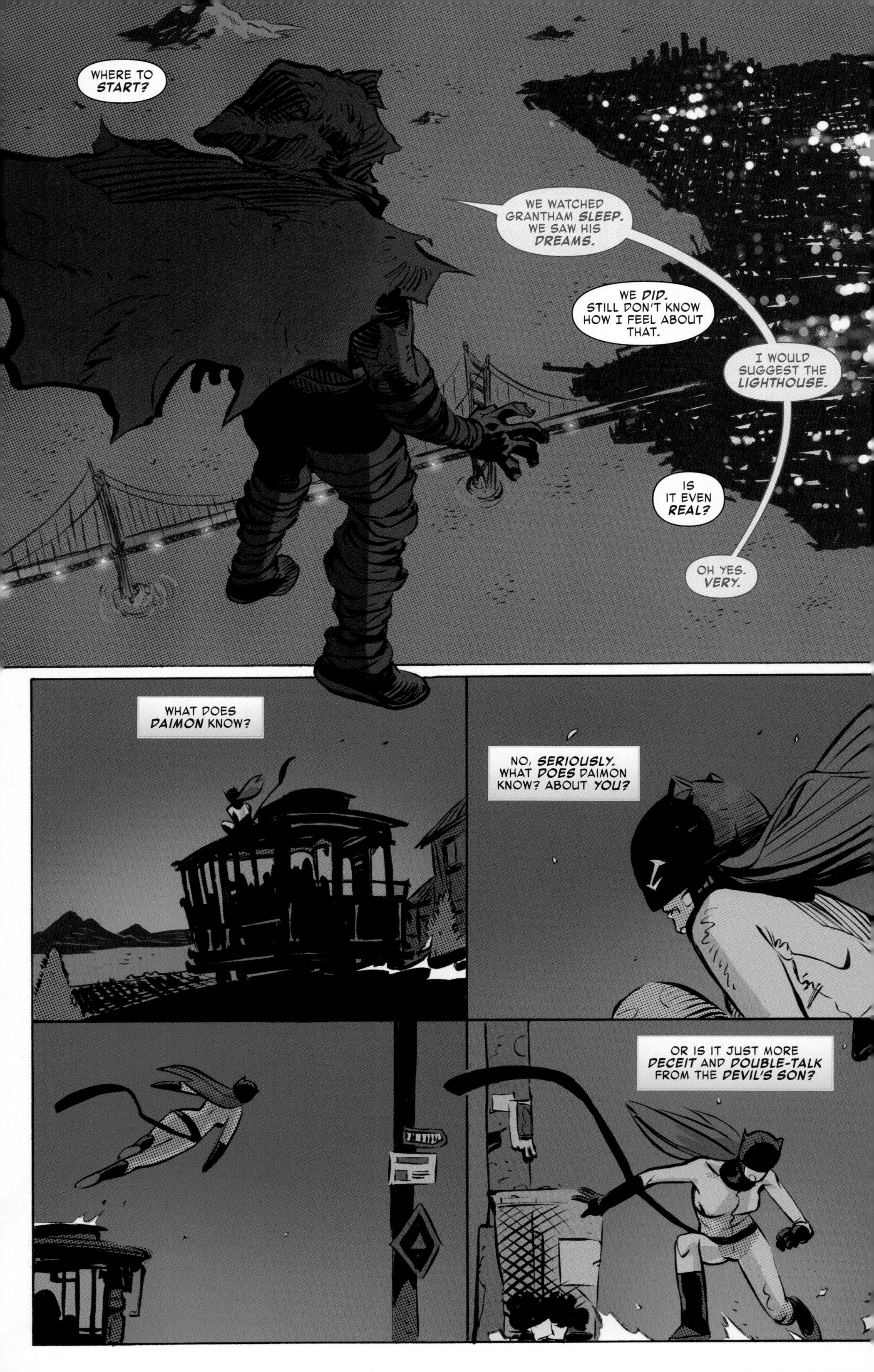
WHERE TO START?
WE WATCHED GRANTHAM SLEEP. WE SAW HIS DREAMS.
WE DID. STILL DON'T KNOW HOW I FEEL ABOUT THAT.
I WOULD SUGGEST THE LIGHTHOUSE.
IS IT EVEN REAL?
OH YES. VERY.
WHAT DOES DAIMON KNOW?
NO, SERIOUSLY. WHAT DOES DAIMON KNOW? ABOUT YOU?
OR IS IT JUST MORE DECEIT AND DOUBLE-TALK FROM THE DEVIL'S SON?

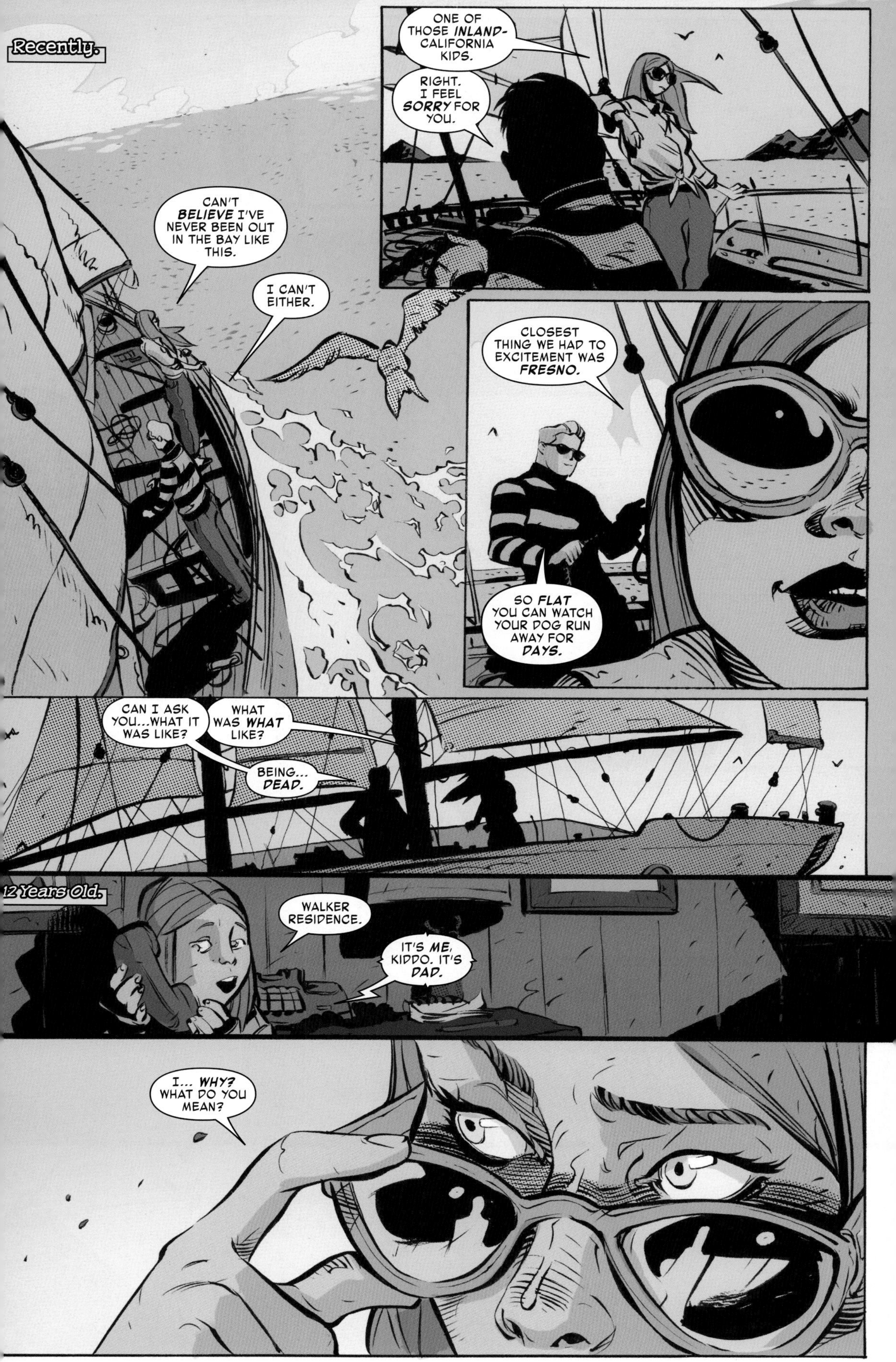
Recently.
CAN'T BELIEVE I'VE NEVER BEEN OUT IN THE BAY LIKE THIS.
I CAN'T EITHER.
ONE OF THOSE INLAND-CALIFORNIA KIDS.
RIGHT. I FEEL SORRY FOR YOU.
CLOSEST THING WE HAD TO EXCITEMENT WAS FRESNO.
SO FLAT YOU CAN WATCH YOUR DOG RUN AWAY FOR DAYS.
CAN I ASK YOU...WHAT IT WAS LIKE?
WHAT WAS WHAT LIKE?
BEING... DEAD.
12 Years Old.
WALKER RESIDENCE.
IT'S ME, KIDDO. IT'S DAD.
I... WHY? WHAT DO YOU MEAN?

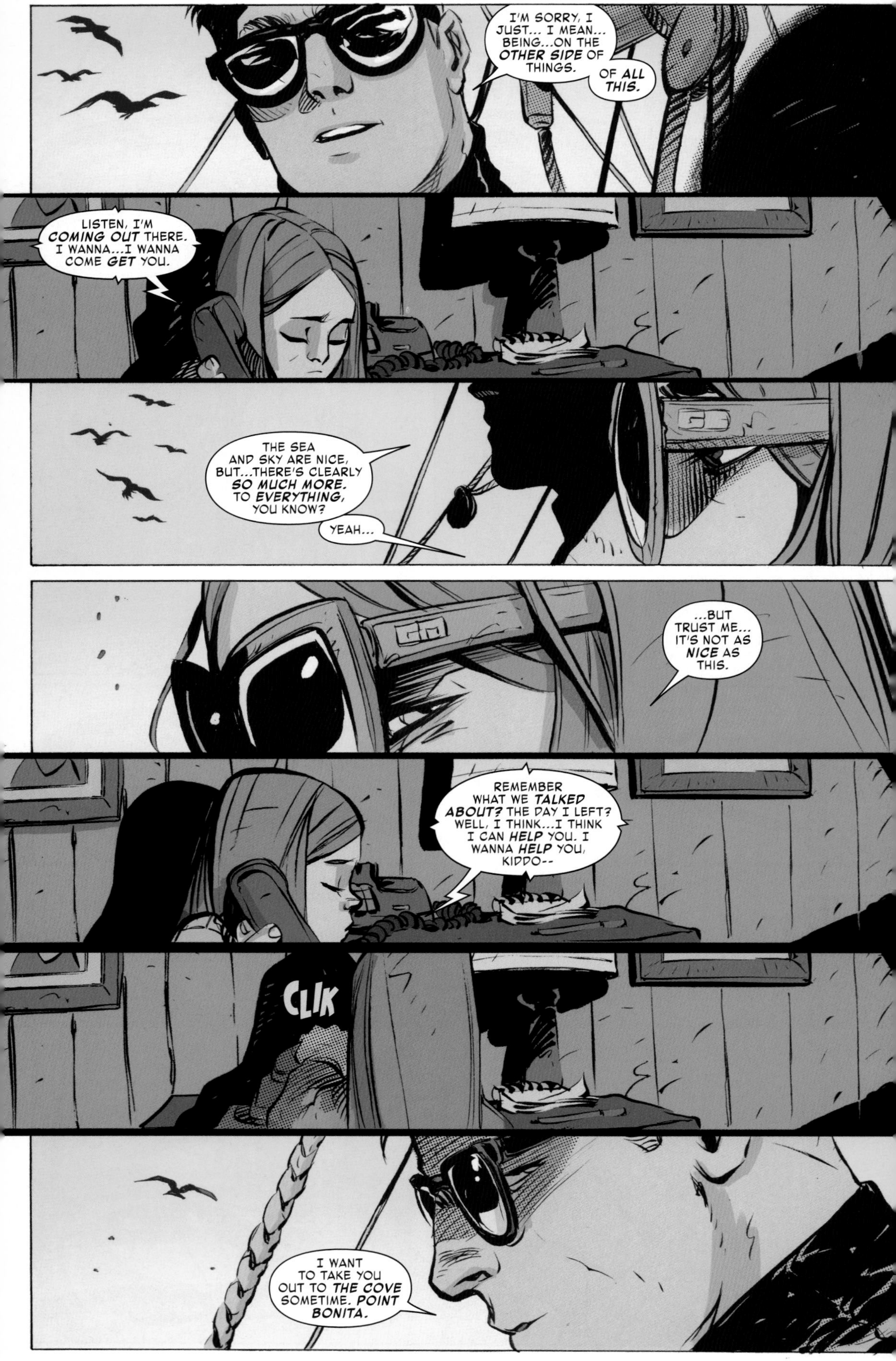
I'M SORRY, I JUST... I MEAN... BEING...ON THE OTHER SIDE OF THINGS.
OF ALL THIS.
LISTEN, I'M COMING OUT THERE. I WANNA...I WANNA COME GET YOU.
THE SEA AND SKY ARE NICE, BUT...THERE'S CLEARLY SO MUCH MORE. TO EVERYTHING, YOU KNOW?
YEAH...
...BUT TRUST ME... IT'S NOT AS NICE AS THIS.
REMEMBER WHAT WE TALKED ABOUT? THE DAY I LEFT? WELL, I THINK...I THINK I CAN HELP YOU. I WANNA HELP YOU, KIDDO--
CLIK
I WANT TO TAKE YOU OUT TO THE COVE SOMETIME. POINT BONITA.

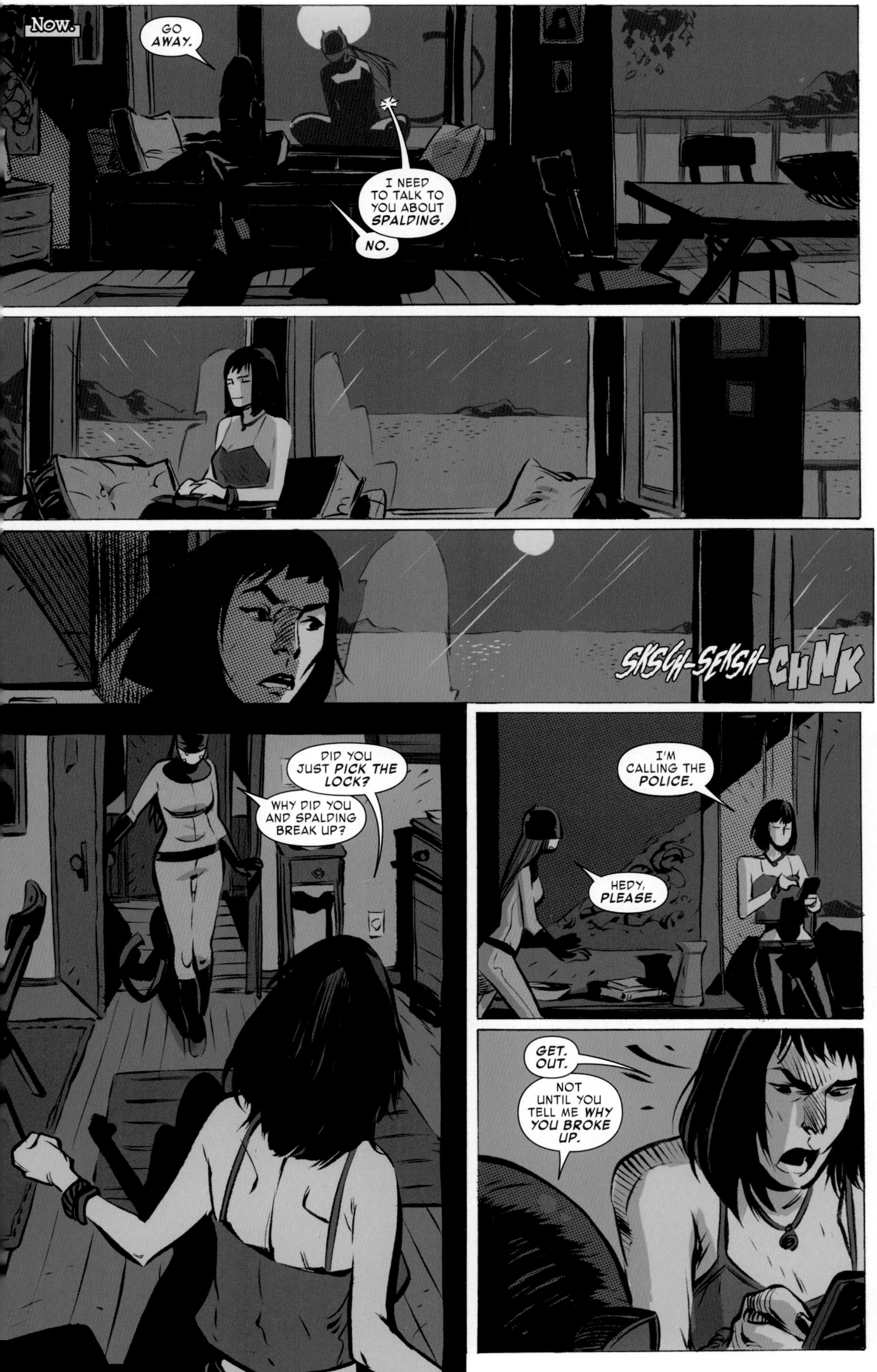
Now.
GO AWAY.
I NEED TO TALK TO YOU ABOUT SPALDING.
NO.
SKSCH-SEKSH-CHNK
DID YOU JUST PICK THE LOCK?
WHY DID YOU AND SPALDING BREAK UP?
I'M CALLING THE POLICE.
HEDY, PLEASE.
GET. OUT.
NOT UNTIL YOU TELL ME WHY YOU BROKE UP.

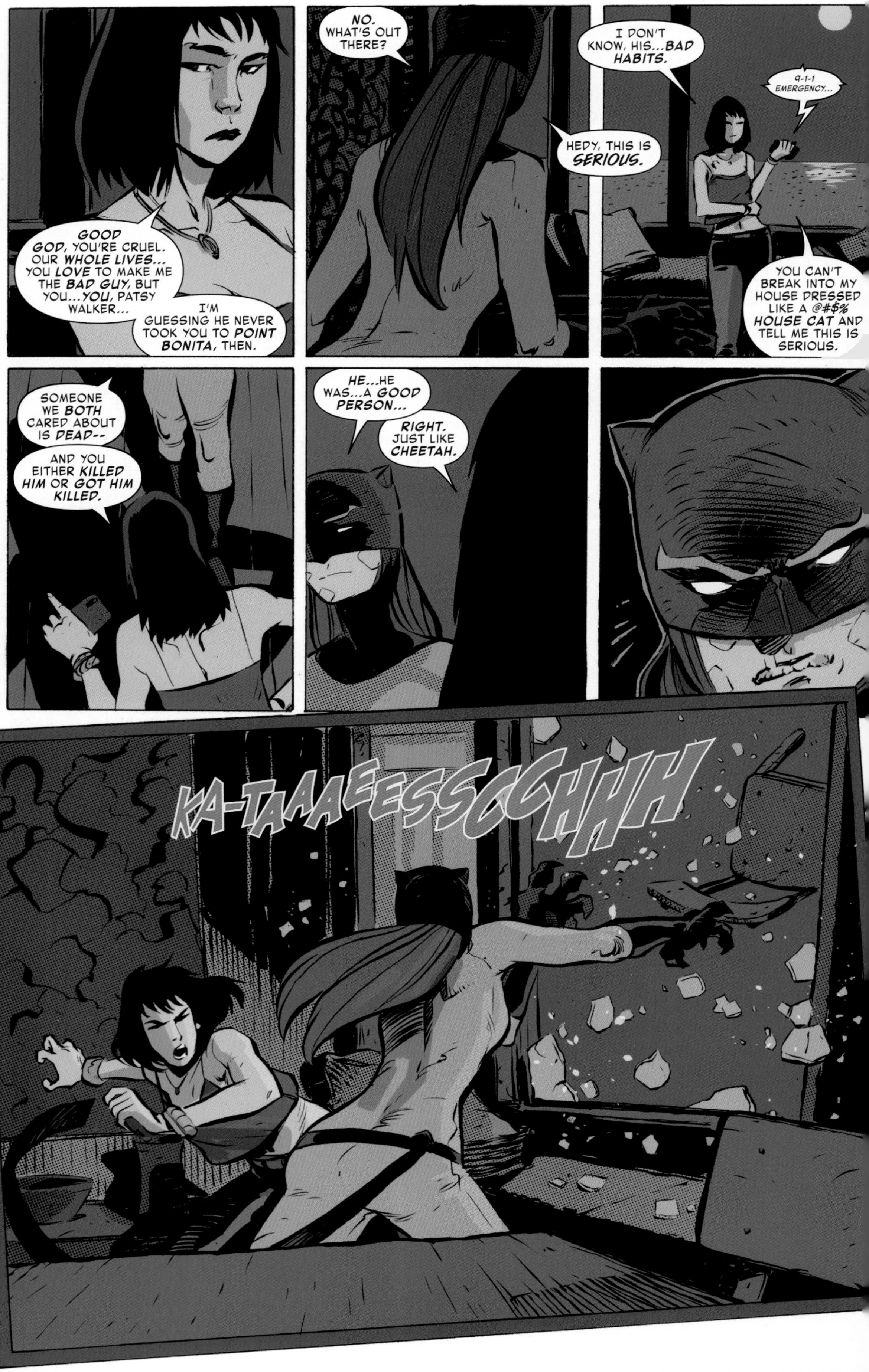

GOOD GOD, YOU'RE CRUEL. OUR WHOLE LIVES... YOU LOVE TO MAKE ME THE BAD GUY, BUT YOU...YOU, PATSY WALKER...
I'M GUESSING HE NEVER TOOK YOU TO POINT BONITA, THEN.
NO. WHAT'S OUT THERE?
I DON'T KNOW, HIS...BAD HABITS.
HEDY, THIS IS SERIOUS.
9-1-1 EMERGENCY...
YOU CAN'T BREAK INTO MY HOUSE DRESSED LIKE A @#$% HOUSE CAT AND TELL ME THIS IS SERIOUS.
SOMEONE WE BOTH CARED ABOUT IS DEAD--
AND YOU EITHER KILLED HIM OR GOT HIM KILLED.
HE...HE WAS...A GOOD PERSON...
RIGHT. JUST LIKE CHEETAH.
KA-TAAAEESSCCHHH

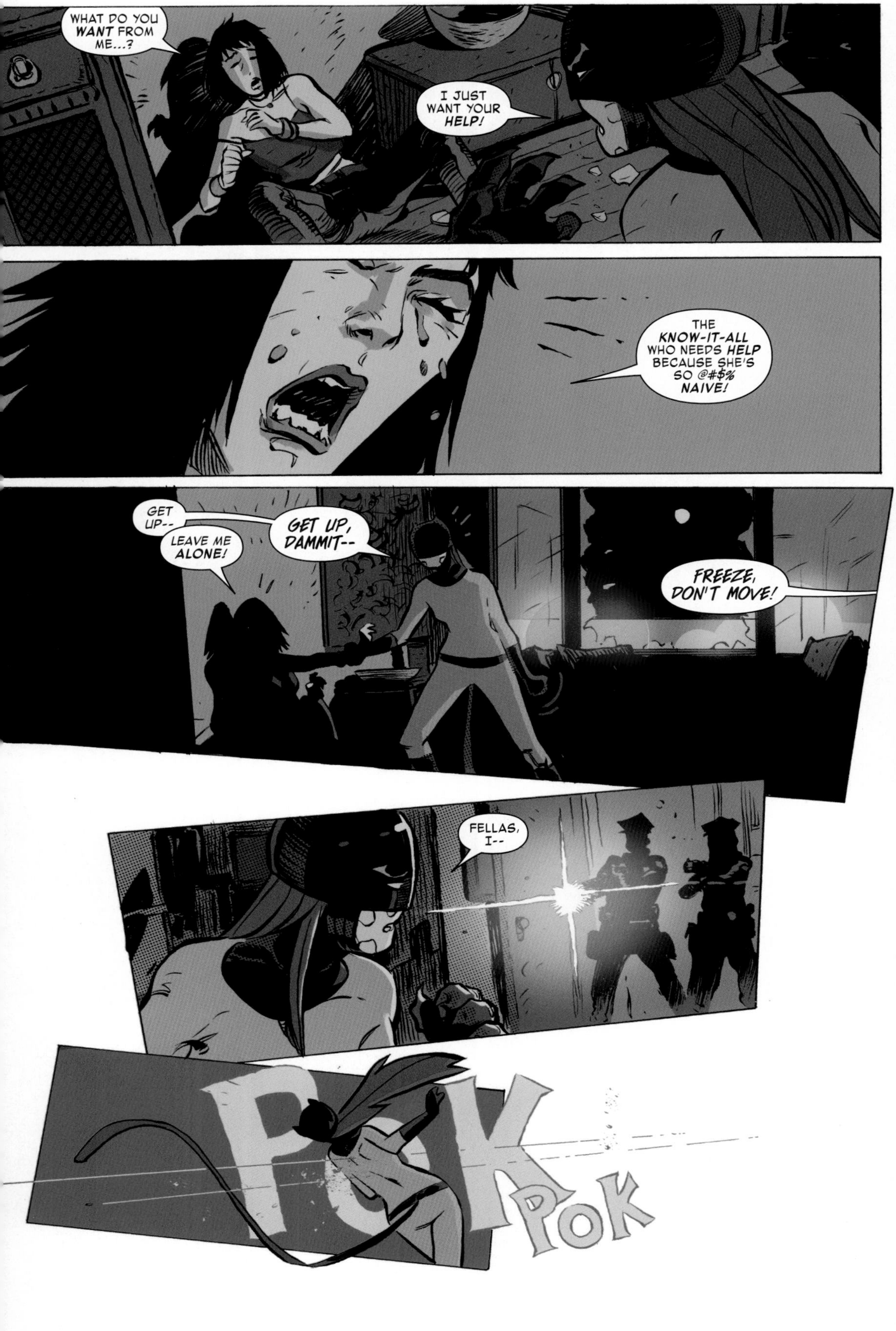
WHAT DO YOU WANT FROM ME...?
I JUST WANT YOUR HELP!
THE KNOW-IT-ALL WHO NEEDS HELP BECAUSE SHE'S SO @#$% NAIVE!
GET UP--
LEAVE ME ALONE!
GET UP, DAMMIT--
FREEZE, DON'T MOVE!
FELLAS, I--
POK
POK

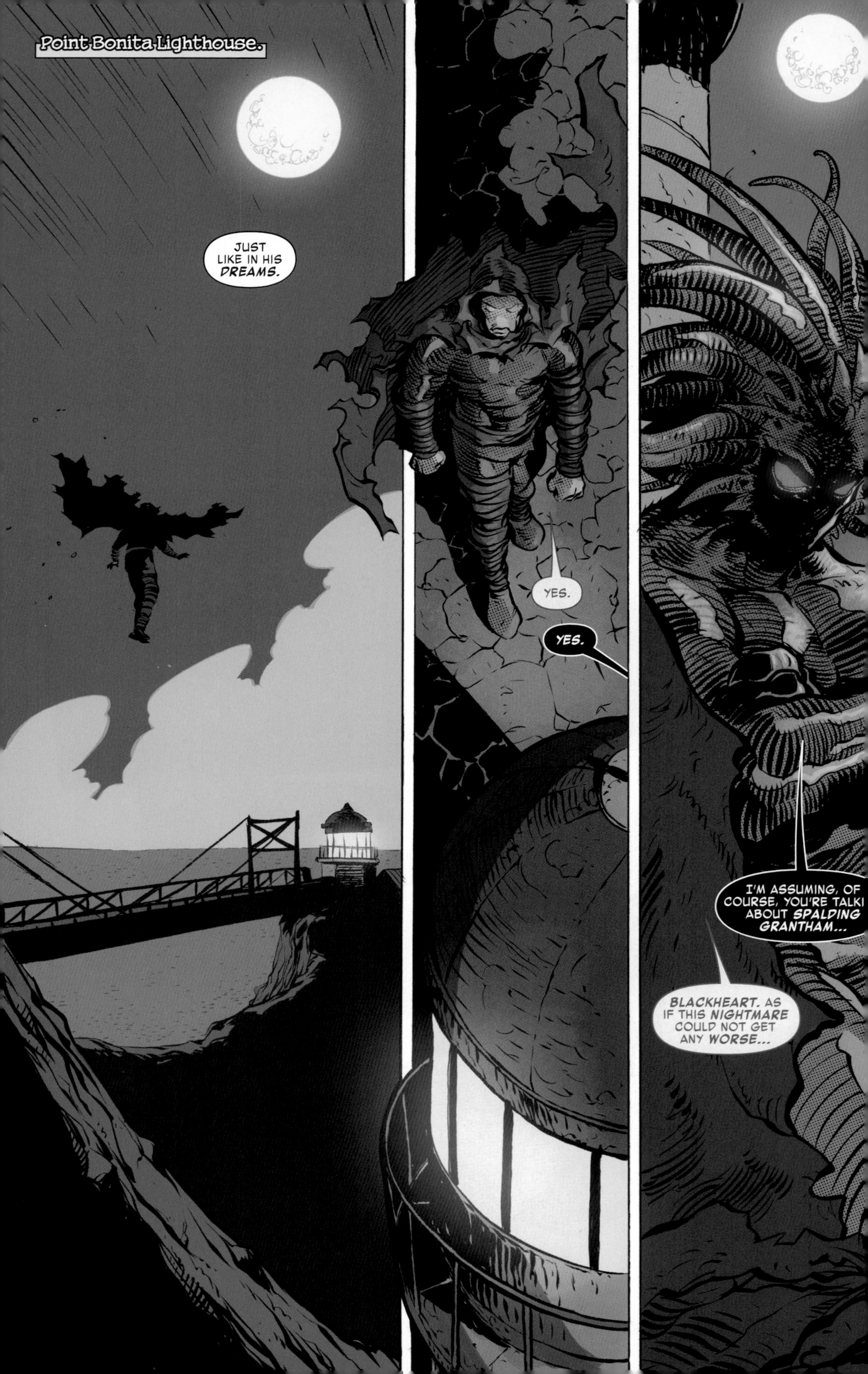
Point Bonita Lighthouse.
JUST LIKE IN HIS DREAMS.
YES.
YES.
I'M ASSUMING, OF COURSE, YOU'RE TALKI ABOUT SPALDING GRANTHAM...
BLACKHEART. AS IF THIS NIGHTMARE COULD NOT GET ANY WORSE...

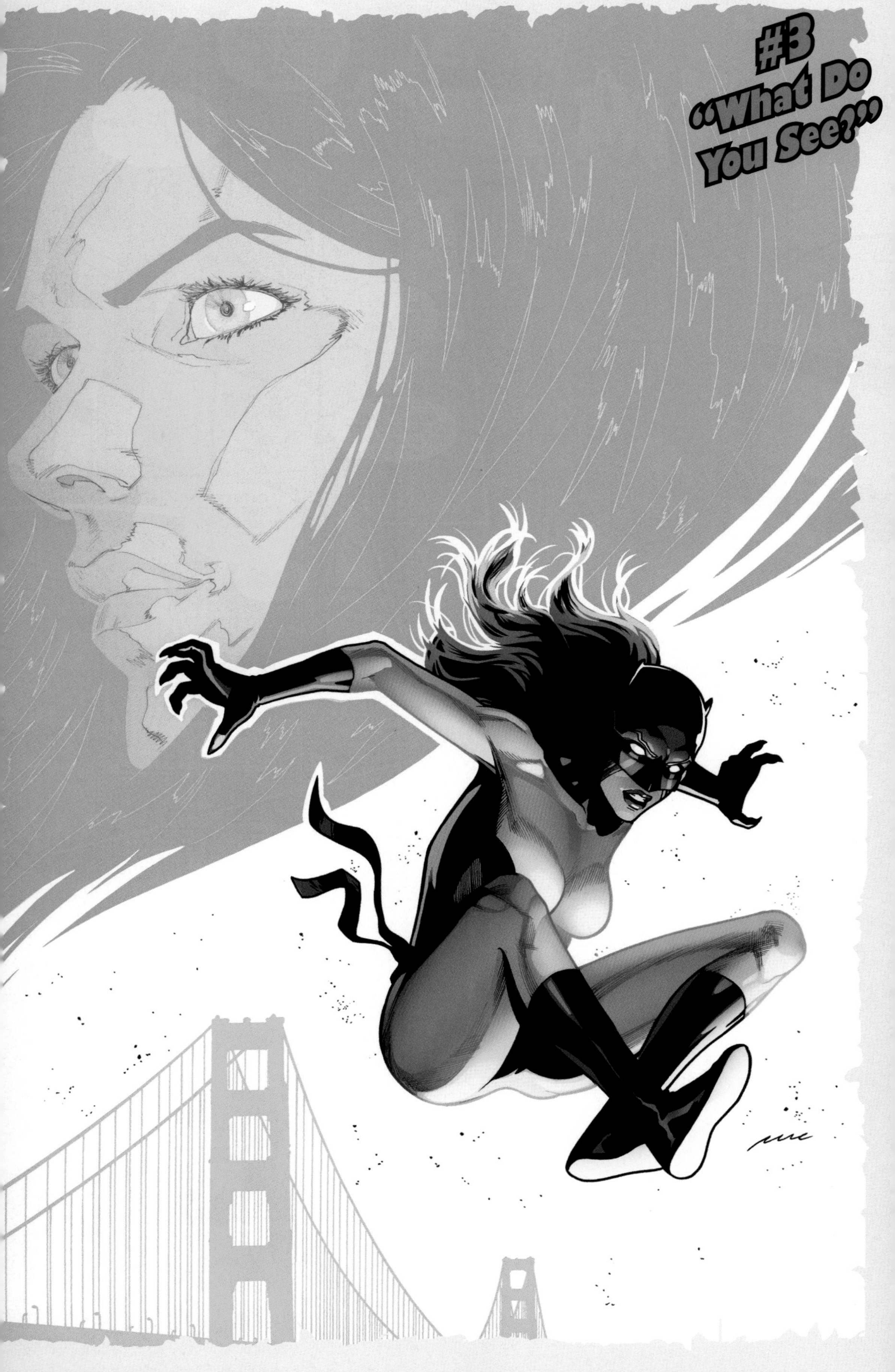
#3
"What Do
You See?"

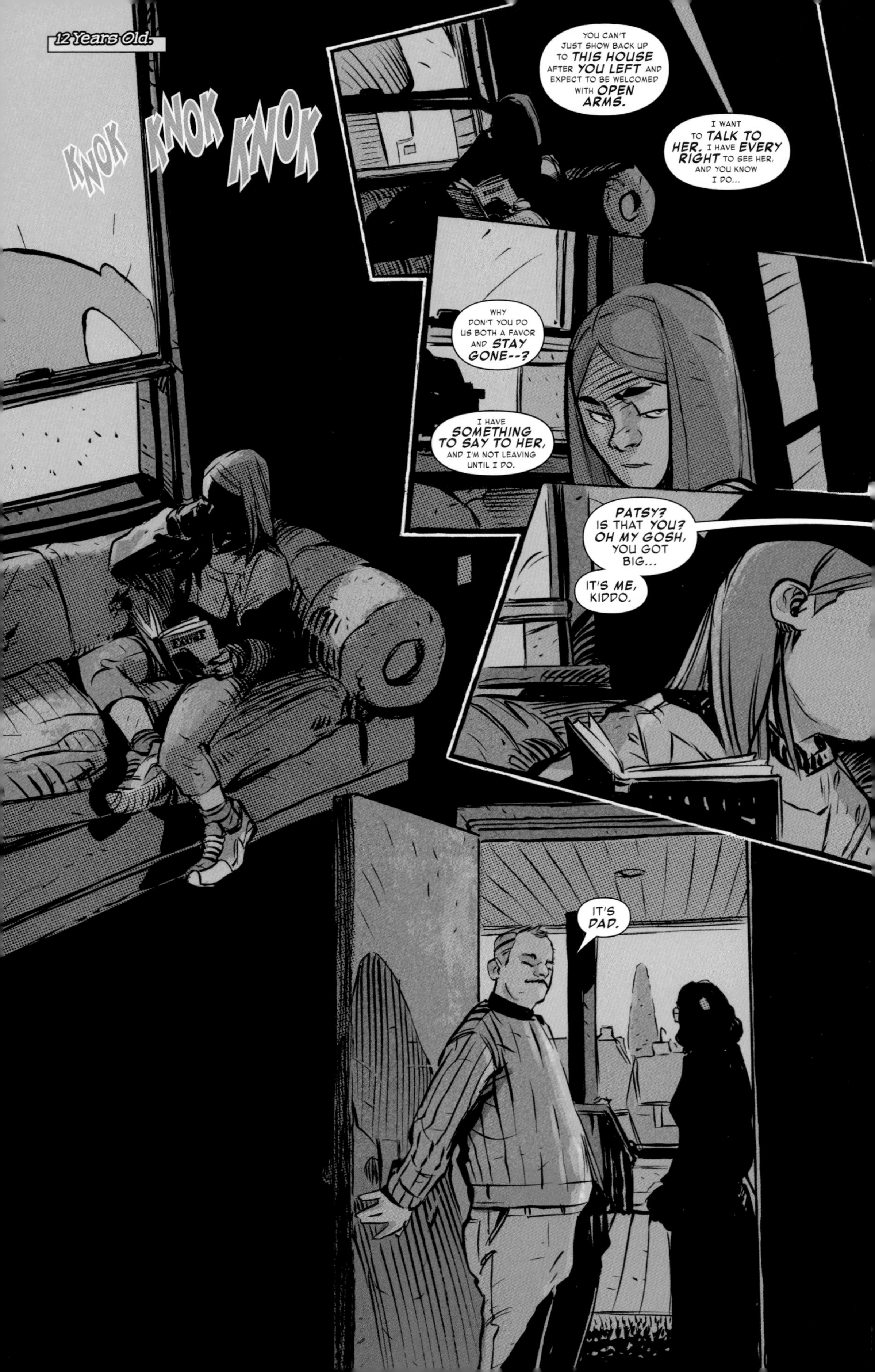
12 Years Old.
KNOK KNOK KNOK
YOU CAN'T JUST SHOW BACK UP TO THIS HOUSE AFTER YOU LEFT AND EXPECT TO BE WELCOMED WITH OPEN ARMS.
I WANT TO TALK TO HER. I HAVE EVERY RIGHT TO SEE HER, AND YOU KNOW I DO...
WHY DON'T YOU DO US BOTH A FAVOR AND STAY GONE--?
I HAVE SOMETHING TO SAY TO HER, AND I'M NOT LEAVING UNTIL I DO.
PATSY? IS THAT YOU? OH MY GOSH, YOU GOT BIG...
IT'S ME, KIDDO.
IT'S DAD.

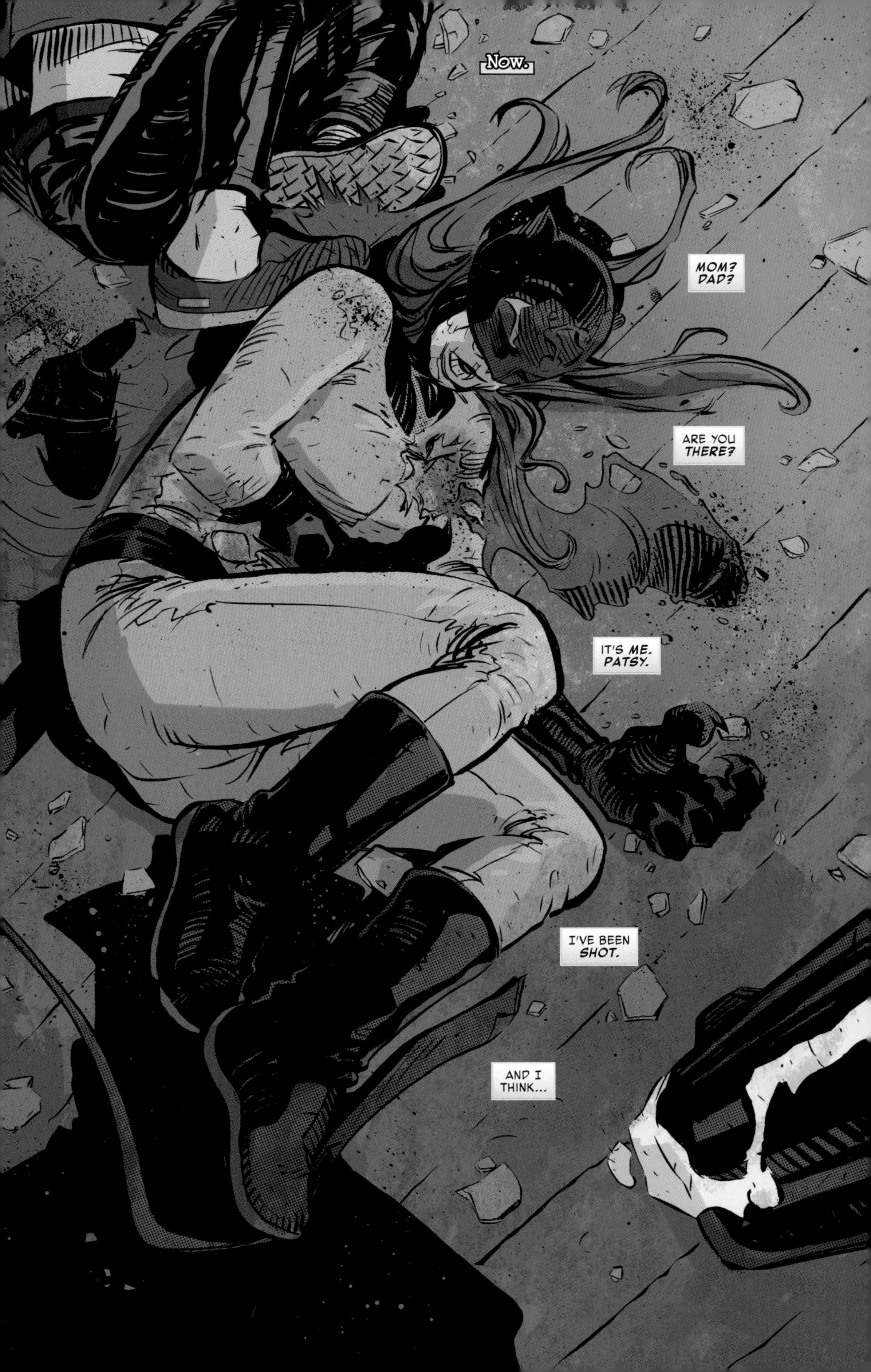
Now.
MOM? DAD?
ARE YOU THERE?
IT'S ME. PATSY.
I'VE BEEN SHOT.
AND I THINK...

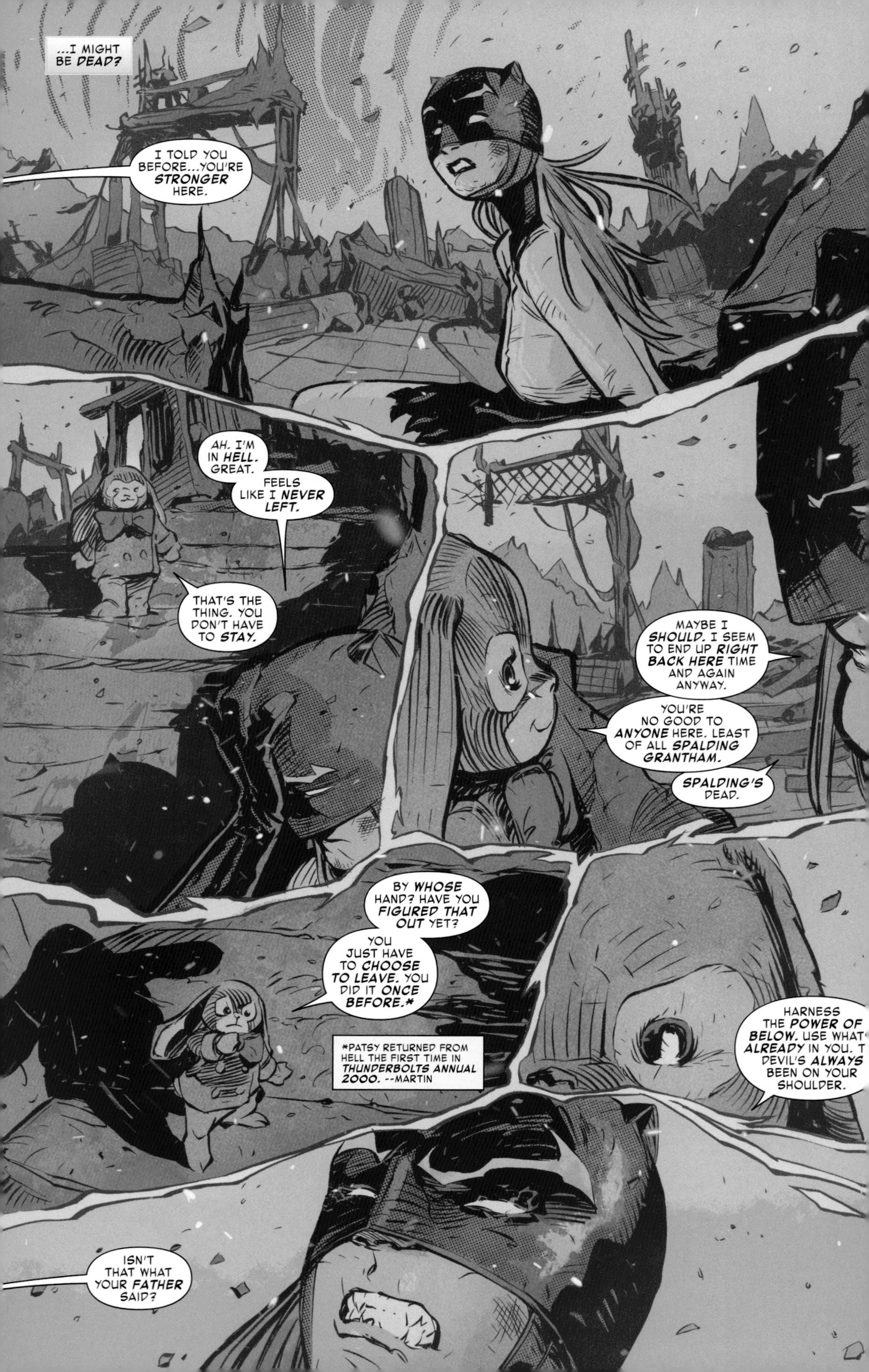
...I MIGHT BE DEAD?
I TOLD YOU BEFORE...YOU'RE STRONGER HERE.
AH. I'M IN HELL. GREAT.
FEELS LIKE I NEVER LEFT.
THAT'S THE THING. YOU DON'T HAVE TO STAY.
MAYBE I SHOULD. I SEEM TO END UP RIGHT BACK HERE TIME AND AGAIN ANYWAY.
YOU'RE NO GOOD TO ANYONE HERE. LEAST OF ALL SPALDING GRANTHAM.
SPALDING'S DEAD.
BY WHOSE HAND? HAVE YOU FIGURED THAT OUT YET?
YOU JUST HAVE TO CHOOSE TO LEAVE. YOU DID IT ONCE BEFORE.*
*PATSY RETURNED FROM HELL THE FIRST TIME IN THUNDERBOLTS ANNUAL 2000. --MARTIN
HARNESS THE POWER OF BELOW. USE WHAT ALREADY IN YOU. T DEVIL'S ALWAYS BEEN ON YOUR SHOULDER.
ISN'T THAT WHAT YOUR FATHER SAID?

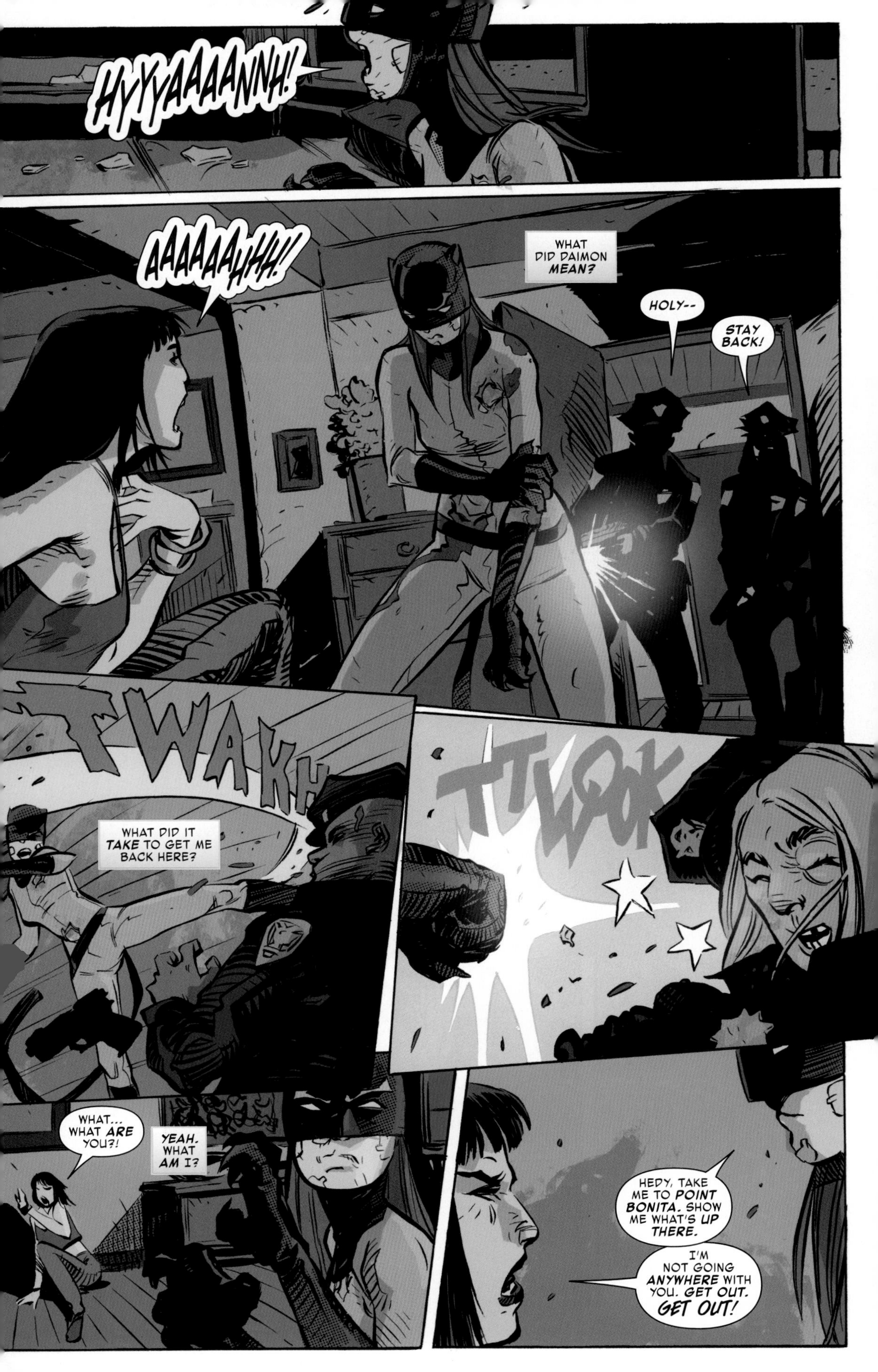
HYYYAAAANNH!
AAAAAAHHH!
WHAT DID DAIMON MEAN?
HOLY--
STAY BACK!
TWAKH
WHAT DID IT TAKE TO GET ME BACK HERE?
TTWOOK
WHAT... WHAT ARE YOU?!
YEAH. WHAT AM I?
HEDY, TAKE ME TO POINT BONITA. SHOW ME WHAT'S UP THERE.
I'M NOT GOING ANYWHERE WITH YOU. GET OUT. GET OUT!

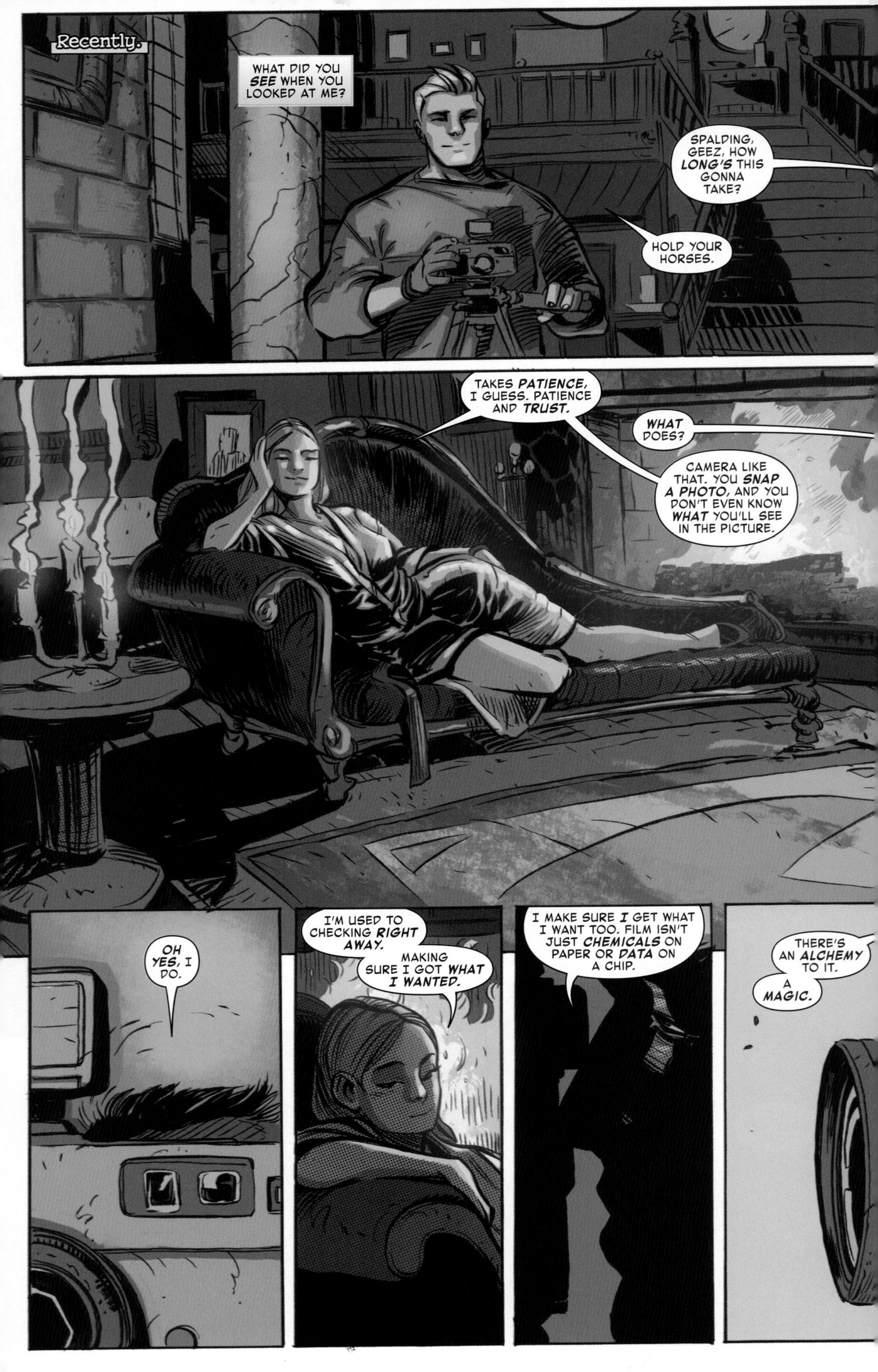

Recently.
WHAT DID YOU SEE WHEN YOU LOOKED AT ME?
SPALDING, GEEZ, HOW LONG'S THIS GONNA TAKE?
HOLD YOUR HORSES.
TAKES PATIENCE, I GUESS. PATIENCE AND TRUST.
WHAT DOES?
CAMERA LIKE THAT. YOU SNAP A PHOTO, AND YOU DON'T EVEN KNOW WHAT YOU'LL SEE IN THE PICTURE.
OH YES, I DO.
I'M USED TO CHECKING RIGHT AWAY.
MAKING SURE I GOT WHAT I WANTED.
I MAKE SURE I GET WHAT I WANT TOO. FILM ISN'T JUST CHEMICALS ON PAPER OR DATA ON A CHIP.
THERE'S AN ALCHEMY TO IT.
A MAGIC.

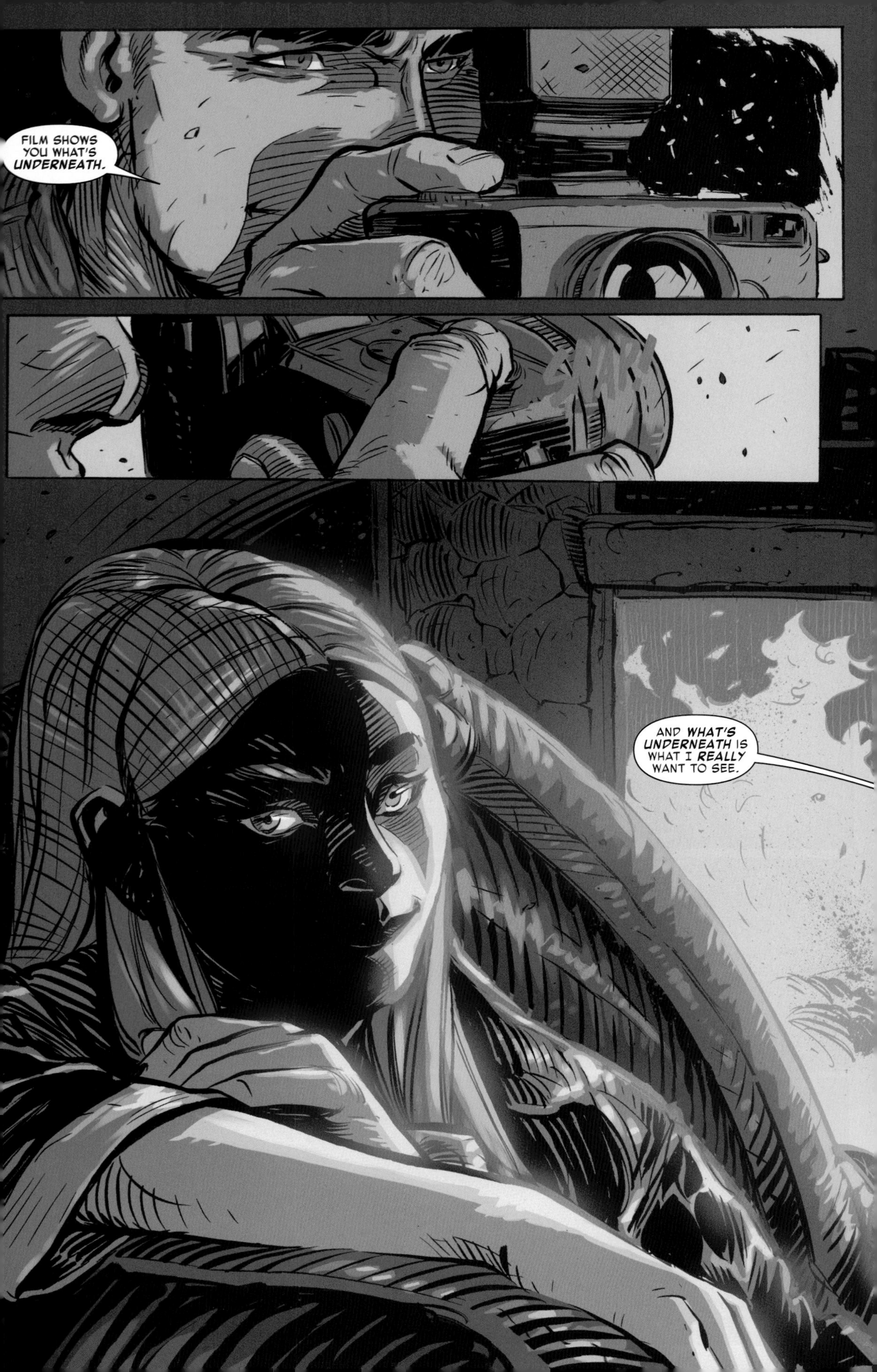
FILM SHOWS YOU WHAT'S *UNDERNEATH*.
AND *WHAT'S UNDERNEATH* IS WHAT I *REALLY* WANT TO SEE.

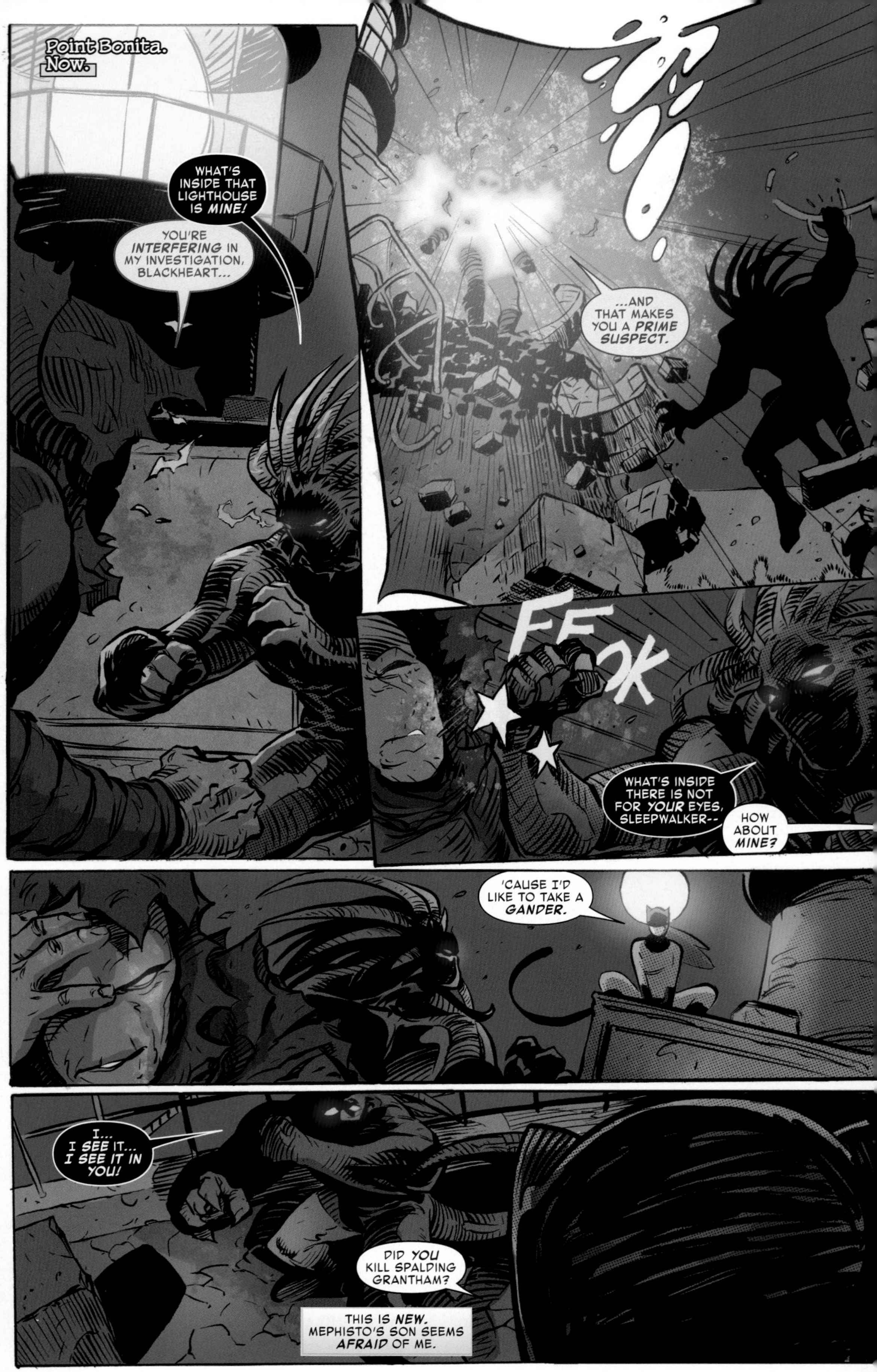
Point Bonita.
Now.
WHAT'S INSIDE THAT LIGHTHOUSE IS MINE!
YOU'RE INTERFERING IN MY INVESTIGATION, BLACKHEART...
...AND THAT MAKES YOU A PRIME SUSPECT.
FFOK
WHAT'S INSIDE THERE IS NOT FOR YOUR EYES, SLEEPWALKER--
HOW ABOUT MINE?
'CAUSE I'D LIKE TO TAKE A GANDER.
I... I SEE IT... I SEE IT IN YOU!
DID YOU KILL SPALDING GRANTHAM?
THIS IS NEW. MEPHISTO'S SON SEEMS AFRAID OF ME.

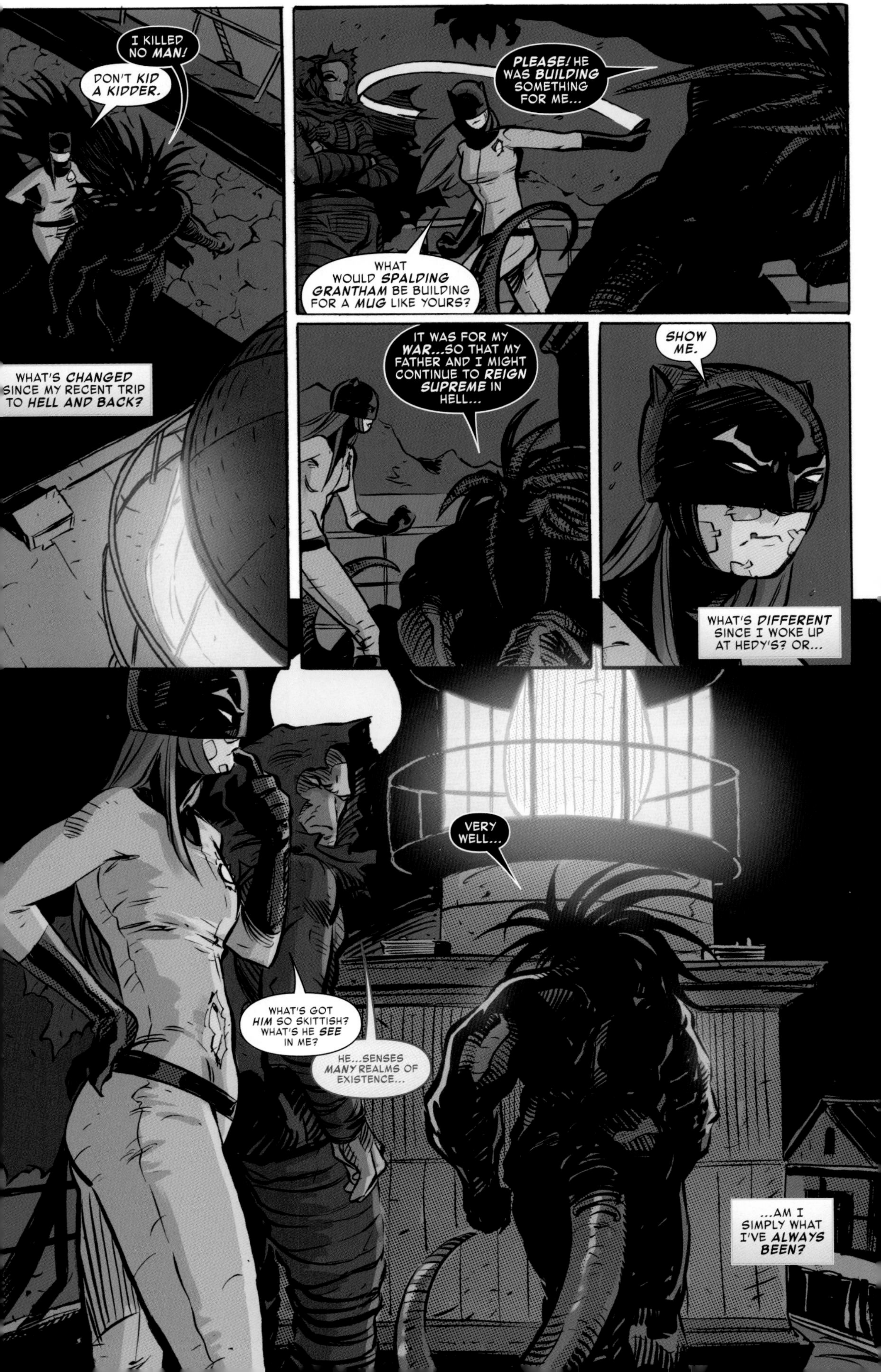
I KILLED NO MAN!
DON'T KID A KIDDER.
PLEASE! HE WAS BUILDING SOMETHING FOR ME...
WHAT WOULD SPALDING GRANTHAM BE BUILDING FOR A MUG LIKE YOURS?
WHAT'S CHANGED SINCE MY RECENT TRIP TO HELL AND BACK?
IT WAS FOR MY WAR...SO THAT MY FATHER AND I MIGHT CONTINUE TO REIGN SUPREME IN HELL...
SHOW ME.
WHAT'S DIFFERENT SINCE I WOKE UP AT HEDY'S? OR...
VERY WELL...
WHAT'S GOT HIM SO SKITTISH? WHAT'S HE SEE IN ME?
HE...SENSES MANY REALMS OF EXISTENCE...
...AM I SIMPLY WHAT I'VE ALWAYS BEEN?

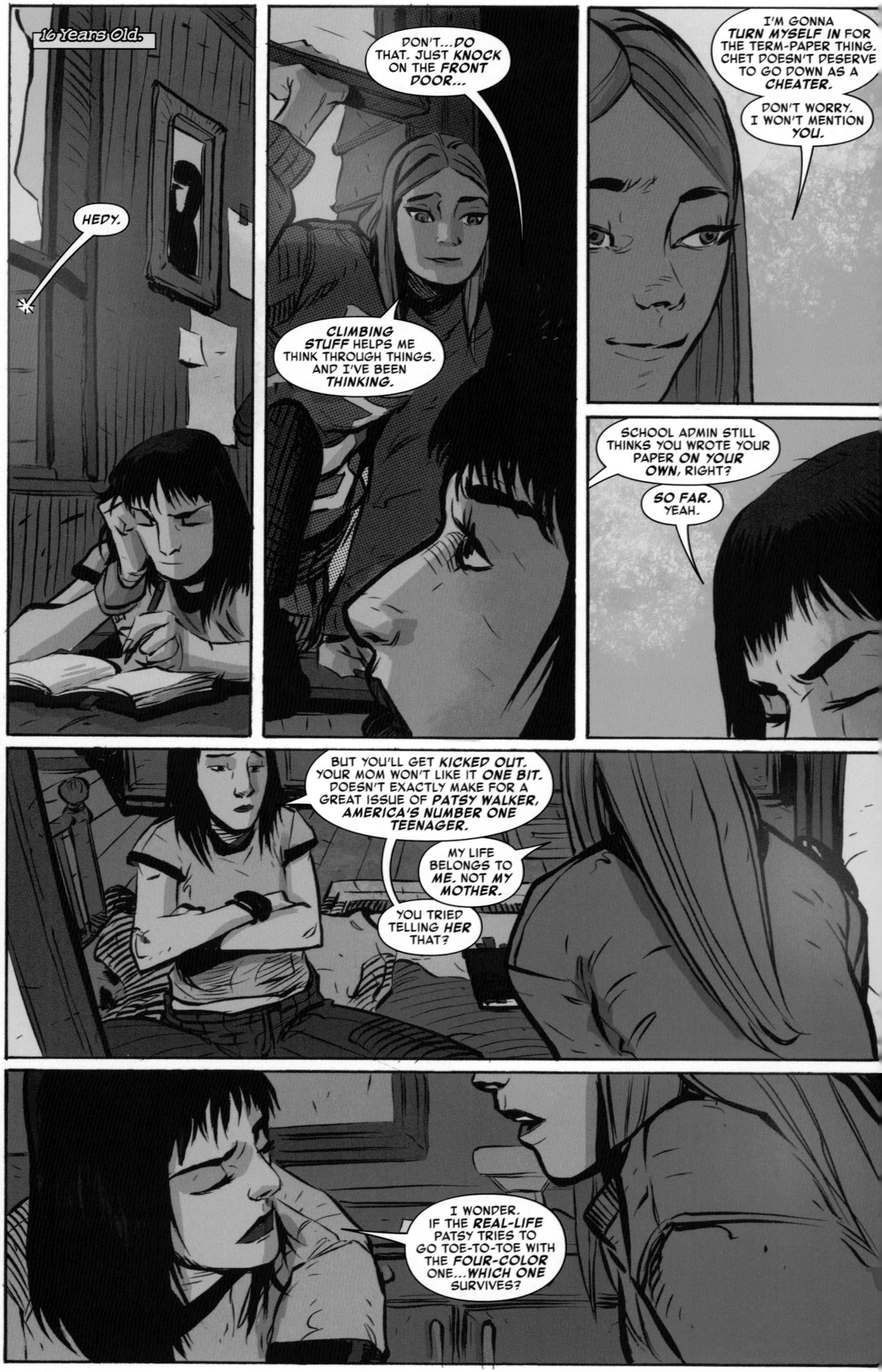
16 Years Old.
HEDY.
DON'T...DO THAT. JUST KNOCK ON THE FRONT DOOR...
CLIMBING STUFF HELPS ME THINK THROUGH THINGS. AND I'VE BEEN THINKING.
I'M GONNA TURN MYSELF IN FOR THE TERM-PAPER THING. CHET DOESN'T DESERVE TO GO DOWN AS A CHEATER.
DON'T WORRY. I WON'T MENTION YOU.
SCHOOL ADMIN STILL THINKS YOU WROTE YOUR PAPER ON YOUR OWN, RIGHT?
SO FAR. YEAH.
BUT YOU'LL GET KICKED OUT. YOUR MOM WON'T LIKE IT ONE BIT. DOESN'T EXACTLY MAKE FOR A GREAT ISSUE OF PATSY WALKER, AMERICA'S NUMBER ONE TEENAGER.
MY LIFE BELONGS TO ME. NOT MY MOTHER.
YOU TRIED TELLING HER THAT?
I WONDER. IF THE REAL-LIFE PATSY TRIES TO GO TOE-TO-TOE WITH THE FOUR-COLOR ONE...WHICH ONE SURVIVES?

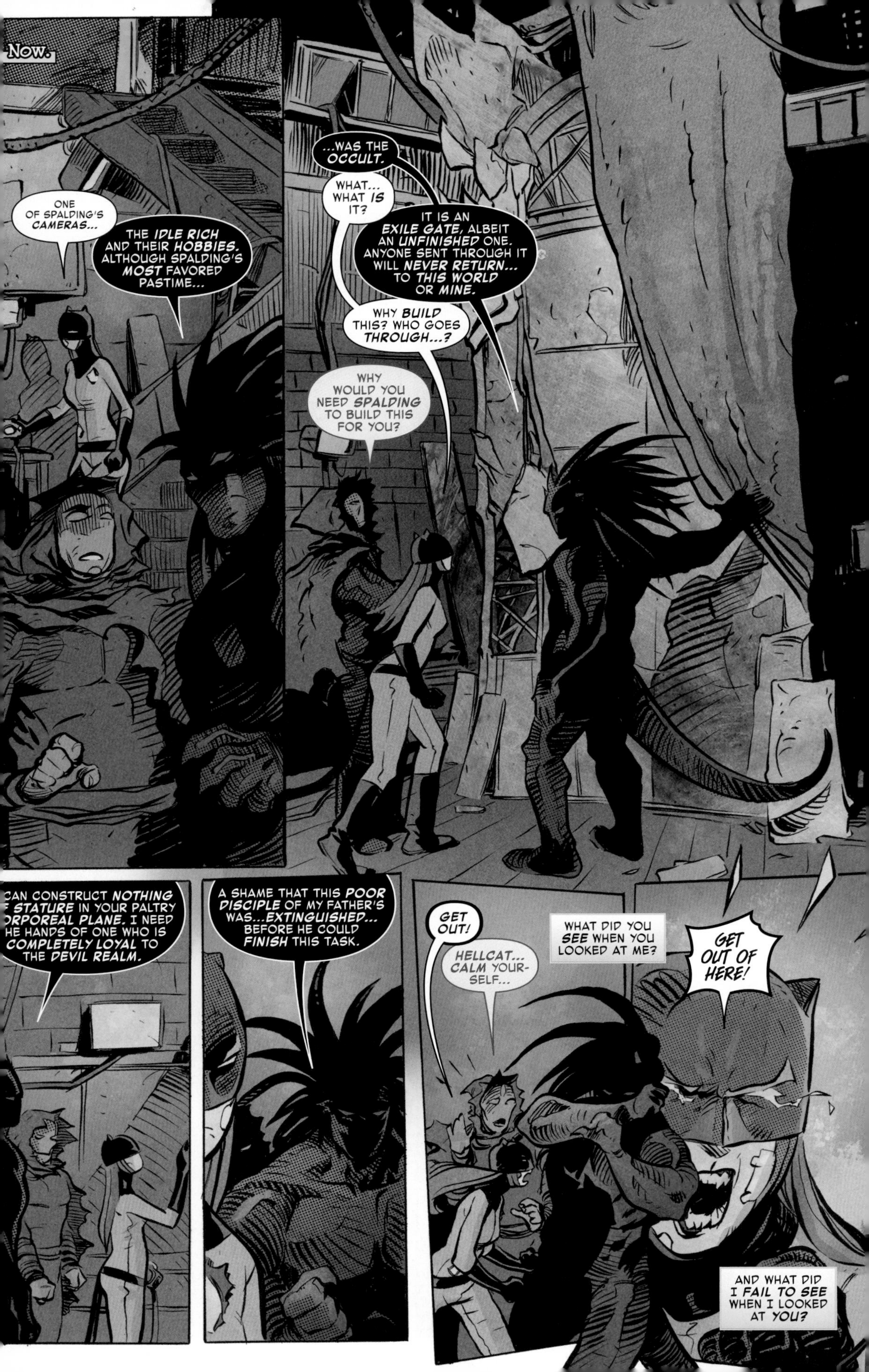

Now.
ONE OF SPALDING'S CAMERAS...
THE IDLE RICH AND THEIR HOBBIES. ALTHOUGH SPALDING'S MOST FAVORED PASTIME...
...WAS THE OCCULT.
WHAT... WHAT IS IT?
IT IS AN EXILE GATE, ALBEIT AN UNFINISHED ONE. ANYONE SENT THROUGH IT WILL NEVER RETURN... TO THIS WORLD OR MINE.
WHY BUILD THIS? WHO GOES THROUGH...?
WHY WOULD YOU NEED SPALDING TO BUILD THIS FOR YOU?
CAN CONSTRUCT NOTHING STATURE IN YOUR PALTRY ORPOREAL PLANE. I NEED HE HANDS OF ONE WHO IS COMPLETELY LOYAL TO THE DEVIL REALM.
A SHAME THAT THIS POOR DISCIPLE OF MY FATHER'S WAS...EXTINGUISHED... BEFORE HE COULD FINISH THIS TASK.
GET OUT!
HELLCAT... CALM YOURSELF...
WHAT DID YOU SEE WHEN YOU LOOKED AT ME?
GET OUT OF HERE!
AND WHAT DID I FAIL TO SEE WHEN I LOOKED AT YOU?

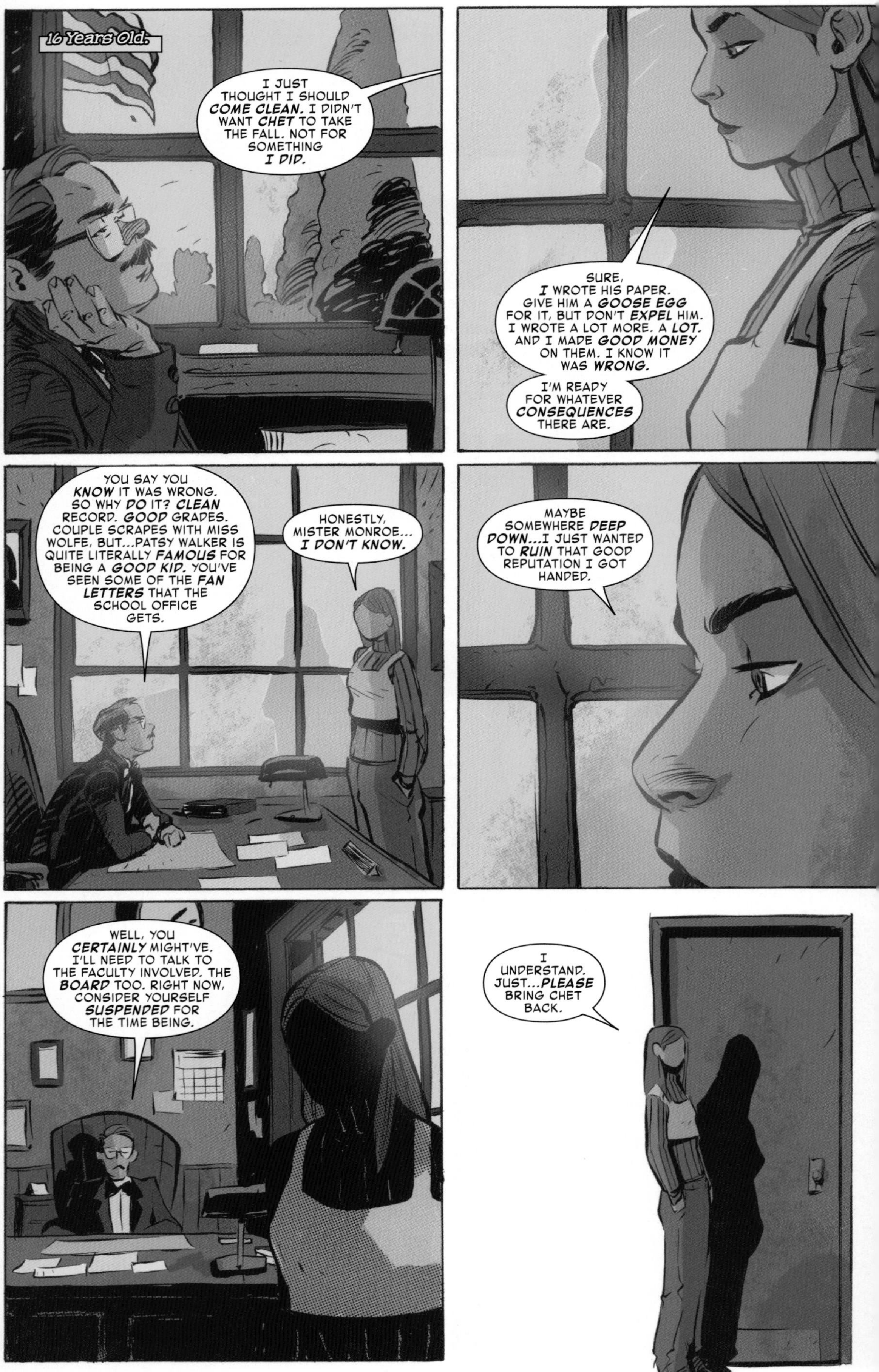
16 Years Old.
I JUST THOUGHT I SHOULD COME CLEAN. I DIDN'T WANT CHET TO TAKE THE FALL. NOT FOR SOMETHING I DID.
SURE, I WROTE HIS PAPER. GIVE HIM A GOOSE EGG FOR IT, BUT DON'T EXPEL HIM. I WROTE A LOT MORE. A LOT. AND I MADE GOOD MONEY ON THEM. I KNOW IT WAS WRONG.
I'M READY FOR WHATEVER CONSEQUENCES THERE ARE.
YOU SAY YOU KNOW IT WAS WRONG. SO WHY DO IT? CLEAN RECORD. GOOD GRADES. COUPLE SCRAPES WITH MISS WOLFE, BUT...PATSY WALKER IS QUITE LITERALLY FAMOUS FOR BEING A GOOD KID. YOU'VE SEEN SOME OF THE FAN LETTERS THAT THE SCHOOL OFFICE GETS.
HONESTLY, MISTER MONROE... I DON'T KNOW.
MAYBE SOMEWHERE DEEP DOWN...I JUST WANTED TO RUIN THAT GOOD REPUTATION I GOT HANDED.
WELL, YOU CERTAINLY MIGHT'VE. I'LL NEED TO TALK TO THE FACULTY INVOLVED. THE BOARD TOO. RIGHT NOW, CONSIDER YOURSELF SUSPENDED FOR THE TIME BEING.
I UNDERSTAND. JUST...PLEASE BRING CHET BACK.

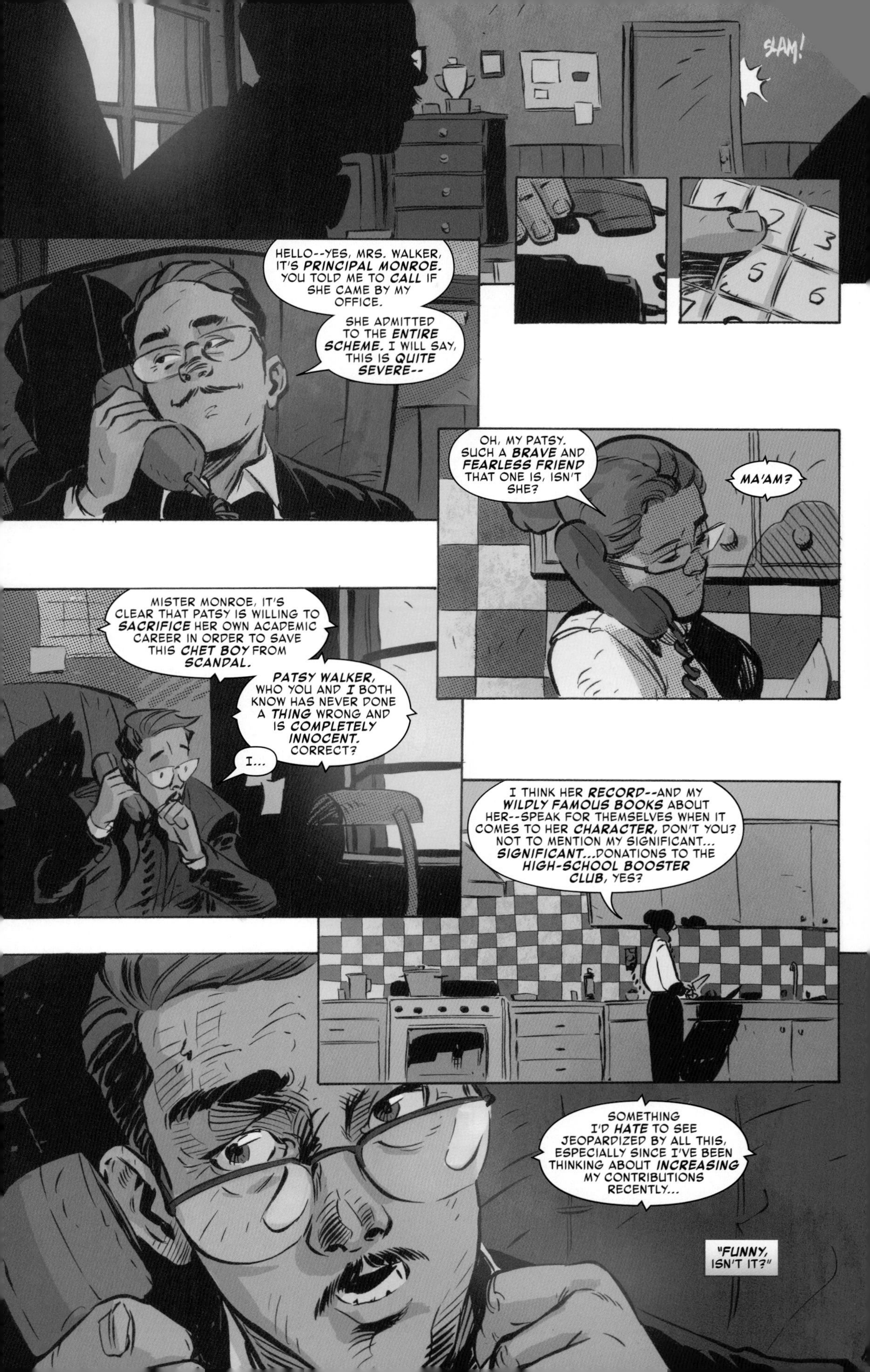
SLAM!
HELLO--YES, MRS. WALKER, IT'S PRINCIPAL MONROE. YOU TOLD ME TO CALL IF SHE CAME BY MY OFFICE.
SHE ADMITTED TO THE ENTIRE SCHEME. I WILL SAY, THIS IS QUITE SEVERE--
OH, MY PATSY. SUCH A BRAVE AND FEARLESS FRIEND THAT ONE IS, ISN'T SHE?
MA'AM?
MISTER MONROE, IT'S CLEAR THAT PATSY IS WILLING TO SACRIFICE HER OWN ACADEMIC CAREER IN ORDER TO SAVE THIS CHET BOY FROM SCANDAL.
PATSY WALKER, WHO YOU AND I BOTH KNOW HAS NEVER DONE A THING WRONG AND IS COMPLETELY INNOCENT. CORRECT?
I...
I THINK HER RECORD--AND MY WILDLY FAMOUS BOOKS ABOUT HER--SPEAK FOR THEMSELVES WHEN IT COMES TO HER CHARACTER, DON'T YOU? NOT TO MENTION MY SIGNIFICANT... SIGNIFICANT...DONATIONS TO THE HIGH-SCHOOL BOOSTER CLUB, YES?
SOMETHING I'D HATE TO SEE JEOPARDIZED BY ALL THIS, ESPECIALLY SINCE I'VE BEEN THINKING ABOUT INCREASING MY CONTRIBUTIONS RECENTLY...
"FUNNY, ISN'T IT?"

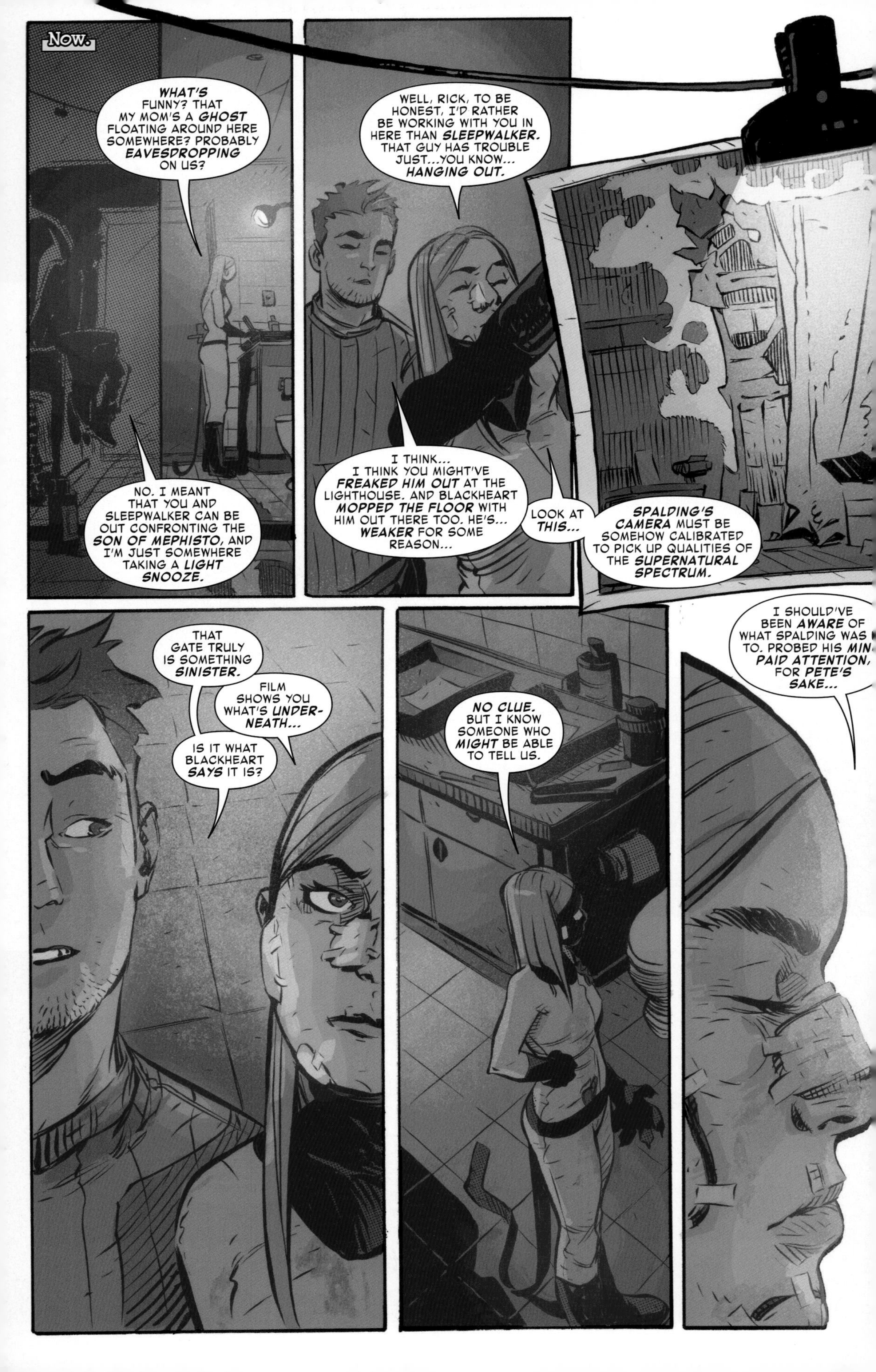
Now.
WHAT'S FUNNY? THAT MY MOM'S A GHOST FLOATING AROUND HERE SOMEWHERE? PROBABLY EAVESDROPPING ON US?
NO. I MEANT THAT YOU AND SLEEPWALKER CAN BE OUT CONFRONTING THE SON OF MEPHISTO, AND I'M JUST SOMEWHERE TAKING A LIGHT SNOOZE.
WELL, RICK, TO BE HONEST, I'D RATHER BE WORKING WITH YOU IN HERE THAN SLEEPWALKER. THAT GUY HAS TROUBLE JUST...YOU KNOW... HANGING OUT.
I THINK... I THINK YOU MIGHT'VE FREAKED HIM OUT AT THE LIGHTHOUSE. AND BLACKHEART MOPPED THE FLOOR WITH HIM OUT THERE TOO. HE'S... WEAKER FOR SOME REASON...
LOOK AT THIS...
SPALDING'S CAMERA MUST BE SOMEHOW CALIBRATED TO PICK UP QUALITIES OF THE SUPERNATURAL SPECTRUM.
THAT GATE TRULY IS SOMETHING SINISTER.
FILM SHOWS YOU WHAT'S UNDER-NEATH...
IS IT WHAT BLACKHEART SAYS IT IS?
NO CLUE. BUT I KNOW SOMEONE WHO MIGHT BE ABLE TO TELL US.
I SHOULD'VE BEEN AWARE OF WHAT SPALDING WAS TO. PROBED HIS MIN PAID ATTENTION, FOR PETE'S SAKE...

BUT I *COULDN'T.* WITH MY MENTAL POWERS *MASKED...* I'LL ADMIT, IT JUST MADE ME *MORE INTRIGUED* BY HIM. MORE *INTERESTED.*

MORE *HUNGRY* TO LEARN ABOUT HIM IN *OTHER* WAYS.

PATSY... IF YOU DON'T MIND MY ASKING... WHAT DROVE YOU... *INSANE?*

LOOK AT RICK. FIRING OFF THE *BIG QUESTIONS* TONIGHT.

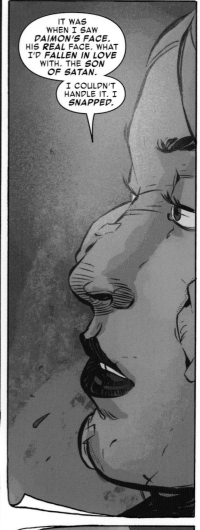

IT WAS WHEN I SAW *DAIMON'S* FACE. HIS *REAL* FACE. WHAT I'D *FALLEN IN LOVE* WITH. THE *SON OF SATAN.*

I COULDN'T HANDLE IT. I *SNAPPED.*

I *TOOK MY OWN LIFE.* I THOUGHT I WAS AS *CORRUPT* AND *HIDEOUS* AS *HE* WAS, JUST BY *ASSOCIATION.*

BUT I *CAME BACK.* HERE I AM. NIFTY *SECOND CHANCES* AND ALL THAT. RIGHT? ALTHOUGH *NOW* I GUESS I'M ON MY *THIRD...*

MAYBE YOU'LL GET A *FULL NINE.*

YOU KNOW, AT *NIGHT,* WHEN I'M IN THE *HOSPITAL* SLEEPING...BUT SLEEPWALKER'S WITH *YOU--* WITH *HELLCAT*--OUT IN THE CITY...

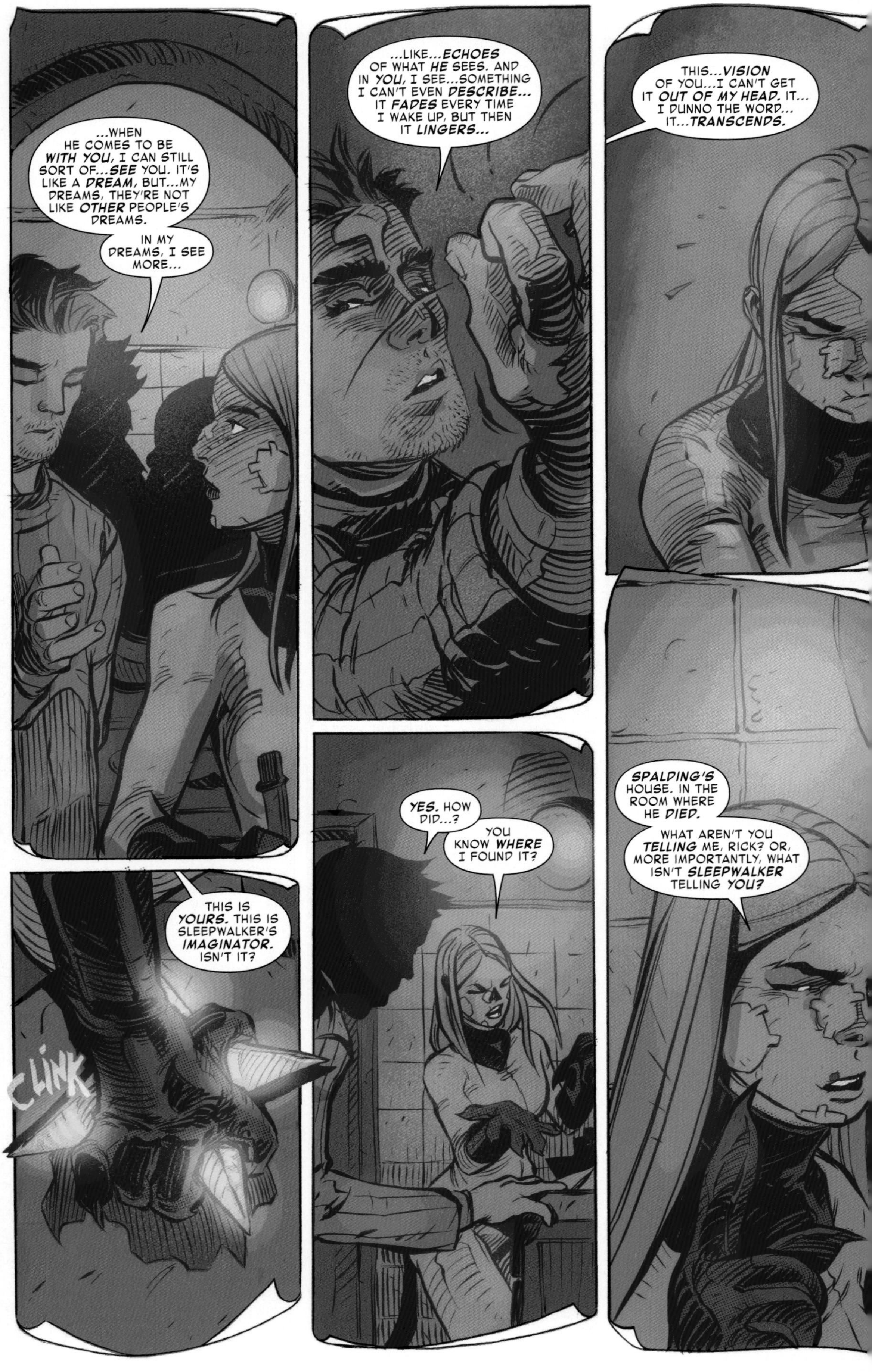
...WHEN HE COMES TO BE WITH YOU, I CAN STILL SORT OF...SEE YOU. IT'S LIKE A DREAM, BUT...MY DREAMS, THEY'RE NOT LIKE OTHER PEOPLE'S DREAMS.
IN MY DREAMS, I SEE MORE...
...LIKE...ECHOES OF WHAT HE SEES. AND IN YOU, I SEE...SOMETHING I CAN'T EVEN DESCRIBE... IT FADES EVERY TIME I WAKE UP, BUT THEN IT LINGERS...
THIS...VISION OF YOU...I CAN'T GET IT OUT OF MY HEAD. IT... I DUNNO THE WORD... IT...TRANSCENDS.
THIS IS YOURS. THIS IS SLEEPWALKER'S IMAGINATOR. ISN'T IT?
CLINK
YES. HOW DID...?
YOU KNOW WHERE I FOUND IT?
SPALDING'S HOUSE. IN THE ROOM WHERE HE DIED.
WHAT AREN'T YOU TELLING ME, RICK? OR, MORE IMPORTANTLY, WHAT ISN'T SLEEPWALKER TELLING YOU?

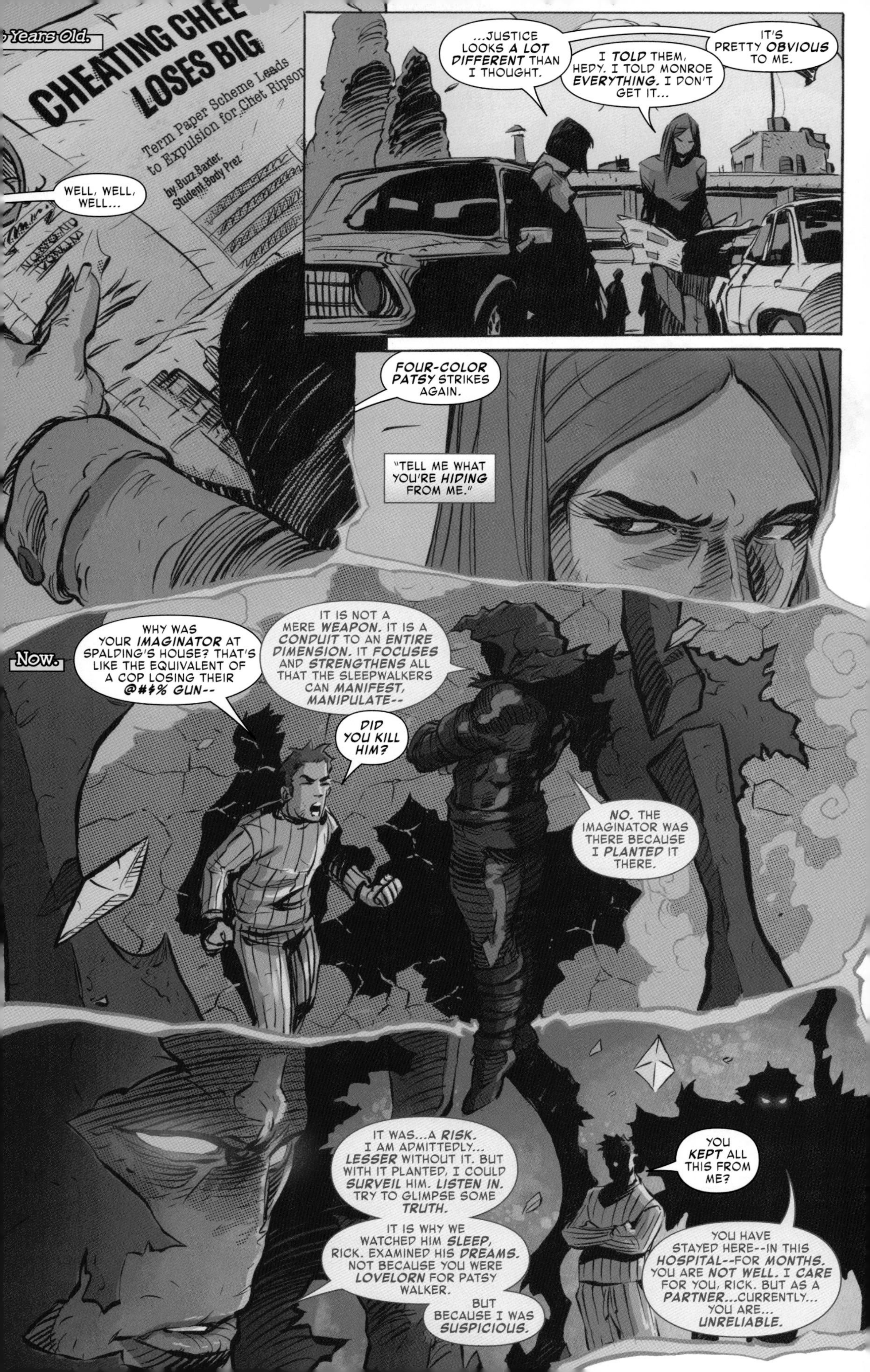

...Years Old.
CHEATING CHEE
LOSES BIG
Term Paper Scheme Leads to Expulsion for Chet Ripson
by Buzz Baxter, Student Body Prez
WELL, WELL, WELL...
...JUSTICE LOOKS A LOT DIFFERENT THAN I THOUGHT.
I TOLD THEM, HEDY. I TOLD MONROE EVERYTHING. I DON'T GET IT...
IT'S PRETTY OBVIOUS TO ME.
FOUR-COLOR PATSY STRIKES AGAIN.
"TELL ME WHAT YOU'RE HIDING FROM ME."
Now.
WHY WAS YOUR IMAGINATOR AT SPALDING'S HOUSE? THAT'S LIKE THE EQUIVALENT OF A COP LOSING THEIR @#$% GUN--
IT IS NOT A MERE WEAPON. IT IS A CONDUIT TO AN ENTIRE DIMENSION. IT FOCUSES AND STRENGTHENS ALL THAT THE SLEEPWALKERS CAN MANIFEST, MANIPULATE--
DID YOU KILL HIM?
NO. THE IMAGINATOR WAS THERE BECAUSE I PLANTED IT THERE.
IT WAS...A RISK. I AM ADMITTEDLY... LESSER WITHOUT IT. BUT WITH IT PLANTED, I COULD SURVEIL HIM. LISTEN IN. TRY TO GLIMPSE SOME TRUTH.
IT IS WHY WE WATCHED HIM SLEEP, RICK. EXAMINED HIS DREAMS. NOT BECAUSE YOU WERE LOVELORN FOR PATSY WALKER.
BUT BECAUSE I WAS SUSPICIOUS.
YOU KEPT ALL THIS FROM ME?
YOU HAVE STAYED HERE--IN THIS HOSPITAL--FOR MONTHS. YOU ARE NOT WELL. I CARE FOR YOU, RICK. BUT AS A PARTNER...CURRENTLY... YOU ARE... UNRELIABLE.

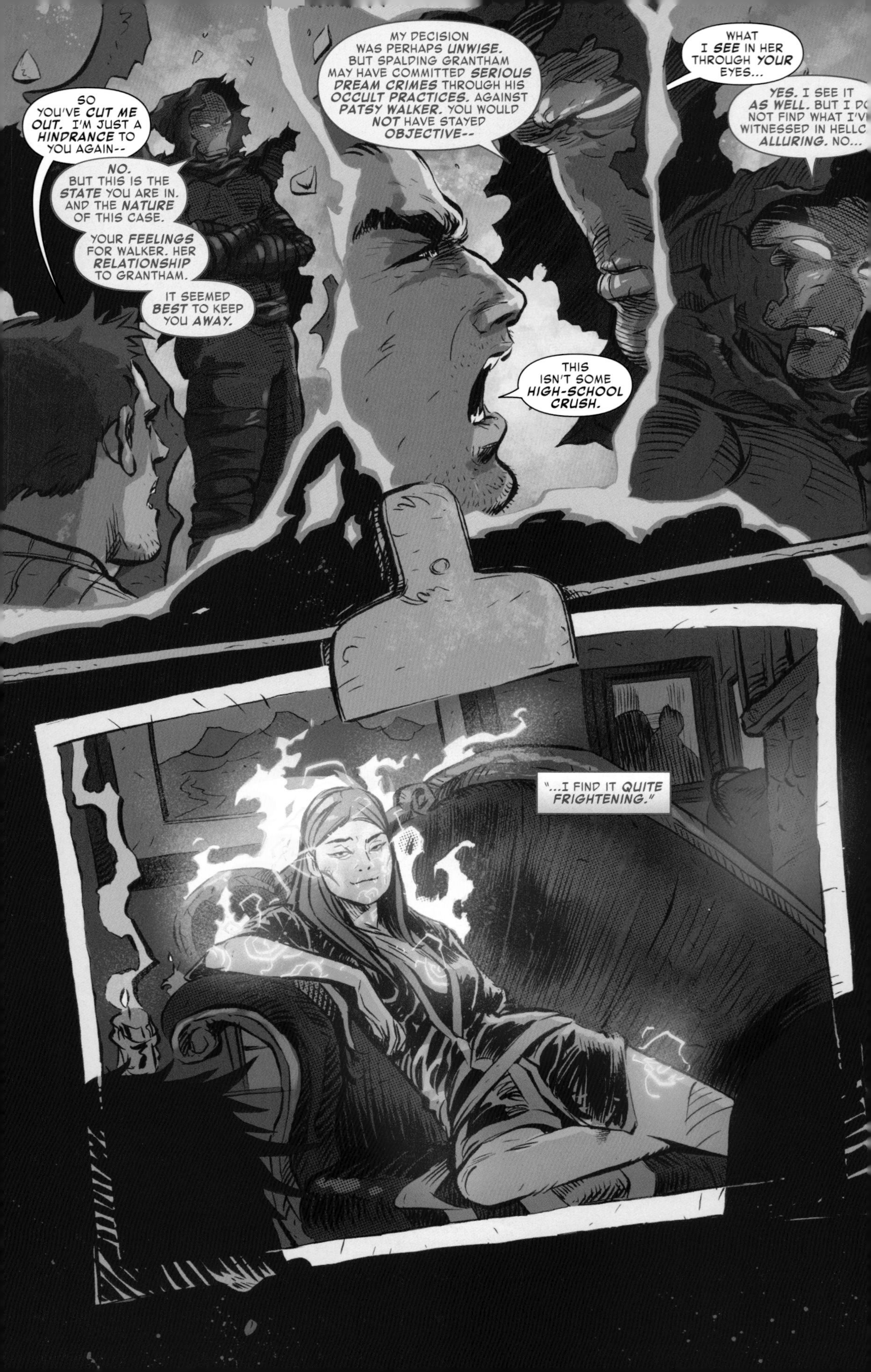
SO YOU'VE CUT ME OUT. I'M JUST A HINDRANCE TO YOU AGAIN--
NO. BUT THIS IS THE STATE YOU ARE IN. AND THE NATURE OF THIS CASE.
YOUR FEELINGS FOR WALKER. HER RELATIONSHIP TO GRANTHAM.
IT SEEMED BEST TO KEEP YOU AWAY.
MY DECISION WAS PERHAPS UNWISE. BUT SPALDING GRANTHAM MAY HAVE COMMITTED SERIOUS DREAM CRIMES THROUGH HIS OCCULT PRACTICES. AGAINST PATSY WALKER. YOU WOULD NOT HAVE STAYED OBJECTIVE--
THIS ISN'T SOME HIGH-SCHOOL CRUSH.
WHAT I SEE IN HER THROUGH YOUR EYES...
YES. I SEE IT AS WELL. BUT I DO NOT FIND WHAT I'VE WITNESSED IN HELL ALLURING. NO...
"...I FIND IT QUITE FRIGHTENING."

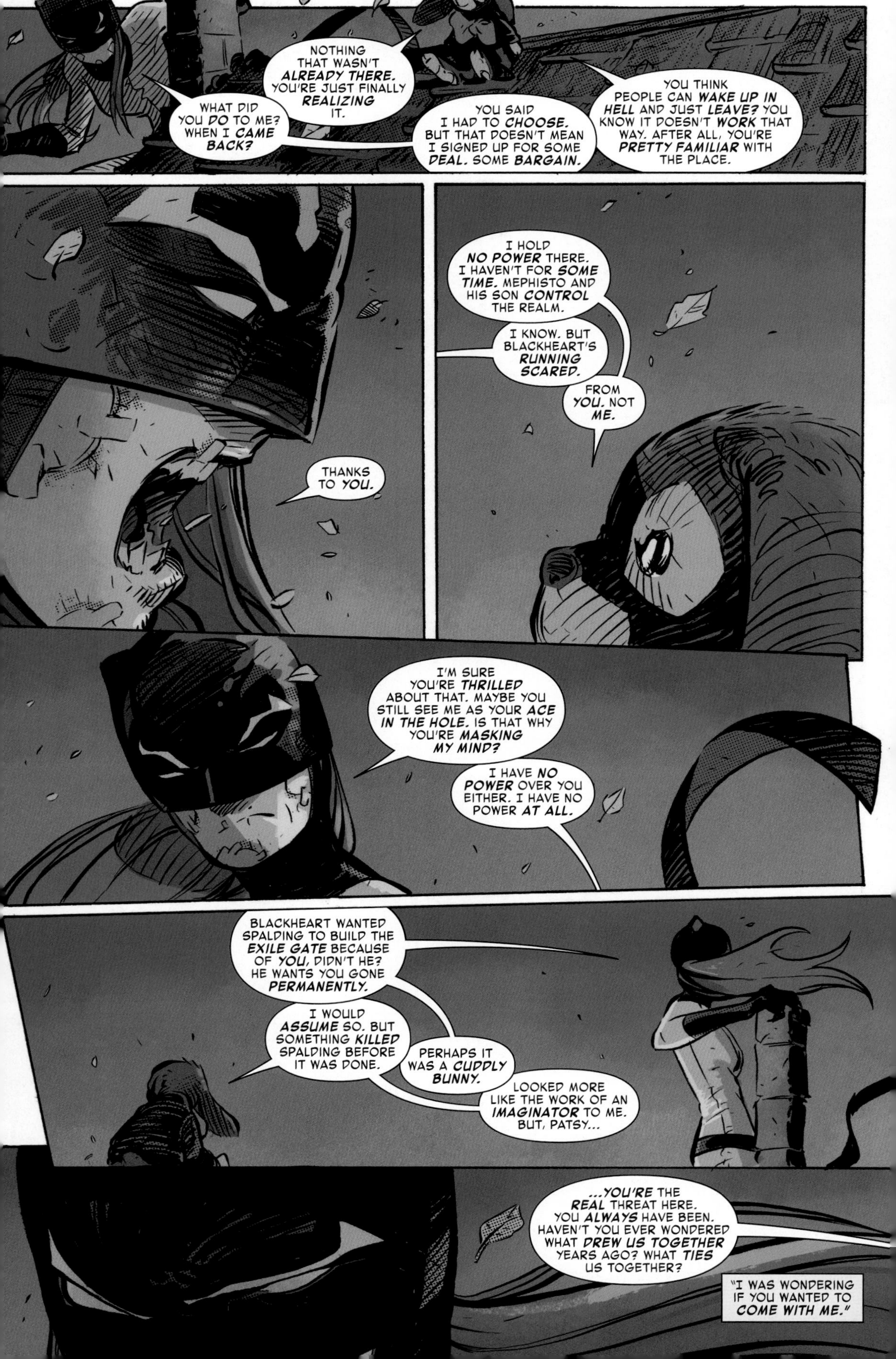
WHAT DID YOU DO TO ME? WHEN I CAME BACK?
NOTHING THAT WASN'T ALREADY THERE. YOU'RE JUST FINALLY REALIZING IT.
YOU SAID I HAD TO CHOOSE. BUT THAT DOESN'T MEAN I SIGNED UP FOR SOME DEAL. SOME BARGAIN.
YOU THINK PEOPLE CAN WAKE UP IN HELL AND JUST LEAVE? YOU KNOW IT DOESN'T WORK THAT WAY. AFTER ALL, YOU'RE PRETTY FAMILIAR WITH THE PLACE.
THANKS TO YOU.
I HOLD NO POWER THERE. I HAVEN'T FOR SOME TIME. MEPHISTO AND HIS SON CONTROL THE REALM.
I KNOW. BUT BLACKHEART'S RUNNING SCARED.
FROM YOU. NOT ME.
I'M SURE YOU'RE THRILLED ABOUT THAT. MAYBE YOU STILL SEE ME AS YOUR ACE IN THE HOLE. IS THAT WHY YOU'RE MASKING MY MIND?
I HAVE NO POWER OVER YOU EITHER. I HAVE NO POWER AT ALL.
BLACKHEART WANTED SPALDING TO BUILD THE EXILE GATE BECAUSE OF YOU, DIDN'T HE? HE WANTS YOU GONE PERMANENTLY.
I WOULD ASSUME SO. BUT SOMETHING KILLED SPALDING BEFORE IT WAS DONE.
PERHAPS IT WAS A CUDDLY BUNNY.
LOOKED MORE LIKE THE WORK OF AN IMAGINATOR TO ME. BUT, PATSY...
...YOU'RE THE REAL THREAT HERE. YOU ALWAYS HAVE BEEN. HAVEN'T YOU EVER WONDERED WHAT DREW US TOGETHER YEARS AGO? WHAT TIES US TOGETHER?
"I WAS WONDERING IF YOU WANTED TO COME WITH ME."

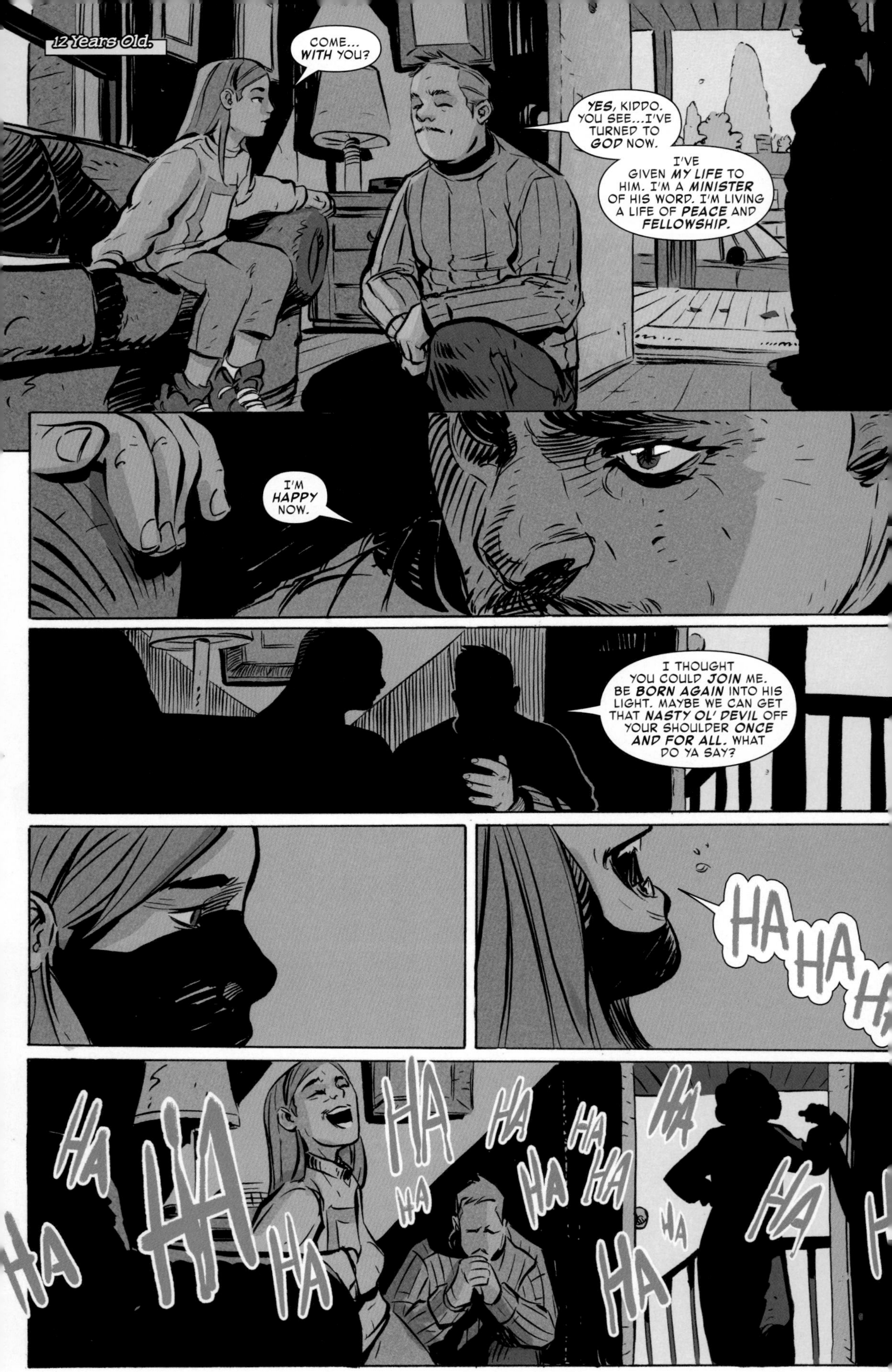
12 Years Old.
COME... WITH YOU?
YES, KIDDO. YOU SEE...I'VE TURNED TO GOD NOW.
I'VE GIVEN MY LIFE TO HIM. I'M A MINISTER OF HIS WORD. I'M LIVING A LIFE OF PEACE AND FELLOWSHIP.
I'M HAPPY NOW.
I THOUGHT YOU COULD JOIN ME. BE BORN AGAIN INTO HIS LIGHT. MAYBE WE CAN GET THAT NASTY OL' DEVIL OFF YOUR SHOULDER ONCE AND FOR ALL. WHAT DO YA SAY?
HA HA
HA HA HA HA HA HA HA HA HA HA HA HA HA HA HA HA HA

THIS COULD BE SOMETHING *POWERFUL*.

I WAS *WONDERING* WHEN YOU'D STOP BY.

AND *YES*. IT *WILL* BE. I'VE FOLLOWED BLACKHEART'S INSTRUCTIONS *TO THE LETTER*.

SOMEONE WHO STEPS THROUGH THIS...THEY'RE *NEVER* COMING BACK.

AND WHAT DO *YOU* GET IN RETURN?

I GET TO *SEE*. EVEN *CLEARER*, INTO THE *DARKNESS*.

BLACKHEART'S A *FOOL*.

I CAN SHOW YOU WHAT TO *REALLY* BUILD.

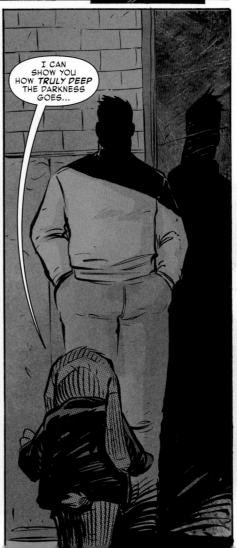

I CAN SHOW YOU HOW *TRULY DEEP* THE DARKNESS GOES...

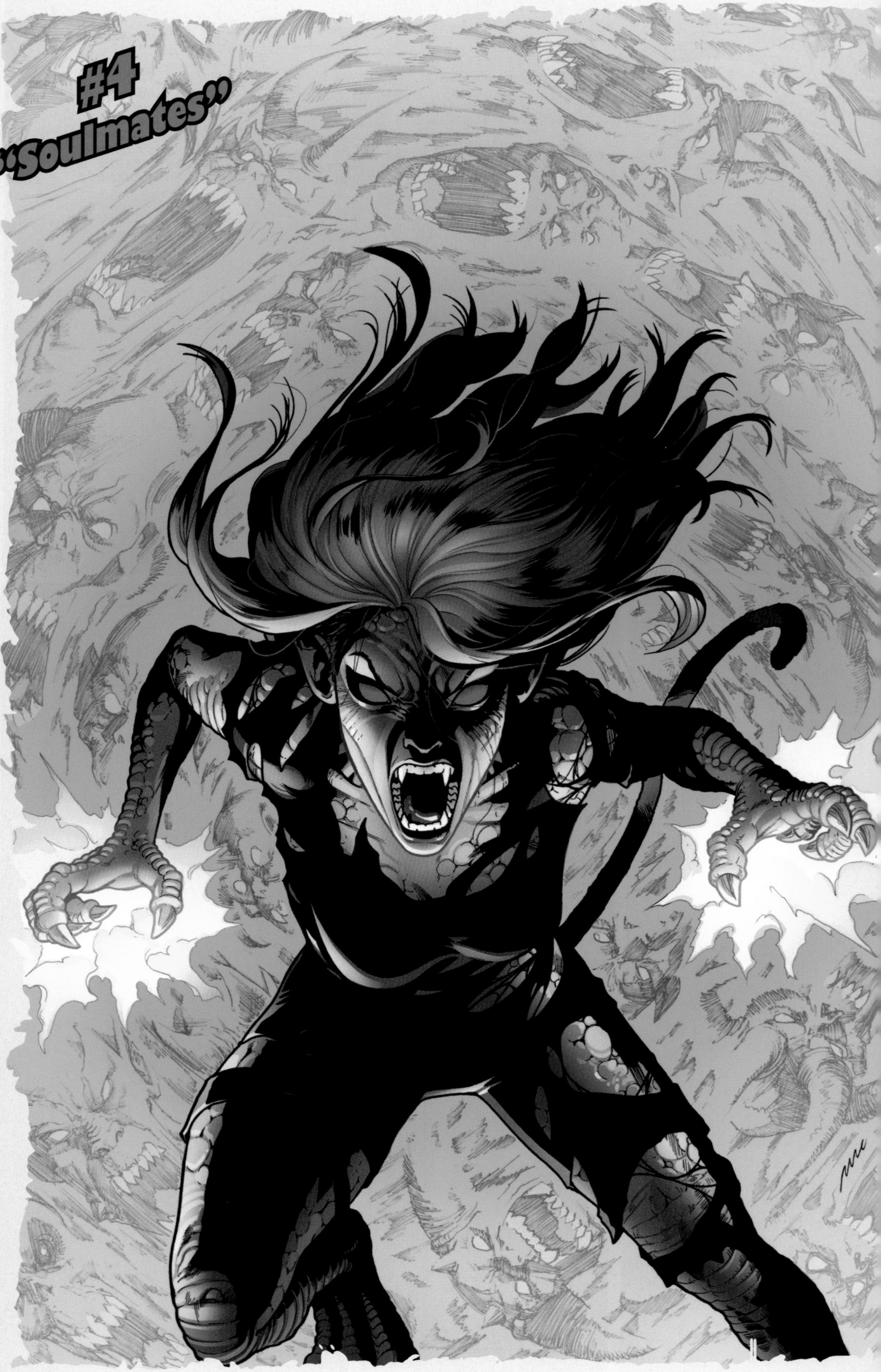
#4
"Soulmates"

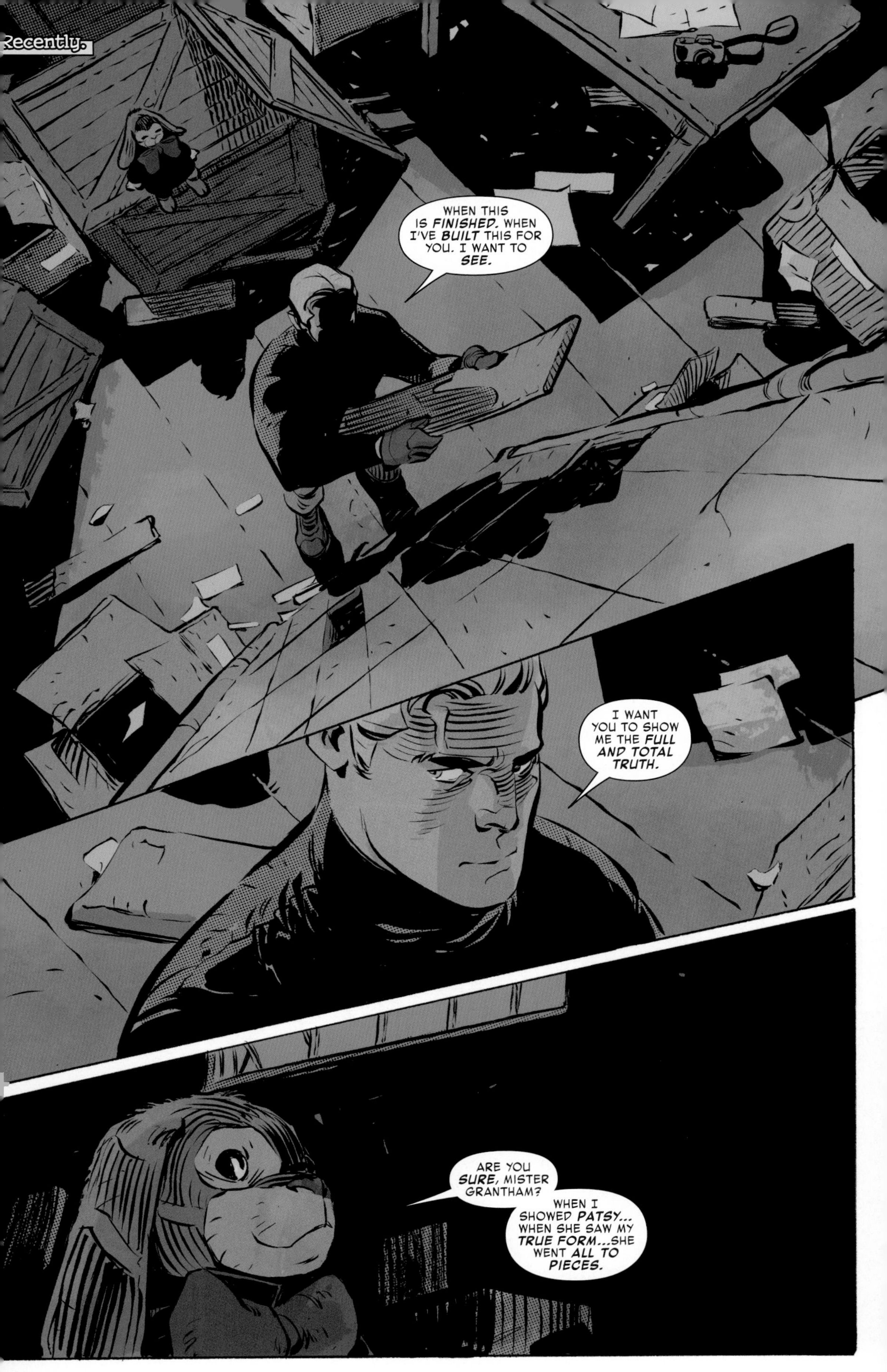
Recently.
WHEN THIS IS FINISHED. WHEN I'VE BUILT THIS FOR YOU. I WANT TO SEE.
I WANT YOU TO SHOW ME THE FULL AND TOTAL TRUTH.
ARE YOU SURE, MISTER GRANTHAM?
WHEN I SHOWED PATSY... WHEN SHE SAW MY TRUE FORM...SHE WENT ALL TO PIECES.

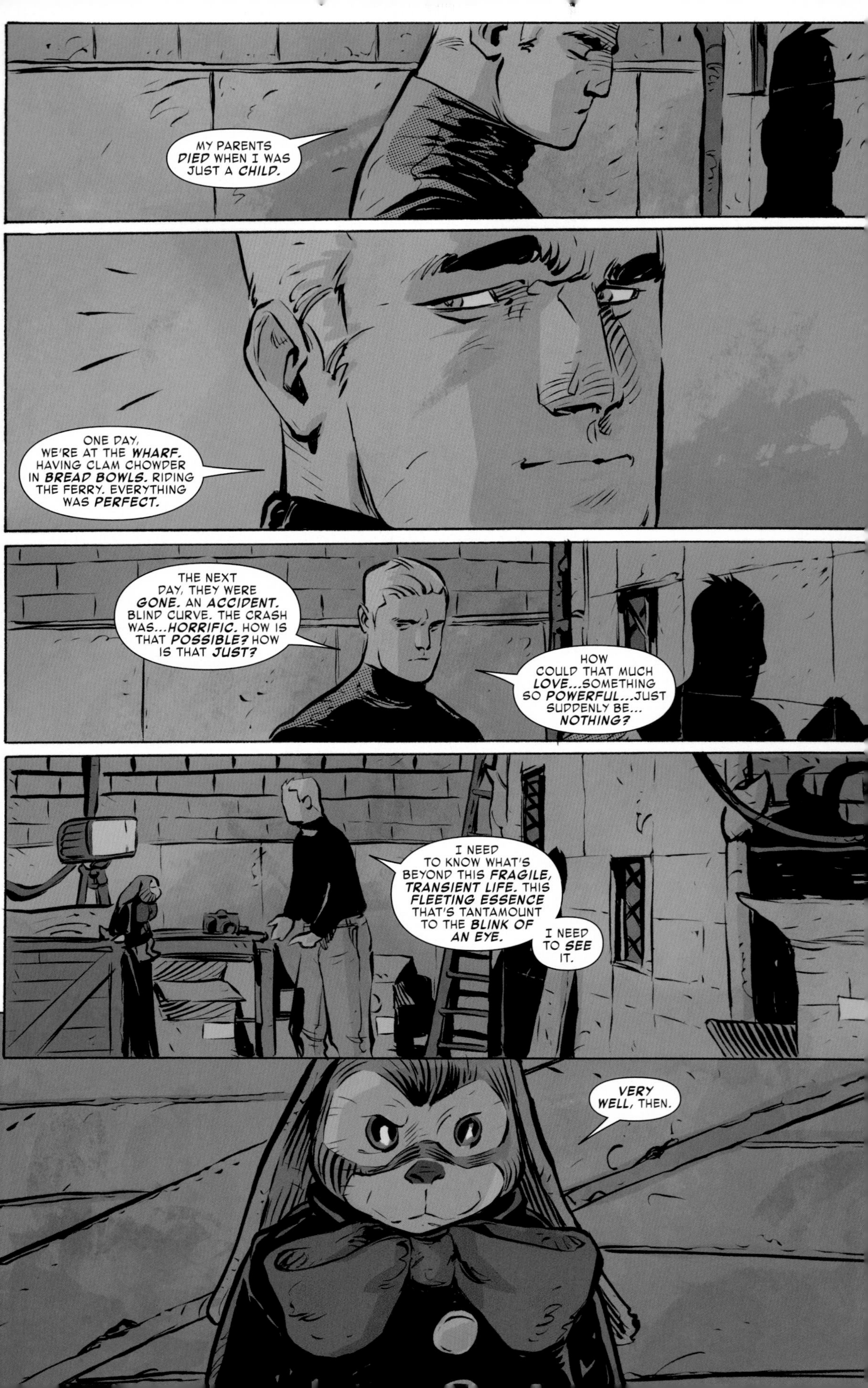
MY PARENTS DIED WHEN I WAS JUST A CHILD.
ONE DAY, WE'RE AT THE WHARF. HAVING CLAM CHOWDER IN BREAD BOWLS. RIDING THE FERRY. EVERYTHING WAS PERFECT.
THE NEXT DAY, THEY WERE GONE. AN ACCIDENT. BLIND CURVE. THE CRASH WAS...HORRIFIC. HOW IS THAT POSSIBLE? HOW IS THAT JUST?
HOW COULD THAT MUCH LOVE...SOMETHING SO POWERFUL...JUST SUDDENLY BE... NOTHING?
I NEED TO KNOW WHAT'S BEYOND THIS FRAGILE, TRANSIENT LIFE. THIS FLEETING ESSENCE THAT'S TANTAMOUNT TO THE BLINK OF AN EYE.
I NEED TO SEE IT.
VERY WELL, THEN.

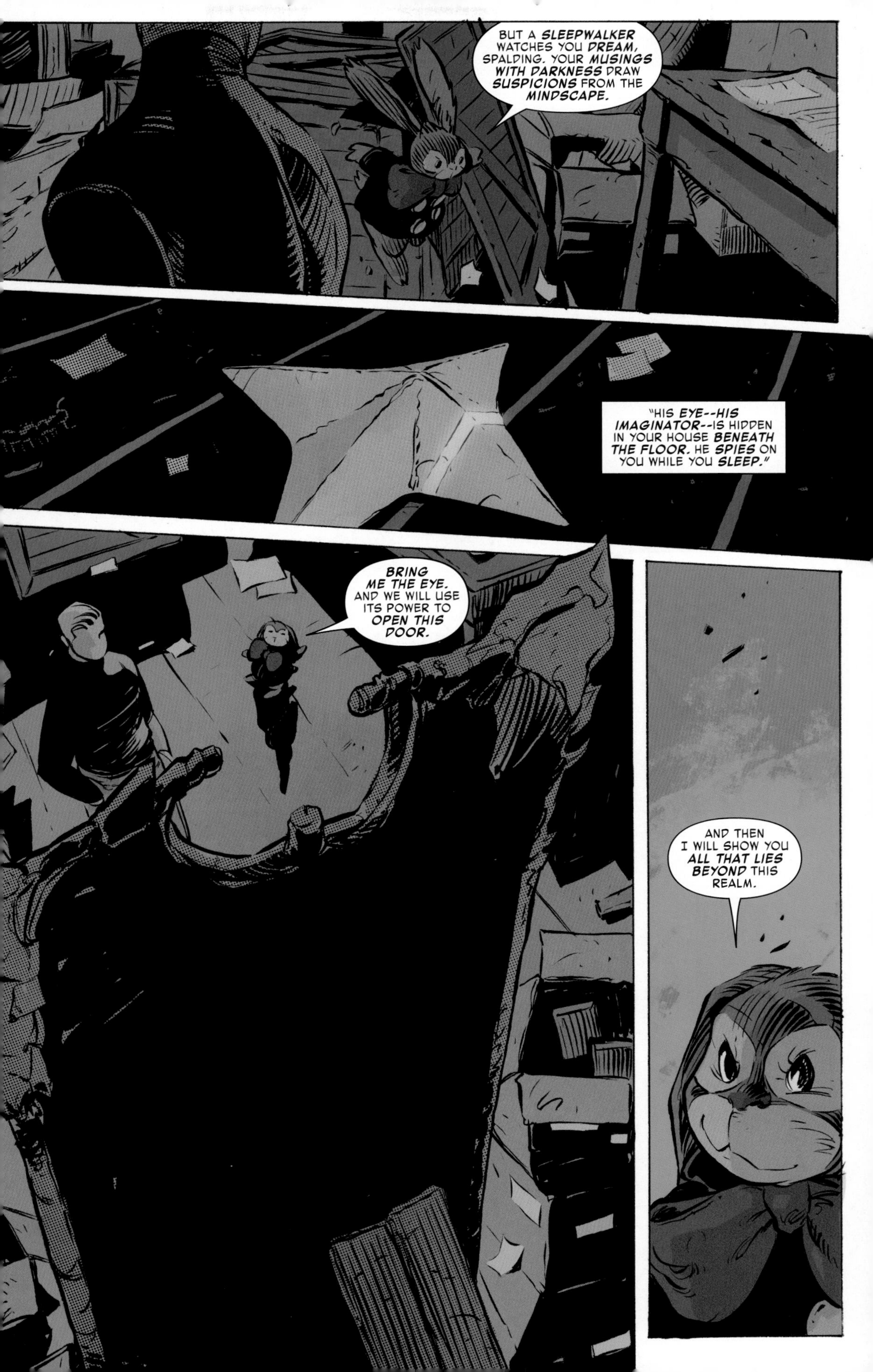
BUT A SLEEPWALKER WATCHES YOU DREAM, SPALDING. YOUR MUSINGS WITH DARKNESS DRAW SUSPICIONS FROM THE MINDSCAPE.
"HIS EYE--HIS IMAGINATOR--IS HIDDEN IN YOUR HOUSE BENEATH THE FLOOR. HE SPIES ON YOU WHILE YOU SLEEP."
BRING ME THE EYE. AND WE WILL USE ITS POWER TO OPEN THIS DOOR.
AND THEN I WILL SHOW YOU ALL THAT LIES BEYOND THIS REALM.

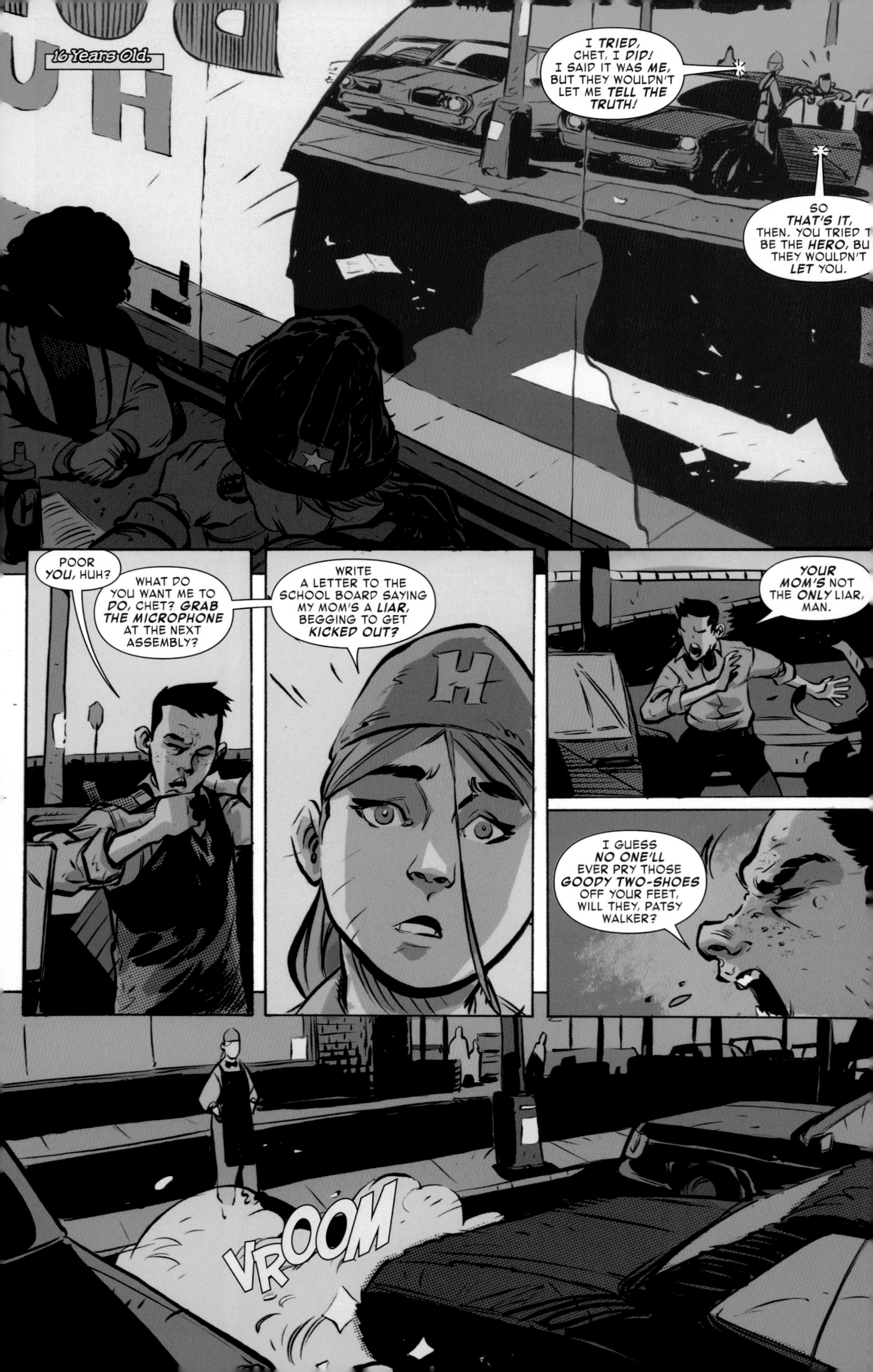

16 Years Old.
I TRIED, CHET, I DID! I SAID IT WAS ME, BUT THEY WOULDN'T LET ME TELL THE TRUTH!
SO THAT'S IT, THEN. YOU TRIED T BE THE HERO, BU THEY WOULDN'T LET YOU.
POOR YOU, HUH?
WHAT DO YOU WANT ME TO DO, CHET? GRAB THE MICROPHONE AT THE NEXT ASSEMBLY?
WRITE A LETTER TO THE SCHOOL BOARD SAYING MY MOM'S A LIAR, BEGGING TO GET KICKED OUT?
YOUR MOM'S NOT THE ONLY LIAR, MAN.
I GUESS NO ONE'LL EVER PRY THOSE GOODY TWO-SHOES OFF YOUR FEET, WILL THEY, PATSY WALKER?
VROOM

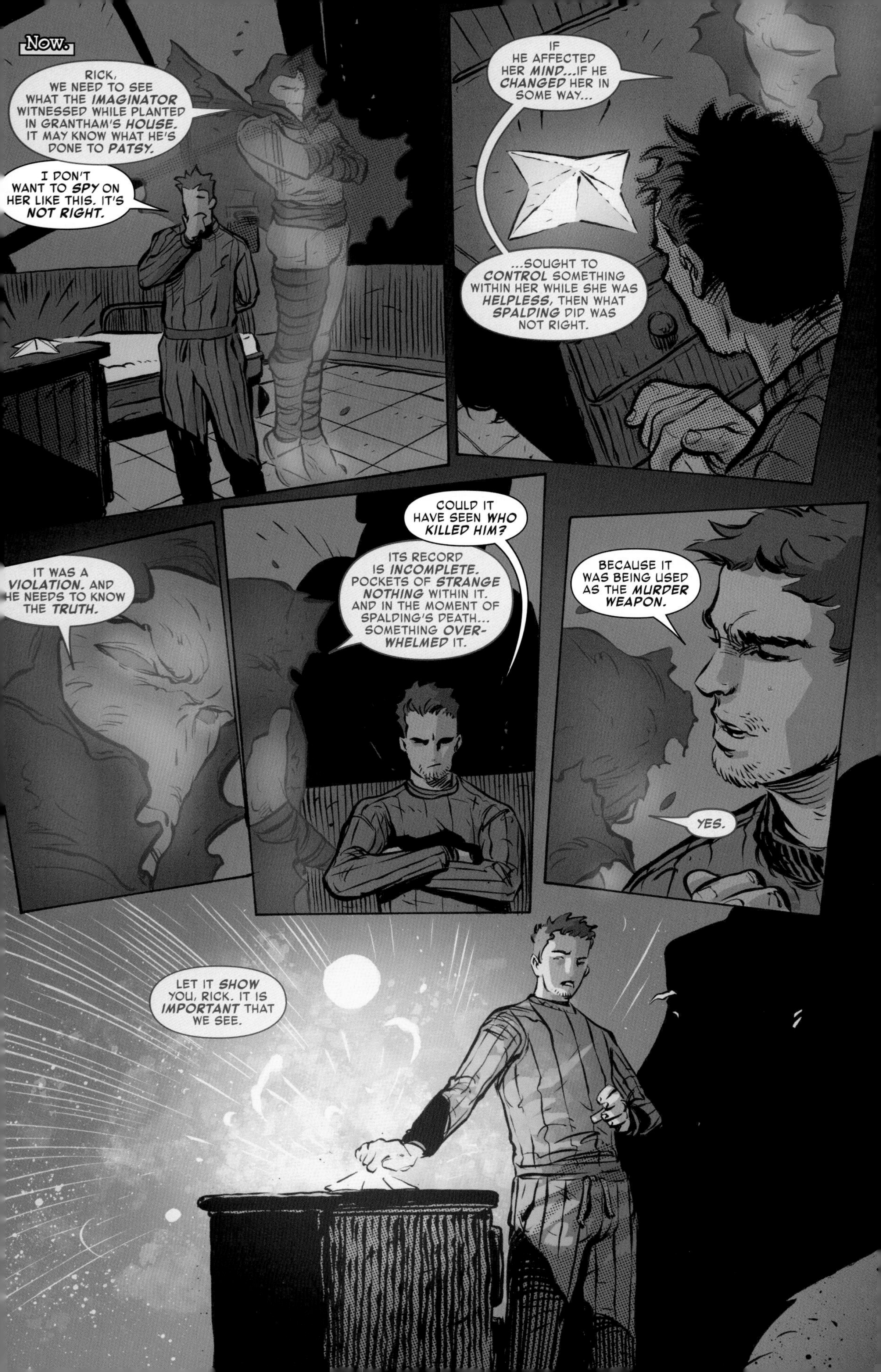
Now.
RICK, WE NEED TO SEE WHAT THE IMAGINATOR WITNESSED WHILE PLANTED IN GRANTHAM'S HOUSE. IT MAY KNOW WHAT HE'S DONE TO PATSY.
I DON'T WANT TO SPY ON HER LIKE THIS. IT'S NOT RIGHT.
IF HE AFFECTED HER MIND...IF HE CHANGED HER IN SOME WAY...
...SOUGHT TO CONTROL SOMETHING WITHIN HER WHILE SHE WAS HELPLESS, THEN WHAT SPALDING DID WAS NOT RIGHT.
IT WAS A VIOLATION. AND HE NEEDS TO KNOW THE TRUTH.
COULD IT HAVE SEEN WHO KILLED HIM?
ITS RECORD IS INCOMPLETE. POCKETS OF STRANGE NOTHING WITHIN IT. AND IN THE MOMENT OF SPALDING'S DEATH... SOMETHING OVER-WHELMED IT.
BECAUSE IT WAS BEING USED AS THE MURDER WEAPON.
YES.
LET IT SHOW YOU, RICK. IT IS IMPORTANT THAT WE SEE.

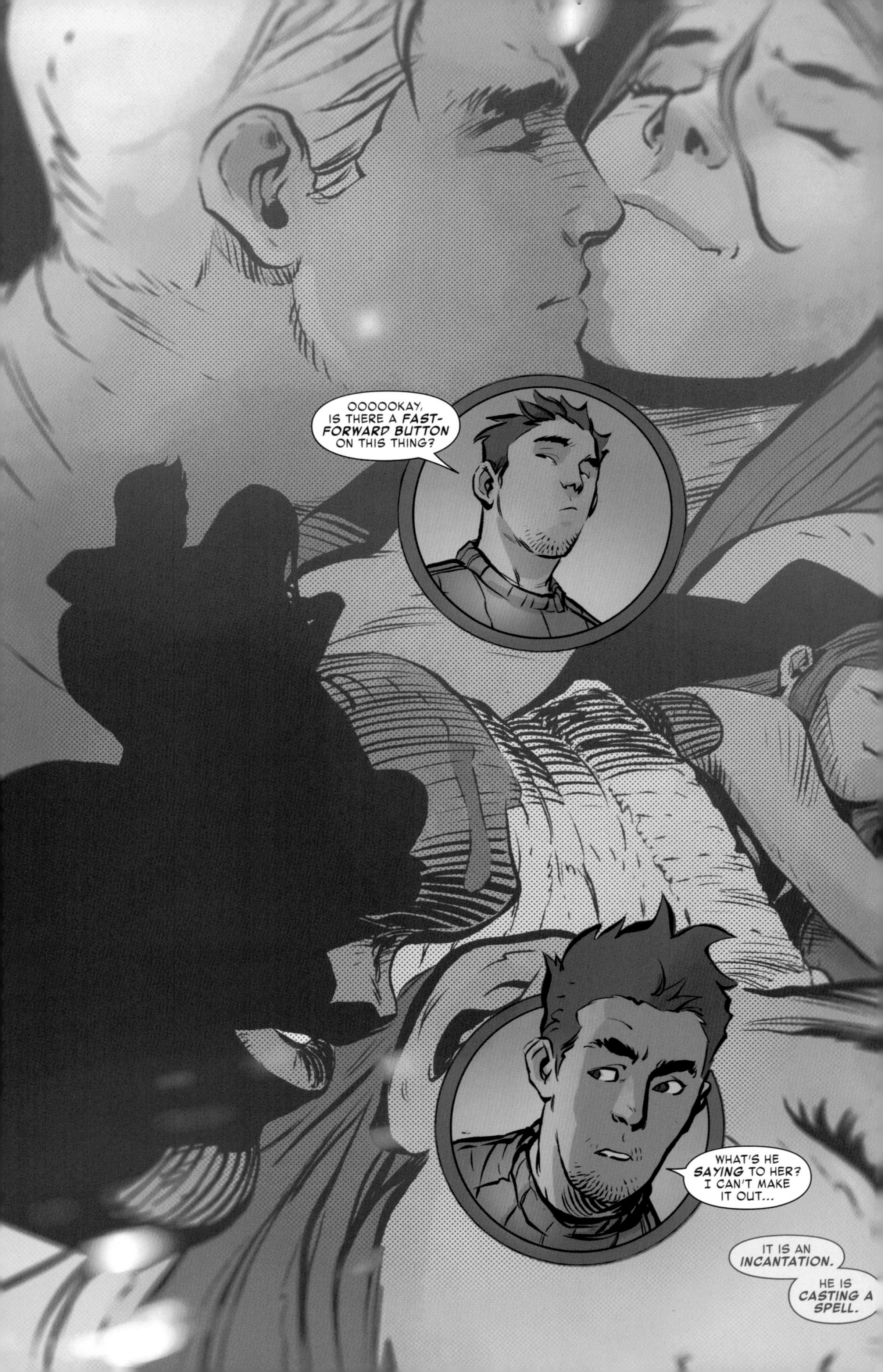
OOOOOKAY, IS THERE A FAST-FORWARD BUTTON ON THIS THING?
WHAT'S HE SAYING TO HER? I CAN'T MAKE IT OUT...
IT IS AN INCANTATION.
HE IS CASTING A SPELL.

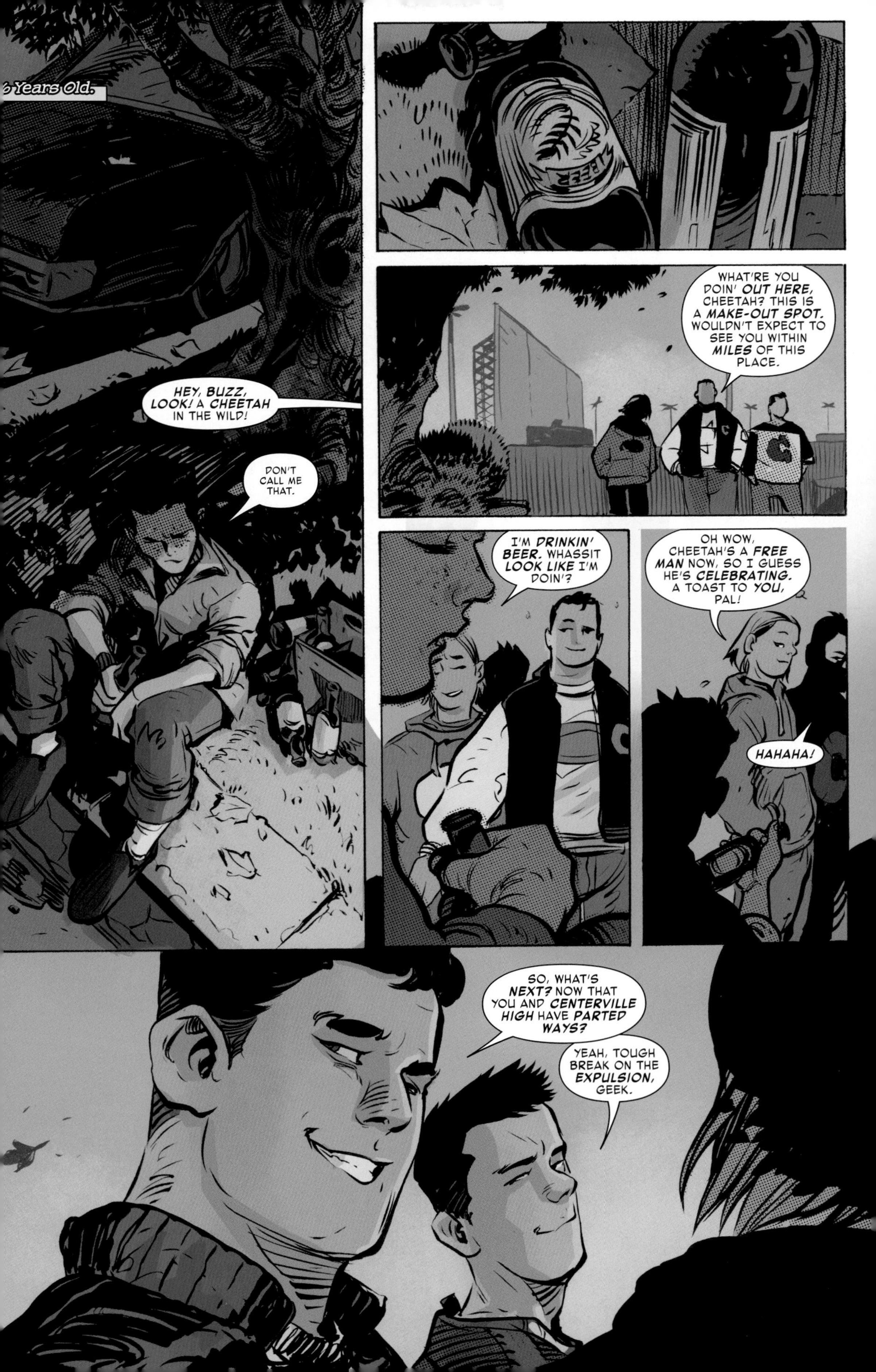

6 Years Old.
HEY, BUZZ, LOOK! A CHEETAH IN THE WILD!
DON'T CALL ME THAT.
WHAT'RE YOU DOIN' OUT HERE, CHEETAH? THIS IS A MAKE-OUT SPOT. WOULDN'T EXPECT TO SEE YOU WITHIN MILES OF THIS PLACE.
I'M DRINKIN' BEER. WHASSIT LOOK LIKE I'M DOIN'?
OH WOW, CHEETAH'S A FREE MAN NOW, SO I GUESS HE'S CELEBRATING. A TOAST TO YOU, PAL!
HAHAHA!
SO, WHAT'S NEXT? NOW THAT YOU AND CENTERVILLE HIGH HAVE PARTED WAYS?
YEAH, TOUGH BREAK ON THE EXPULSION, GEEK.

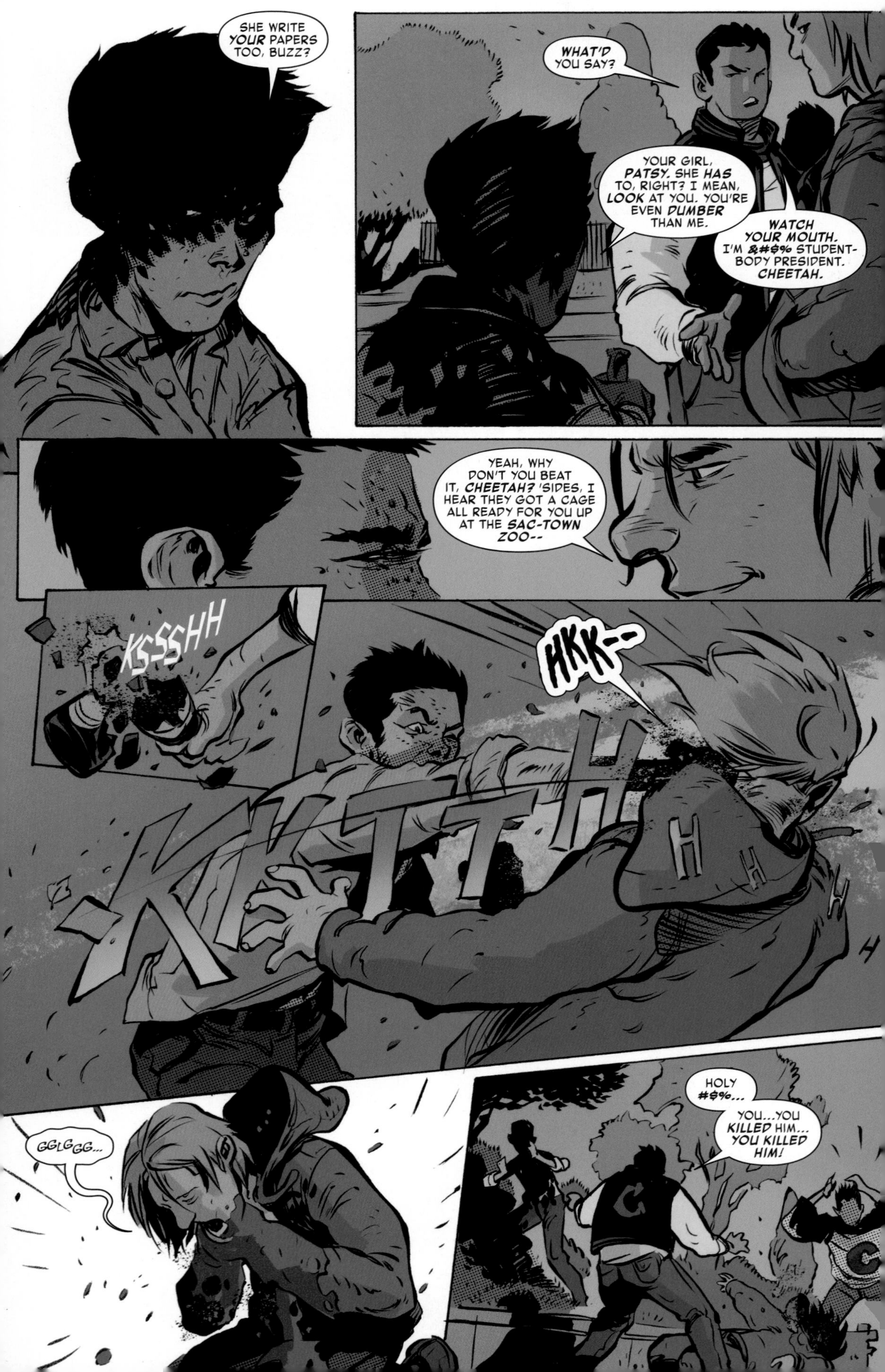
SHE WRITE YOUR PAPERS TOO, BUZZ?
WHAT'D YOU SAY?
YOUR GIRL, PATSY. SHE HAS TO, RIGHT? I MEAN, LOOK AT YOU. YOU'RE EVEN DUMBER THAN ME.
WATCH YOUR MOUTH. I'M &#$% STUDENT-BODY PRESIDENT. CHEETAH.
YEAH, WHY DON'T YOU BEAT IT, CHEETAH? 'SIDES, I HEAR THEY GOT A CAGE ALL READY FOR YOU UP AT THE SAC-TOWN ZOO--
KSSSHH
HKK--
KHTTHHHHH
GGLGGG...
HOLY #$%...
YOU...YOU KILLED HIM... YOU KILLED HIM!

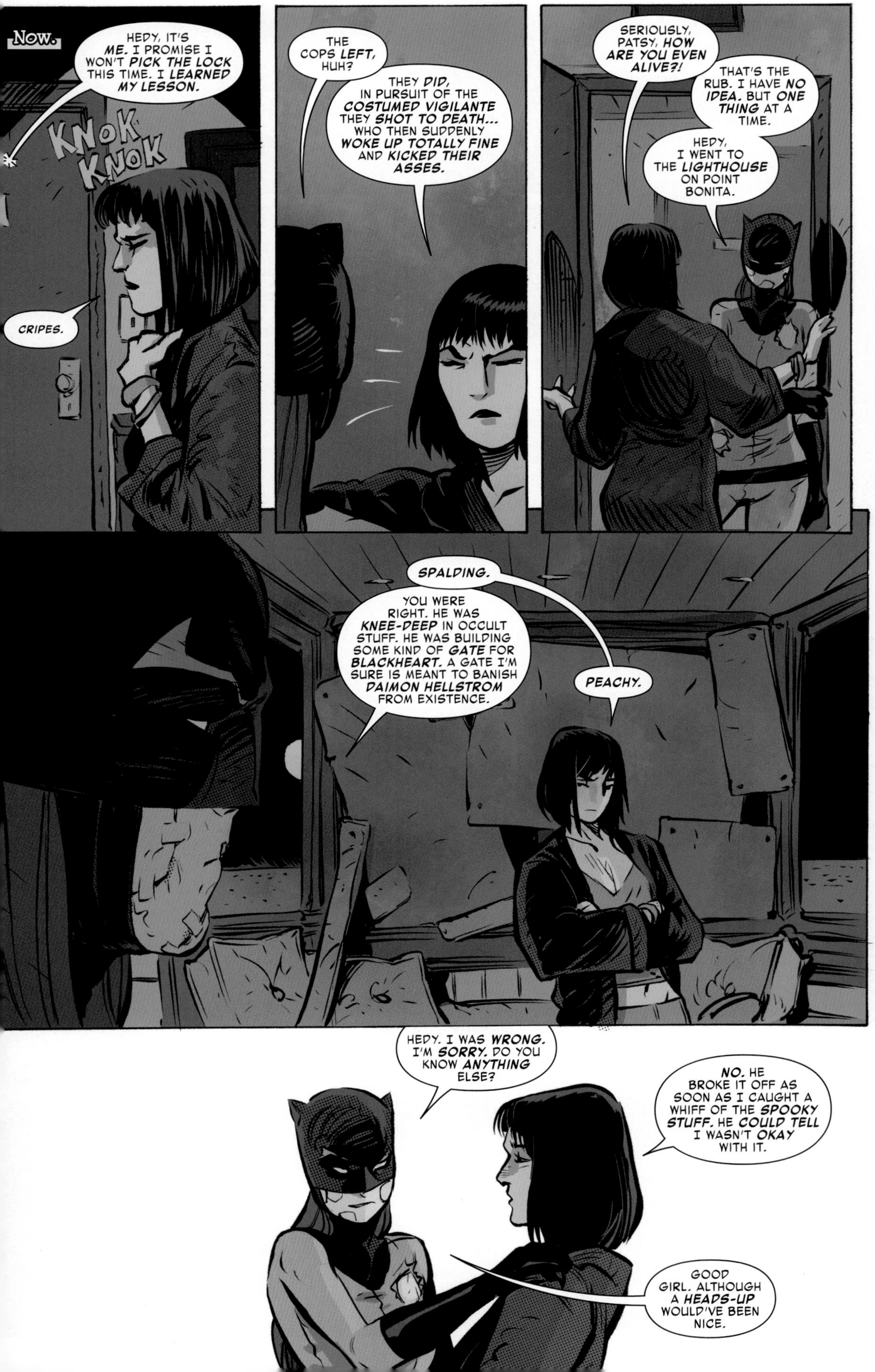
NOW.
HEDY, IT'S ME. I PROMISE I WON'T PICK THE LOCK THIS TIME. I LEARNED MY LESSON.
KNOK KNOK
CRIPES.
THE COPS LEFT, HUH?
THEY DID, IN PURSUIT OF THE COSTUMED VIGILANTE THEY SHOT TO DEATH... WHO THEN SUDDENLY WOKE UP TOTALLY FINE AND KICKED THEIR ASSES.
SERIOUSLY, PATSY, HOW ARE YOU EVEN ALIVE?!
THAT'S THE RUB. I HAVE NO IDEA. BUT ONE THING AT A TIME.
HEDY, I WENT TO THE LIGHTHOUSE ON POINT BONITA.
SPALDING.
YOU WERE RIGHT. HE WAS KNEE-DEEP IN OCCULT STUFF. HE WAS BUILDING SOME KIND OF GATE FOR BLACKHEART. A GATE I'M SURE IS MEANT TO BANISH DAIMON HELLSTROM FROM EXISTENCE.
PEACHY.
HEDY. I WAS WRONG. I'M SORRY. DO YOU KNOW ANYTHING ELSE?
NO. HE BROKE IT OFF AS SOON AS I CAUGHT A WHIFF OF THE SPOOKY STUFF. HE COULD TELL I WASN'T OKAY WITH IT.
GOOD GIRL. ALTHOUGH A HEADS-UP WOULD'VE BEEN NICE.

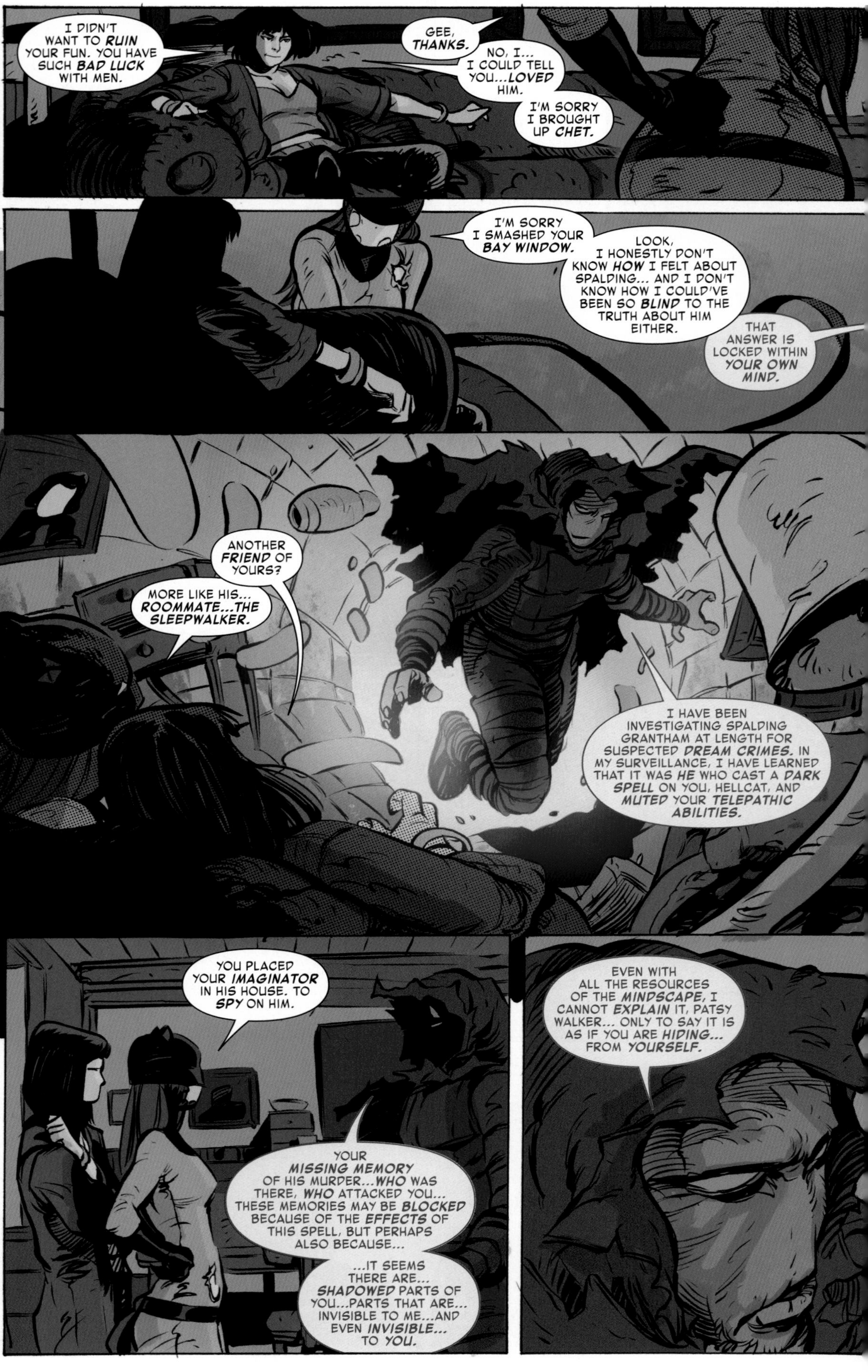

I DIDN'T WANT TO RUIN YOUR FUN. YOU HAVE SUCH BAD LUCK WITH MEN.
GEE, THANKS.
NO, I... I COULD TELL YOU...LOVED HIM.
I'M SORRY I BROUGHT UP CHET.
I'M SORRY I SMASHED YOUR BAY WINDOW.
LOOK, I HONESTLY DON'T KNOW HOW I FELT ABOUT SPALDING... AND I DON'T KNOW HOW I COULD'VE BEEN SO BLIND TO THE TRUTH ABOUT HIM EITHER.
THAT ANSWER IS LOCKED WITHIN YOUR OWN MIND.
ANOTHER FRIEND OF YOURS?
MORE LIKE HIS... ROOMMATE...THE SLEEPWALKER.
I HAVE BEEN INVESTIGATING SPALDING GRANTHAM AT LENGTH FOR SUSPECTED DREAM CRIMES. IN MY SURVEILLANCE, I HAVE LEARNED THAT IT WAS HE WHO CAST A DARK SPELL ON YOU, HELLCAT, AND MUTED YOUR TELEPATHIC ABILITIES.
YOU PLACED YOUR IMAGINATOR IN HIS HOUSE. TO SPY ON HIM.
YOUR MISSING MEMORY OF HIS MURDER...WHO WAS THERE, WHO ATTACKED YOU... THESE MEMORIES MAY BE BLOCKED BECAUSE OF THE EFFECTS OF THIS SPELL, BUT PERHAPS ALSO BECAUSE...
...IT SEEMS THERE ARE... SHADOWED PARTS OF YOU...PARTS THAT ARE... INVISIBLE TO ME...AND EVEN INVISIBLE... TO YOU.
EVEN WITH ALL THE RESOURCES OF THE MINDSCAPE, I CANNOT EXPLAIN IT, PATSY WALKER... ONLY TO SAY IT IS AS IF YOU ARE HIDING... FROM YOURSELF.

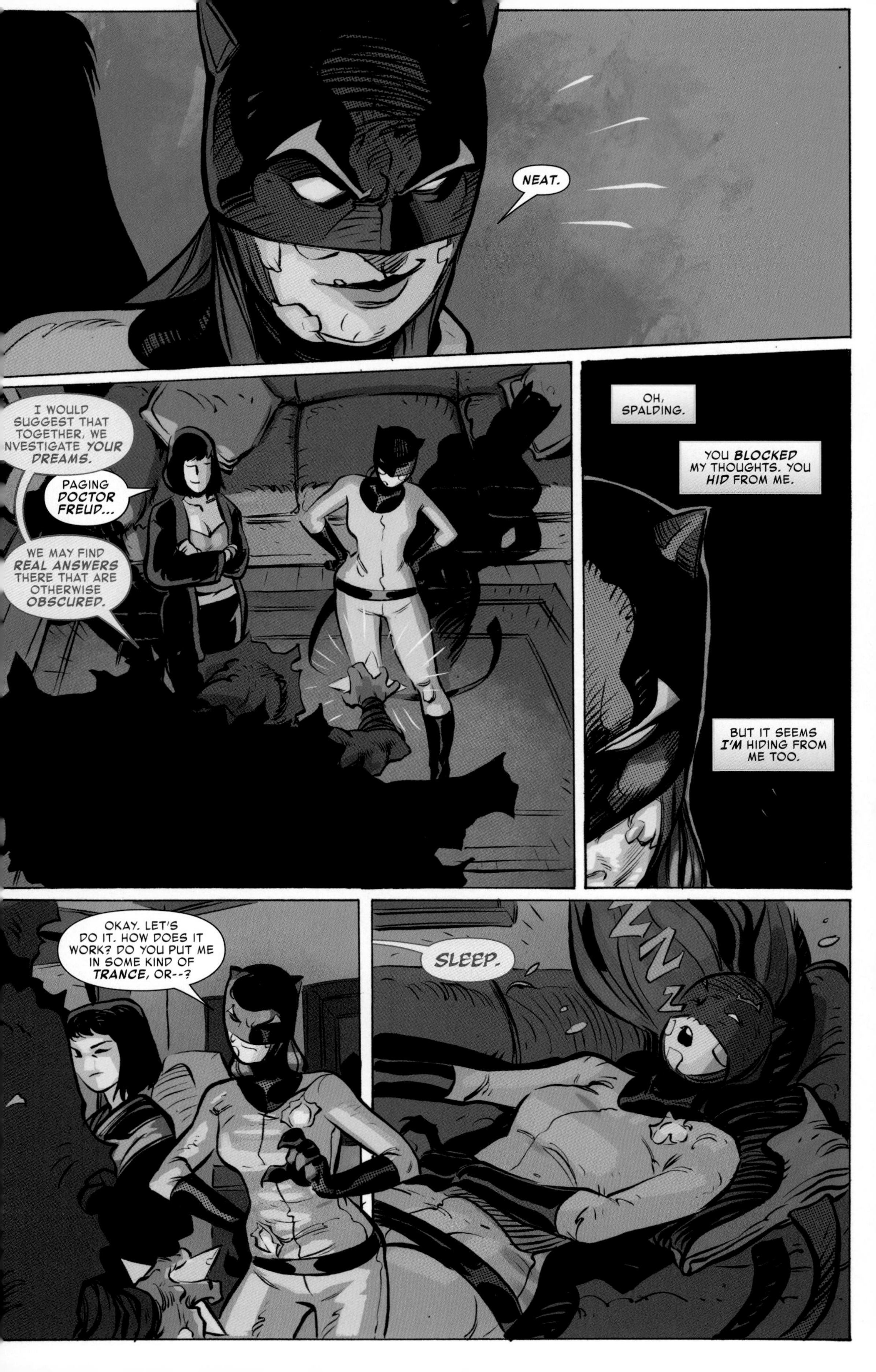
NEAT.
I WOULD SUGGEST THAT TOGETHER, WE NVESTIGATE YOUR DREAMS.
PAGING DOCTOR FREUD...
WE MAY FIND REAL ANSWERS THERE THAT ARE OTHERWISE OBSCURED.
OH, SPALDING.
YOU BLOCKED MY THOUGHTS. YOU HID FROM ME.
BUT IT SEEMS I'M HIDING FROM ME TOO.
OKAY. LET'S DO IT. HOW DOES IT WORK? DO YOU PUT ME IN SOME KIND OF TRANCE, OR--?
SLEEP.

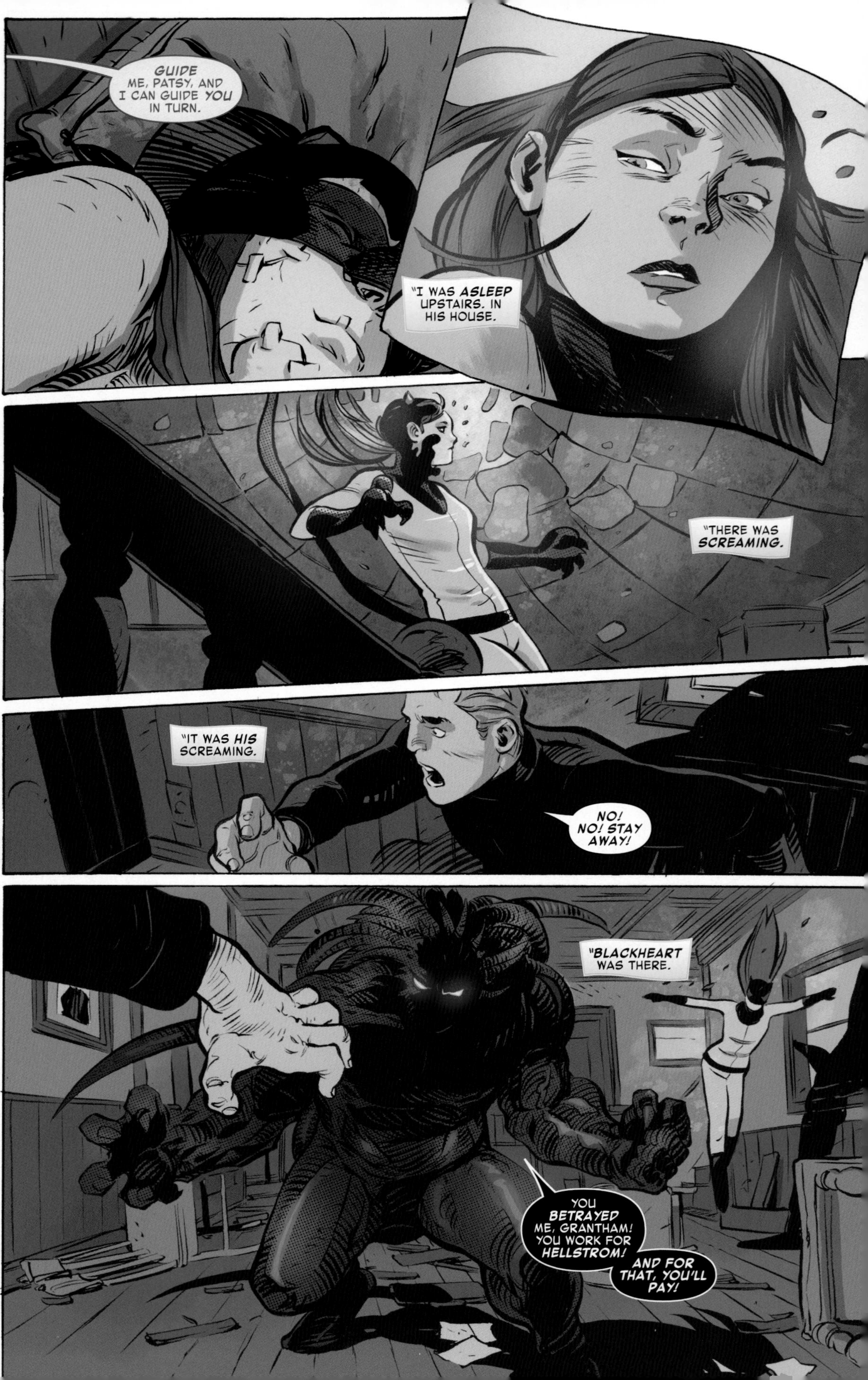
GUIDE ME, PATSY, AND I CAN GUIDE YOU IN TURN.
"I WAS ASLEEP UPSTAIRS. IN HIS HOUSE.
"THERE WAS SCREAMING.
"IT WAS HIS SCREAMING.
NO! NO! STAY AWAY!
"BLACKHEART WAS THERE.
YOU BETRAYED ME, GRANTHAM! YOU WORK FOR HELLSTROM!
AND FOR THAT, YOU'LL PAY!

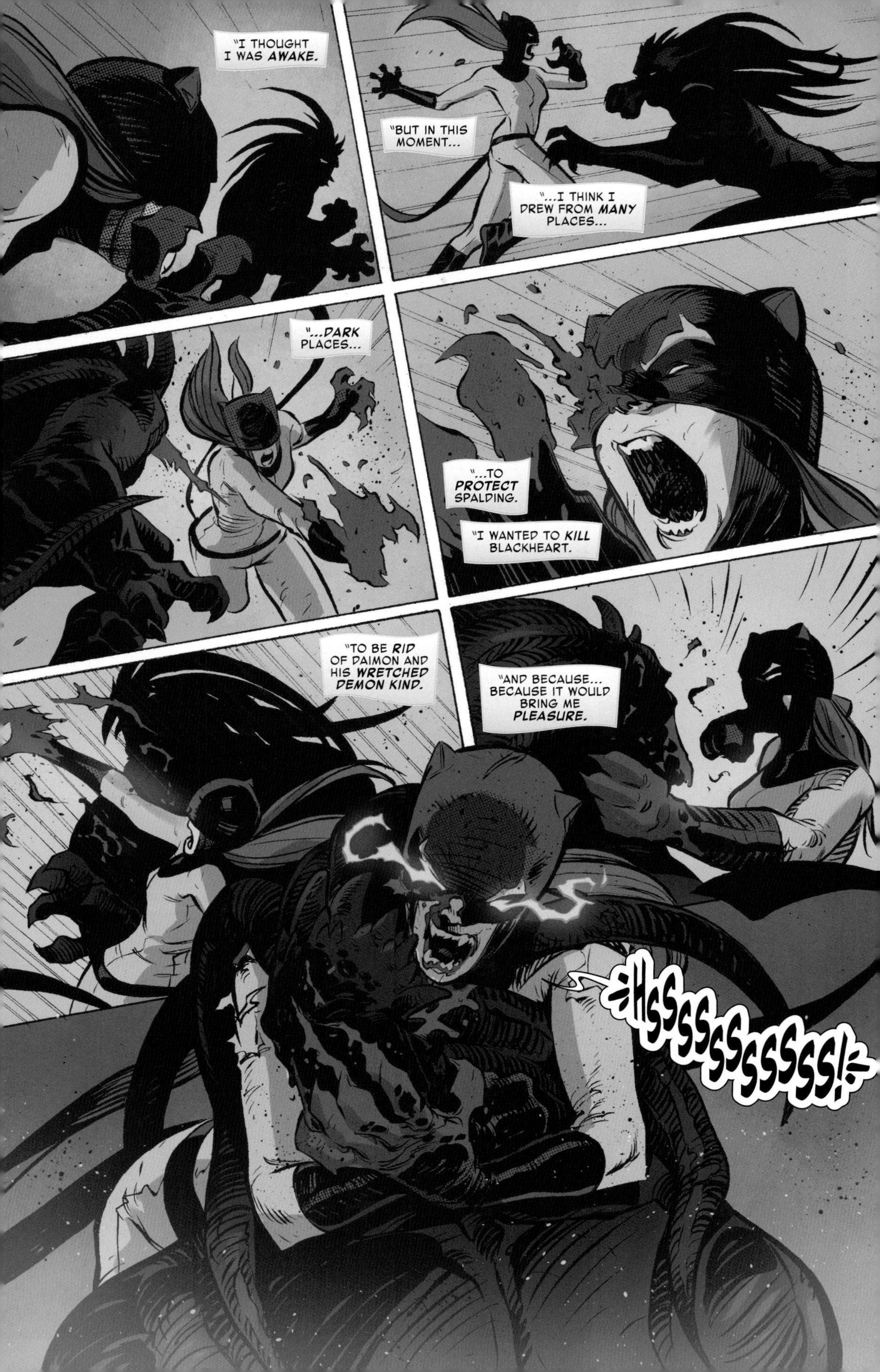
"I THOUGHT I WAS AWAKE.
"BUT IN THIS MOMENT...
"...I THINK I DREW FROM MANY PLACES...
"...DARK PLACES...
"...TO PROTECT SPALDING.
"I WANTED TO KILL BLACKHEART.
"TO BE RID OF DAIMON AND HIS WRETCHED DEMON KIND.
"AND BECAUSE... BECAUSE IT WOULD BRING ME PLEASURE.
HSSSSSSSSSSS!

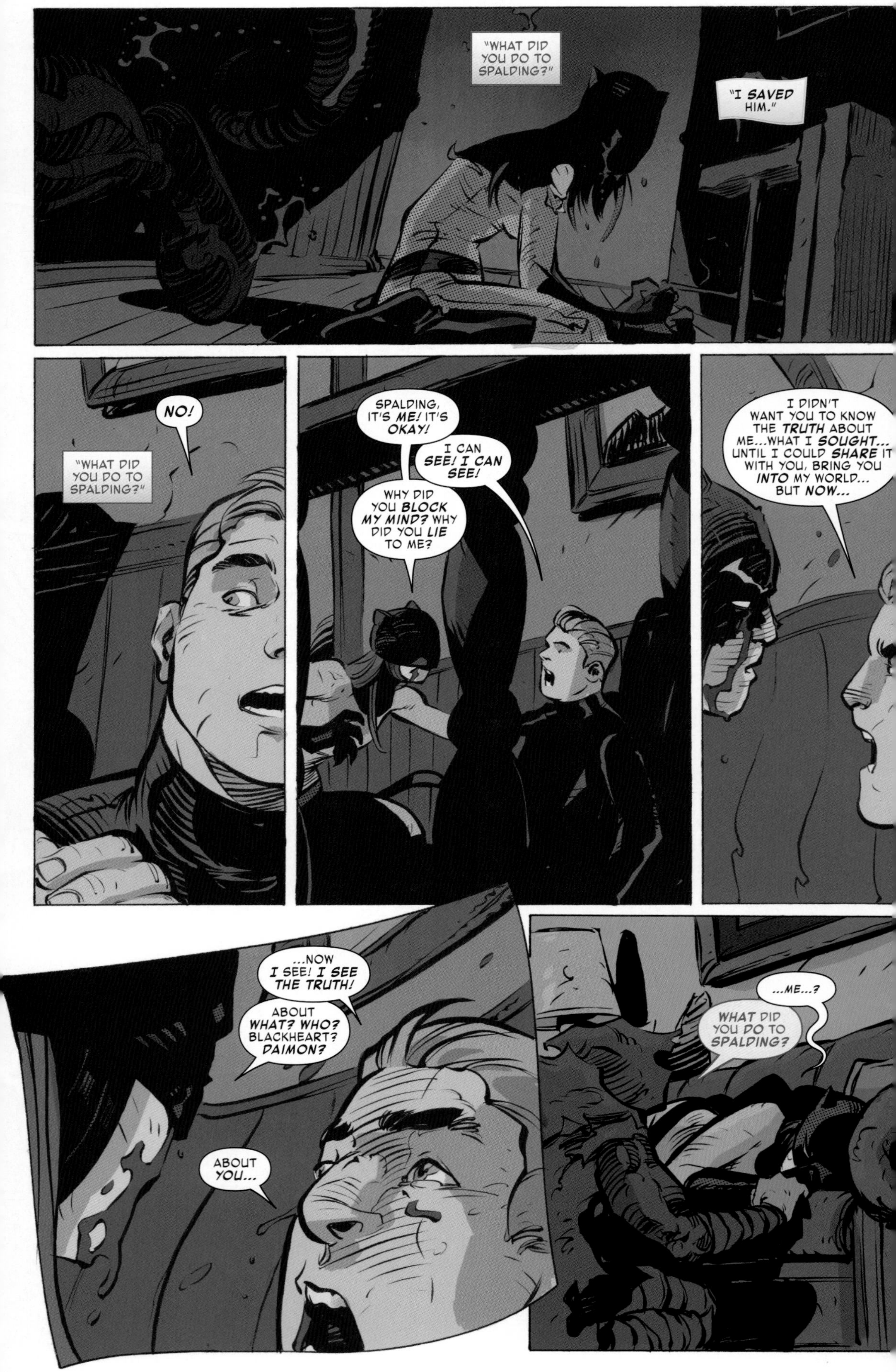
"WHAT DID YOU DO TO SPALDING?"
"I SAVED HIM."
NO!
"WHAT DID YOU DO TO SPALDING?"
SPALDING, IT'S ME! IT'S OKAY!
I CAN SEE! I CAN SEE!
WHY DID YOU BLOCK MY MIND? WHY DID YOU LIE TO ME?
I DIDN'T WANT YOU TO KNOW THE TRUTH ABOUT ME...WHAT I SOUGHT... UNTIL I COULD SHARE IT WITH YOU, BRING YOU INTO MY WORLD... BUT NOW...
...NOW I SEE! I SEE THE TRUTH!
ABOUT WHAT? WHO? BLACKHEART? DAIMON?
ABOUT YOU...
...ME...?
WHAT DID YOU DO TO SPALDING?

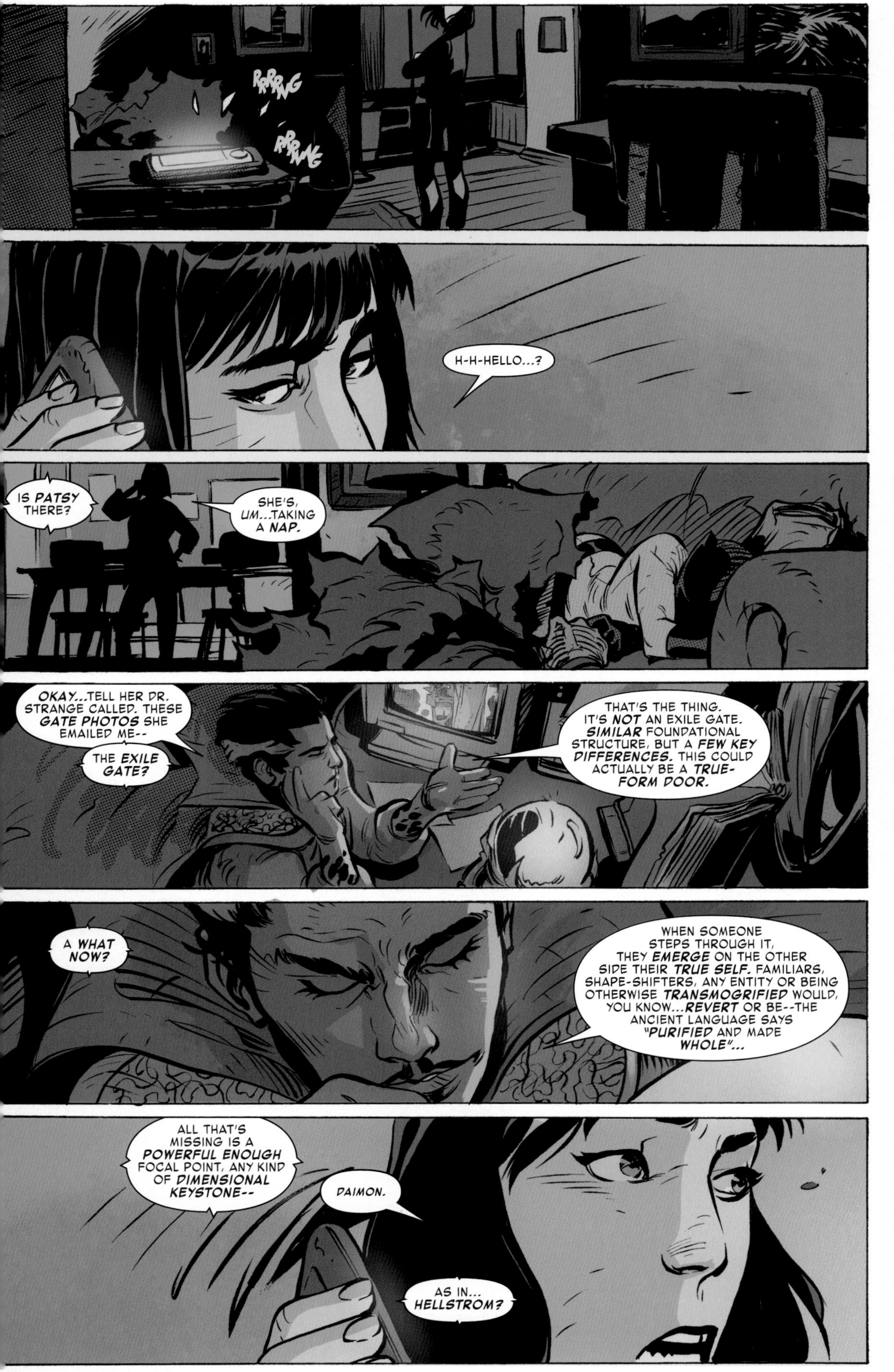
RRRRNG
RRRRNG
H-H-HELLO...?
IS PATSY THERE?
SHE'S, UM...TAKING A NAP.
OKAY...TELL HER DR. STRANGE CALLED. THESE GATE PHOTOS SHE EMAILED ME--
THE EXILE GATE?
THAT'S THE THING. IT'S NOT AN EXILE GATE. SIMILAR FOUNDATIONAL STRUCTURE, BUT A FEW KEY DIFFERENCES. THIS COULD ACTUALLY BE A TRUE-FORM DOOR.
A WHAT NOW?
WHEN SOMEONE STEPS THROUGH IT, THEY EMERGE ON THE OTHER SIDE THEIR TRUE SELF. FAMILIARS, SHAPE-SHIFTERS, ANY ENTITY OR BEING OTHERWISE TRANSMOGRIFIED WOULD, YOU KNOW...REVERT OR BE--THE ANCIENT LANGUAGE SAYS "PURIFIED AND MADE WHOLE"...
ALL THAT'S MISSING IS A POWERFUL ENOUGH FOCAL POINT, ANY KIND OF DIMENSIONAL KEYSTONE--
DAIMON.
AS IN... HELLSTROM?

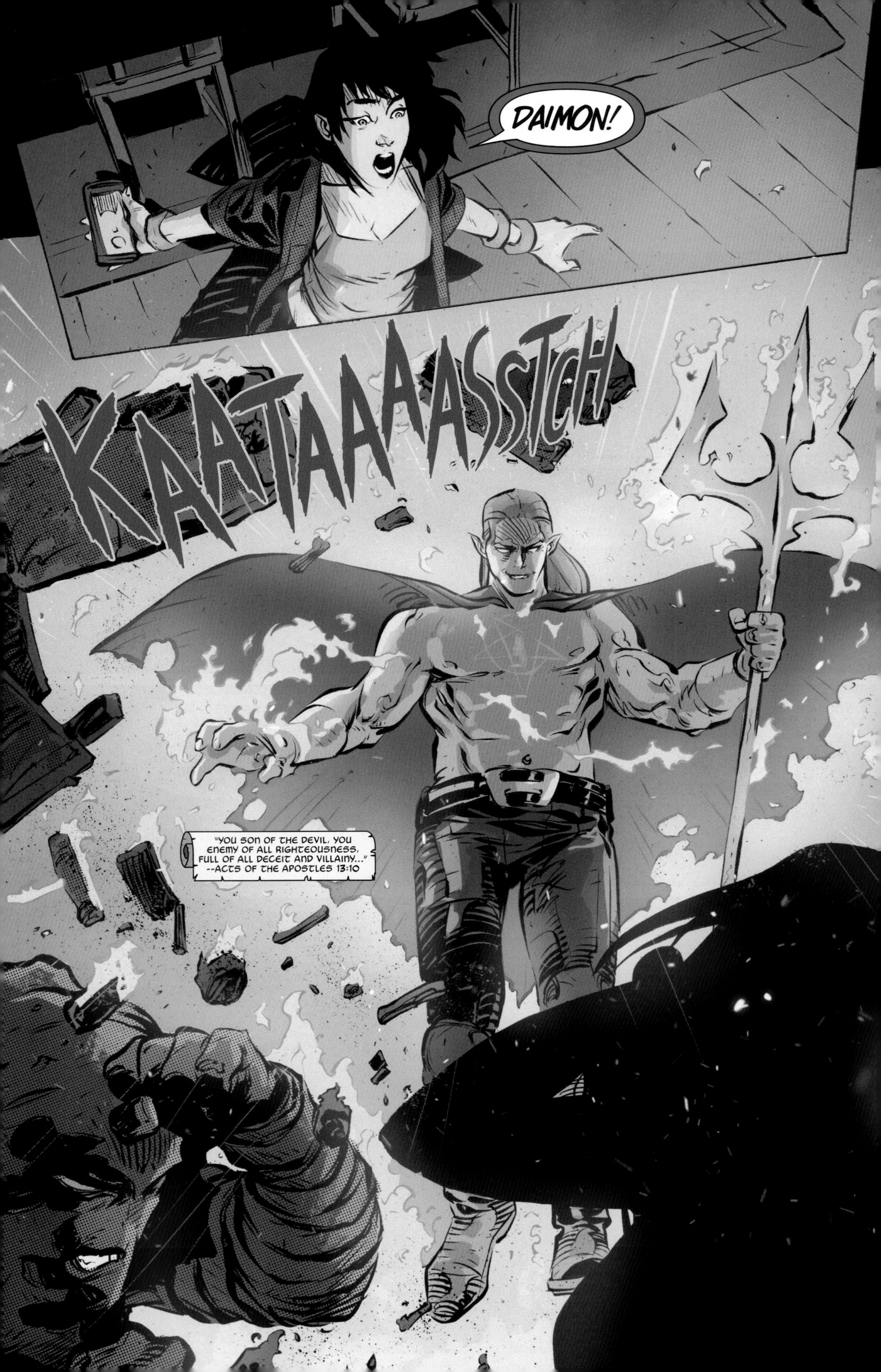
DAIMON!
KAATAAAASSTCH
"YOU SON OF THE DEVIL, YOU ENEMY OF ALL RIGHTEOUSNESS, FULL OF ALL DECEIT AND VILLAINY..." --ACTS OF THE APOSTLES 13:10

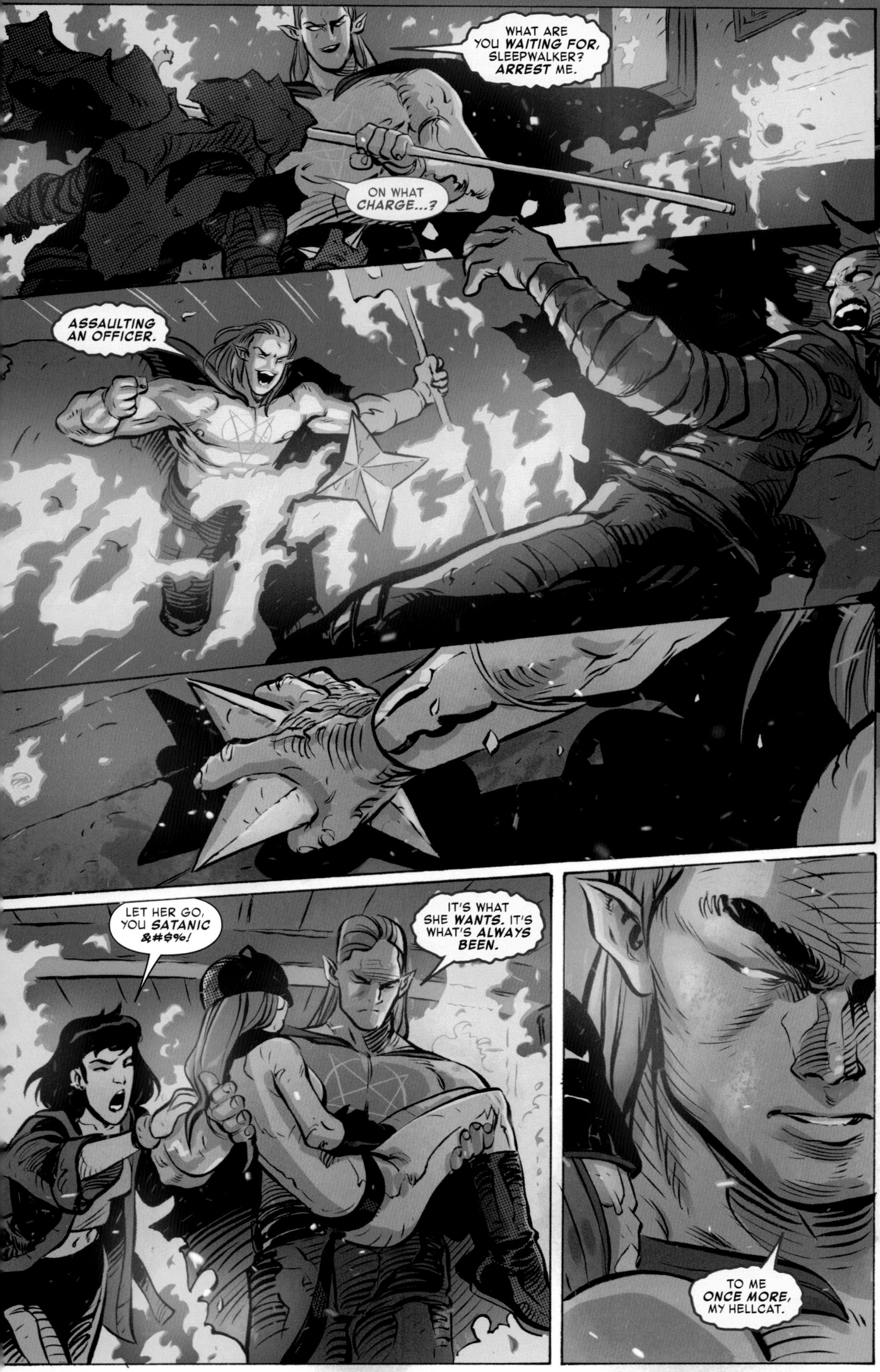
WHAT ARE YOU WAITING FOR, SLEEPWALKER? ARREST ME.
ON WHAT CHARGE...?
ASSAULTING AN OFFICER.
LET HER GO, YOU SATANIC &#$%!
IT'S WHAT SHE WANTS. IT'S WHAT'S ALWAYS BEEN.
TO ME ONCE MORE, MY HELLCAT.

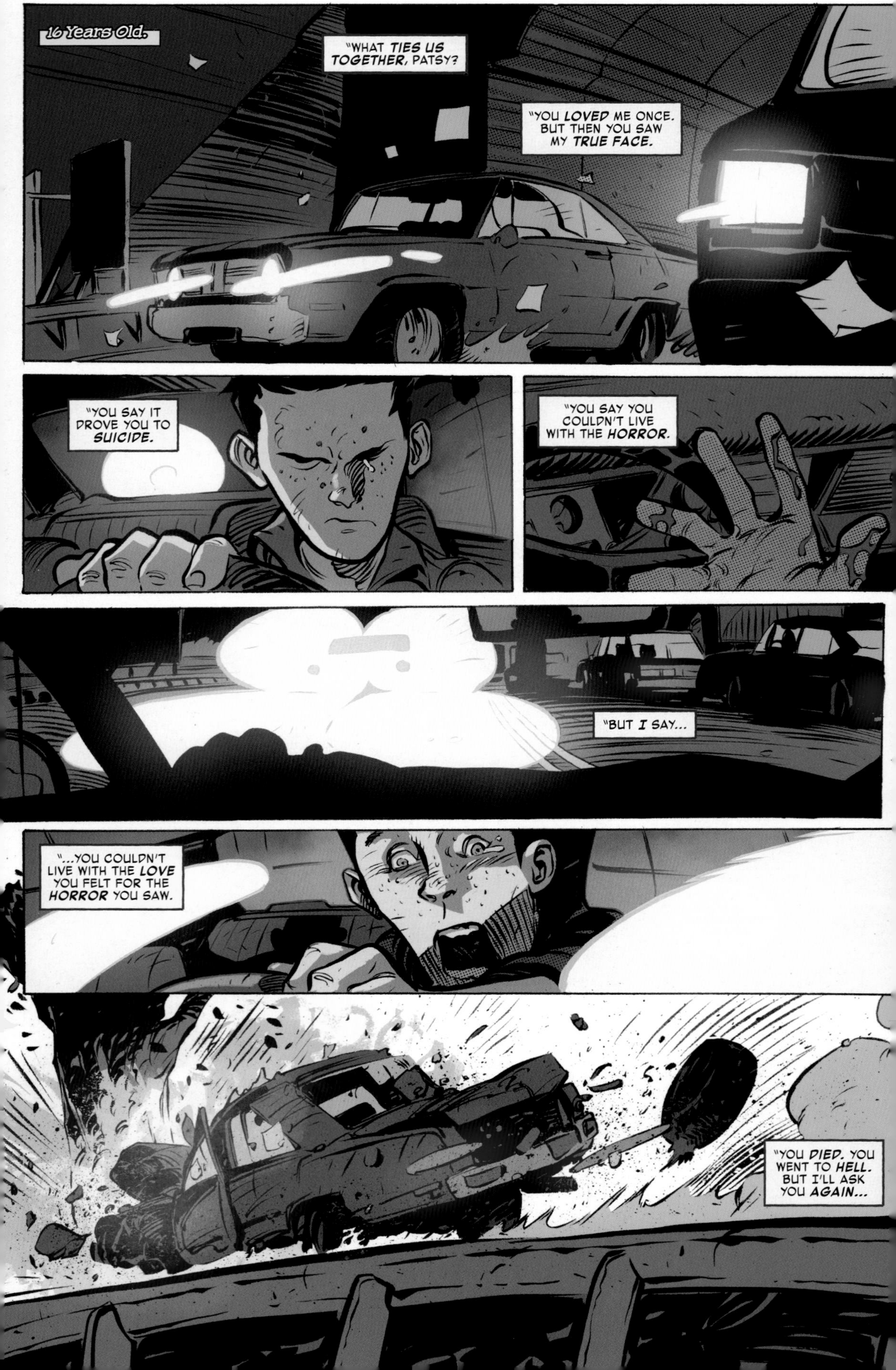
16 Years Old.
"WHAT TIES US TOGETHER, PATSY?
"YOU LOVED ME ONCE. BUT THEN YOU SAW MY TRUE FACE.
"YOU SAY IT DROVE YOU TO SUICIDE.
"YOU SAY YOU COULDN'T LIVE WITH THE HORROR.
"BUT I SAY...
"...YOU COULDN'T LIVE WITH THE LOVE YOU FELT FOR THE HORROR YOU SAW.
"YOU DIED. YOU WENT TO HELL. BUT I'LL ASK YOU AGAIN...

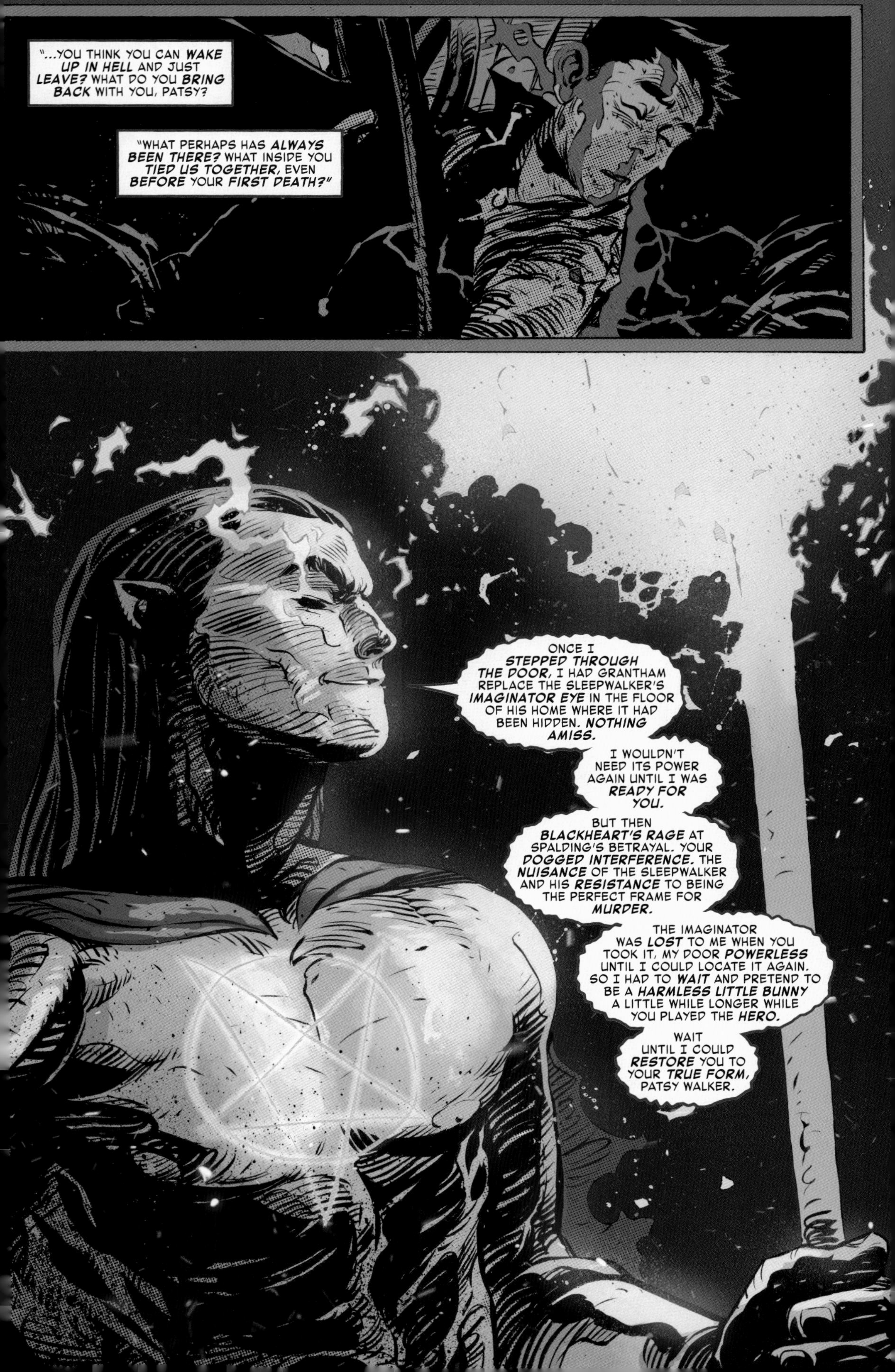
"...YOU THINK YOU CAN WAKE UP IN HELL AND JUST LEAVE? WHAT DO YOU BRING BACK WITH YOU, PATSY?
"WHAT PERHAPS HAS ALWAYS BEEN THERE? WHAT INSIDE YOU TIED US TOGETHER, EVEN BEFORE YOUR FIRST DEATH?"
ONCE I STEPPED THROUGH THE DOOR, I HAD GRANTHAM REPLACE THE SLEEPWALKER'S IMAGINATOR EYE IN THE FLOOR OF HIS HOME WHERE IT HAD BEEN HIDDEN. NOTHING AMISS.
I WOULDN'T NEED ITS POWER AGAIN UNTIL I WAS READY FOR YOU.
BUT THEN BLACKHEART'S RAGE AT SPALDING'S BETRAYAL. YOUR DOGGED INTERFERENCE. THE NUISANCE OF THE SLEEPWALKER AND HIS RESISTANCE TO BEING THE PERFECT FRAME FOR MURDER.
THE IMAGINATOR WAS LOST TO ME WHEN YOU TOOK IT, MY DOOR POWERLESS UNTIL I COULD LOCATE IT AGAIN. SO I HAD TO WAIT AND PRETEND TO BE A HARMLESS LITTLE BUNNY A LITTLE WHILE LONGER WHILE YOU PLAYED THE HERO.
WAIT UNTIL I COULD RESTORE YOU TO YOUR TRUE FORM, PATSY WALKER.

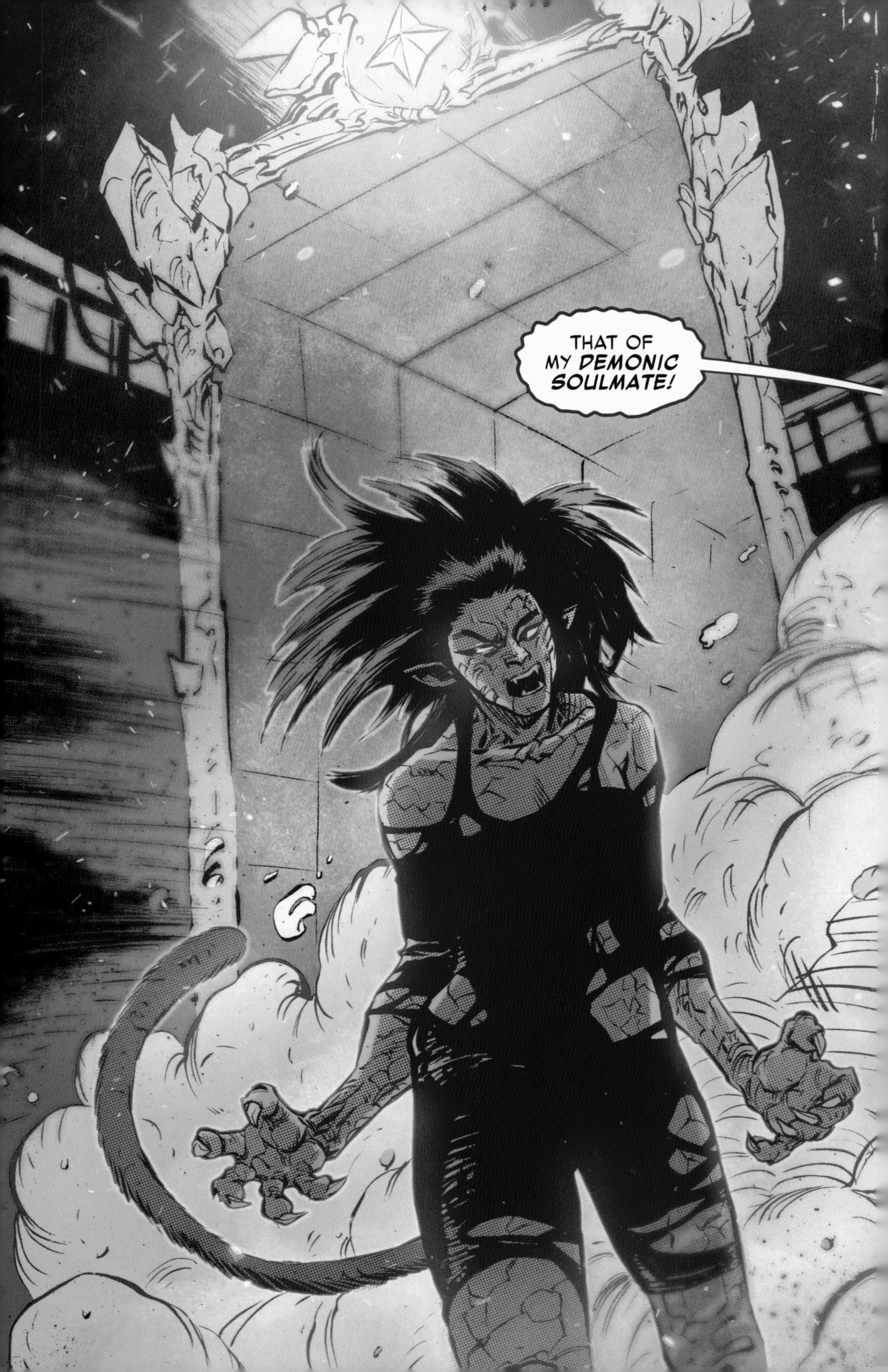
THAT OF MY DEMONIC SOULMATE!

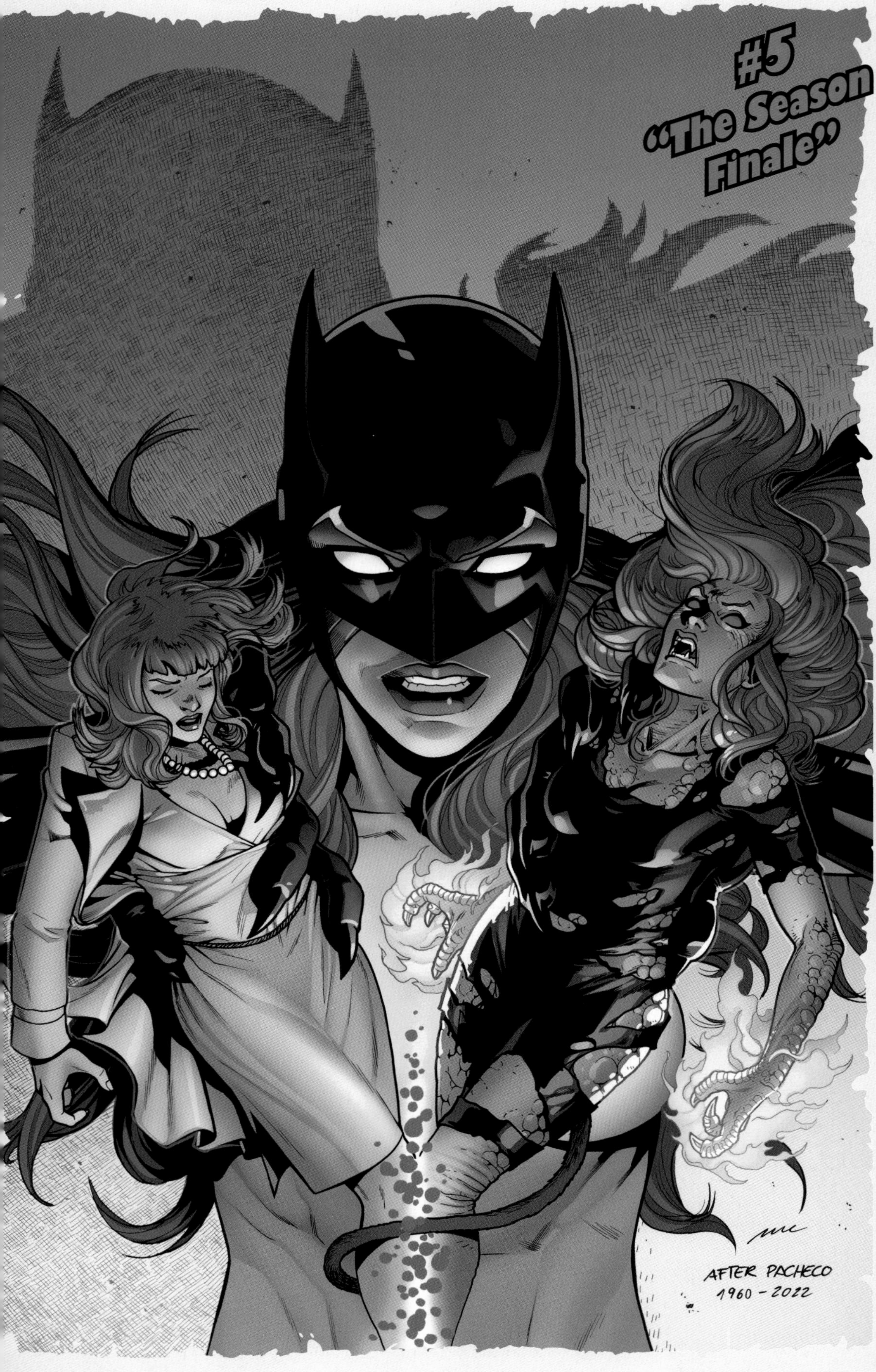
#5
"The Season Finale"
AFTER PACHECO
1960 - 2022

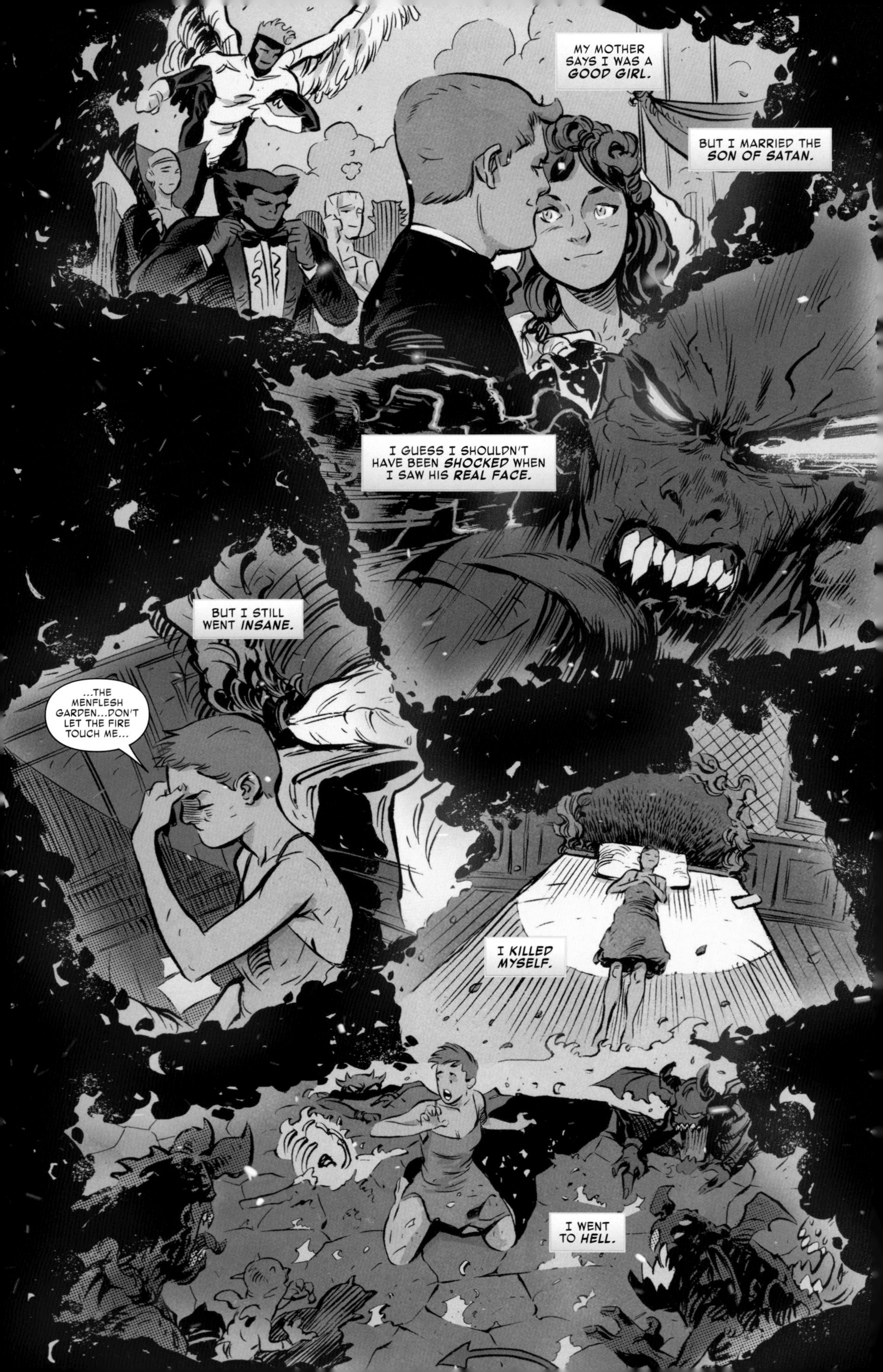
MY MOTHER SAYS I WAS A GOOD GIRL.
BUT I MARRIED THE SON OF SATAN.
I GUESS I SHOULDN'T HAVE BEEN SHOCKED WHEN I SAW HIS REAL FACE.
BUT I STILL WENT INSANE.
...THE MENFLESH GARDEN...DON'T LET THE FIRE TOUCH ME...
I KILLED MYSELF.
I WENT TO HELL.

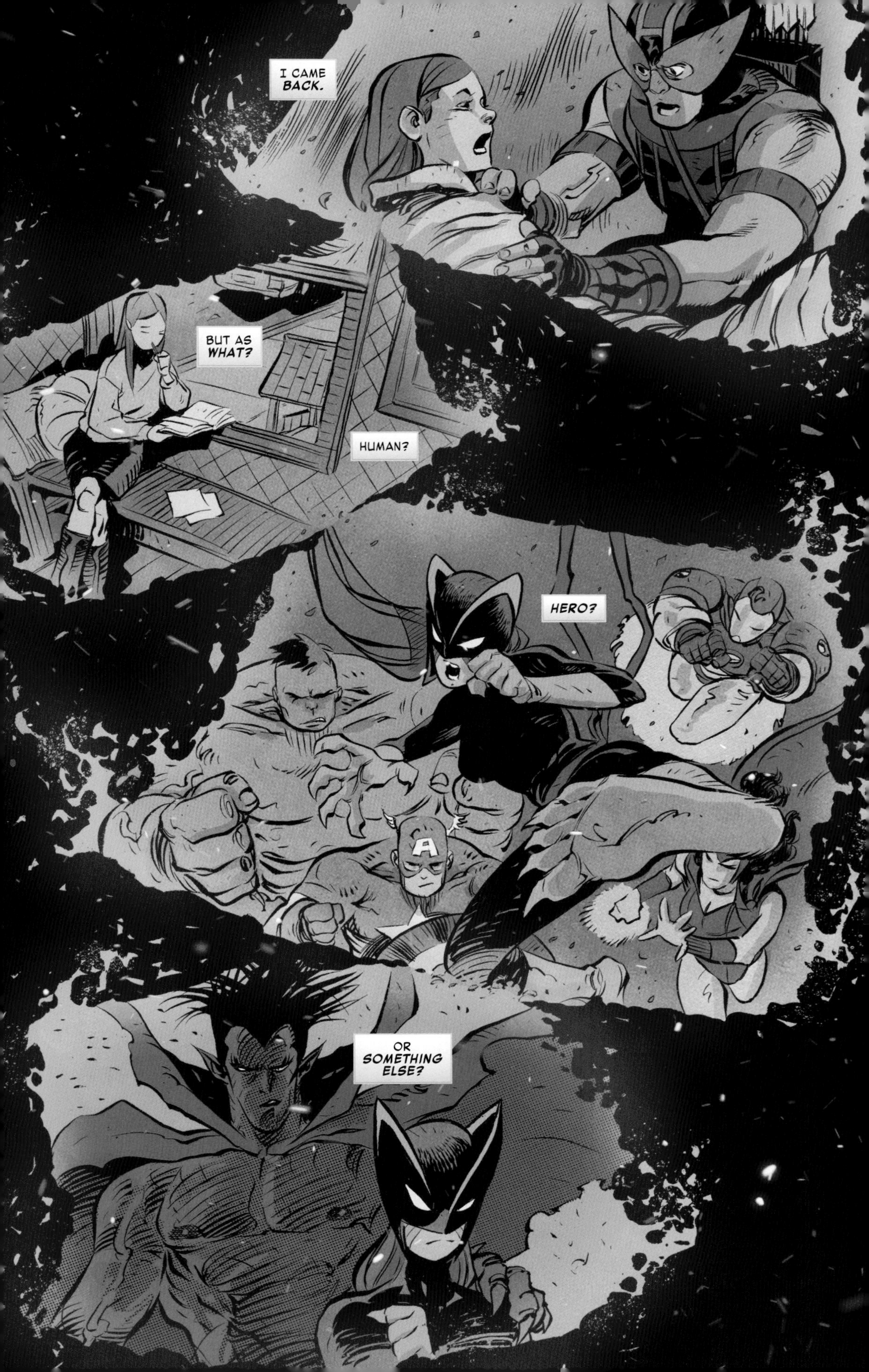
I CAME BACK.
BUT AS WHAT?
HUMAN?
HERO?
OR SOMETHING ELSE?

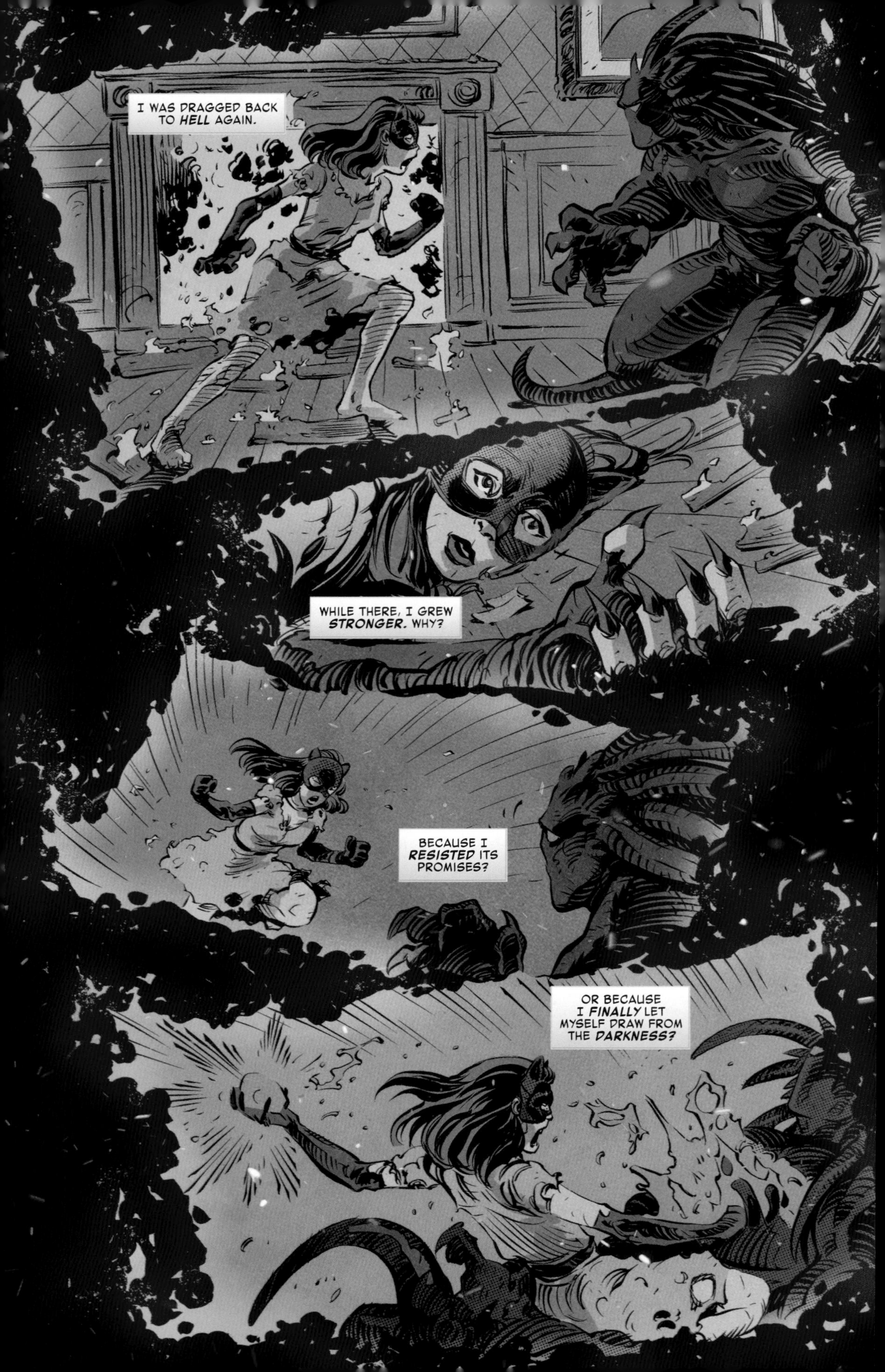
I WAS DRAGGED BACK TO HELL AGAIN.
WHILE THERE, I GREW STRONGER. WHY?
BECAUSE I RESISTED ITS PROMISES?
OR BECAUSE I FINALLY LET MYSELF DRAW FROM THE DARKNESS?

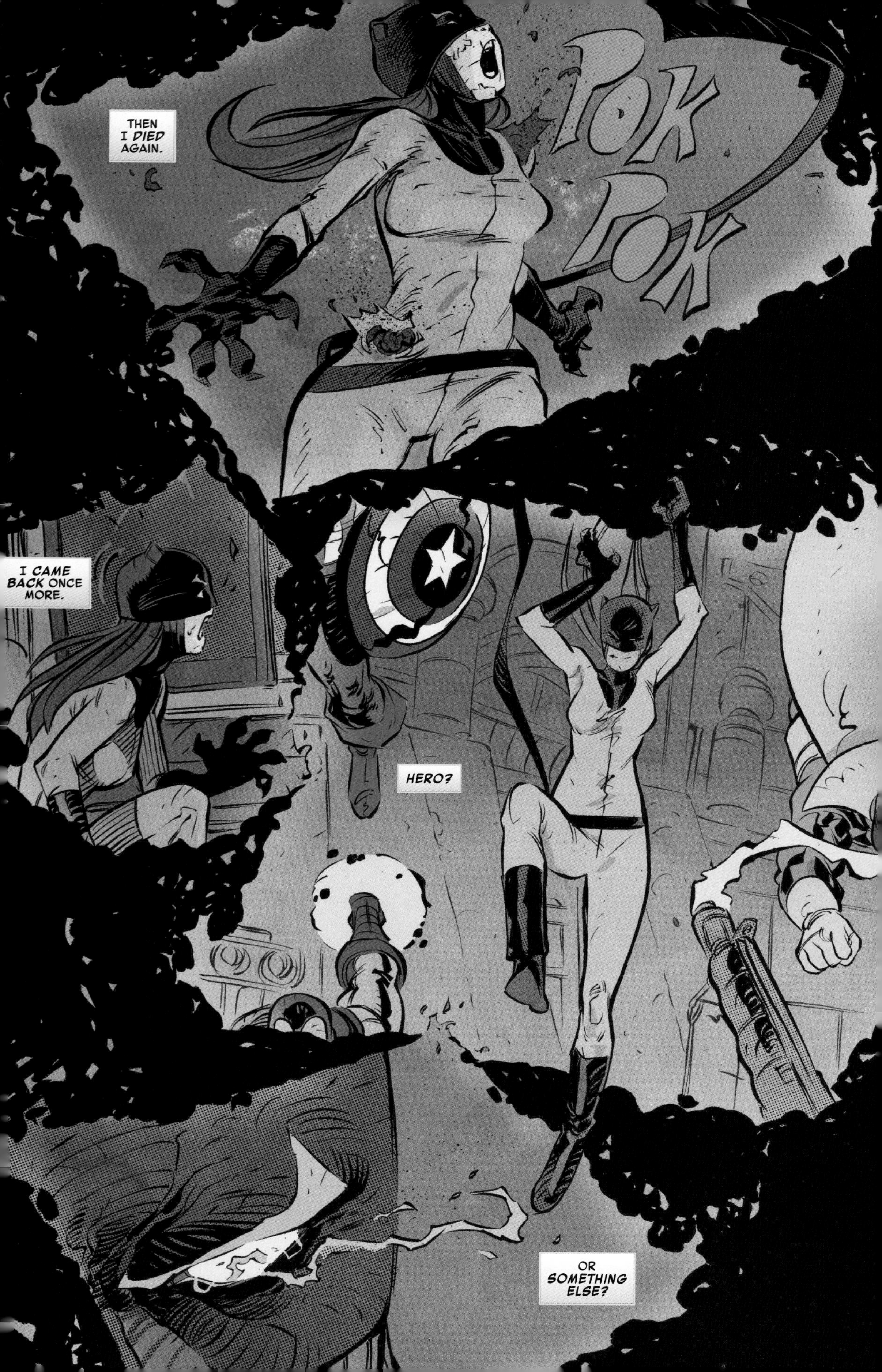
THEN I DIED AGAIN.
POK POK POK
I CAME BACK ONCE MORE.
HERO?
OR SOMETHING ELSE?

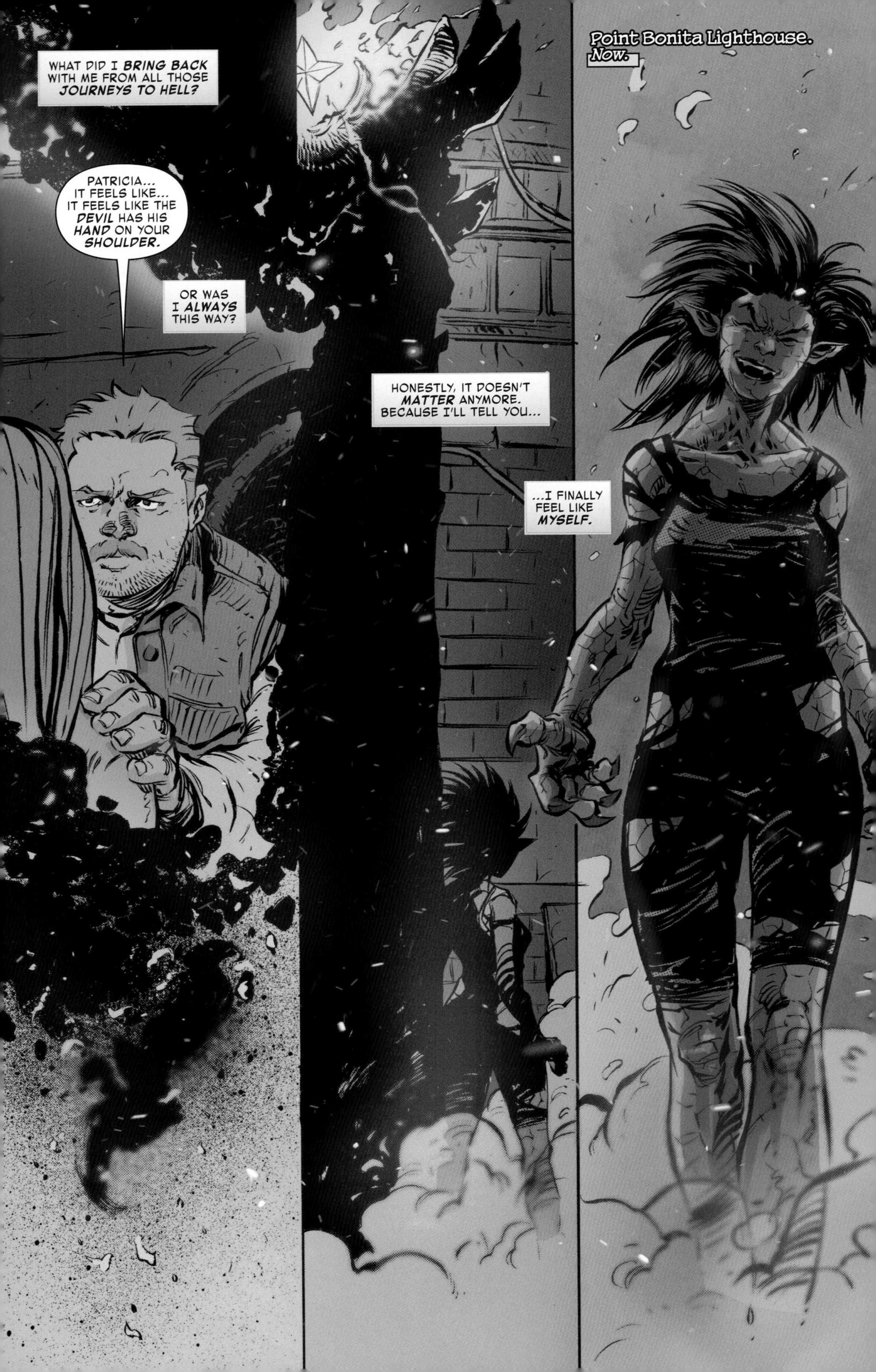
WHAT DID I BRING BACK WITH ME FROM ALL THOSE JOURNEYS TO HELL?
PATRICIA... IT FEELS LIKE... IT FEELS LIKE THE DEVIL HAS HIS HAND ON YOUR SHOULDER.
OR WAS I ALWAYS THIS WAY?
HONESTLY, IT DOESN'T MATTER ANYMORE. BECAUSE I'LL TELL YOU...
Point Bonita Lighthouse.
Now.
...I FINALLY FEEL LIKE MYSELF.

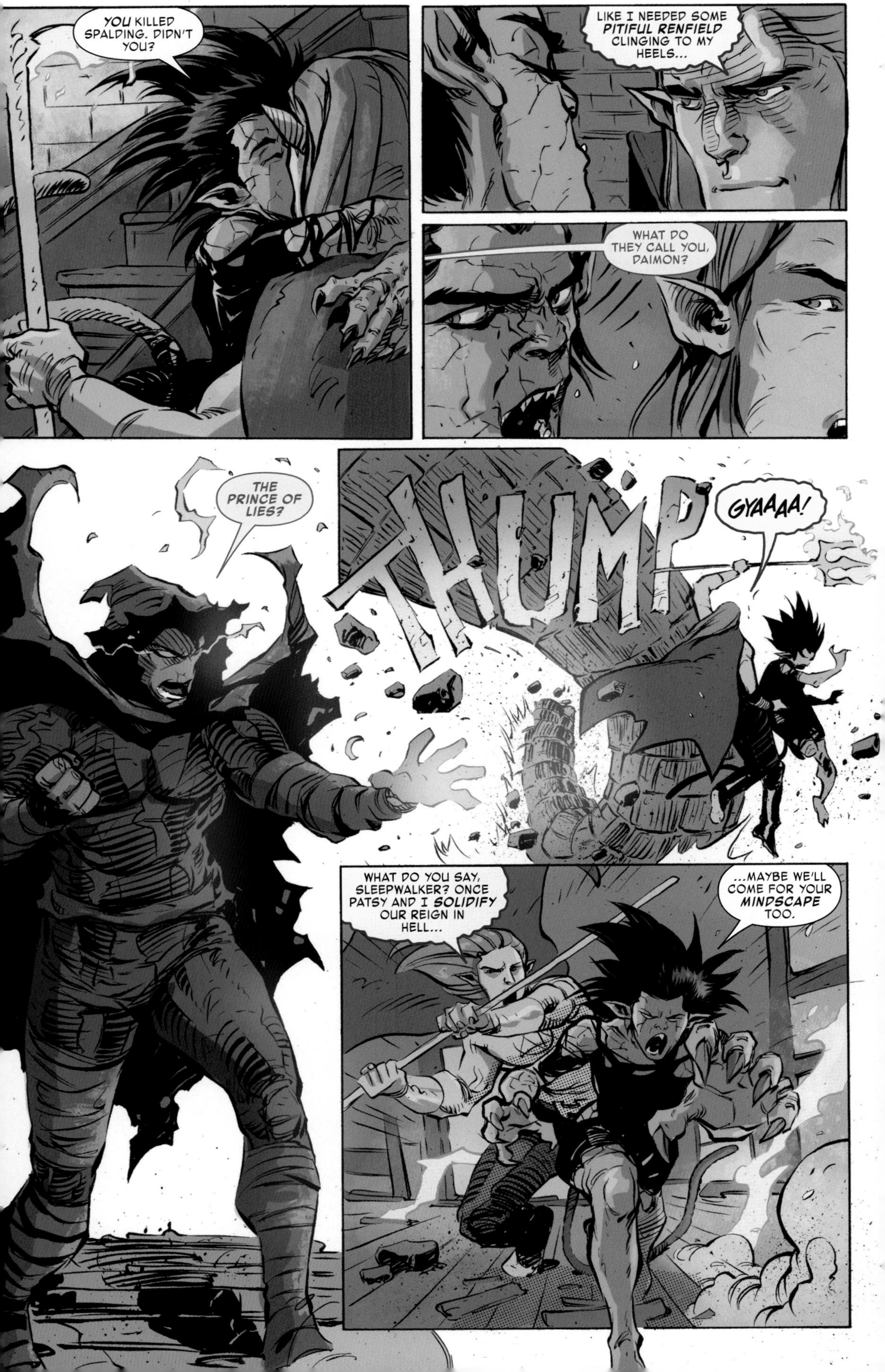
YOU KILLED SPALDING. DIDN'T YOU?
LIKE I NEEDED SOME PITIFUL RENFIELD CLINGING TO MY HEELS...
WHAT DO THEY CALL YOU, DAIMON?
THE PRINCE OF LIES?
THUMP
GYAAAA!
WHAT DO YOU SAY, SLEEPWALKER? ONCE PATSY AND I SOLIDIFY OUR REIGN IN HELL...
...MAYBE WE'LL COME FOR YOUR MINDSCAPE TOO.

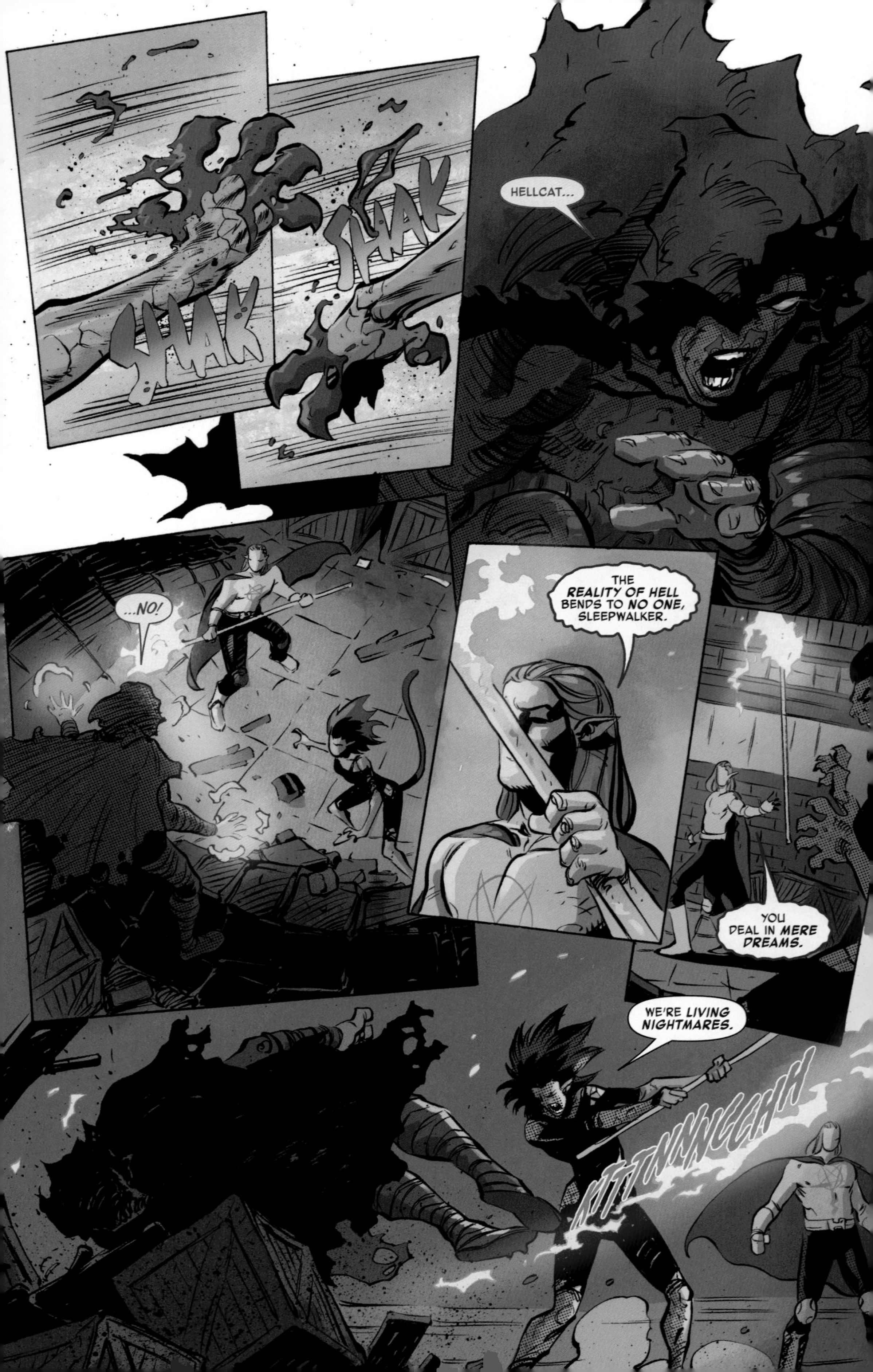
SHAK
SHAK
HELLCAT...
...NO!
THE REALITY OF HELL BENDS TO NO ONE, SLEEPWALKER.
YOU DEAL IN MERE DREAMS.
WE'RE LIVING NIGHTMARES.
KTTTNNNCCHH

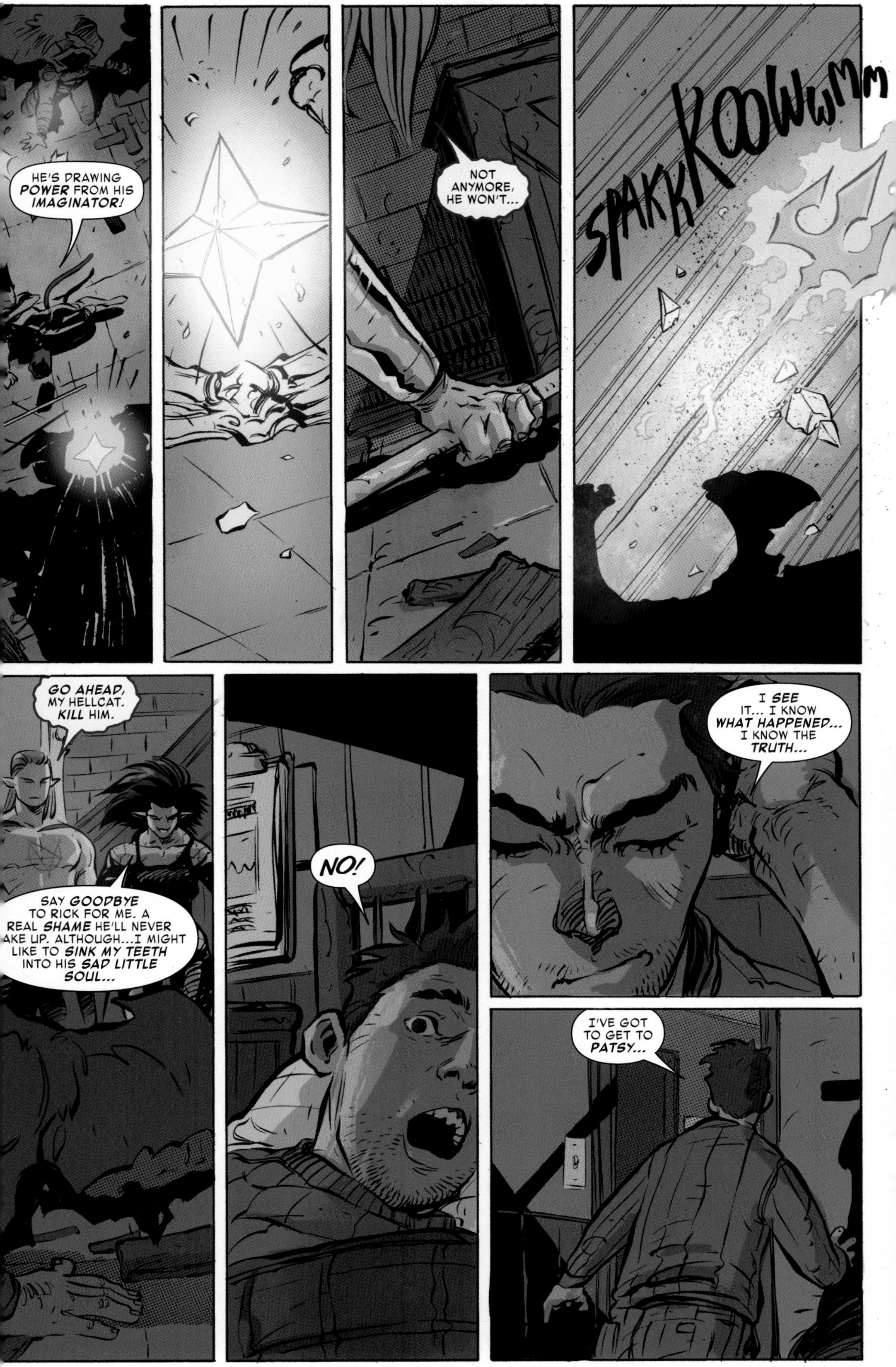
HE'S DRAWING POWER FROM HIS IMAGINATOR!
NOT ANYMORE, HE WON'T...
SPAKKROOWWMM
GO AHEAD, MY HELLCAT. KILL HIM.
SAY GOODBYE TO RICK FOR ME. A REAL SHAME HE'LL NEVER AKE UP. ALTHOUGH...I MIGHT LIKE TO SINK MY TEETH INTO HIS SAD LITTLE SOUL...
NO!
I SEE IT... I KNOW WHAT HAPPENED... I KNOW THE TRUTH...
I'VE GOT TO GET TO PATSY...

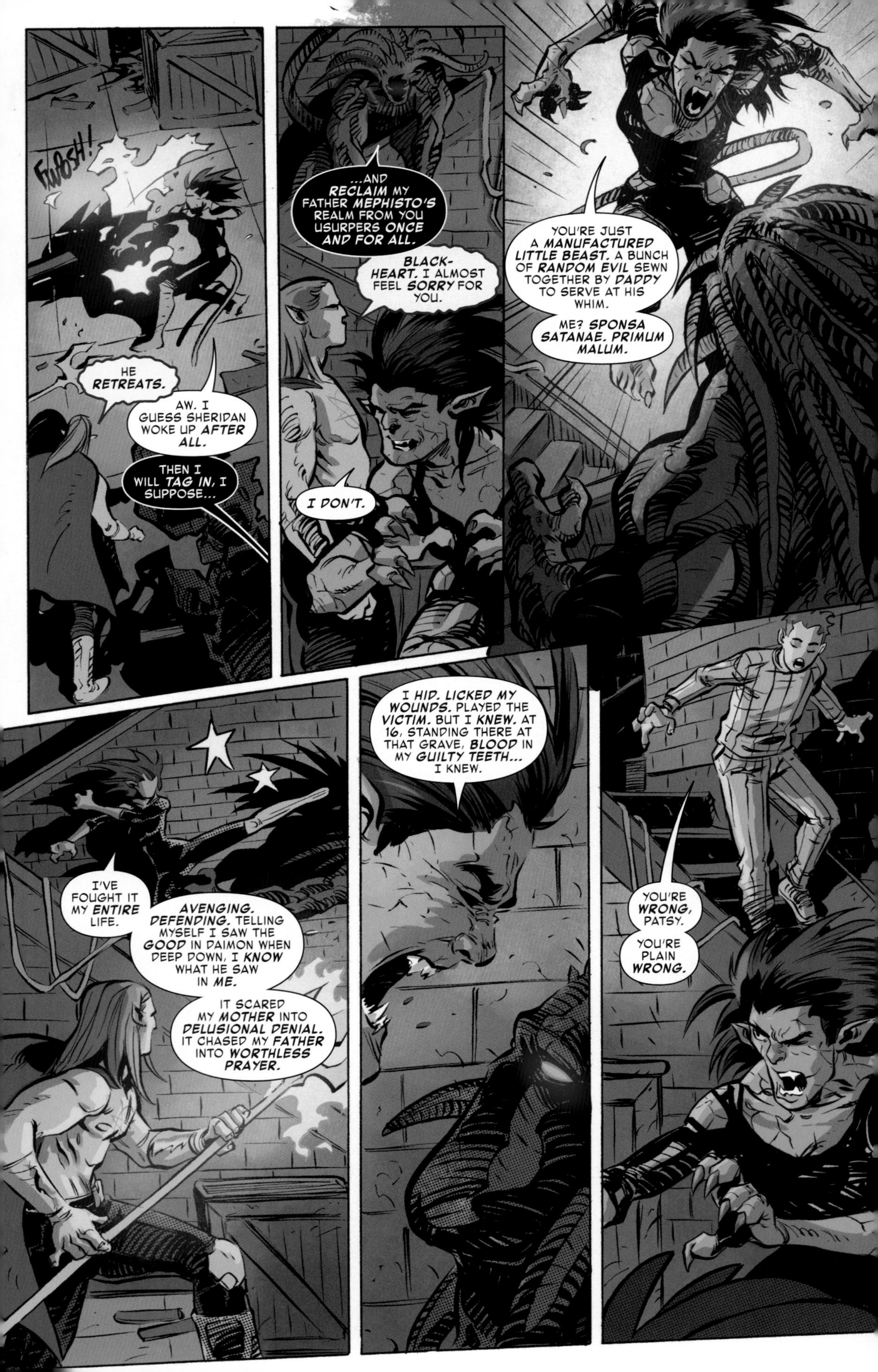
FWOOSH!
HE RETREATS.
AW. I GUESS SHERIDAN WOKE UP AFTER ALL.
THEN I WILL TAG IN, I SUPPOSE...
...AND RECLAIM MY FATHER MEPHISTO'S REALM FROM YOU USURPERS ONCE AND FOR ALL.
BLACK-HEART. I ALMOST FEEL SORRY FOR YOU.
I DON'T.
YOU'RE JUST A MANUFACTURED LITTLE BEAST. A BUNCH OF RANDOM EVIL SEWN TOGETHER BY DADDY TO SERVE AT HIS WHIM.
ME? SPONSA SATANAE. PRIMUM MALUM.
I'VE FOUGHT IT MY ENTIRE LIFE.
AVENGING. DEFENDING. TELLING MYSELF I SAW THE GOOD IN DAIMON WHEN DEEP DOWN, I KNOW WHAT HE SAW IN ME.
IT SCARED MY MOTHER INTO DELUSIONAL DENIAL. IT CHASED MY FATHER INTO WORTHLESS PRAYER.
I HID. LICKED MY WOUNDS. PLAYED THE VICTIM. BUT I KNEW. AT 16, STANDING THERE AT THAT GRAVE, BLOOD IN MY GUILTY TEETH... I KNEW.
YOU'RE WRONG, PATSY.
YOU'RE PLAIN WRONG.

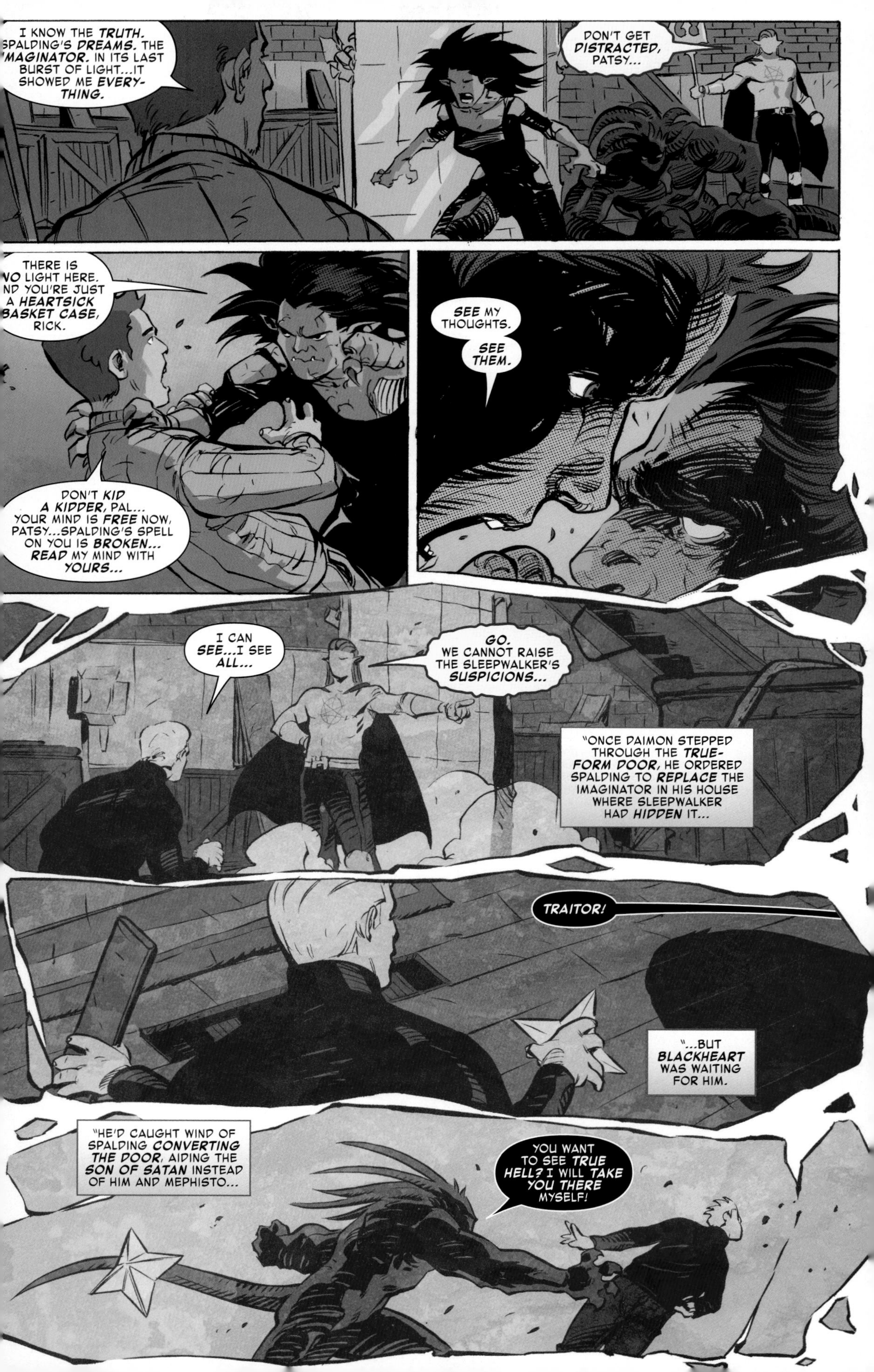
I KNOW THE TRUTH. SPALDING'S DREAMS. THE IMAGINATOR. IN ITS LAST BURST OF LIGHT...IT SHOWED ME EVERYTHING.
DON'T GET DISTRACTED, PATSY...
THERE IS NO LIGHT HERE. AND YOU'RE JUST A HEARTSICK BASKET CASE, RICK.
DON'T KID A KIDDER, PAL... YOUR MIND IS FREE NOW, PATSY...SPALDING'S SPELL ON YOU IS BROKEN... READ MY MIND WITH YOURS...
SEE MY THOUGHTS.
SEE THEM.
I CAN SEE...I SEE ALL...
GO. WE CANNOT RAISE THE SLEEPWALKER'S SUSPICIONS...
"ONCE DAIMON STEPPED THROUGH THE TRUE-FORM DOOR, HE ORDERED SPALDING TO REPLACE THE IMAGINATOR IN HIS HOUSE WHERE SLEEPWALKER HAD HIDDEN IT...
TRAITOR!
"...BUT BLACKHEART WAS WAITING FOR HIM.
"HE'D CAUGHT WIND OF SPALDING CONVERTING THE DOOR, AIDING THE SON OF SATAN INSTEAD OF HIM AND MEPHISTO...
YOU WANT TO SEE TRUE HELL? I WILL TAKE YOU THERE MYSELF!

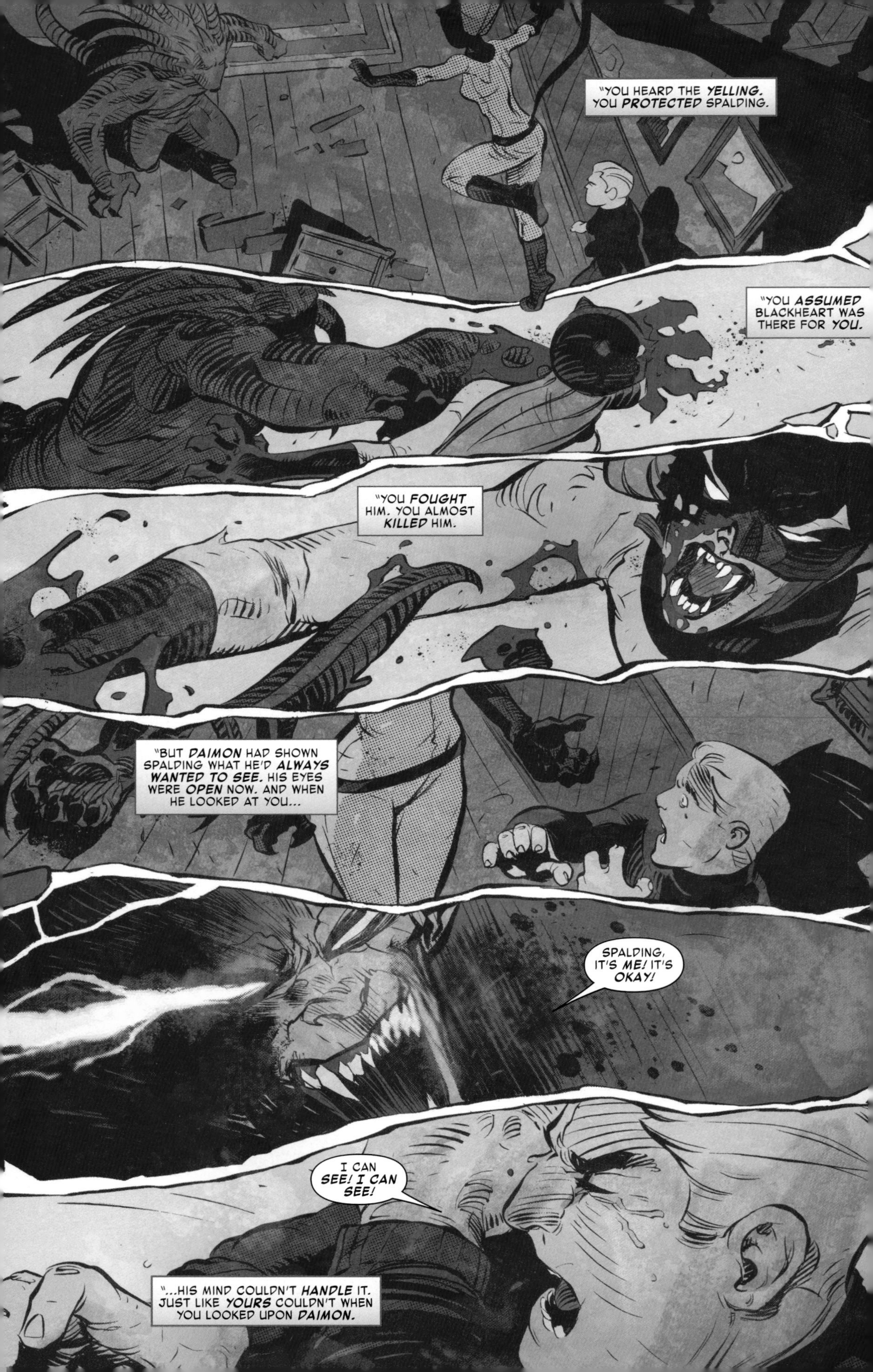
"YOU HEARD THE YELLING. YOU PROTECTED SPALDING.
"YOU ASSUMED BLACKHEART WAS THERE FOR YOU.
"YOU FOUGHT HIM. YOU ALMOST KILLED HIM.
"BUT DAIMON HAD SHOWN SPALDING WHAT HE'D ALWAYS WANTED TO SEE. HIS EYES WERE OPEN NOW. AND WHEN HE LOOKED AT YOU...
SPALDING, IT'S ME! IT'S OKAY!
I CAN SEE! I CAN SEE!
"...HIS MIND COULDN'T HANDLE IT. JUST LIKE YOURS COULDN'T WHEN YOU LOOKED UPON DAIMON.

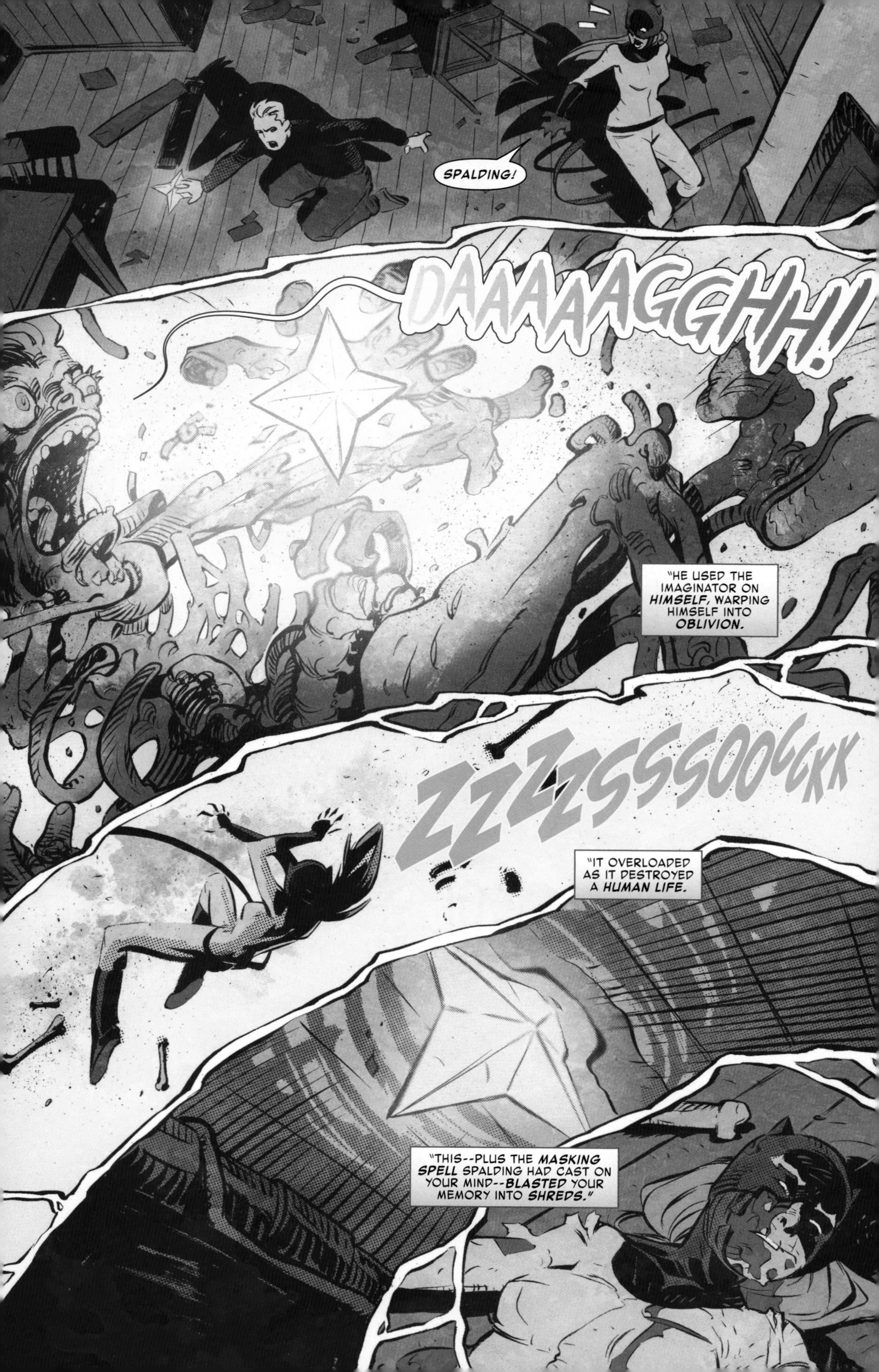
SPALDING!
DAAAAAAGGHH!
"HE USED THE IMAGINATOR ON HIMSELF, WARPING HIMSELF INTO OBLIVION.
ZZZZSSSSOOOCKK
"IT OVERLOADED AS IT DESTROYED A HUMAN LIFE.
"THIS--PLUS THE MASKING SPELL SPALDING HAD CAST ON YOUR MIND--BLASTED YOUR MEMORY INTO SHREDS."

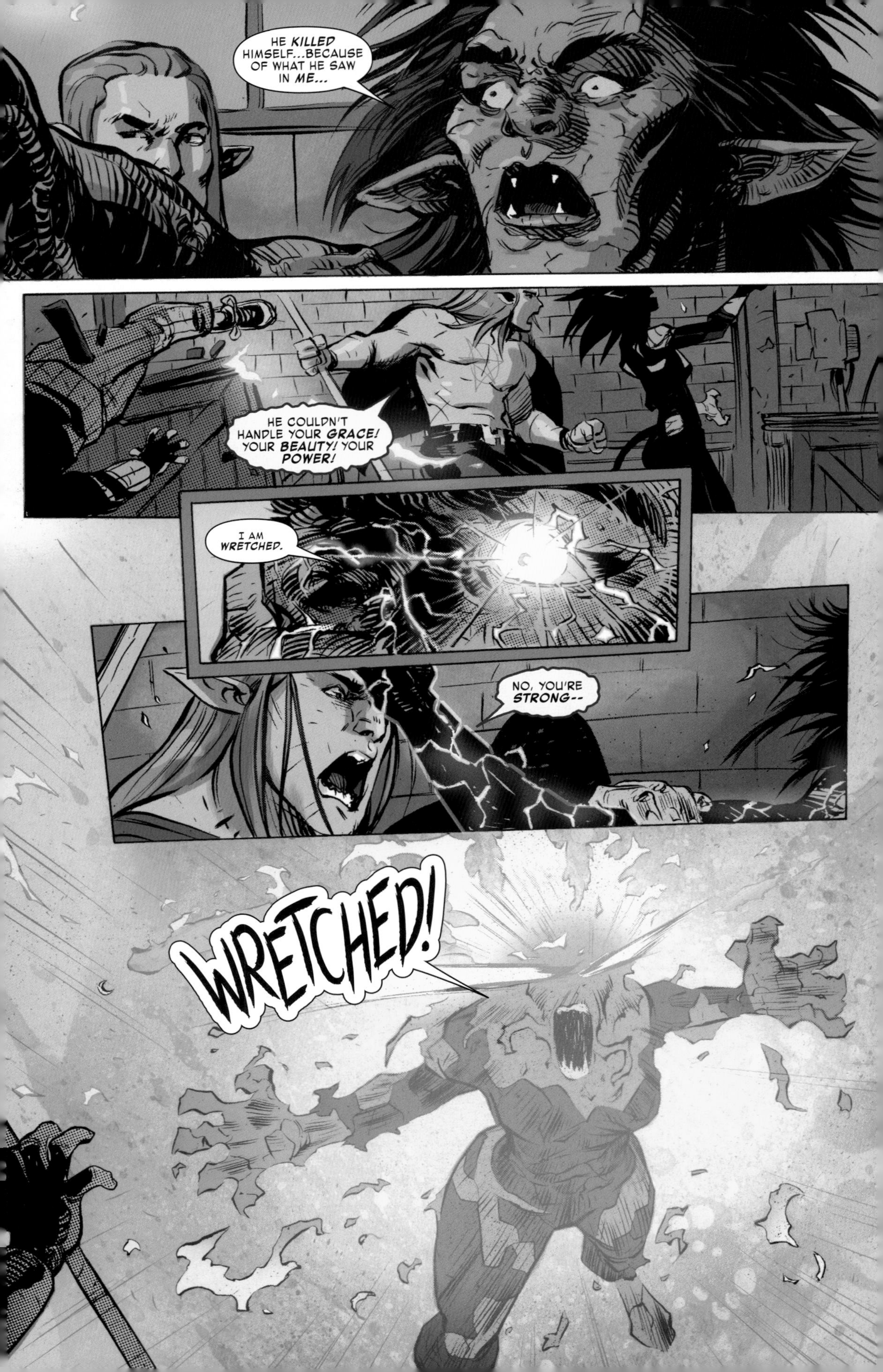
HE KILLED HIMSELF...BECAUSE OF WHAT HE SAW IN ME...
HE COULDN'T HANDLE YOUR GRACE! YOUR BEAUTY! YOUR POWER!
I AM WRETCHED.
NO, YOU'RE STRONG--
WRETCHED!

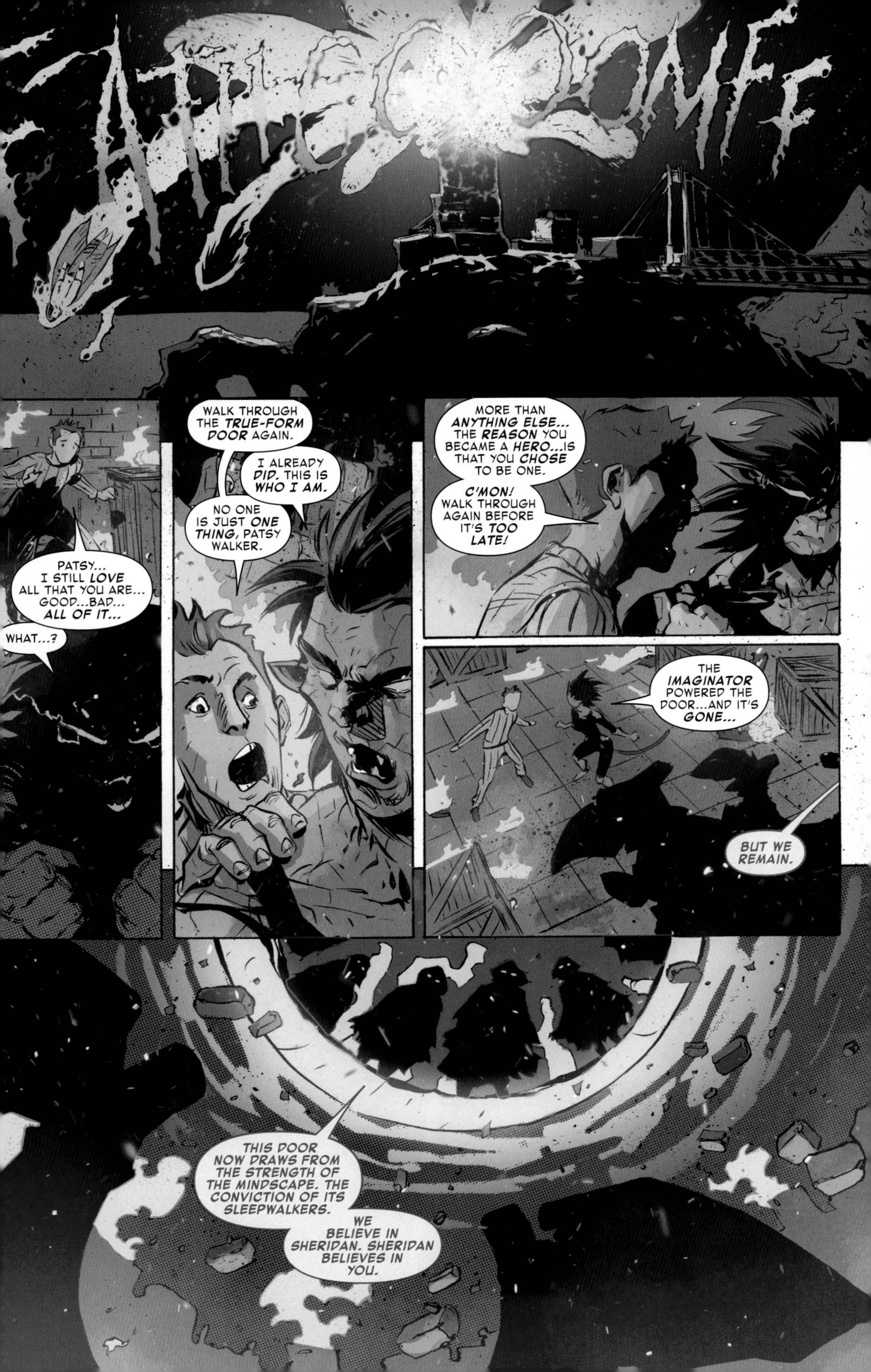
WALK THROUGH THE TRUE-FORM DOOR AGAIN.
I ALREADY DID. THIS IS WHO I AM.
NO ONE IS JUST ONE THING, PATSY WALKER.
PATSY... I STILL LOVE ALL THAT YOU ARE... GOOD...BAD... ALL OF IT...
WHAT...?
MORE THAN ANYTHING ELSE... THE REASON YOU BECAME A HERO...IS THAT YOU CHOSE TO BE ONE.
C'MON! WALK THROUGH AGAIN BEFORE IT'S TOO LATE!
THE IMAGINATOR POWERED THE DOOR...AND IT'S GONE...
BUT WE REMAIN.
THIS DOOR NOW DRAWS FROM THE STRENGTH OF THE MINDSCAPE. THE CONVICTION OF ITS SLEEPWALKERS.
WE BELIEVE IN SHERIDAN. SHERIDAN BELIEVES IN YOU.

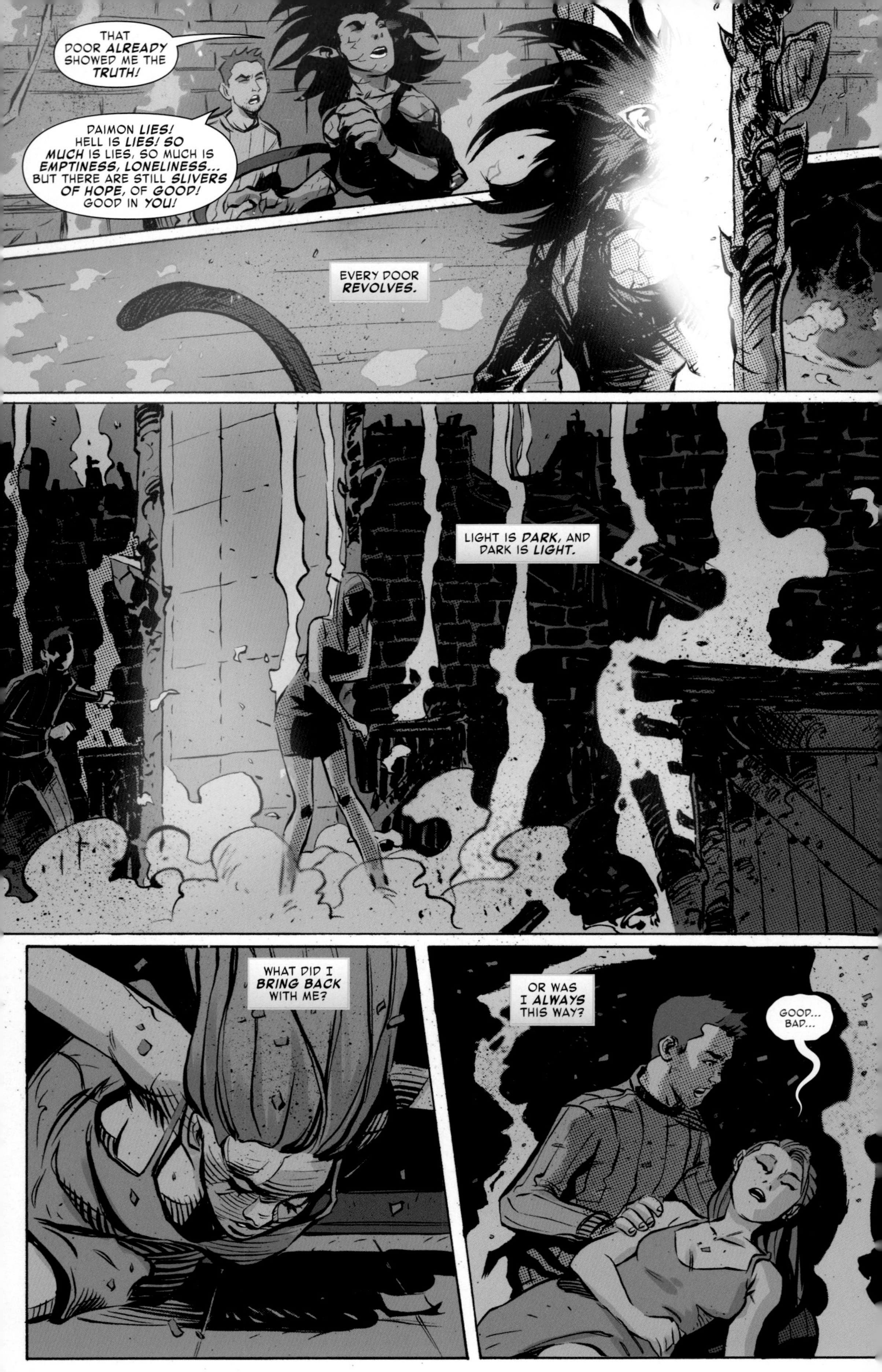

THAT DOOR ALREADY SHOWED ME THE TRUTH!
DAIMON LIES! HELL IS LIES! SO MUCH IS LIES, SO MUCH IS EMPTINESS, LONELINESS... BUT THERE ARE STILL SLIVERS OF HOPE, OF GOOD! GOOD IN YOU!
EVERY DOOR REVOLVES.
LIGHT IS DARK, AND DARK IS LIGHT.
WHAT DID I BRING BACK WITH ME?
OR WAS I ALWAYS THIS WAY?
GOOD... BAD...

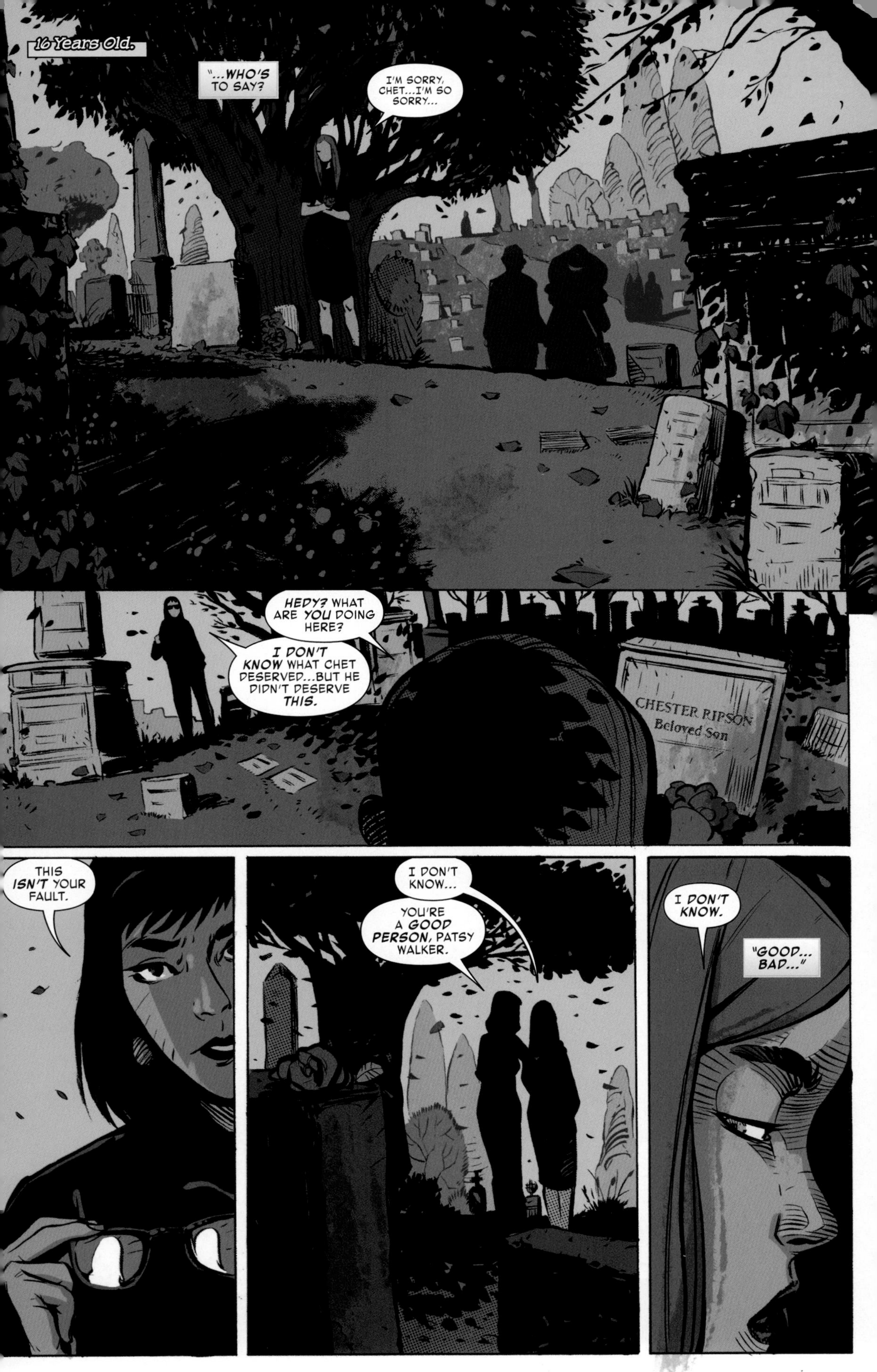
16 Years Old.
"...WHO'S TO SAY?
I'M SORRY, CHET...I'M SO SORRY...
HEDY? WHAT ARE YOU DOING HERE?
I DON'T KNOW WHAT CHET DESERVED...BUT HE DIDN'T DESERVE THIS.
CHESTER RIPSON Beloved Son
THIS ISN'T YOUR FAULT.
I DON'T KNOW...
YOU'RE A GOOD PERSON, PATSY WALKER.
I DON'T KNOW.
"GOOD... BAD..."

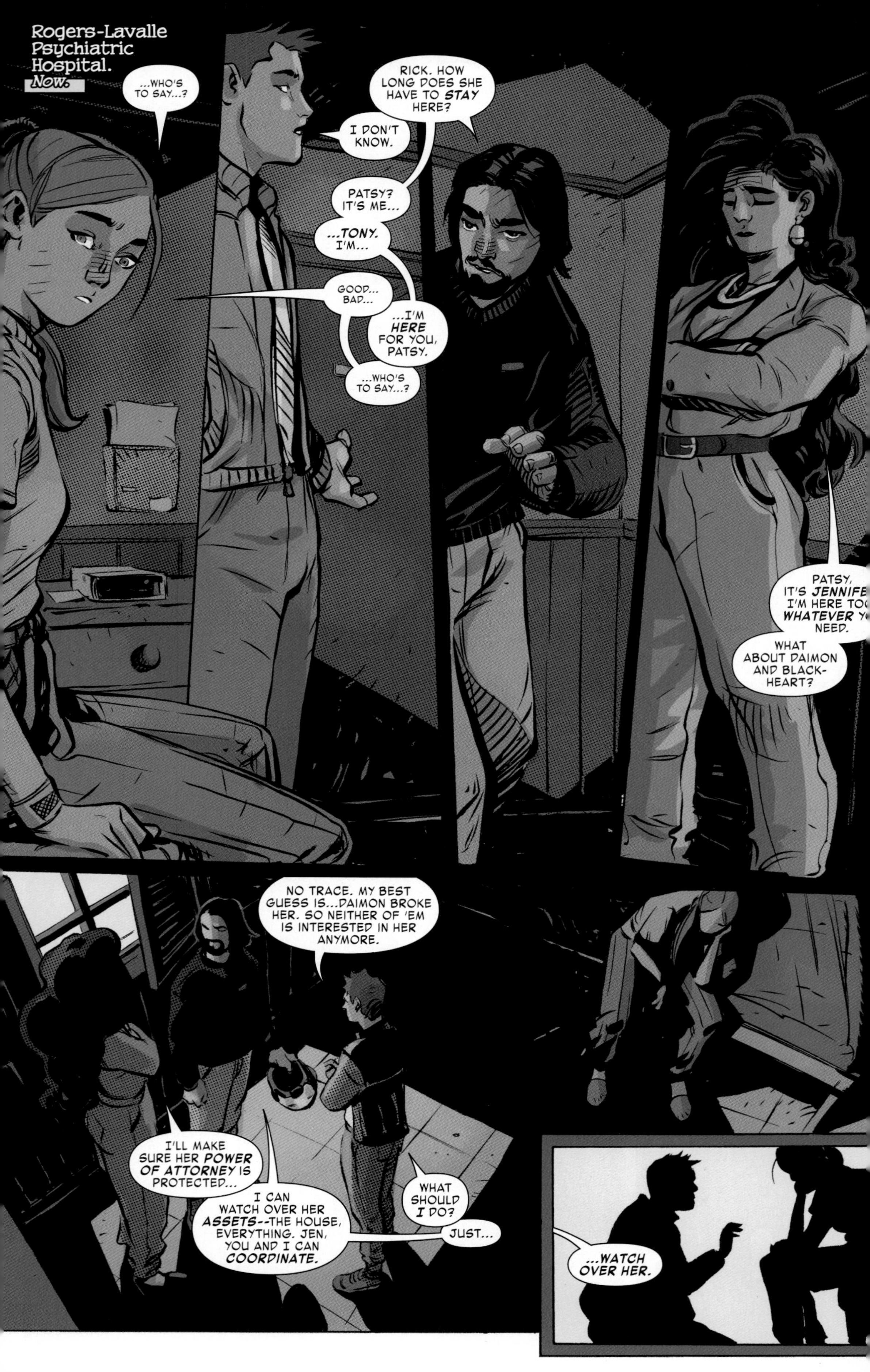
Rogers-Lavalle Psychiatric Hospital. Now.
...WHO'S TO SAY...?
RICK. HOW LONG DOES SHE HAVE TO STAY HERE?
I DON'T KNOW.
PATSY? IT'S ME...
...TONY. I'M...
GOOD... BAD...
...I'M HERE FOR YOU, PATSY.
...WHO'S TO SAY...?
PATSY, IT'S JENNIFE I'M HERE TO WHATEVER Y NEED.
WHAT ABOUT DAIMON AND BLACK-HEART?
NO TRACE. MY BEST GUESS IS...DAIMON BROKE HER. SO NEITHER OF 'EM IS INTERESTED IN HER ANYMORE.
I'LL MAKE SURE HER POWER OF ATTORNEY IS PROTECTED...
I CAN WATCH OVER HER ASSETS--THE HOUSE, EVERYTHING. JEN, YOU AND I CAN COORDINATE.
WHAT SHOULD I DO?
JUST...
...WATCH OVER HER.

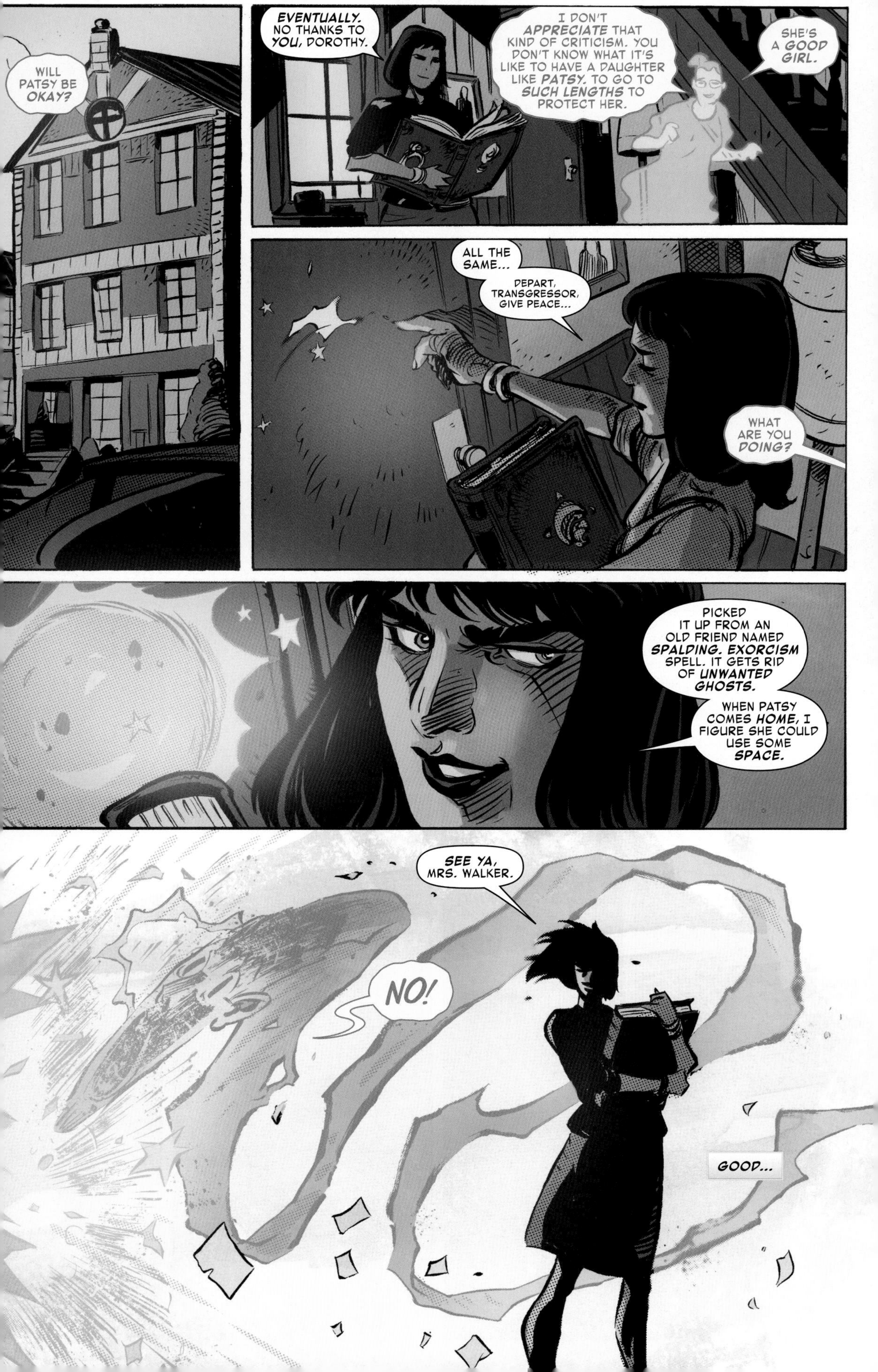
WILL PATSY BE OKAY?
EVENTUALLY. NO THANKS TO YOU, DOROTHY.
I DON'T APPRECIATE THAT KIND OF CRITICISM. YOU DON'T KNOW WHAT IT'S LIKE TO HAVE A DAUGHTER LIKE PATSY. TO GO TO SUCH LENGTHS TO PROTECT HER.
SHE'S A GOOD GIRL.
ALL THE SAME...
DEPART, TRANSGRESSOR, GIVE PEACE...
WHAT ARE YOU DOING?
PICKED IT UP FROM AN OLD FRIEND NAMED SPALDING. EXORCISM SPELL. IT GETS RID OF UNWANTED GHOSTS.
WHEN PATSY COMES HOME, I FIGURE SHE COULD USE SOME SPACE.
SEE YA, MRS. WALKER.
NO!
GOOD...

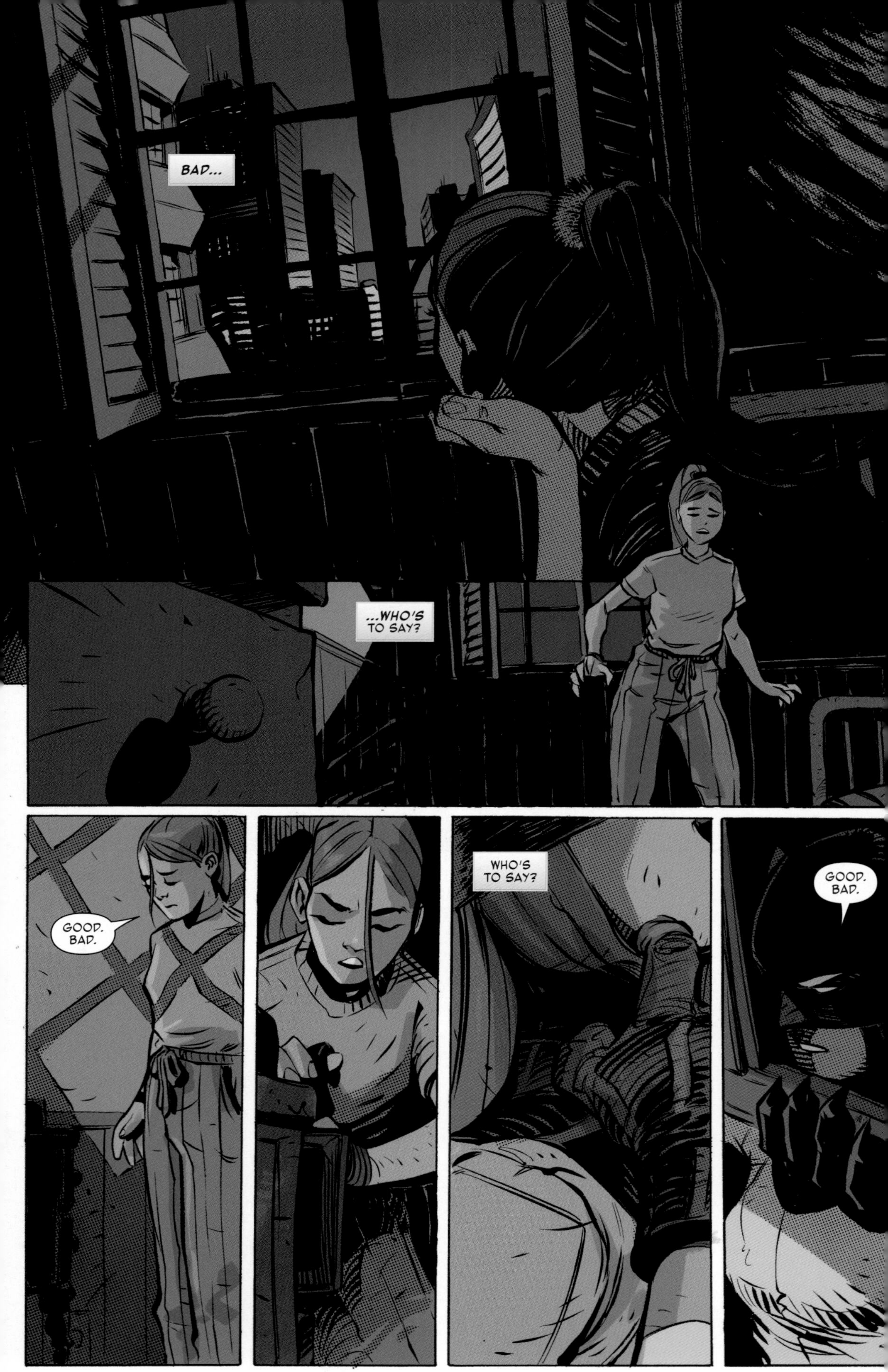
BAD...
...WHO'S TO SAY?
GOOD. BAD.
WHO'S TO SAY?
GOOD. BAD.

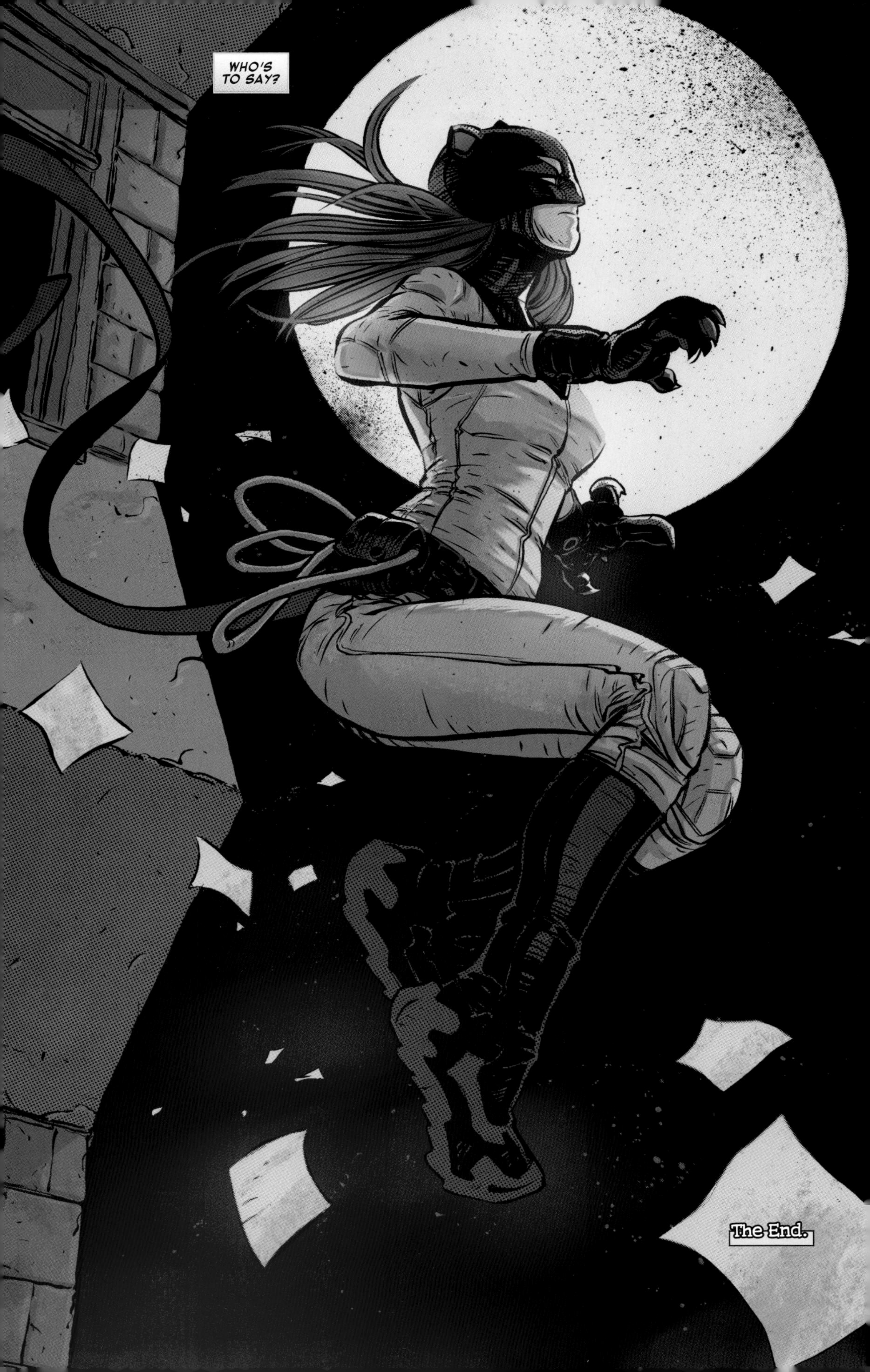
WHO'S TO SAY?
The End.

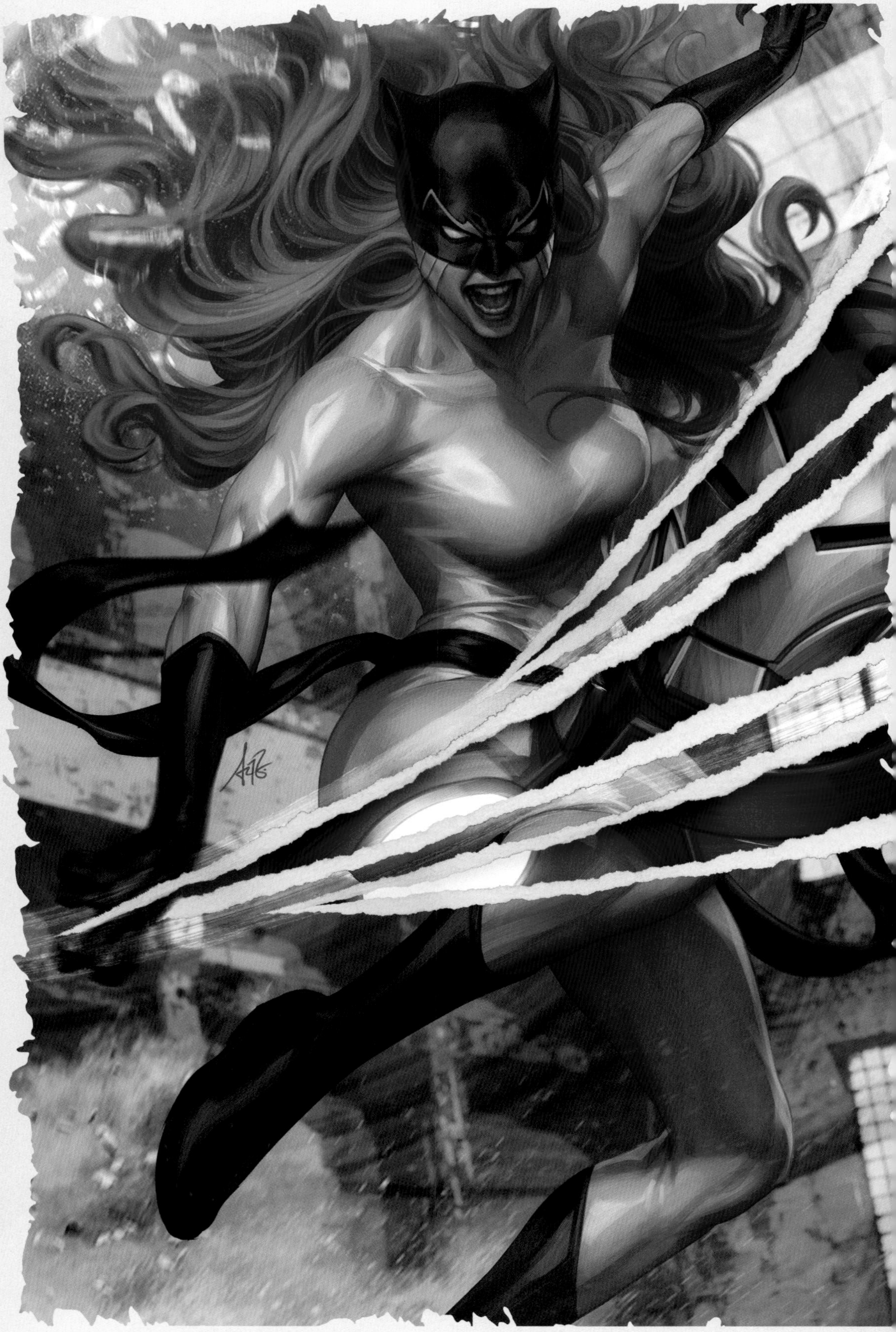

IRON MAN/HELLCAT ANNUAL #1 VARIANT BY
STANLEY "ARTGERM" LAU

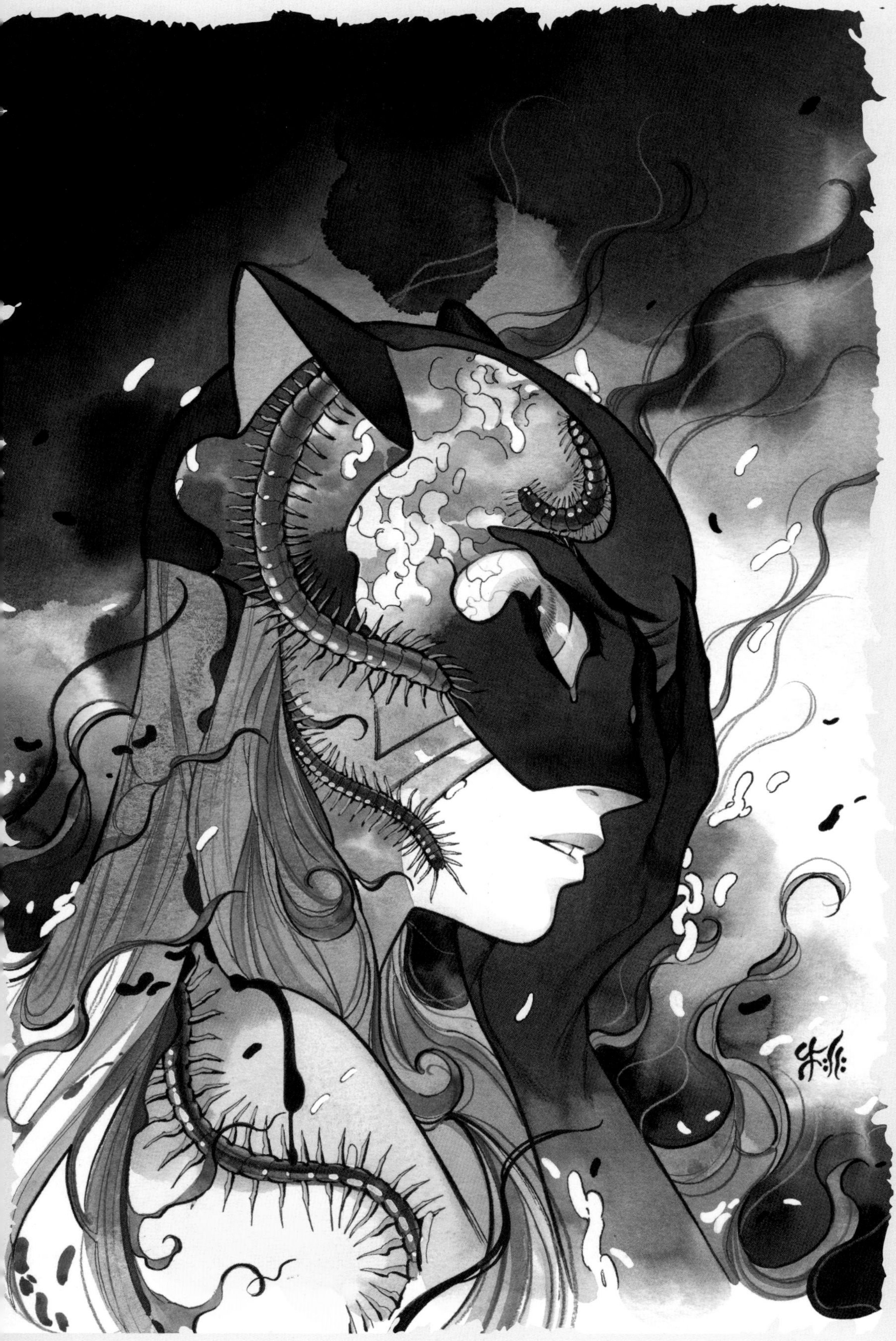

IRON MAN/HELLCAT ANNUAL #1 VARIANT BY
PEACH MOMOKO

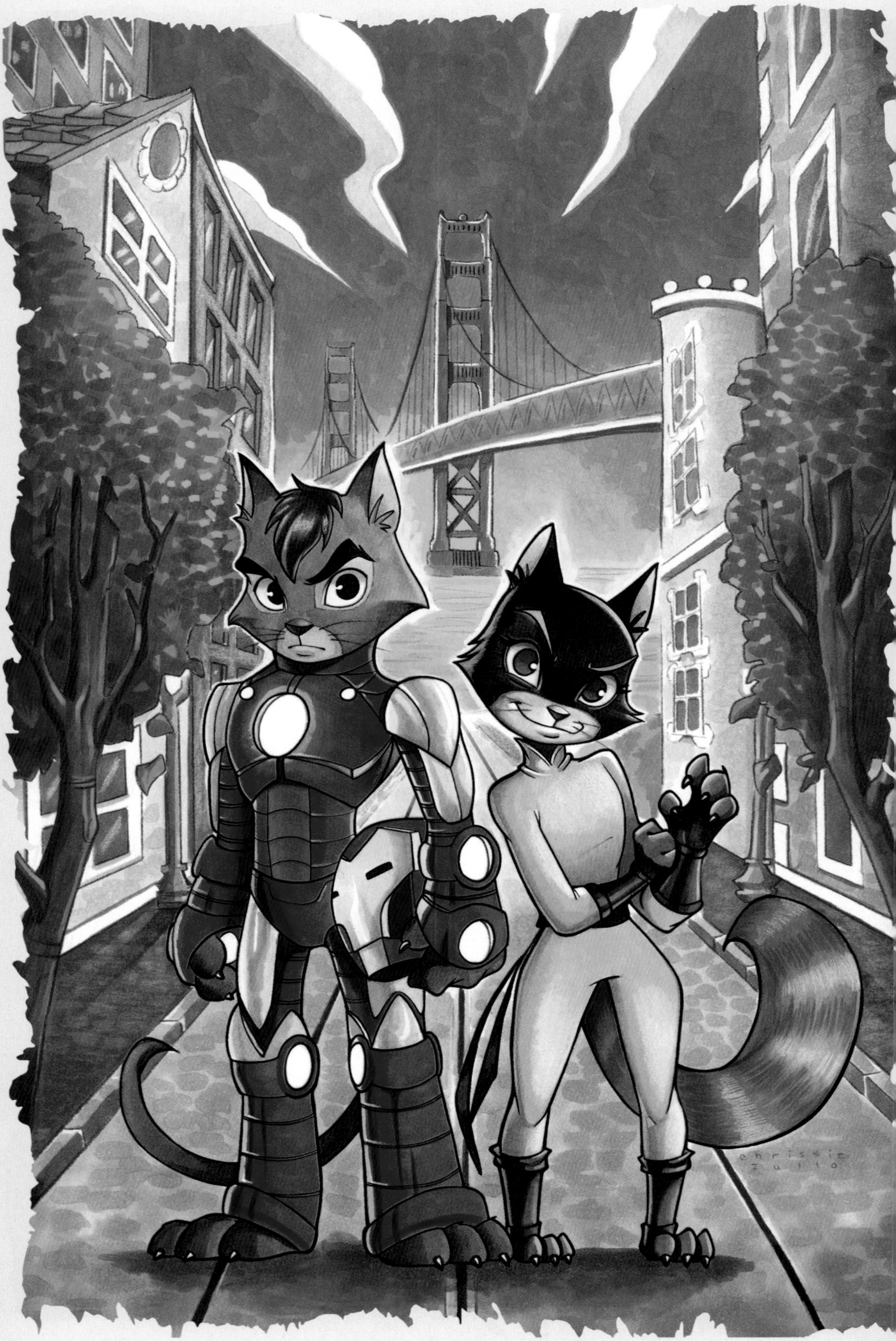
chrissie zullo

IRON MAN/HELLCAT ANNUAL #1 VARIANT BY
CHRISSIE ZULLO

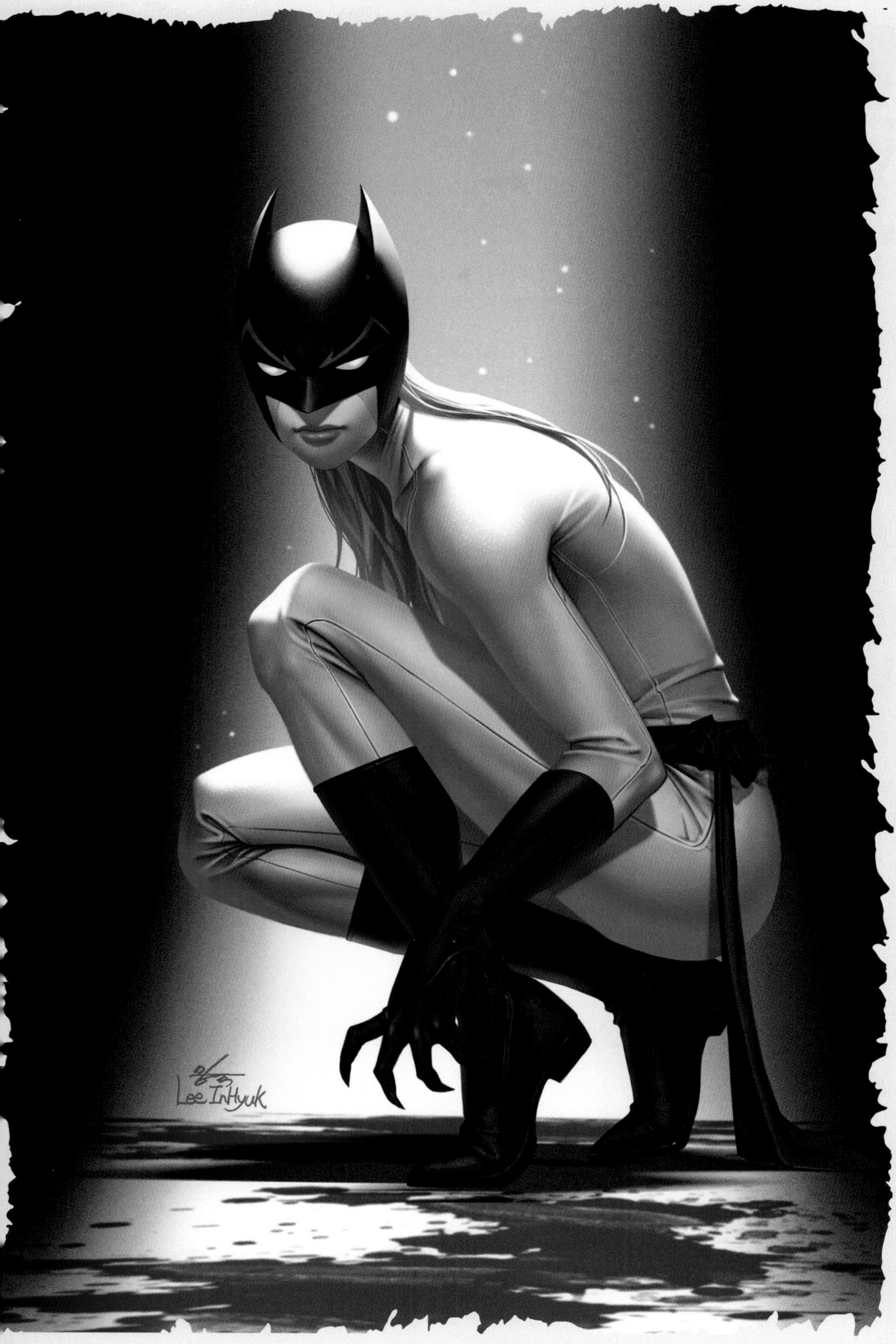
Lee InHyuk

HELLCAT #1 VARIANT BY
INHYUK LEE

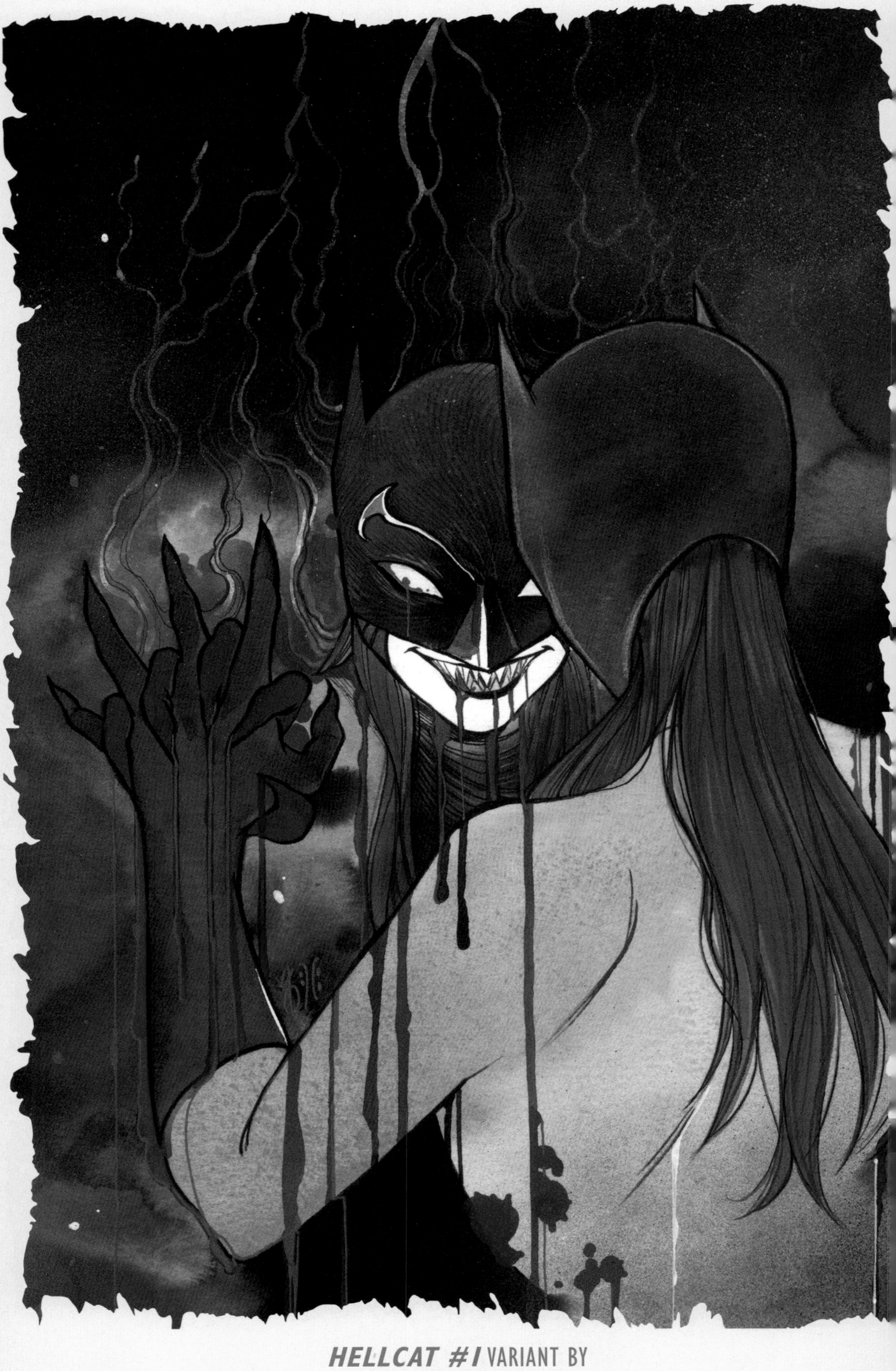

HELLCAT #1 VARIANT BY
PEACH MOMOKO

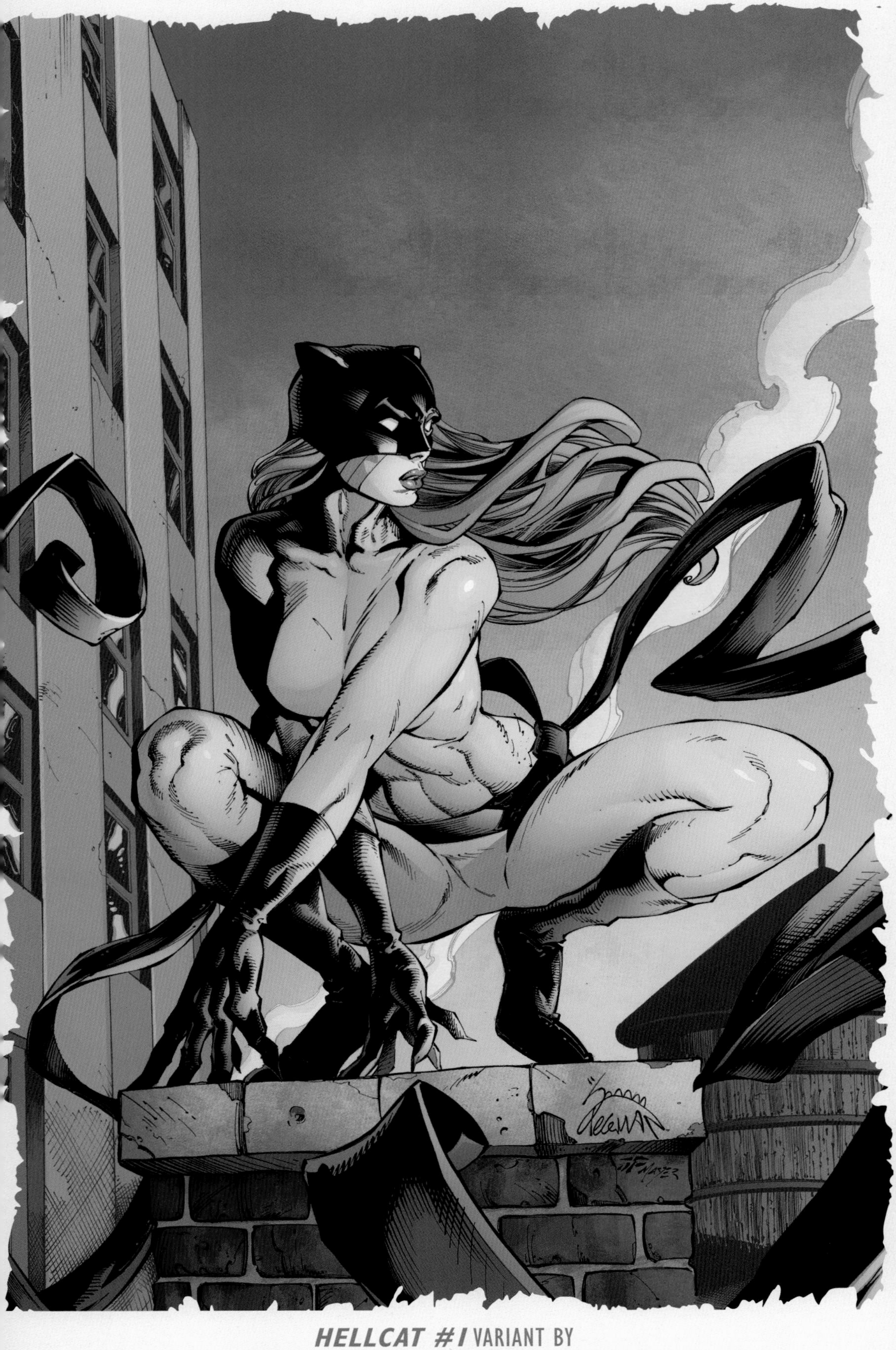

HELLCAT #1 VARIANT BY
RYAN STEGMAN, JP MAYER & DAVE McCAIG

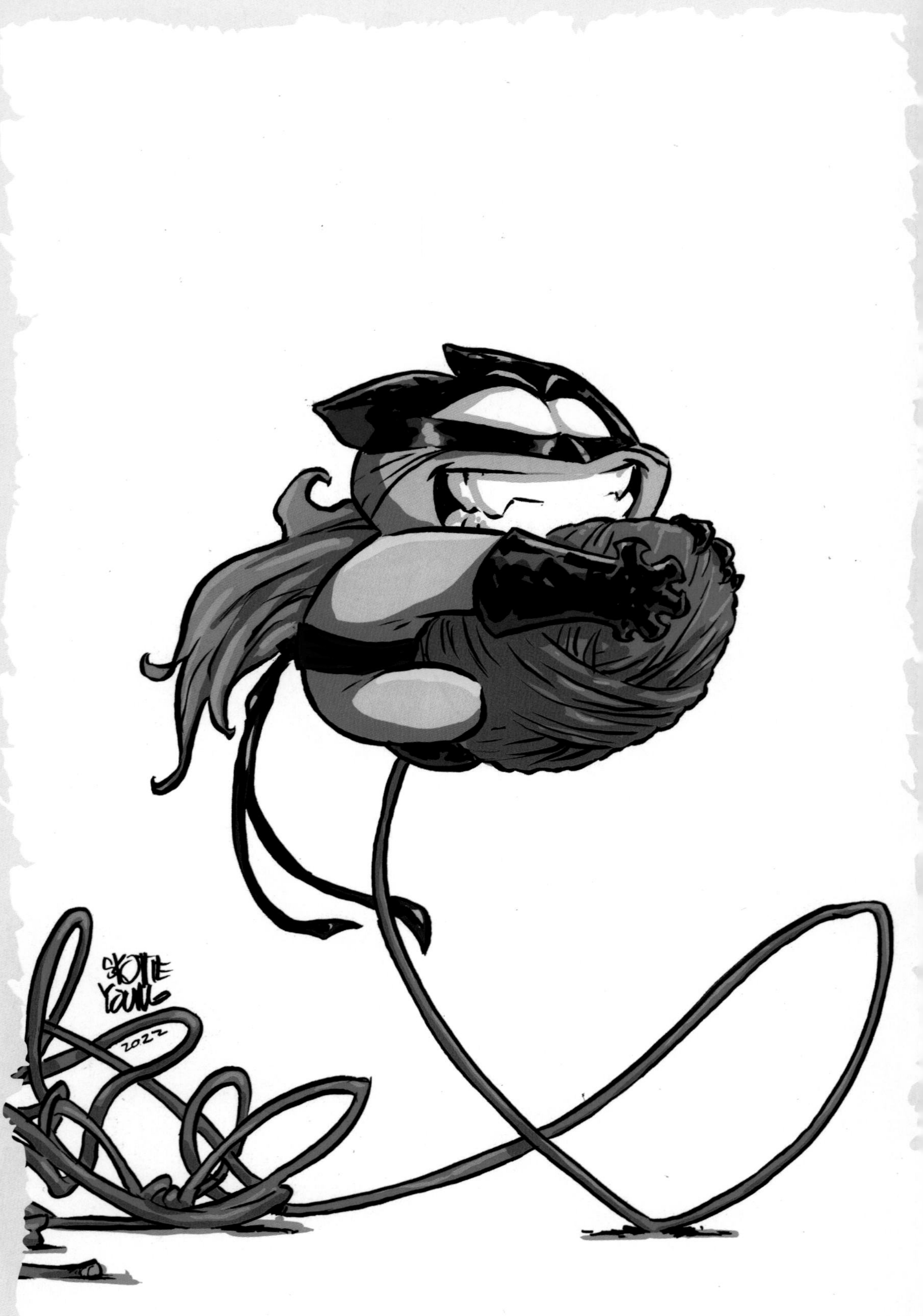
SKOTTIE
YOUNG
2022

HELLCAT #1 VARIANT BY
SKOTTIE YOUNG

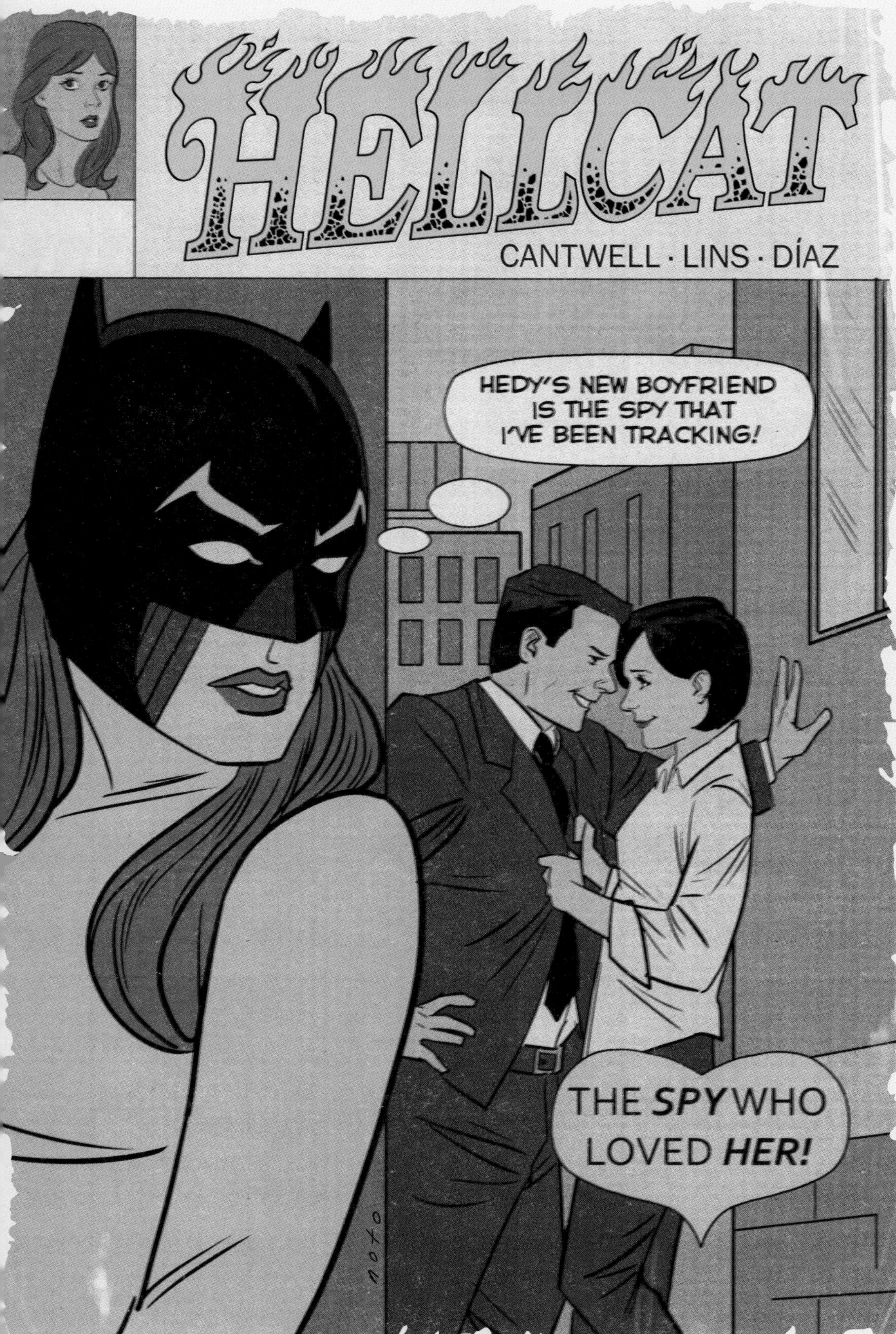
HELLCAT
CANTWELL · LINS · DÍAZ
HEDY'S NEW BOYFRIEND IS THE SPY THAT I'VE BEEN TRACKING!
THE SPY WHO LOVED HER!
noto

HELLCAT #2 VARIANT BY
PHIL NOTO

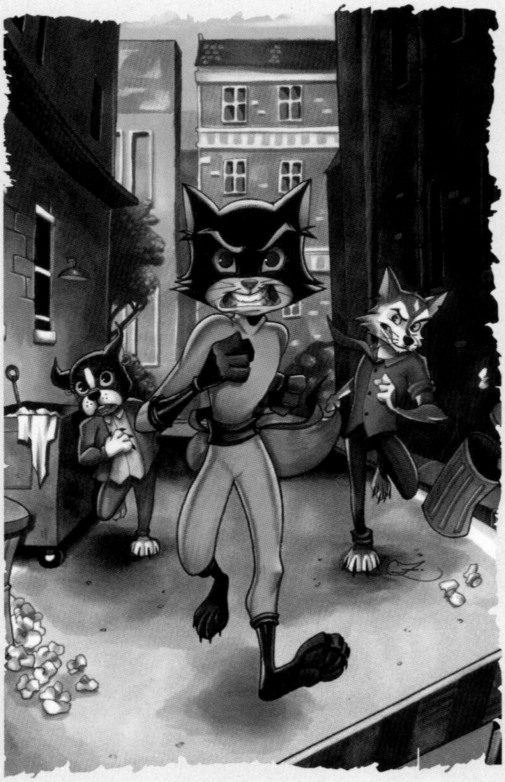

HELLCAT #2 VARIANT BY
CHRISSIE ZULLO

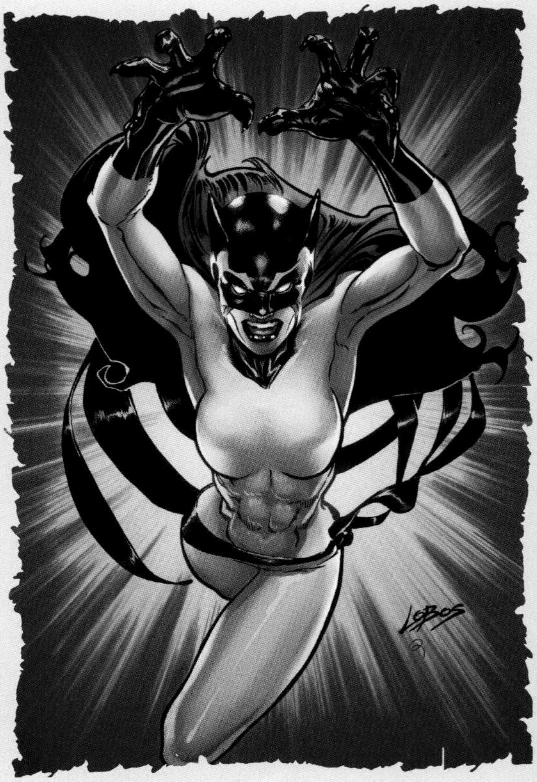
LOBOS

HELLCAT #2 VARIANT BY
PABLO VILLALOBOS & RACHELLE ROSENBERG

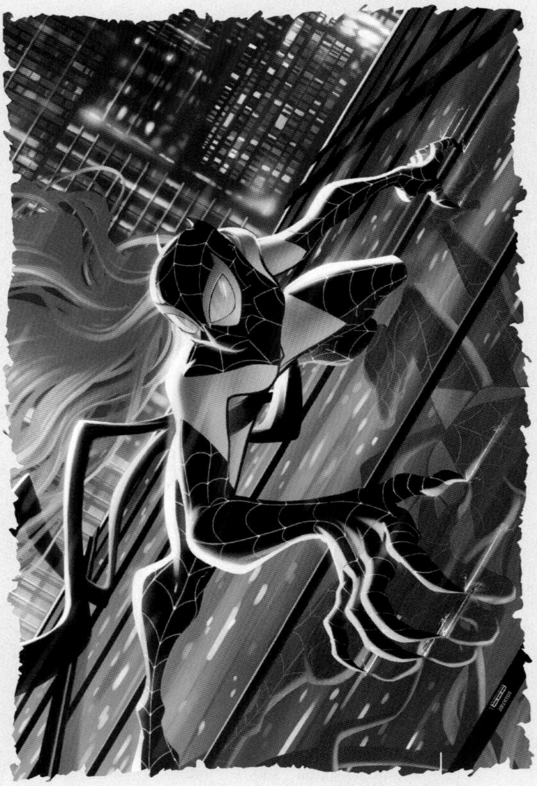

HELLCAT #3 SPIDER-VERSE VARIANT BY
DAVID BALDEÓN

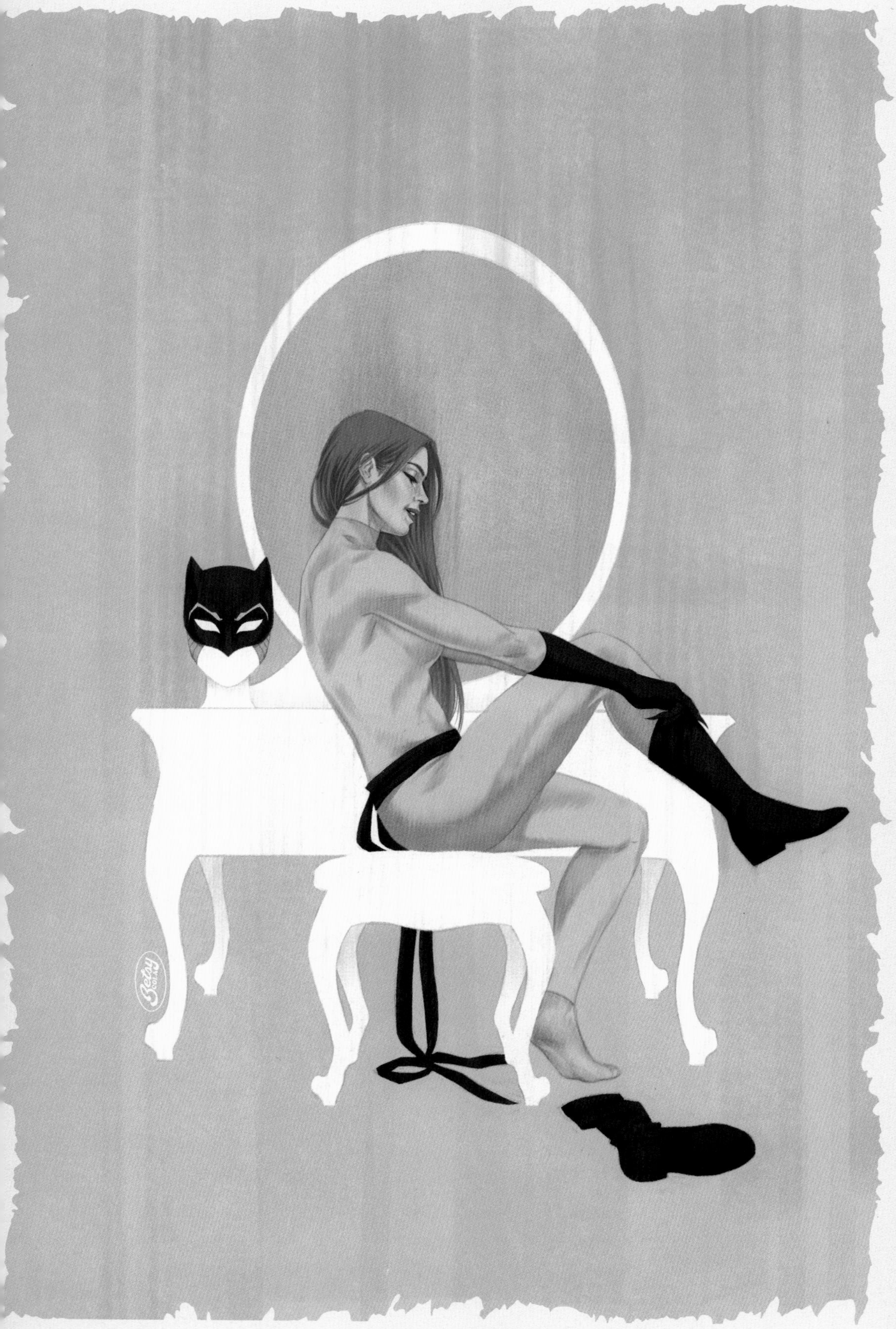

HELLCAT #3 VARIANT BY
BETSY COLA

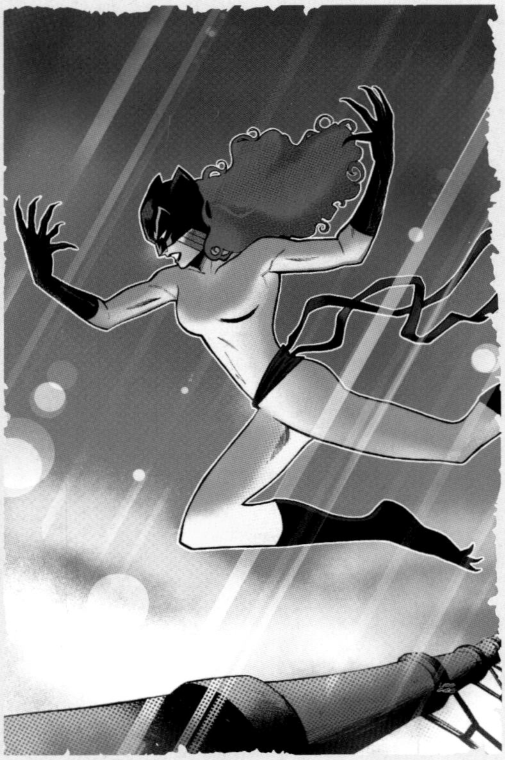

HELLCAT #3 VARIANT BY
LEE GARBETT

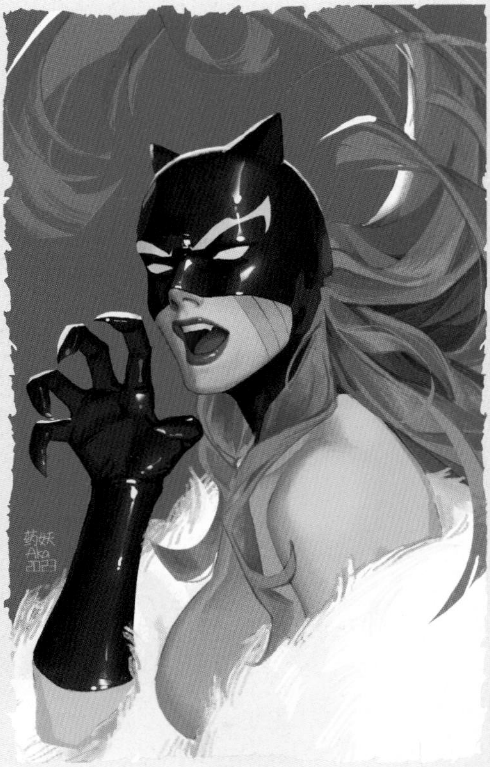

HELLCAT #4 VARIANT BY
AKA

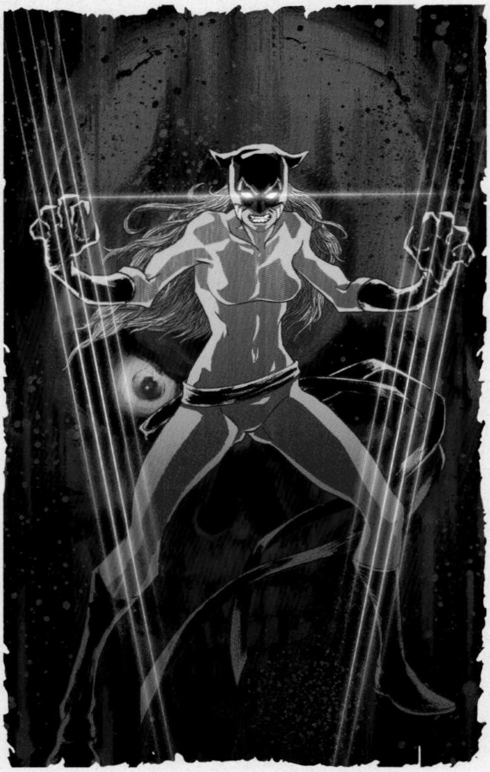

HELLCAT #4 VARIANT BY
SUPERLOG